Advancing 1

Monetary Policy

Tobias **Adrian**

Douglas **Laxton**

Maurice **Obstfeld**

Editors

Authors: Tobias Adrian, Rania Al-Mashat, Rahul Anand, Andrew Berg, Kevin Clinton, Giovanni Dell'Ariccia, Fernando Duarte, Federico Grinberg, Vikram Haksar, Darryl King, Douglas Laxton, Tommaso Mancini-Griffoli, Maurice Obstfeld, Rafael Portillo, and Hou Wang

INTERNATIONAL MONETARY FUND

© 2018 International Monetary Fund
Cover design: Jessie Sanchez Art & Design

Cataloging-in-Publication Data
Joint Bank-Fund Library

Names: Adrian, Tobias, editor. | Laxton, Douglas, editor. | Obstfeld, Maurice, editor. | International Monetary Fund.
Title: Advancing the frontiers of monetary policy / Tobias Adrian, Douglas Laxton, and Maurice Obstfeld, editors ; authors: Tobias Adrian [and eleven others].
Description: Washington, DC : International Monetary Fund, 2018 | Includes bibliographical references.
Identifiers: ISBN 9781484325940 (Paper) | 9781484344484 (ePub) | 9781484344491(Mobipocket) | 9781484344521 (PDF)
Subjects: LCSH: Monetary policy. | Inflation targeting.
Classification: LCC HG230.3.E96 2018

Recommended citation: Adrian, Tobias, Douglas Laxton, and Maurice Obstfeld, eds. 2018. *Advancing the Frontiers of Monetary Policy.* Washington, DC: International Monetary Fund.

ISBN 978-1-48432-5940 (Paper)
978-1-48434-4484 (ePub)
978-1-48434-4491 (Mobipocket)
978-1-48434-4521 (PDF)

Please send orders to:

International Monetary Fund, Publication Services
P.O. Box 92780, Washington, DC 20090, U.S.A.
Tel.: (202) 623-7430 Fax: (202) 623-7201
E-mail: publications@imf.org
Internet: www.elibrary.imf.org
www.bookstore.imf.org

Contents

Foreword

Inflation is no longer a problem that dominates people's minds these days. Other economic issues in 2018 have a far higher profile in the public debate—employment, trade, technological change, industrial restructuring, inequality, aging populations, and sluggish growth, to name a few. Yet in the 1970s and 1980s, inflation was a first-order problem. The change followed the emergence of a consensus that the main objective of monetary policy is to establish a low, stable rate of inflation. In line with this, many countries have adopted an explicit numerical target—2 percent is popular—as the basis for monetary policy.

New Zealand led the way in the late 1980s, using inflation targeting as an initiative to end its chronic and severe inflation problem. Canada soon followed. The priority in the early years was to establish the credibility of the initial targets among a skeptical public. Policymakers, therefore, set interest rates high enough to make sure that they achieved, or overachieved, the initial targets. Despite outspoken criticism of the high interest rates and the losses of output and employment that followed, the inflation targeters stood their ground. By the mid-1990s, disinflation was sufficient to grab the attention of the public and to lead the way to a permanent decline in inflation expectations. Meanwhile, the losses of output proved to be temporary—just as the theory of the expectations-augmented Phillips curve had predicted. Other countries noticed, and by the turn of the century numerous central banks were pursuing an inflation target.

Within a few years they had broadly established confidence in stable long-term inflation. Shocks to the inflation rate over which monetary policy has no effective control, for example, from sudden changes in energy prices, no longer shifted long-term expectations. Policymakers could now adopt a more flexible approach in responding to disturbances to the rate of inflation with more weight on stabilizing the level of output. Flexible inflation targeting would allow a one-off change in the inflation rate to accommodate the relative price change, but not a lasting change. A consistent policy that returns inflation to a steady low rate over the medium term is the ultimate foundation for public confidence in this outcome. In a seminal contribution, Lars Svensson proposed for this purpose that central banks aim at achieving their own forecast of the inflation path. Inflation-forecast targeting provides, in effect, a systematic way to implement the otherwise vague notion of flexible inflation targeting.

For a good number of years before 2008 the framework worked well, avoiding recessions and keeping inflation on track. The record since the 2008–09 global financial crisis has, however, been disappointing. The response of monetary policy to subpar output and below-target inflation has been stymied by the effective lower bound on the nominal interest rate (a number near zero). The situation calls for coordinated deployment of all relevant policies, in particular fiscal stimulus, where the public sector balance sheet is in good shape, and structural

reforms, including strengthening financial systems and deploying macroprudential tools. The authors of this volume nevertheless argue that monetary policy can
make a positive contribution. Management of expectations is the core of the
matter. To this end, they recommend increased central bank transparency with
respect to economic forecasts, and more assertive policy actions.

More generally, the book considers how to structure an inflation-forecast-targeting regime that will work well in good and bad times. It describes how policymakers might systematically formulate responses to inflation shocks, with due
regard to the consequences for output. Moreover, the book introduces a novel
rationale for taking financial conditions into account when setting monetary
policy, and looks more broadly at effective operational frameworks and communication strategies. The authors draw on contributions they have made to the
practice of inflation-forecast targeting. Their experience at central banks in
advanced and emerging market economies as well as in low-income countries
gives their analysis a pragmatic viewpoint. They use model simulations along with
case studies to illustrate their arguments. At the same time, the treatment of the
issues is not highly technical and remains accessible to a wide audience, including
central bankers and other policymakers, business journalists, financial market
analysts, and students.

Carla Grasso
Deputy Managing Director and Chief Administrative Officer
International Monetary Fund

Preface

This book was based, to a large extent, on our experience working with a large number of central banks on their inflation-forecast-targeting frameworks. Rania Al-Mashat, Ali Alichi, Michal Andrle, Jaromir Benes, Andrew Berg, Aleš Bulíř, Kevin Clinton, Aaron Drew, Charles Freedman, Tibor Hlédik, Tomás Holub, Benjamin Hunt, Tore Anders Husebø, Ondra Kamenik, Joannes Mongardini, Rafael Portillo, David Rose, Jack Selody, David Vávra, Hou Wang, Jiaxiong Yao, and Fan Zhang, among others, provided important contributions on technical assistance missions. Rebecca Eyassu, Yiqun Li, and Cristina Quintos provided excellent administrative and research assistance. We would also like to thank Olivier Blanchard, Jorg Decressin, and Gian Maria Milesi-Ferretti for encouraging us to complete this project. Linda Griffin Kean in the Editorial and Publications Division of the IMF's Communications Department oversaw the editing and production of this book.

Abbreviations

CNB	Czech National Bank
CPI	consumer price index
DSGE	dynamic stochastic general equilibrium
Fed	US Federal Reserve System
FPAS	forecasting and policy analysis system
GaR	growth at risk
IFB	inflation-forecast based
PCE	personal consumption expenditures
QPM	quarterly projection model
RBI	Reserve Bank of India
VaR	value at risk
VAR	vector autoregression

Contributors

EDITORS

Tobias Adrian is the Financial Counsellor and the Director of the Monetary and Capital Markets Department of the IMF. Before joining the IMF in January 2017, he served as Senior Vice President and Associate Director of Research at the Federal Reserve Bank of New York, where he helped lead the New York Fed's work on financial stability policy and monetary policy. He previously conducted economic research at the National Bureau of Economic Research in Cambridge, Massachusetts, and at the Centre for European Policy Studies in Brussels. He earned his PhD in economics from the Massachusetts Institute of Technology (MIT) and his MSc from the London School of Economics and Political Science. He also earned postgraduate degrees from Goethe University in Frankfurt and Dauphine University in Paris. He taught economics at MIT, Princeton University, and New York University. His economic analyses have been published in such scholarly journals as the *American Economic Review, Journal of Financial Economics,* and *Journal of Finance.*

Douglas Laxton is the Division Chief of the Economic Modeling Division in the Research Department of the IMF, which develops modern macro models to support the IMF's surveillance activities. He joined the IMF's Research Department in 1993 and has held numerous positions, including Advisor to the IMF's Economic Counsellor. He has worked with many central banks developing forecasting and policy analysis systems to support inflation-forecast targeting frameworks. He has written on a wide range of topics but focuses his time on building multicountry models, including, more recently, models with strong macro-financial linkages designed to support macroprudential policies. He has also developed models of the oil market to support the IMF's surveillance activities. Prior to joining the IMF, Mr. Laxton held numerous positions in the Research Department at the Bank of Canada (1981–93) and was responsible for developing its modeling framework to support inflation targeting. Mr. Laxton completed graduate work in economics in 1981 at the University of Western Ontario. For more details see www.douglaslaxton.org.

Maurice Obstfeld has been the Economic Counsellor and Director of Research of the IMF since September 2015, on leave from the University of California, Berkeley. At Berkeley, he is the Class of 1958 Professor of Economics and former Chair of the Department of Economics (1998–2001). He arrived at Berkeley in 1991 as a professor, following permanent appointments at Columbia (1979–86) and the University of Pennsylvania (1986–89), and a visiting appointment at Harvard University (1989–90). He received his PhD in economics from MIT in

1979 after attending the University of Pennsylvania (BA, 1973) and King's College, Cambridge University (MA, 1975). From July 2014 to August 2015, Dr. Obstfeld served as a member of President Obama's Council of Economic Advisers. He was previously an honorary advisor to the Bank of Japan's Institute of Monetary and Economic Studies (2002–14). He is a Fellow of the Econometric Society and the American Academy of Arts and Sciences. Among Dr. Obstfeld's honors are Tilburg University's Tjalling C. Koopmans Asset Award, the John von Neumann Award of the Rajk Laszlo College for Advanced Studies (Budapest), and the Kiel Institute's Bernhard Harms Prize. He has delivered a number of distinguished lectures, including the American Economic Association's annual Richard T. Ely Lecture, the L. K. Jha Memorial Lecture of the Reserve Bank of India, and the Frank D. Graham Memorial Lecture at Princeton University. Dr. Obstfeld has served on the Executive Committee and as Vice President of the American Economic Association. He has consulted and taught at the IMF and numerous central banks around the world. He is also the coauthor of two leading textbooks on international economics, *International Economics* (10th edition, 2014, with Paul Krugman and Marc Melitz) and *Foundations of International Macroeconomics* (1996, with Kenneth Rogoff), as well as more than 100 research articles on exchange rates, international financial crises, global capital markets, and monetary policy.

AUTHORS

Rania Al-Mashat is an Advisor in the IMF's Research Department. In this position, she has made significant contributions to the technical assistance and capacity development work of the Research Department, leading technical assistance missions to central banks in various regions and engaging in several outreach activities. She has worked on a number of research projects, focusing on, among other topics, financial stability, potential output, and central bank transparency. These responsibilities tap her years of experience serving as Sub-Governor for Monetary Policy at the Central Bank of Egypt (2005–16). During her tenure, she helped modernize the bank's monetary policy strategy and manage the country's macroeconomic transition, and acted as the primary liaison between the central bank and the IMF. She has had several board affiliations, including with the Egyptian Stock Exchange, the General Authority for Free Zones and Investment in Egypt, the Arab International Bank, the Middle East Economic Association, and the Arab Investment Bank. Prior to joining the Central Bank of Egypt, she was a Senior Economist at the IMF and covered a number of emerging Asian economies, including India and Vietnam, with research focused on monetary policy formulation and transmission as well as structural reforms. She has received numerous awards and recognitions for her research efforts and contributions to public work, including being selected a Young Global Leader by the World Economic Forum and chosen to be a part of their Expert Network in 2017, and being selected among the top 50 most influential women in the Egyptian economy during 2015. She is a member of Bruegel's scientific council and a Research Fellow at the Economic Research Forum for the Arab countries, Iran, and Turkey. She was a lecturer at the Egyptian Banking

Institute and an adjunct professor of economics at the American University in Cairo. She holds a PhD in economics from the University of Maryland.

Rahul Anand is Assistant to the Director in the IMF's Institute for Capacity Development. He previously worked in the African Department and the Asia and Pacific Department, covering South Africa, India, and Sri Lanka. His research spans a range of areas, including general equilibrium modeling to study monetary policy issues in emerging markets, macro-critical structural reforms, subsidy reforms, and growth-enhancing structural transformation. Before joining the IMF in 2010, he held various senior positions in India as a member of the Indian Administrative Service designing, implementing, and monitoring government economic programs and policies. He holds a PhD from Cornell University and a master's degree from Harvard University.

Andrew Berg is Deputy Director of the IMF's Institute for Capacity Development. He holds a PhD in economics from MIT and an undergraduate degree from Harvard University. He first joined the IMF in 1993, and most recently served in the Research Department as Chief of the Development Macroeconomic Division and before that in the African Department, including as Chief of the Regional Studies Division and as Mission Chief to Malawi. He has also worked at the US Treasury and as an associate of Jeffrey Sachs. He has published articles on, among other topics, growth accelerations, the macroeconomics of aid, predicting currency crises, inequality and growth, public investment and debt sustainability, artificial intelligence and inequality, and monetary policy in low-income countries.

Kevin Clinton works as a consultant for the IMF and the World Bank, following a long career as Research Adviser at the Bank of Canada, in departments responsible for monetary policy modeling and strategy, financial markets and policy implementation, and international issues. Since 1990 he has participated in technical assistance missions to central banks in Asia, the Caribbean, Central and Eastern Europe, and South America. His recent publications, coauthored with teams led by Douglas Laxton, focus on the implementation of inflation-forecast targeting. Earlier articles are published in various journals, including the *American Economic Review*, *Canadian Journal of Economics*, *Journal of Finance*, *Journal of Political Economy*, and in various Bank of Canada publications. Mr. Clinton studied at the London School of Economics, and completed a PhD at Western University; he has taught at the University of Maryland, Queen's, and Carleton.

Giovanni Dell'Ariccia is Deputy Director of the IMF's Research Department. He supervises the department's work on financial, macroprudential, and monetary policy issues, including the activities of the Macro-Financial Division. Previously, he worked in the Asia and Pacific Department on assignments on Thailand, Singapore, and Hong Kong Special Administrative Region. He received his undergraduate degree in economics from Sapienza Università di Roma and a PhD in economics from MIT. His research interests include banking, the macroeconomics of credit, monetary policy, international finance, and conditionality in international lending and aid programs. He has published extensively in major economics and finance journals on issues ranging from bank competition under asymmetric information to credit booms and the relationship between monetary policy and bank risk-taking. He is a Research Fellow at the Centre for Economic Policy Research.

Fernando Duarte is an Economist in the Capital Markets Function at the Federal Reserve Bank of New York, with main research interests in inflation, asset pricing, and the connections between macroeconomics and finance. He obtained his PhD in economics from MIT in 2011.

Federico Grinberg is an Economist in the Monetary and Capital Markets Department of the IMF, working on monetary policy. He previously worked in the IMF's European Department. He earned a PhD in economics from the University of California, Los Angeles, in 2015, and holds a BSc in economics from the University of Buenos Aires, Argentina.

Vikram Haksar is an Assistant Director in the IMF's Strategy Policy and Review Department. In this role, he manages work on global surveillance and Group of 20 prospects and the IMF's engagement on finance and technology. He was previously the IMF's Mission Chief for Brazil and Mexico, leading the team that set up the IMF's $70 billion flexible credit line agreement with Mexico in 2009. He earlier worked on emerging market economies in Asia and Eastern Europe and was the IMF's Resident Representative in the Philippines. He received his PhD from Cornell University.

Darryl King is the Deputy Division Chief of the Central Bank Operations Division of the Monetary and Capital Markets Department of the IMF. He previously managed the implementation of monetary and foreign exchange policies at the Reserve Bank of New Zealand and was a member of the Monetary Policy Committee. Since joining the IMF in the late 1990s he has worked extensively with central banks in the areas of monetary and foreign exchange operations, market development, and financial stability. He is also involved in policy work and is one of the authors of the 2015 IMF paper "Evolving Monetary Policy Frameworks in Low-Income and Other Developing Countries," and recently led a team that developed a framework for central bank intervention in securities markets.

Tommaso Mancini-Griffoli is a Deputy Division Chief in the Monetary and Capital Markets Department of the IMF, in charge of work on monetary policy. He has advised country authorities and published on issues related to unconventional monetary policies, monetary policy spillovers, exchange rate regimes and interventions, and evolving monetary policy frameworks. Prior to joining the IMF, he was a Senior Economist in the Research and Monetary Policy Division of the Swiss National Bank, where he advised the Board on quarterly monetary policy decisions. He spent prior years in the private sector at Goldman Sachs, the Boston Consulting Group, and technology start-ups in Silicon Valley. He holds a PhD from the Graduate Institute in Geneva, a master's from the London School of Economics, and a bachelor's from Stanford University.

Rafael Portillo has worked in the Western Hemisphere, Monetary and Capital Markets, African, and Research Departments of the IMF. From 2016–17 he worked at the Joint Vienna Institute. His work has focused on macroeconomic modeling and monetary policy issues through surveillance, research, and technical assistance. Mr. Portillo has coauthored several IMF policy papers, working papers, and academic publications. He received his PhD in economics in 2006 from the University of Michigan and also holds degrees from the Université Paris I Panthéon-Sorbonne and the Université Paris IX Dauphine.

Hou Wang is an Economist in the Research Department of the IMF. Since she joined the IMF, she has worked with many central banks developing models to support inflation-forecast-targeting frameworks. She has also worked on multi-country dynamic stochastic general equilibrium models to support the IMF's surveillance activities. She holds a PhD in economics from the Johns Hopkins University.

PART I

The Frontiers of Monetary Policymaking

CHAPTER 1

An Overview of Inflation-Forecast Targeting

Tobias Adrian, Douglas Laxton, and Maurice Obstfeld

In 1990, the Reserve Bank of New Zealand became the first central bank to announce an inflation target, followed a year later by the Bank of Canada. This was a significant step toward demystifying the objectives of monetary policy, and it signaled the start of a remarkable transition toward central bank transparency.

During the 1980s, global monetary policy objectives were diffuse, characterized by loose commitments to price stability and high employment, and central banks' operational procedures were somewhat obscure. But by the mid-2000s, after the series of changes set in motion by New Zealand and Canada, many central banks used explicit inflation targets to govern monetary policy, informed by a structured framework of forecasting and policy analysis.

In the earliest phase, inflation-targeting central banks gave high priority to establishing the credibility of the new regime by adopting a rigid policy stance to ensure that inflation would not exceed the initial annual targets. This tough approach did succeed in bringing inflation expectations down. It soon became clear, however, that a more flexible approach that put more weight on output stability would be more effective and sustainable.[1] Instead of rigidly targeting inflation from one year to the next, the key to maintaining credibility would be to react effectively and visibly to any deviation in order to return inflation to target over a medium-term horizon. Best practice would involve a flexible approach, taking account of the implications of policy actions for both output and inflation.

Swedish economist Lars Svensson (1997) developed the concept of inflation-forecast targeting, which provides a systematic way to implement the notion of flexible inflation targeting.[2] Svensson points out that the central bank's

---

[1]Output and employment are used interchangeably because these two variables are closely correlated over the business cycle.

[2]The term "inflation targeting" is often interpreted as strict adherence to a particular inflation rate. Here, the term "flexible inflation targeting" is used to describe a policy regime under which the central bank pursues the primary objective of maintaining low and stable inflation while taking

inflation forecast represents an ideal conditional intermediate target because it takes account of all available information, including the preferences of the policymakers and their views on how the economy works. Practitioners have come to view inflation-forecast targeting as an efficient and systematic way to make flexible inflation targeting operational. In the United States, the Federal Reserve gradually adopted a substantively similar approach under its dual mandate to stabilize prices and maximize employment, announcing a 2 percent inflation target in 2012. Although the Fed does not classify itself as an inflation targeter, the post-2012 regime embodies the fundamental principles of inflation-forecast targeting (Alichi and others 2015).

This book tracks the development of monetary policy over the past quarter century through the prism of the evolution of inflation-forecast targeting.

PRINCIPLES AND PRACTICES

Principles and practices of inflation-forecast targeting are covered in Part II (Chapters 2–8). These chapters also describe some of the history since 1990, during which a striking consensus emerged that the main objective of monetary policy should be a low, stable rate of inflation with an explicit, fixed, long-term target rate. The actual numerical settings for this objective fall within a narrow range, with most advanced economies opting for 2 percent and others between 2 and 4 percent.

Compare this with the late 1980s, when central banks pursued multiple objectives. Many policy analysts in advanced economies argued that maintaining high levels of output and employment should be at the fore. Only New Zealand had an explicit inflation target. Two popular options for a nominal anchor were either a fixed exchange rate against a low-inflation currency or a target growth rate for one of many alternative monetary aggregates. Emerging market economies often prioritized stabilizing the exchange rate or a "managed float."[3] Yet repeated experience in the wake of asymmetric economic shocks showed that a flexible exchange rate provided a useful means of adjustment, and the evidence refuted the notion of stable and exploitable links between monetary aggregates and goal variables like inflation and output.

As described in Chapter 2, announcing a target for the inflation rate was a major step toward demystifying the objective of monetary policy and making central bank operations more transparent, which is important given that inflation levels affect everybody in a significant way. Regarding the policy instrument, generally accepted practice today in advanced economies has the central bank

---

into account other objectives such as output or employment and ensuring that pursuit of those other objectives remains consistent with the primary inflation objective.

[3]Some countries have used an exchange rate peg as a strategy to stop very high inflation (Calvo and Vegh 1999). However, success requires a quick transition to exchange rate flexibility as soon as a measure of credibility is achieved, to prevent a misalignment. An overvalued currency can be very harmful for macroeconomic and financial stability.

announce its setting for a key short-term interest rate, immediately after the monetary policy committee holds a rate-setting meeting. In some small, very open economies, the central bank may use the exchange rate as a systematic instrument to influence output and inflation (for example, Singapore).

In low-income countries that lack well-functioning financial markets, the exchange rate and monetary aggregates may conceivably be the only effective policy levers. In addition, even in economies where the normal instrument is a short-term interest rate, under exceptional circumstances, for example, at the effective lower bound of the policy interest rate, the central bank may use the exchange rate as a less conventional instrument—Svensson (2001) makes a theoretical argument for such a tactic, while the Czech National Bank provides an example of its actual use. Clarity of purpose and execution underlie the principles of inflation-forecast targeting as spelled out in Chapter 2.

Monetary policy involves managing public expectations. Chapter 3 explains how a transparent inflation-forecast-targeting framework helps policymakers manage expectations in support of an environment of steady low inflation. Establishing a firm nominal anchor under inflation targeting means ensuring that expectations for long-term inflation hold steady at the target rate, notwithstanding short-term fluctuations in the actual rate. In the earliest phase of inflation targeting, the Reserve Bank of New Zealand and the Bank of Canada put a high priority on establishing the credibility of the new regime. To this end, and in recognition of the history of inflation in these countries and considerable skepticism about the new regime, they adopted rigid policy stances to ensure that inflation would not exceed the initial annual targets.

The tough approach did indeed bring inflation expectations down over a few years, in line with the targets. However, it also started to become clear that a more flexible approach, that put more weight on output stability in the short term, would be more effective and sustainable. Given that most countries see substantial variations around the target from year to year, the key to maintaining credibility is to react effectively and visibly to any deviations in order to return inflation to the target over the medium term. Simultaneously with this realization, as noted, Svensson's (1997) concept of inflation-forecast targeting provided a systematic way to implement the notion of flexible inflation targeting.

Of course, if policy is to return inflation to target following a disturbance, the policy instrument must have the power to influence goal variables appropriately. The effectiveness of the policy interest rate also depends on managing expectations. Households and firms borrow and lend at longer terms than the very short term of the policy rate. To affect inflation and output, a change in the policy rate must therefore shift the whole yield curve by changing expectations of future short-term rates.[4] Chapter 3 summarizes the strong evidence that expectations

---

[4]Woodford (2005) highlights that managing expectations is a key task in the practice of central banking. Clinton and others (2015) discuss practical issues involved with developing analytical frameworks and monetary policy models to support inflation-forecast-targeting regimes.

have been better anchored in economies where monetary policy follows inflation-forecast-targeting principles.

One development that was less visible but no less essential for the conduct of policy was the establishment inside central banks of forecasting and policy analysis systems for the implementation of inflation targeting (Chapter 4). The Reserve Bank of New Zealand and the Bank of Canada soon recognized that, for inflation targeting, they needed a structure to supply the relevant economic information—forecasts, risk analyses, implications of alternative strategies, and so on—on a schedule determined by monetary policy committee decision meetings. These systems involve a team of economists with skills in macroeconomic modeling and forecasting; a core macroeconomic model; and an adequate, easily updated, macroeconomic database (Laxton, Rose, and Scott 2009). Timely, relevant forecasts and policy simulations for the deliberations of the monetary policy committee require an efficient production process, which includes adherence to a tight schedule of iterations and open communications between forecasters and policymakers. The internal reallocation of central bank resources along these lines again represents a tremendous generational change: the maintenance of a fixed exchange rate, or of a given rate of money growth, had demanded much less in the way of updated economic information or analytical frameworks to help address policy issues.

The core macroeconomic model captures the main aspects of the complex transmission mechanism from the policy interest rate to output and inflation and takes account of a myriad of other factors that might influence these goal variables, using judgmental input from sectoral experts. An essential feature is an endogenous policy interest rate, such that following a disturbance, the interest rate systematically responds to bring inflation back to the target within a medium-term horizon. The coefficients of the policy reaction function reflect policymakers' preferences about the short-term trade-off between inflation and output—for example, a higher weight on the current divergence of inflation from target would imply a faster return toward the target rate following a supply shock, at the cost of a sharper widening of the output gap.

Chapter 5 examines the operational control of the monetary policy instrument in both advanced and low-income countries. The framework in advanced and most emerging market economies hinges on the provision of balances for the settlement of interbank payments (that is, bank reserves), for which the central bank is the unique source. The central bank also sets the terms of provision through a "corridor" of rates on its accounts: the overnight lending rate (traditionally called the discount rate) is the ceiling of the corridor, whereas the central bank deposit rate (for excess balances) sets the floor. This corridor sets a band for the policy rate—that is, the very short-term money market rate targeted by policy. Various facilities and processes—including averaging for reserve requirements and official repo operations—ensure that the actual policy rate stays close to the announced rate, which is usually the center of the band. This operational arrangement has been more complicated in the wake of the global financial crisis, however. The policy rate in many countries has been stuck for extended periods at the effective lower bound. Under this constraint, monetary policy-makers have deployed less conventional instruments to provide monetary ease, for example, quantitative easing, and setting the policy rate at the floor of the rate corridor; in addition, banks have held large balances of excess reserves at the central bank. In all circumstances, the efficacy of monetary policy can be enhanced by clear communications about how the central bank is using the policy instrument.

It goes without saying that economic performance benefits enormously from a safe and efficient financial system. Since the global financial crisis, central banks have used their public communications to raise the profile of the objective of financial stability. There is little dispute about the need for the postcrisis tightening of microprudential regulations, including increased capital require-ments and stress testing for systemically important institutions. Likewise, there has been widespread support for the introduction of a macroprudential instrument—namely, cyclically variable capital requirements—to moderate excessive credit growth in the system as a whole. There is controversy, however, about the extent to which monetary policy should be used to address perceived financial imbalances. Chapter 6 argues that monetary policy should, as a rule, stick to targeting inflation, for which it has a strong comparative advantage, and that prudential policy instruments (micro and macro) should be used to deal with financial stability issues. That said, it is important that central banks con-tinue to extend their analytical frameworks as new evidence emerges on macro-financial linkages. Many central banks around the world publish financial stability reports that feed into prudential and monetary policy decisions. Furthermore, financial conditions play an increasingly important role in the monetary policy process, because they contain powerful information about future economic conditions, particularly downside risks. In general, indices of financial conditions gauge how easily money and credit flow through the econ-omy via financial markets by examining indicators such as borrowing costs, risk spreads, asset price volatility, exchange rates, inflation rates, and commodity prices. Chapter 7 provides a reduced-form monetary policy model with an explicit role for financial conditions in determining the conditional distribution of future GDP. The approach rationalizes why central banks need to monitor financial conditions to manage the output-inflation trade-off.

Improved communications have helped promote increased transparency (Chapter 8). Senior policymakers hold press conferences and address a variety of audiences immediately after policy decisions to explain their rationale explicitly in terms of the efficient achievement of the inflation target. Monetary Policy Reports, usually quarterly, provide more detailed justification for the central bank's actions.[5] Websites provide rapid public access to the latest information and policy statements, as well as to staff research. A key piece of information published by inflation-forecast-targeting central banks is the macroeconomic

---

[5]Some central banks refer to these reports as inflation reports.

forecast on which actual decisions are based. The model-based forecast yields a coherent macroeconomic narrative linking the current and forecast settings of the interest rate instrument to the goal variables of inflation and output. Most central banks publish just a verbal, qualitative description of the forecast policy rate path. Their view is that the policy rate must be free to respond at any future monetary policy committee meeting to all possible contingencies and that they do not want to confuse the public by appearing to have a commitment of some kind toward the interest rate (Freedman and Laxton 2009). However, some leading-edge central banks release their full forecast, including the projected path of the policy rate.[6] The publication of confidence bands and alternative scenarios embodying different sets of assumptions can help underline the uncertainties that attend the forecast and the conditionality of the interest rate path. In all cases, under inflation-forecast targeting, the central bank indicates to the public not simply a possible path for the future policy rate but also a sense of how this path might change in response to a variety of developments. One of the arguments put forward throughout this book is that an inflation-forecast-targeting framework seamlessly accommodates the introduction of financial conditions, as financial variables help in forecasting downside risks to GDP. More generally, financial vulnerability as monitored in financial stability reports is a key component of the macroeconomic information set. At the same time, we are not arguing for a separate financial stability objective for monetary policy, because that can create thorny communications and credibility issues for the central bank. But even central banks that implicitly place a small weight on output stabilization in their objective function will find the incorporation of financial conditions to be crucial. Indeed, financial conditions are mentioned with increasing frequency in monetary policy statements.

COUNTRY EXPERIENCES

Part III (Chapters 9–12) explores aspects of inflation-forecast targeting in four countries: Canada, the Czech Republic, India, and the United States. The very different structures and issues of these economies illustrate the adaptability of the inflation-forecast-targeting regime. The first three had a history of unstable inflation that led to unanchored, drifting expectations, and widespread skepticism greeted the initial announcements of numerical targets for inflation control. By contrast, the United States adopted an explicit numerical objective after long-term inflation expectations had become anchored at low levels.

The discussion starts, in Chapter 9, with Canada, which in 1991 was the first of these four countries to adopt inflation targeting.[7] The mandate of the Bank of Canada includes objectives for stabilizing both output and inflation. Flexible inflation targeting, which takes account of the lagged effects of monetary policy

---

[6]Svensson (2007) argues for publishing the central bank's forecast interest rate path.

[7]For a discussion of the history of inflation targeting in Canada, see Lane (2015).

on inflation and output and the short-term trade-offs between these goal variables, is squarely in line with this mandate. The economic conjuncture in the early 1990s was relatively favorable to an inflation control program: there was a recession, but not a profound economic upheaval. More fundamentally for the ongoing practice of inflation targeting, a large volume of research had established a good understanding of underlying variables, such as the real equilibrium interest rate and potential output growth, and of key relationships, such as the sensitivity of aggregate demand to interest rates in the aggregate demand function, and the short-term trade-off between output and inflation in the Phillips curve. The Bank of Canada had developed a model, QPM, well-suited for inflation targeting, with forward-looking, model-consistent expectations and an endogenous interest rate determined by a policy reaction function (Black and others 1994). Existing forecasting procedures at the Bank of Canada provided the basis of an efficient forecasting and policy analysis system. And the Bank of Canada drew on the experience of the Reserve Bank of New Zealand.

The main job of the policymakers at first was to lower long-term inflation expectations to the middle of the ultimate target range of 1–3 percent and to stabilize them there. Inflation fell somewhat more quickly than the announced targets envisaged. While this helped quickly dispel much of the skepticism, consensus long-term forecasts of inflation stabilized at 2 percent only after the 1995 federal government budget, which put the public finances on a clearly sustainable path.

Fast-forward to 2017. After a quarter-century the Canadian monetary framework has been well tested and, without question, proven sound. Inflation has varied around 2 percent; expectations of long-term inflation have been steady at that rate; and, compared to other advanced economies, output and employment have been relatively stable. Nevertheless, increased transparency about the future path of the policy rate—a step that can be called *conventional forward guidance*—would increase the effectiveness of monetary policy. Conventional forward guidance would involve routine publication of the forecast path of the policy rate and other relevant macroeconomic variables (for example, output gap and inflation) following the central bank's policy decision meetings.

A risk-avoidance strategy seems best for Canada to keep the economy well away from bad equilibriums. These would involve destabilized expectations—for example, high and variable inflation or deflation. Technically, within a model, such a strategy is represented by loss-minimizing monetary policy with a quadratic loss function that puts an increasingly heavy penalty on deviations from the inflation target and from potential output. This implies strong, prompt policy actions whenever a shock threatens to put the economy into a dark corner. Noting that the Canadian public-sector balance sheet remains quite strong, fiscal stimulus is recommended in the event of a major negative demand shock when the policy interest rate is close to the effective lower bound. More generally, the argument is that coherent and coordinated deployment of all the main policy instruments is more likely to generate self-fulfilling expectations of a good outcome than the use of monetary policy alone.

In the Czech Republic of the 1990s, matters were more difficult by orders of magnitude (Chapter 10). The economy was in the middle of a transformation from a state-run to a market-based system. Mass privatization of former state enterprises was under way. A fixed exchange rate led to the rapid accumulation of foreign exchange reserves. Although the central bank had installed an operating framework based on reserve requirements, open-market operations, and daily monitoring of reserve provision, it could not completely sterilize this inflow; the banking system became flush with excess liquidity. Inflation seemed stuck in the high single digits. Banking regulation and supervision were at a rudimentary stage. A banking crisis and capital flight in 1997 forced the abandonment of the pegged rate for the koruna.

The Czech National Bank decided quite quickly in favor of inflation targeting for the nominal anchor, but this was neither an easy nor an uncontroversial decision. There were doubts that conventional monetary policy was effective at all, in view of the incomplete transition to a market economy. Prices for many important consumer items were to be deregulated in the years ahead, which would mean sporadic jumps in the consumer price index.[8] And again, the history of inflation made for widespread skepticism about the central bank's announcement of targets for inflation reduction and stabilization.

Just as in Canada, however, inflation fell quickly after the targets for inflation reduction were announced, largely because a recession was already under way. This grabbed the public's attention and weakened the inflationary mindset. While this was happening, the Czech National Bank moved with all due speed on two fronts.

First, it installed a forecasting and policy analysis system, with forecasts deriving from a macroeconomic model with forward-looking expectations and an endogenous, policy-determined interest rate. IMF technical assistance is part of this story (Coats, Laxton, and Rose 2003).

Second, the Czech National Bank embarked on an open communications policy. The central bank emphasized early that its inflation targeting was not about rigidly hitting annual targets but about eventually returning inflation to target following any disturbance, taking account of the implications for output. This clear commitment to an inflation-forecast-targeting approach helped solidify its credibility.

The system has worked well. Although at times inflation has been way off the official target, Czech National Bank actions have brought inflation back into line over the medium term. If the foundation for confidence in the system has been that inflation does not long stray from target, transparent communications have made sure that the public understands that this is not by accident and that deliberate, systematic monetary policy actions are indeed responsible. The use of

---

[8]The Czech National Bank dealt with the transitional price-decontrol issue by defining the initial targets in terms of *net inflation*, which excluded the impact of changes in administered prices.

models in the forecasting and policy analysis system has allowed policymakers to provide a coherent macroeconomic narrative in support of their policy actions.

The Czech National Bank is today an international leader in central bank transparency. It is one of the few to publish the complete results of the model-based forecast used as input for policy decisions. This includes the projected path of the short-term interest rate. The public obtains the main quantitative information underlying each policy decision with minimal delay. Expectations of long-term inflation remain stable at 2 percent, notwithstanding the volatility caused by shocks to oil and food prices.

Chapter 11 traces monetary policy in India. The government and the Reserve Bank of India announced an inflation target range of 2–6 percent in 2016. Monetary policy had previously been based on a multiple-indicator approach, which failed to stabilize inflation: the rate of inflation had varied between 5 and 16 percent in the 20 years 1990–2010, and between 8 and 13 percent in the 5 years 2010–15. Thus, the Reserve Bank of India has faced a far more difficult legacy of inflation expectations than the Bank of Canada or the Czech National Bank.

There have been additional issues specific to India. Food prices account for 50 percent of the basket of goods that comprise the consumer price index. This has short-term and long-term aspects. The short-term aspect is that large year-to-year cycles in food prices often result from variations in harvest conditions (especially the monsoon rains), or from speculative hoarding by wholesalers, or from government interventions (minimum support prices, minimum wage regulations). This has made it difficult for the public and policymakers alike to perceive the influence of monetary policy on the inflation rate. Part of the reason for the large historical influence of food prices on inflation was that central bank policy did not effectively contain the second-round effects. People therefore came to expect that a food price shock would influence the inflation rate over an extended period. In India, slow adjustment of regulated prices does mean that the impact of a food price shock inevitably occurs over a considerable stretch of time: the risk that this will be misinterpreted as a durable rise in the inflation rate underscores the importance of establishing credibility for the new regime and of clear communications. Model simulations underline the need to prevent a shock from affecting long-term expectations in a situation where monetary policy credibility is imperfect. In practice, well-established inflation-forecast-targeting regimes have achieved a major dampening of the pass-through of one-off inflation shocks.

The long-term aspect is that, because of rising real incomes and structural shifts, the relative price of food has shown a trend increase. This is an issue for the definition of the long-term target. The presence of a permanent relative food price increase would justify a somewhat higher target for headline inflation, to avoid the risk of negative core inflation during a cyclical downturn. This is consistent with the choice of 4 percent as the long-term target; that is, two points above the typical target in advanced economies.

Another issue in India has been the uncertain transmission mechanism of monetary policy. This was a problem too in New Zealand and the Czech

Republic, which began inflation targeting during a profound structural transformation. However, weakness of the transmission mechanism has been palpably more severe in India. In contrast to the more advanced economies, changes in Indian policy rates have had little effect on the administered interest rates of the commercial banks—that much of the system is state owned may be a factor. The exchange rate has responded rather sluggishly to changed policy rates, slowing the external channel of policy transmission. Foreign capital flows at times have had strong effects on domestic credit conditions at variance with monetary policy objectives. Statutory preemptions protect the availability of credit to certain types of borrowers (for example, in agriculture). A considerable segment of the population still does not have access to regular financial institutions despite tremendous progress over the last decade, and resorts to informal local lenders whose charges do not reflect the policy rates.

The Reserve Bank of India has developed macroeconomic models that incorporate these special features. Models that incorporate a credibility-building process are appropriate: in this process, expectations of long-term inflation converge on the official target rate only to the extent that the actual inflation rate does not stray far from the target. Weaknesses in policy transmission have effects that come out clearly in policy simulations: following shocks that threaten to push inflation off target, the appropriate interest rate responses may have to be larger than those typical in advanced economies.

Despite the special problems, early results from inflation-forecast targeting in India seem positive. As happened in several advanced economies after the adoption of explicit long-term targets, inflation has dropped substantially. This should raise confidence in the new regime. The system has yet to be tested, however, by a major shock to food prices. It remains to be seen whether, following such an event, long-term inflation expectations will remain anchored by the official targets.

Chapter 12 reviews recent monetary policy in the United States. The Federal Reserve has not formally adopted inflation targeting, but the Federal Open Market Committee's (FOMC's) 2012 clarification of the dual mandate for price stability and maximum employment was tantamount to a statement of inflation-forecast targeting. The FOMC announced, in effect, a target of 2 percent for the inflation rate, and nonquantitative commitment to maximum employment. The communications issues associated with forward guidance on the federal funds rate and quantitative easing are worth examination. These unconventional monetary instruments have been broadly successful in the purpose for which they were designed—that is, to reduce longer-term interest rates and ease the supply of bank credit after the funds rate had been cut to its effective lower bound. Nevertheless, as for Canada, this chapter recommends a strategy of prompt, aggressive responses to shocks that might push the economy into the trap of a bad equilibrium. The argument put forward in this book also calls for a further step forward in transparency for this already quite transparent central bank: publication of all key macroeconomic variables from the staff forecast, including the forecast path of the policy rate.

A WIDENED PERSPECTIVE FOR INFLATION-FORECAST TARGETING

Chapter 13 reviews the monetary policy challenges faced by low-income countries. Some are of a more severe form than those described above confronting India, or the Czech Republic in the 1990s. They include the predominance of supply shocks, the uncertainties regarding the monetary transmission mechanism in a context of structural transformation, and limited access to the formal financial sector. Other issues include limited and noisy macroeconomic and financial data, large exposure to domestic and foreign shocks, recurrent pressures arising from shifts in fiscal policy, and monetary policy regimes centered around exchange rate objectives or guidelines for monetary aggregates, which can make policy more opaque and reduce its effectiveness. The chapter makes the case that adopting key elements of inflation-forecast targeting—for example, an explicit commitment to a numerical long-term inflation target, and a strengthened policy interest rate instrument—can help central banks in these countries articulate clear policy responses, despite the challenging environment. And in fact, several of them are in the process of doing just that, with IMF support, notably in the area of forecasting and policy analysis system development.

Chapter 14 summarizes the main conclusion of the book, that inflation-forecast targeting can provide, and has provided, a robust and adaptable nominal anchor in countries with a wide variety of economic structures and circumstances. Because no alternative monetary regime has been as successful in this respect, or as durable, inflation-forecast targeting can be considered the state of the art for monetary policy. Like any exploration of frontiers, however, it is a project in progress.

REFERENCES

Alichi, A., K. Clinton, C. Freedman, M. Juillard, O. Kamenik, D. Laxton, J. Turunen, and H. Wang. 2015. "Avoiding Dark Corners: A Robust Monetary Policy Framework for the United States." IMF Working Paper 15/134, International Monetary Fund, Washington, DC.

Black, R., D. Laxton, D. Rose, and R. Tetlow. 1994. "The Steady-State Model: SSQPM, the Bank of Canada's New Quarterly Projection Model." Bank of Canada Technical Report 72, Part 1, Bank of Canada, Ottawa.

Calvo, G.A., and C. Vegh. 1999. "Inflation Stabilization and BOP Crises in Developing Countries." NBER Working Paper 6925, National Bureau of Economic Research, Cambridge, MA.

Clinton, K., C. Freedman, M. Juillard, O. Kamenik, D. Laxton, and H. Wang. 2015. "Inflation-Forecast Targeting: Applying the Principle of Transparency." IMF Working Paper 15/132, International Monetary Fund, Washington, DC.

Coats, W., D. Laxton, and D. Rose. 2003. *The Czech National Bank's Forecasting and Policy Analysis System.* Prague: Czech National Bank.

Freedman, C., and D. Laxton. 2009. "Why Inflation Targeting?" IMF Working Paper 09/86, International Monetary Fund, Washington, DC.

Lane, T. 2015. "Inflation Targeting—A Matter of Time." Bank of Canada, Conference presentation, Halifax, Nova Scotia, October.

Laxton, D., D. Rose, and A. Scott. 2009. "Developing a Structured Forecasting and Policy Analysis System to Support Inflation-Forecast Targeting (IFT)." IMF Working Paper 09/65, International Monetary Fund, Washington, DC.

Svensson, L. E. O. 1997 "Inflation Forecast Targeting: Implementing and Monitoring Inflation Targets." *European Economic Review* 41 (6): 1111–46.

————. 2001. "The Zero Bound in an Open Economy: A Foolproof Way of Escaping from a Liquidity Trap." *Monetary and Economic Studies* (Special Edition), February.

————. 2007. "Monetary Policy and the Interest Rate Path." Speech presented at Danske Bank, Stockholm, August 22.

Woodford, M. 2005. "Central-Bank Communication and Policy Effectiveness." Paper presented at the Federal Reserve Bank of Kansas City Symposium, Jackson Hole, Wyoming, August 25–27.

PART II

Principles and Practices of Inflation-Forecast Targeting

CHAPTER 2

First Principles

RANIA AL-MASHAT, KEVIN CLINTON, DOUGLAS
LAXTON, AND HOU WANG

Inflation targeting implies inflation-forecast targeting. —L. E. O. Svensson (1997)

Inflation-forecast targeting represents the frontier of flexible inflation targeting. This chapter reviews its development as a monetary policy regime, particularly how that development was influenced by trends in economic theory, by pragmatic learning-by-doing, and by the experience of inflation-targeting central banks.[1] Box 2.1 provides some examples of how certain central banks transitioned to full-fledged inflation-forecast targeting.

THEORY AND PRACTICE

The volatile inflation of the 1970s made a lasting impression on the central bankers who came to run monetary policy in the succeeding decades. Two post–World War II regimes had failed to keep inflation under control. The Bretton Woods system, with fixed exchange rates pegged to the US dollar as the reserve currency, relied too optimistically on low inflation in the United States and did not provide an efficient means for adjusting to asymmetric international shocks. After the breakdown of the Bretton Woods system in the early 1970s, monetarist-inspired policies were adopted, directed at stable money growth, but these rapidly fizzled out, undone by financial innovations and instability in the demand for money. Neither system provided a reliable nominal anchor.

Lower but chronic inflation in the 1980s seemed to fit the Kydland and Prescott (1977) time-consistency theory, which predicted that discretionary monetary policy has a bias toward inflation because of the perennial temptation to boost output through surprise bursts of monetary expansion. To solve this alleged problem, Barro and Gordon (1983) proposed removing discretion from the central bank, to constrain it to a time-consistent price-stability objective. The idea did not resonate with central bankers, who were aware from experience that tactical room was needed to deal with complex and unpredictable developments. But they did see the practical logic in a binding commitment to price stability, defined as a state in which people expect a low rate of increase in consumer prices to

---

[1]This section draws on Alichi and others (2015) and Clinton and others (2015).

prevail over time. The practical issue raised by the time-consistency theory therefore became how to establish the credibility of the goal while retaining discretionary control over monetary policy instruments.

The Reserve Bank of New Zealand (RBNZ) introduced inflation targets as the foundation for its monetary policy in the heyday of time-consistency theory. However, this landmark reform was driven more by a pragmatic effort to address the country's chronic inflation problem than by any academic trend. Indeed, from the viewpoint of time-consistency theory, announcing a numerical target for low inflation was an incomplete solution to the alleged dilemma. Missing was a constraint to credibly commit the central bank to the target, that is, to prevent short-term actions to boost inflation and output.

Whether the theory was valid or not, the preceding decades of unstable inflation did mean that inflation-targeting policymakers faced a large initial credibility problem. They therefore put great store in getting inflation down to a rate no higher than the initial numerical targets. The RBNZ started out in 1990 with a rigid approach that succeeded in producing a rapid decline in inflation, down in fact to the long-term target, but also produced a recession. The approach paid insufficient attention to the lagged effects of policy actions. The short targeting horizon led to instability, with volatility in the policy interest rate, in the exchange rate (which at the time the RBNZ manipulated through interest-rate differentials as the effective policy instrument), and in output.

The Bank of Canada, which adopted explicit inflation-reduction targets a year later, also implemented a very tight monetary policy stance to bring inflation down fast. In the Canadian case, the focus on short-term results led to a steep recession and a slow recovery.

By the late 1990s, after inflation stabilized at the low target rates, it became clearer that the key to establishing confidence was not rigid adherence to numerical targets from one year to the next, but rather a transparent strategy to eliminate over time any deviations that arose. The idea of transparency as a credibility-building device moved to the forefront. Announcing an explicit numerical target was itself a major step toward clarifying what monetary policy was aiming to achieve. Central banks took further steps to open their communications through regular monetary policy reports (which are sometimes called inflation reports), speeches by senior officials on strategy, media briefings after interest rate decision meetings, and so on.

By the turn of the millennium, one could argue that the transparent pursuit of a low-inflation objective by politically accountable central banks had provided a solution to the time-consistency problem. That is, inflation targeting had apparently removed inflation bias from discretionary policy. Another interpretation of the evidence would be that successful control over inflation in many countries during the 1990s (not just in inflation-targeting countries) refuted the time-consistency theory: Central banks were showing no sign of reneging in favor of short-term output goals. Indeed, policymakers in general, governments as well as central banks, did not display the short-sighted bias at the heart of the argument. Governments left and right of center have since supported the low-inflation

Box 2.1. Learning from Experience

In 1990, New Zealand was the first country to embark on inflation targeting. Today it has a full-fledged inflation-forecast targeting (IFT) regime, and its monetary policy credibility has deepened over time.

As the pioneer, the Reserve Bank of New Zealand (RBNZ) had to learn by doing. Inflation fell quickly, to less than 2 percent in 1992, but the use of the exchange rate as the main policy instrument led to instrument instability. The RBNZ introduced the first fully structured framework for conducting policy under IFT, the forecasting and policy analysis system (FPAS), in 1997, and jumped straight to IFT, with immediate full disclosure of the central bank forecast. The RBNZ's implementation of the FPAS benefited from the experience of the Bank of Canada, which adopted the FPAS on its initial move to inflation targeting in 1991. Elements of Canada's FPAS—which includes a forward-looking forecasting model— were already being put in place as part of the existing policy of price stability, which was not defined numerically but was understood to involve a long-term objective for inflation below 2 percent. The program announced in early 1991 had an eventual target of 2 percent, which has been unchanged since. It took several years to anchor expectations, but after fiscal policy was put on a sustainable footing in 1995, long-term inflation expectations soon stabilized at the 2 percent target rate.

The Czech Republic adopted inflation targeting in 1998. The preceding year had brought the collapse of a fixed exchange rate policy and widespread bank failures. There were lingering difficulties in the transition to the post-communist market economy, with important prices yet to be liberalized. Inflation had been in the upper single digits since 1993 and was accelerating at the time inflation targeting was adopted. With assistance from Bank of Canada staff and the IMF, by 2002 the Czech National Bank was using a purpose-built FPAS with a model-based forecast. The Czech National Bank began publishing its quarterly forecast in detail, including the forecast path for the interest rate, in 2008. Surveys of inflation expectations for the past decade have shown strong public confidence in the 2 percent target.

The RBNZ and the Czech National Bank remain today at the forefront of monetary policy transparency.

objective, albeit in different ways: by a formal instruction where the central bank does not have goal independence (for example, the United Kingdom), by an endorsement where it does (for example, the Czech Republic), or by a statement of agreement where the government and central bank jointly assume responsibility for the goal (for example, Canada).

Under typical arrangements for inflation targeting, the central bank is accountable for its conduct of monetary policy to the government or parliament and, implicitly, to the public. This means that the central bank must have *instrument independence*—that is, unfettered authority to adjust its policy instruments sufficiently aggressively to anchor inflation and inflation expectations.[2] In large part because of the clear delegation of responsibility, implementation of inflation targeting has been accompanied by a vast increase in the transparency of the

[2]Some central banks, in addition, have *goal independence*—they may set their own objectives (Fischer 1995).

conduct of monetary policy, a good thing from the viewpoint of democratic governance. Central bank independence is not an end but a means to protect monetary stability from the risks of short-term political interference. On these grounds, the decisions of the central bank should be subject to political scrutiny, not day by day, but at regular intervals. If inflation targeting is a system of constrained discretion, then accountability provides the means to ensure that discretion is used within the designated constraints and to the specified ends. Accountability without transparency means nothing.[3]

Moreover, during the 1990s, central bankers realized that the better their policies were understood, the more effective they were—a remarkable turnaround within one generation for a profession formerly reputed (not entirely fairly) for its secrecy.[4] Regarding publication of explicit numerical forecasts, the debate has been about how much to disclose—in particular, which elements of the quarterly macroeconomic forecast the central bank should release. Publishing the forecast for inflation and output has not been controversial because policymakers have to show the public they have a plan for keeping inflation on target and that the plan recognizes the potential short-term implications for output.

In an influential contribution, Svensson (1997) pointed out that the central bank's inflation forecast represents an ideal conditional intermediate target, since it takes into account all available information, including the preferences of policymakers and their views on how the economy works. This implies balancing the deviations of inflation from target against deviations of output from potential—in effect recognizing a dual mandate in the implementation of policy.

The history of inflation targeting and of its transition to full-fledged inflation-forecast targeting follows a line of openness or accountability. Milestones along the way have been the following:

- The announcement of targets with a multiyear horizon—clarity on targets
- Precision on the policy interest rate setting—clarity on the instrument[5]
- Transparent communications on policy implementation[6]
- Publication of a complete macro forecast (including inflation)—clarity about the intermediate target
- Publication of a conditional forecast path, alternative scenarios, and confidence bands for the short-term interest rate (full-fledged IFT)

---

[3]Bernanke and others (1999) and Freedman and Laxton (2009) discuss the themes of this paragraph in more depth.

[4]Compare Acheson and Chant (1973) with Chant (2003).

[5]For most advanced economies, a short-term interest rate is used as the policy instrument. However, when central banks have been constrained by the effective lower bound, they have used either large-scale asset purchases (Chapter 12 on the United States) or the exchange rate (Chapter 10 on the Czech Republic). In some countries where their economies are very open (such as Singapore), the more effective instrument could be the exchange rate instead of the short-term interest rate even during normal times.

[6]See Chapter 5 for discussions related to monetary policy operations.

Newcomers to inflation targeting do not have to pass each one of these milestones; the road has been tested and smoothed over several decades. Depending on the available technical capacity, a central bank can enter the road at any point. An international survey of inflation targeters revealed that all started from unpromising initial conditions (Batini and Laxton 2007). None began with a reputation for stable low inflation. Many were emerging from a crisis that had shaken confidence in the monetary authorities (Czech Republic, Sweden, United Kingdom). Some were in the midst of economy-wide structural changes that would completely alter the transmission of monetary policy (Czech Republic, New Zealand). Special problems in certain countries enfeebled the monetary transmission mechanism (for example, dollarization in Peru and severe financial fragility in the Czech Republic). Among the early adopters, only the Bank of Canada had anything close to a forecasting and policy analysis system that was up to the task—a common omission being the lack of an appropriate policy model. None had the external communications program required to explain to a broad public how the monetary policy objective was to be achieved and maintained. Experience therefore denies that there is a demanding list of prerequisites—if you can conduct useful monetary policy at all, you can adopt inflation targeting. However, it is the case that central banks that adopted inflation targets quickly put in place a suitable framework for making the regime effective, even if those frameworks remain works in progress.

The level of development of the economy, and the technical tools available to the central bank, might well affect what form of inflation-targeting regime is most appropriate. For example, in an emerging market economy the central bank might not yet have a model on which it wants to rely for publishing forecasts, whereas the US Federal Reserve has for many years possessed robust, technical models that would support full and formal disclosure.

THE NUMERICAL LONG-TERM TARGET

Over the long term, the main choice variable for an independent monetary policy is the rate of inflation, at least in major advanced economies functioning without disruptive upheavals. If the mandate of the central bank has price stability as the overriding objective, defining an operational objective entails specifying the rate of increase in consumer prices deemed to be consistent with price stability.

Summers (1991), in a contribution that preceded the widespread adoption of inflation targets, lays out the main considerations. High rates of inflation—in the double digits or higher—impose significant costs on the economy through reduced growth, allocative inefficiencies, distortions to the tax system, inequitable redistributions of income, and labor market strife (see, for example, Sarel 1995). The evidence on the economic costs of slightly lower long-term rates of inflation—say, from 2 to 8 percent—is less clear-cut. However, a zero rate of increase for the consumer price index (CPI) over the long term would not be a good target, for a number of reasons. Measurement error produces an upward bias in the official, published CPI, so that a zero target would effectively mean deliberate long-term deflation, rather than price stability (Boskin and others 1996). A very low positive

CPI target—less than 1 percent—would be more consistent with literal price stability, but it would imply that the economy undergo deflation almost half the time. And deflation in advanced economies has usually (although not always) been associated with bad outcomes for employment and growth. For example, other chapters of this book explore how deflation, combined with the floor on the interest rate, may become a trap for the economy, locking in chronic underperformance.

Most advanced economies have settled on a long-term official target rate of 2 percent. This is ample to cover the upward measurement bias, and until the global financial crisis, it seemed high enough to avoid the deflation trap. Since then, however, prolonged below-target inflation and weak growth have led many economists to recommend a higher target (see Williams 2009, 2016; Blanchard, Dell'Ariccia, and Mauro 2010; Clinton and others 2010; Ball 2014; Kiley and Roberts 2017). A key underlying factor in their arguments is that the real equilibrium interest rate has fallen substantially this century, and may not be much above zero. With a near-zero floor on the nominal interest rate, and 2 percent expected inflation in the long term, conventional monetary policy would be hard pressed to provide appropriate stimulus in a recession. If the long-term target were, say, 1 to 2 percentage points higher, then conventional interest rate policy would be that much more effective in real terms. Proponents point out that the evidence does not suggest that such an increase in the target rate of inflation would have long-term negative effects on output.

Major central banks, however, have stuck with their original targets. Raising them would raise questions of credibility and time consistency. For example, having committed to a target of 2 percent for the long term, after you raise the target to 3 or 4 percent how do you convince the public that you will not raise it to 5 percent or 6 percent whenever it seems expedient?[7] More fundamentally, many central bankers take a conservative view of the mandate for price stability— and this conservatism may itself be an asset worth preserving for the credibility of policy (Rogoff 1985).

Lower-income countries experience larger inflation rate shocks than advanced economies because of the larger proportion of fresh food and energy in the consumer basket. Prices of these staples are subject to volatility resulting from developments in international markets, from year-to-year variations in harvests, and in some situations from changes in government controls. Divergences between core inflation (which excludes fresh food and energy) and headline inflation are wider than in advanced economies. This might justify a somewhat higher target for headline inflation (Chapter 11 covers the case of India).

While recognizing the initial success of inflation targeting, there were suggestions beginning in the late 1990s that price-level-path targeting might be an approach that is more consistent with the mandate for price stability, which is

---

[7]Structured research to compare the benefits and costs of choosing a particular inflation target is essential. For example, the Bank of Canada invites and conducts research every five years leading up to the Renewal of the Inflation-Control Target agreement between the Canadian government and the central bank.

largely meant to mean reducing long-term uncertainty over price levels. This approach has been put forward by several academics (Svensson 1999; Cecchetti and Kim 2005) and central bankers (King 1999; Dodge 2005).

The potential benefits of price-level-path targeting were again highlighted in response to the poor economic recovery after the global financial crisis. For example, Coibion, Gorodnichenko, and Wieland (2012) and Williams (2016) suggested that price-level-path targeting would have provided a framework to allow central banks to use their instruments more aggressively to eliminate economic slack faster by planning to have "lower-for-longer" interest rates and temporarily overshoot their long-term inflation objectives.

The Bank of Canada launched an ambitious research effort to investigate the possibility of price-level-path targeting in the renewal of the inflation-control target framework in 2006. Informed by the research, the bank reached the view that realizing the theoretical net benefits of the approach would likely be challenging in practice (Bank of Canada 2011). Interestingly, from the adoption of a 2 percent inflation target in the fourth quarter of 1999 until the global financial crisis, Canadian prices strayed very little from the trend path implied by the 2 percent inflation target, and they tended to revert to that path after temporary deviations—something that looks like a successful price-level-path targeting regime. Kamenik and others (2013) study the Canada case and show that some planned overshooting (or undershooting) of inflation over the target may be consistent with optimal monetary policy under uncertainty.

SOME PRINCIPLES OF INFLATION-FORECAST TARGETING

Underlying inflation-forecast targeting is the principle that, given a long-term objective for the rate of inflation, the central bank's own forecast of inflation is an optimal, conditional, intermediate target. This is because the forecast, in principle, embodies all the relevant information available to the central bank, including knowledge of the policymakers' preferences about the trade-off between deviations of inflation from target and output from potential and the bank's view of the monetary policy transmission mechanism.

The basic features of inflation-forecast targeting are these:

- Monetary policy uses the instruments (typically the policy interest rate) to achieve an official low-inflation target over the medium term (within about two years in practice).
- The central bank's economic forecast contains a path to the official target that is an ideal intermediate target for managing the short-term output-inflation trade-off.
- The staff forecast is a key input into the decision of the monetary policy committee, but only one input among others—committee members need not agree with the forecast and can incorporate other information into their decision-making.

- The staff uses a core model, with standard macroeconomic properties, to derive the forecast. The model-based forecast provides a basis both for policy decisions and for explaining the economic logic underlying these decisions in public communications. (The forecast path for the short-term interest rate—the policy instrument—is endogenous in the model, with the rate varying to achieve the long-term inflation target and to eliminate any output gap).

The last point should be emphasized: the policy interest rate responds to eliminate any deviations between actual inflation and its objective.

The forecasting and policy analysis system organizes the quarterly forecasting exercise around a core projection model (Laxton, Rose, and Scott 2009; see also Chapter 4). The typical core model is a quarterly macroeconomic model of moderate size that incorporates the central bank's knowledge of the policy transmission channels. It contains a reaction function for the policy interest rate that captures the preferences of the policymakers relative to the short-term trade-offs between the variability of inflation, output, and the interest rate.

Having an efficient forecasting and policy analysis system is essential. The staff presents a baseline forecast and alternative forecasts based on different assumptions about the economy or the policy reaction function. The monetary policy committee in effect receives a menu of alternative forecast paths for the policy rate. Each interest rate decision stems from the committee's view of the best path of the policy rate over the medium term, taking into consideration both the short-term trade-off against output that is implied and the requirement to ensure that actual inflation does not deviate too much from target over the medium term.

Many of today's inflation-targeting central banks, under this definition, would be considered inflation-forecast targeters. Examples of established and credible inflation-forecast-targeting central banks are the RBNZ, the Bank of Canada, the Central Bank of Chile, and the Czech National Bank. Developing a forecasting and policy analysis system from scratch has become easier because of the increased opportunities to learn from others. Indeed, as Norges Bank has shown, it has become possible for newer entrants to leapfrog the pack and jump straight to the frontier.

The pragmatic requirements within the central bank for an operational inflation-forecast-targeting regime are these:

- A structured forecasting and policy analysis system maintains relevant databases and produces a model-based staff forecast and associated economic analysis on a regular schedule.

- Policymakers and technical staff maintain communications to ensure that the forecast addresses the main broad concerns of the monetary policy committee.

- The forecast team presents policymakers with the forecast—which at least once a quarter would come from a full forecasting exercise, or in between from an update just to the main variables—shortly before each rate-setting meeting.

Inflation-forecast targeting also implies a transparent communications strategy. A typical schedule following a policy decision is as follows:

- The same-day announcement (press release) sketches a brief rationale.

- The central bank governor gives a review of the policy decision and the economic outlook at a press conference. Staff members may answer the more technical questions.

- A monetary policy report or inflation report explains in greater depth the rationale for the policy actions. The report provides the baseline forecast path, usually quarterly, for the main goal variables, inflation and output growth, and for other macroeconomic variables. The latter include a conditional forecast for the short-term interest rate, for most central banks just in general qualitative terms, but for the *avant-garde* of inflation-forecast targeters it is an explicit numerical path.

- Presentations and publications underline conditionality and uncertainty by showing confidence bands around the baseline for relevant variables and by considering alternative scenarios with different assumptions for specific shocks germane to the economic conjuncture. These exercises do not just warn of the risks, they also give the public insight into how the central bank might respond to a range of shocks.

THE NOMINAL ANCHOR: AN ENDOGENOUS POLICY RESPONSE

The credibility of the long-term inflation target underpins inflation-forecast targeting. Everything pivots around the anchor provided by the firm public expectation that monetary policy will keep inflation stable and near the official target rate. This in turn requires that policy responds systematically to the requirements of this objective. Figure 2.1 depicts a model of the process.

With a forward-looking policy, the expected path of the policy interest rate is adjusted when unanticipated disturbances hit the economy in an attempt to bring inflation back to the target while keeping disruptions to output to a minimum. This policy feedback, through an endogenous short-term interest rate, is represented by the red dashed arrows in Figure 2.1. It ensures that the nominal anchor holds.

In the general situation, where the actual inflation rate differs from the long-term target, monetary policymakers have a choice as to how to respond. The approach may be more or less rapid, depending on the preferences regarding the short-term output-inflation trade-off. It might involve a smooth approach or a planned overshoot. Out of the available options, the central bank will implement the one that "looks best," that is, the one that reflects its judgment as to the best

Figure 2.1. Inflation-Forecasting Targeting: Feedback Response and Transmission

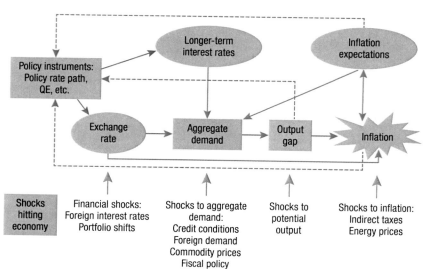

Source: Authors' construction.
Note: QE = quantitative easing.

outcome relative to the trade-offs between inflation and output and the variability of the interest rate.[8]

For example, consider a positive shock to energy prices. If policymakers put a high relative weight on stabilizing the inflation rate, they will respond with a relatively sharp increase in the policy rate to return inflation quickly to target and implicitly accept the negative short-term consequences for output as a necessary cost. The forecast team would take account of the ramifications on all external variables, for example, the demand from trading partners, and then use the core model to simulate the impact on the domestic economy. The baseline forecast, using the standard policy response of the model, would imply an interest rate path that, over the medium term, returns inflation to its long-term target rate, while taking into account the trade-off between the costs induced by inflation being away from target and the costs of output gaps. Other policy responses might also be simulated to provide policymakers with a menu of options. In each case, an entire chronology would be created for future short-term interest rates,

---

[8]For a discussion of the theory and practice of flexible inflation targeting, see Svensson (2010). In part, the judgment is equivalent to choosing among outcomes that impose a different weight on the relative importance of the deviation of output from potential relative to the deviation of inflation from its target along the path back to equilibrium. Qvigstad (2005) provides a Norwegian central banker's pragmatic description of this choice.

of which the next rate-setting decision would be the first step. The forecast team might also provide forecasts based on several scenarios in which very different assumptions are used for oil prices or, for that matter, for other exogenous variables. Associated with each simulation would be confidence bands for the key variables, reflecting the normal range of random factors that may affect the forecast. In making their decision, policymakers would decide on one of the alternative endogenous paths for the interest rate.

A full description of the central bank's policy decision would entail the entire future path of the policy rate, not just the current level of the policy rate. The likely course of the interest rate would be a theme for the subsequent round of external communications, through post-decision-meeting media briefings and press conferences, the monetary policy (or inflation) report, and so on. In the most transparent case, the central bank would publish the endogenous path for the short-term interest rate along with the confidence band.[9]

Expectations of future policy rate movements over the short to medium term play a crucial role in the transmission mechanism, as depicted by the blue arrows pointing at the ovals labelled *Longer-term interest rates* and *Exchange rate*. The cost of borrowing for businesses and households is not the very short-term rate directly controlled by the central bank. They borrow at longer terms. Policy affects the rates they pay more through the impact of the policy rates expected in the future, and hence the level of the whole yield curve, than through the current policy rate itself. This is reflected in the rectangle for the "Policy Rate Path"—the *whole path* expected for the medium term, not just the current setting, is what counts.

Use of an exogenous interest rate path (including a path derived from current market forward rates) in a forecast is inconsistent with inflation targeting. If the figure were modified to represent an exogenous interest rate path, the red dashed feedback arrows would be erased.

CONCLUSIONS

Inflation-forecast targeting constitutes a transparent, flexible approach to inflation targeting. Academic theorizing has influenced its development, but practical experience has built the main foundation of its principles.

Inflation-forecast targeting does not require rigid actions designed to hit the target from year to year. The approach recognizes that monetary policy has objectives for output and employment in the short to medium term, as well as for inflation, and that monetary policy takes effect with a considerable lag. Since the central bank's own forecast accounts for all relevant information, including policymakers' preferences about the short-term trade-off between output and employment, it is an ideal intermediate target for monetary policy.

---

[9]For example, see Clinton and others (2017) for a discussion of the Czech experience with publishing the path of the policy rate.

A guiding principle is that inflation-forecast targeting establishes confidence that inflation will converge to the official target rate. For this, the central bank must consistently use the policy instrument to return inflation to target. Since it may take a year or two to eliminate a substantial deviation, actual inflation might be off-target for prolonged periods. When the public understands this, long-term expectations hold firm to the target even through fluctuations in the actual rate of price increases—and the nominal anchor is stable. To this end, transparent communications are important, as discussed in detail in Chapter 8.

Efficient implementation relies on a forecasting and policy analysis system that is designed specifically to support inflation-forecast targeting. An essential part of this is a macroeconomic forecasting model in which the policy interest rate is determined by a systematic policy reaction. The instrument must respond to any disturbance to keep inflation on track to reaching the fixed official target.

Some important conditions must be met for inflation-forecast targeting to work effectively. These include a well-functioning monetary transmission mechanism, central bank instrument independence, and no fiscal dominance (Batini, Kuttner, and Laxton 2005). However, when monetary policy is constrained because interest rates remain at or close to zero (the "effective lower bound"), use of unconventional monetary policy instruments may be required as well as a fiscal backstop. These issues are discussed in detail in the chapters on Canada (Chapter 9) and the United States (Chapter 10).

REFERENCES

Acheson, K., and J. Chant. 1973. "Bureaucratic Theory and the Choice of Central Bank Goals." *Journal of Money, Credit and Banking* 5 (2): 637–55.

Alichi, A., K. Clinton, C. Freedman, M. Juillard, O. Kamenik, D. Laxton, J. Turunen, and H. Wang. 2015. "Avoiding Dark Corners: A Robust Monetary Policy Framework for the United States." IMF Working Paper 15/134, International Monetary Fund, Washington, DC.

Ball, L. 2014. "The Case for a Long-Run Inflation Target of Four Percent." IMF Working Paper 14/92, International Monetary Fund, Washington, DC.

Bank of Canada. 2011. "Renewal of the Inflation-Control Target: Background Information," November.

Barro, R., and D. Gordon. 1983. "Rules, Discretion, and Reputation in a Model of Monetary Policy." *Journal of Monetary Economics* 12 (1): 101–21.

Batini, N., K. Kuttner, and D. Laxton. 2005. "Does Inflation Targeting Work in Emerging Markets?" Chapter 4 of the September 2005 *World Economic Outlook*, International Monetary Fund, Washington, DC.

Batini, N., and D. Laxton. 2007. "Under What Conditions Can Inflation Targeting Be Adopted? The Experience of Emerging Markets." In *Monetary Policy Under Inflation Targeting*, edited by F. S. Mishkin and K. Schmidt-Hebbel. Chile: Banco Central de Chile.

Bernanke, B. S., T. Laubach, F. S. Mishkin, and A. S. Posen. 1999. *Inflation Targeting: Lessons from the International Experience*. Princeton, NJ: Princeton University Press.

Blanchard, O., G. Dell'Ariccia, and P. Mauro. 2010. "Rethinking Macroeconomic Policy." IMF Staff Position Note 10/03, February. International Monetary Fund, Washington, DC.

Boskin, M., E. Dulberger, R. Gordon, Z. Griliches, and D. Jorgenson. 1996. "Toward a More Accurate Measure of the Cost of Living." Report of the Advisory Commission on the Consumer Price Index, December. United States Senate, Washington, DC.

Cecchetti, S., and J. Kim. 2005. "Inflation Targeting, Price Path Targeting, and Output Variability." In *The Inflation Targeting Debate*, ed. by B. Bernanke and M. Woodford, 173–200. Chicago: University of Chicago Press

Chant, J. 2003. "The Bank of Canada: Moving towards Transparency." *Bank of Canada Review* Spring: 5–13.

Clinton, K., C. Freedman, M. Juillard, O. Kamenik, D. Laxton, and H. Wang. 2015. "Inflation-Forecast Targeting: Applying the Principle of Transparency." IMF Working Paper 15/132, International Monetary Fund, Washington, DC.

Clinton, K., R. Garcia-Saltos, M. Johnson, O. Kamenik, and D. Laxton. 2010. "International Deflation Risks under Alternative Macroeconomic Policies." *Journal of the Japanese and International Economies* 24 (2): 140–77.

Clinton, K., T. Hlédik, T. Holub, D. Laxton, and H. Wang. 2017. "Czech Magic: Implementing Inflation-Forecast Targeting at the CNB." IMF Working Paper 17/21, International Monetary Fund, Washington, DC.

Coibion, O., Y. Gorodnichenko, and J. Wieland. 2012. "The Optimal Inflation Rate in New Keynesian Models: Should Central Banks Raise Their Inflation Targets in Light of the ZLB?" *Review of Economic Studies* 79: 1371–406.

Dodge, D. 2005. "Our Approach to Monetary Policy: Inflation Targeting." Remarks to the Regina Chamber of Commerce, Regina, Saskatchewan.

Fischer, S. 1995. "Modern Approaches to Central Banking." NBER Working Paper 5064. National Bureau of Economic Research, Cambridge, MA.

Freedman, C., and D. Laxton. 2009. "Inflation Targeting Pillars: Transparency and Accountability." IMF Working Paper 09/262, International Monetary Fund, Washington, DC.

Kamenik, O., H. Kiem, V. Klyuev, and D. Laxton. 2013. "Why Is Canada's Price Level So Predictable?" *Journal of Money Credit and Banking* 45 (1): 71–85.

Kiley, M., and J. Roberts. 2017. "Monetary Policy in a Low Interest Rate World." Brookings Papers on Economic Activity Conference Drafts, March 23–24.

King, M. 1999. "Challenges to Monetary Policy: New and Old." In *New Challenges for Monetary Policy*, proceedings of the Federal Reserve Bank of Kansas City Symposium, August, 11–57.

Kydland, F., and E. Prescott. 1977. "Rules Rather than Discretion: The Inconsistency of Optimal Plans." *Journal of Political Economy* 85 (3): 473–92.

Laxton, D., D. Rose, and A. Scott. 2009. "Developing a Structured Forecasting and Policy Analysis System to Support Inflation-Forecast Targeting (IFT)." IMF Working Paper 09/65, International Monetary Fund, Washington, DC.

Qvigstad, J. F. 2005. "When Does an Interest Rate Path 'Look Good'? Criteria for an Appropriate Future Interest Rate Path – A Practician's Approach." Norges Bank Staff Memo 2005/6, Norges Bank, Oslo.

Rogoff, K. 1985. "The Optimal Degree of Commitment to an Intermediate Monetary Target." *Quarterly Journal of Economics* 100 (4): 1169–89.

Sarel, M. 1995. "Nonlinear Effects of Inflation on Economic Growth." IMF Working Paper 95/56, June, International Monetary Fund, Washington, DC.

Summers, L. 1991. "Panel Discussion: Price Stability: How Should Long-Term Monetary Policy Be Determined?" *Journal of Money, Credit and Banking* 23 (3), Part 2, August.

Svensson, L. E. O. 1997. "Inflation Forecast Targeting: Implementing and Monitoring Inflation Targets." *European Economic Review* 41 (6): 1111–46.

———. 1999. "Inflation Targeting as a Monetary Policy Rule." *Journal of Monetary Economics* 43 (3): 607–54.

———. 2010. "Inflation Targeting." In *Handbook of Monetary Economics*, edited by Benjamin M. Friedman, and Michael Woodford. Volume 3B, Chapter 22.

Williams, J.C. 2009. "Heeding Daedalus: Optimal Inflation and the Zero Lower Bound." *Brookings Papers on Economic Activity* 2.

———. 2016. "Monetary Policy in a Low R-Star World." FRBSF Economic Letter 23, Federal Reserve Bank of San Francisco, San Francisco, CA.

CHAPTER 3

Managing Expectations

RANIA AL-MASHAT, KEVIN CLINTON, DOUGLAS
LAXTON, AND HOU WANG

*For not only do expectations about policy matter, but, at least under current conditions,
very little else matters. —M. Woodford (2005)*

The essence of useful monetary policy is effectively managing expectations. This
applies both to the policy objectives and to the policy instruments.

The primary, long-term objective of monetary policy is to achieve a sustained
environment of low inflation (see, for example, Summers 1991). There is no
useful long-term trade-off between inflation and the level of output or employment. Technology, demographics, legal and regulatory structures, education,
natural resources, government taxes and spending, national savings and investment, and other nonmonetary factors determine the latter variables.

Bad monetary policy—resulting in unstable or high inflation or deflation—
could get in the way of good performance in the real sector. But if the price level
is predictable, as it would be in a sustained environment of low inflation, monetary policy does not have a first-order effect on the long-term level of output. The
important practical choice for the long-term objective for monetary policy is
therefore—explicitly or implicitly—the numerical target for the long-term rate of
inflation. For those central banks with a mandate to pursue price stability, this
may be rephrased to say that the main practical choice is the definition of price
stability as the long-term measured rate of price increase. No practical difference
need exist between an explicit inflation target and an explicit price stability objective. Regimes that have an explicit objective, however, differ substantively in their
transparency and accountability from those that do not—and they differ in their
credibility and effectiveness.

POLICY INSTRUMENTS

To achieve the single policy objective of a sustained environment of low inflation
requires at least one policy instrument. The main monetary policy instrument
over the short or medium term is usually the key short-term interest rate controlled by the central bank. Modern theoretical models and topical discussions of
policy actions focus almost exclusively on this instrument, except under unusual
circumstances (which are discussed later in this book). The exchange rate gets a

Figure 3.1. Phillips Curve Adjustment to Inflation-Reduction Target: Perfect versus Imperfect Policy Credibility

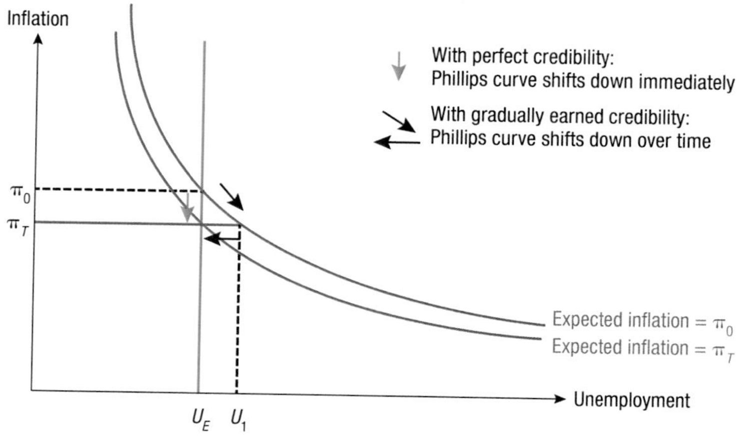

Source: Authors' construction.

lot of attention too, but deliberate manipulation of the exchange rate, independent of the interest rate, is feasible only over brief periods in a world of high capital mobility. In a small or mid-size economy, the world interest rate and a risk premium set the domestic interest rate via capital mobility. In the long term, the central bank controls neither the interest rate nor the exchange rate.

Through what instrument then does the central bank control the long-term inflation rate? The answer is expectations, and expectations alone. One objective, low inflation, matches one instrument, the management of expectations.

The inflation equation in a conventional macroeconomic model, an expectations-augmented Phillips curve, illustrates the point. It writes current inflation as a function of expected inflation and the output gap. In the long-term equilibrium, actual inflation is equal to expected inflation, and the output gap is zero. The solid red lines in Figure 3.1 illustrate this, using the unemployment rate to represent the output gap: the long-term equilibrium has inflation at the target rate π_T, and unemployment at the long-term equilibrium rate U_E.

Eventually, the expected rate of inflation prevails, with the Phillips curve vertical at the equilibrium rate of unemployment. From this viewpoint, the main job of monetary policy is to ensure that expectations hold firm at the target rate—in other words, that people have confidence that inflation will continue into the indefinite future at the officially announced rate.

But suppose that at the introduction of a target, inflation has varied around a higher rate, and that expectations have gelled at this rate, π_0. To get from there to the new equilibrium at the target rate will in general involve a cost in terms of above-equilibrium unemployment. For example, with the initial Phillips curve,

Figure 3.2. Phillips Curve: Stable versus Variable Unemployment Rate

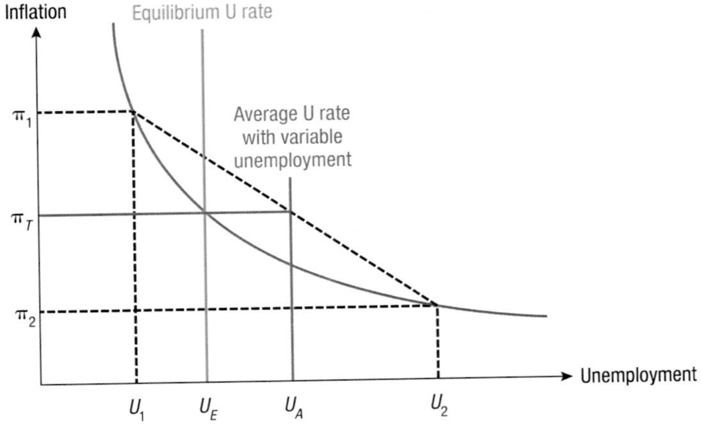

consistent with long-term expected inflation at π_0, the central bank may tighten to get immediately to the announced target, π_T. The short-term Phillips curve indicates that this implies raising unemployment to U_1. Holding inflation at the target rate for long enough will ensure that eventually expectations fall into line. The Phillips curve shifts down, and resettles at the long-term equilibrium, with the unemployment gap back to zero, as indicated by the black arrows. Depending on how the public's expectations adjust, this process may involve a prolonged unemployment gap. However, in a hypothetical case where the central bank's announcements have perfect credibility, expectations will go immediately to the target rate, at no unemployment cost, as per the red arrow. During the adjustment to a new inflation target the unemployment cost is lower the more rapidly public expectations adapt to the target, underscoring their key role in transition states.

In addition, the effectiveness of the policy transmission mechanism depends on well-managed expectations. Figure 3.2 illustrates the importance of this point.

As before, the long-term equilibrium is at the target rate of inflation π_T and equilibrium unemployment rate U_E. However, shocks are always hitting the economy, such that monetary policy cannot hold inflation on target all the time, but only on average. In the figure, half the time inflation is at π_1, with unemployment U_1; and half the time at π_2, U_2. On average inflation is on target. But the average unemployment rate is above the deterministic equilibrium rate because of the nonlinearity of the standard Phillips curve: the average U_A lies on the chord between the two short-term equilibrium points on the curve.[1] More generally, the

---

[1]Debelle and Laxton (1997) make this point, distinguishing the natural rate of unemployment from the rate consistent with non-accelerating inflation.

wider the cyclical fluctuations in the economy, the greater the deadweight loss of output over time. It follows that the more effective monetary policy is as a countercyclical tool, the lower this cost. And in turn, the effectiveness of the policy instrument for this purpose again depends on managing expectations.

If monetary policy interest rate actions are to influence output, it is essential that changes in the policy rate, a very short-term money market rate itself of little relevance to most economic activity, cause changes in the same direction in the longer-term rates at which households and firms borrow and lend. This implies that current changes in the policy rate must, if they are to influence macroeconomic variables at all, affect expectations of the future path of the policy rate.

Thus, managing expectations is crucial in both the long term and the short term. But how best to do this? In the real world, official announcements alone do not work: policymakers earn (or lose) credibility by acting predictably over time to produce results consistent with their declared objectives (or not).

TRANSPARENCY: PUBLISHED INTEREST RATE FORECASTS

Full transparency is the simplest way for the central bank to reinforce confidence in the long-term inflation target and to encourage movements in longer-term interest rates. The argument has long been accepted in regard to the objective: inflation-targeting central banks have always insisted that they will achieve their long-term targets and have used all the communications tools at their disposal to convince the public to expect long-term inflation at the target rate, including from the outset a published forecast path on which a medium-term target is also achieved.

In addition, over the short to medium term, publication of the central bank's own forecast path for the endogenous policy rate, along with other main variables in its macroeconomic forecast, strengthens the policy transmission mechanism. A few central banks have already adopted this approach, including the Reserve Bank of New Zealand and the Czech National Bank. Despite a worry that the public might interpret publication of an interest rate forecast as some kind of commitment on the policy rate, financial markets have readily understood that the rate forecast is subject to change, conditional on unpredictable economic developments.[2] The management of expectations through full disclosure of the forecast interest rate path is called *conventional forward guidance*, to distinguish it from the ad hoc forward guidance that the Federal Reserve and many other central banks have used since the global financial crisis.

Since it typically takes several years for the effects of policy interest actions to be realized, in the forecast a variety of future paths will be consistent with achieving the official inflation target, some more quickly than others. The path chosen by policymakers would reflect their preferences regarding the short-term trade-off

---

[2]Freedman and Laxton (2009) discuss this issue in more depth.

between inflation and output. For example, in response to a supply shock, a higher weight on output stability would imply smoother adjustments of the interest rate in response to a given deviation from the inflation target, and a slower return to the target. At any decision point, policymakers must therefore have in mind a time profile for the future policy rate—a conditional path, to be sure, which will change as new data arrive.

Publication of this path would help move expected short-term rates, and hence the whole term structure of interest rates, in support of the transmission mechanism. In terms of objectives, the payoff from this reinforcement of policy effectiveness would be a reduced cost of eliminating deviations of actual inflation from the long-term target rate, or equivalently, an improved short-term output-inflation trade-off (Blanchard and Galí 2007; Laxton and N'Diaye 2002). A connected, but somewhat distinct, argument in favor of publishing the forecast interest rate path is that the information further improves the accountability of the central bank.

EXIT POLICY

If monetary policy leaves expectations of inflation free to wander, the economy can become trapped in a bad *quasi-equilibrium*—either very high and unstable inflation or very low inflation (at the worst, deflation)—from which conventional monetary policies offer at best a very costly exit or at worst no exit at all. It is a quasi-equilibrium in that it would not be restored following a lucky shock that put the economy onto a preferred path. These situations call for a coordinated attack using all the main instruments of policy—fiscal, structural, and monetary.[3] But a transparent, assertive stance from the central bank can make a big difference. The essence, for better or for worse, is managing expectations—as illustrated in Box 3.1.

One dark corner, which quite a few central banks confront when they first adopt an inflation-targeting regime, is an inflationary environment where people have become accustomed to rapidly rising prices over many years. They have no reason to trust promises from the central bank to disinflate the economy. A tightened monetary stance may result in a steep drop in output, with little to show in the way of lower inflation for years. Unless policymakers have unusually long horizons, the visible output and employment costs of disinflation would exceed the distant perceived benefits. The public would understand the policymakers' dilemma. As a result, a time-consistent inflationary equilibrium persists, which policymakers have no apparent incentive to change and which people expect to continue. This may be like the situation before India introduced inflation targeting. At the outset of the new regime, the Reserve Bank of India had to change skeptical perceptions about its willingness, or ability, to reduce inflation to the official target range and keep it there.

---

[3]Gaspar and others (2016) present the argument in the context of below-target inflation, and wide output gaps, in some large advanced economies.

The dark corner on the other side of the room—a deflation trap—is even more difficult to escape. In the worst-case scenario, conventional monetary policy becomes completely ineffective. The central bank would cut the nominal policy rate to or near zero (the effective lower bound), attempting to stimulate activity and stabilize prices. But with negative and declining inflation the real interest rate (nominal rate minus expected inflation) may be substantially positive and rising. The economy sinks into a hole. Symptoms of this kind have been evident in Japan since 1990. And for some years after the global financial crisis other advanced economies, notably the euro area, experienced a mild but still chronic version of the syndrome—with low inflation, rather than deflation, and a persistent negative output gap.

For almost 10 years, major central banks have maintained policy interest rates at historically low levels, sometimes below zero. With rates slightly above the effective lower bound, policymakers have had little room for further cuts. To provide further monetary stimulus, central banks have used forward guidance for the policy interest rate and quantitative easing through large-scale asset purchases. The intent has been to reduce longer-term rates by a provisional commitment to keep the policy rate low for an extended period or by reducing the term premium in bond yields. Both forward guidance and quantitative easing mainly influence bond rates and primarily through expectations—they strengthen prospects that future short-term rates will remain at the floor for a long period.

To judge from the extremely low levels to which yields fell after these policy actions, forward guidance and quantitative easing did in fact provide monetary policy with additional instruments to reduce borrowing costs. Moreover, positive macroeconomic outcomes—increased output and a decline in unemployment—suggest that these less conventional measures had some effect. In the case of the United States, the Federal Reserve's actions along these lines contributed to the steady recovery after 2009. The problem in most economies was that the stimulus to output was not strong enough.

Under inflation-forecast targeting, forward guidance can be considered an ongoing process in which the central bank provides a continuous flow of information on its current policy actions and on its view of what medium-term actions may be appropriate. During a period in which the effective lower bound is indeed binding and where the main danger is deflation the central bank would publish a forecast with an endogenous interest rate near the floor for long enough to get inflation back on track. To the extent that the forecast affects market expectations, it will move medium- and long-term rates down, in line with the objective of shifting the economy away from the low-inflation trap.

Publication of the forecast is thus an instrument that helps policy achieve its objectives, in effect like the Fed's forward guidance.[4] However, the strategy of the most transparent inflation-forecast-targeting central banks emerges from a

---

[4]Bernanke (2013) provides an authoritative description of the evolution of forward guidance at the Fed.

Box 3.1. Policy Expectations May Absorb or Amplify Shocks

Figure 3.1.1 illustrates a contractionary shock. In response, in normal times, the central bank would cut the policy rate. The effect on the economy depends on how people interpret this action.

Credibility results in shock absorption. If the rate hike is perceived as the assertive response of a credible central bank, inflation expectations for the longer term remain stable, and the policy action lowers the real interest rate.

In addition, uncovered interest parity implies a depreciation in the real exchange rate:

$$\downarrow \sum_{j=0}^{k} r_{t+j} = [z_{t+k+1} - \uparrow z_t] + \sum_{j=0}^{k} \left\{ r_{t+j}^f + u_{t+j} \right\} \qquad (3.1.1)$$

Notation: r, real interest rate; z, real exchange rate (up means a depreciation); r^f, foreign real interest rate; μ, country risk premium.

A similar argument applies to asset prices, which would also rise. The easier monetary conditions, and the induced wealth effect, stimulate demand, and narrow—eventually eliminating—the negative output gap. Inflation returns without unusual delay to the long-term target rate.

Lack of credibility, however, can lead to shock amplification.

In the unusual time of a low-inflation trap, with the interest rate at the effective lower bound, the risk of a worse outcome is greater. With falling expectations of inflation, or rising expectations of deflation, the real interest rate would increase, the real exchange rate would appreciate, and asset prices would fall:

$$\uparrow r_t = i_t - \downarrow E_t \pi_{t+1} \qquad (3.1.2)$$

This is the classic deflation trap. An assertive reflationary policy stance is then required. Since the nominal interest rate can go no lower, the central bank must persuade people not only that the nominal interest rate will remain at the floor for an extended period and that the rate of inflation will rise over the medium term (possibly above the long-term target), but also that the rate of inflation will eventually return to target. Clearly, everything depends on the ability of the monetary policymakers to manage the expectations of the public.

Figure 3.1.1. Expectations as Absorbers or Amplifiers Follow a Contractionary Shock

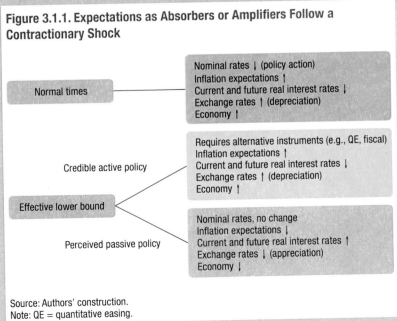

Source: Authors' construction.
Note: QE = quantitative easing.

framework that applies always, not just during a dark corner. The principle that underlies the effectiveness of forward guidance applies more generally: if the markets understand where monetary policy is heading, they are likely to move interest rates in a direction that supports policy. It follows that releasing that path would be the single most obvious way of clarifying for the public the policy implications of the economic outlook. Moreover, the ongoing nature of the commitment under inflation-forecast targeting provides assurance that the response to shocks in the future will be just as vigorous, since the central bank communicates to the public not just a conditional path for the future policy rate, but also a rationale for it, and a sense of how this expected path might change when unexpected developments arise. This underlines the conditionality of the current central bank forecast at the same time that it is strengthening confidence in the long-term outlook.

EVIDENCE ON MANAGING EXPECTATIONS UNDER INFLATION TARGETING

Given the susceptibility of an economy to many kinds of disturbances, the inflation rate is bound to vary from year to year, and it will sometimes deviate substantially from the objective of the central bank, regardless of the policy regime or the skill of the policymakers. Targeting errors need not, however, undermine the credibility of monetary policy. The foundation for the credibility is not so much precision in achieving an announced objective—although that would surely help—but instead the expectation that monetary policy will systematically respond to any deviations in such a way that the long-term objective will be achieved. The evidence in the following subsections suggests that a well-designed and well-executed inflation-targeting regime instills such confidence. It also suggests that in the early, credibility-building phase any failure to follow through on the commitment to a policy response consistent with the inflation target can cause confusion and destabilize expectations—with a costly macroeconomic impact.

United Kingdom 1997

This episode provided an early indication of the power of a credible inflation targeting announcement (Escolano and others 2000). Before 1997 the United Kingdom had a peculiar inflation-targeting arrangement: the Chancellor of the Exchequer (finance minister), not the Bank of England, set the policy interest rate. In May 1997, a reform transferred this responsibility to the Monetary Policy Committee of the central bank. The reform also provided for increased transparency and accountability. It required publication of minutes of the monthly Monetary Policy Committee meeting. The target shifted, from a 1–4 percent range, to the midpoint of that range, 2.5 percent. And if inflation diverges over a year from the target, the governor now must write an open letter to the Chancellor explaining why and outlining what the Monetary Policy

Figure 3.3. Inflation Expectations 10 Years ahead in the United Kingdom, 1995–99
(Percent)

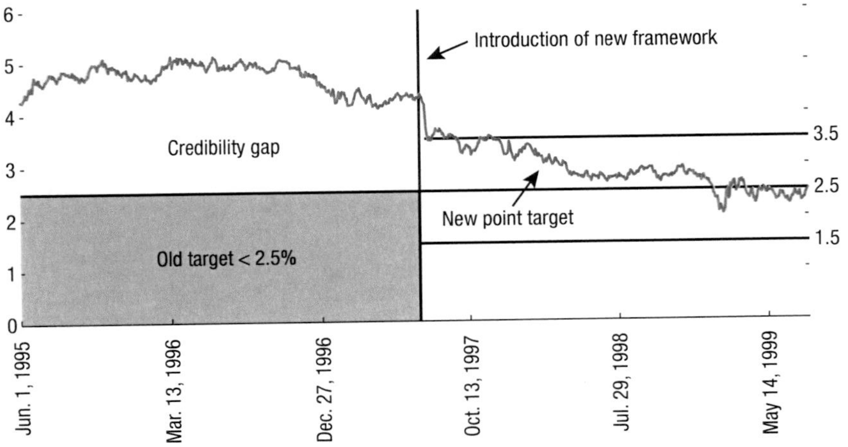

Source: Escolano and others 2000.

Committee will do to rectify the deviation. In brief, the reform set up an ortho-dox inflation-targeting policy framework, with instrument independence for the central bank.

The inflation premium on long-term bond yields declined. Ten-year inflation expectations, as gauged by the difference in yields between nominal and indexed bonds, dropped from more than 4 percent to 2.5 percent (the target rate)—and they stabilized around that rate (Figure 3.3). The announcement of the reform provided a large boost to confidence in monetary policy, eliminating the credibil-ity gap evident in bond yields, even before the regime had demonstrated it would deliver on its commitments.

Emerging Market Economies

During the great moderation period before 2008, inflation performance across advanced economies was uniformly good, with no large difference between infla-tion targeters and others. The differences among emerging market economies, however, were substantial. Batini, Kuttner, and Laxton (2005) find that within this group inflation targeting was associated with lower inflation, lower inflation expectations, and lower inflation volatility compared with countries that did not adopt inflation targeting. Inflation targeting did not appear to hurt output, or other dimensions of economic performance—for example, the volatility of inter-est rates, exchange rates, and international reserves.

Figure 3.4. Israel: Interest Rates, Inflation, and Exchange Rates, 2001–04
(Percent)

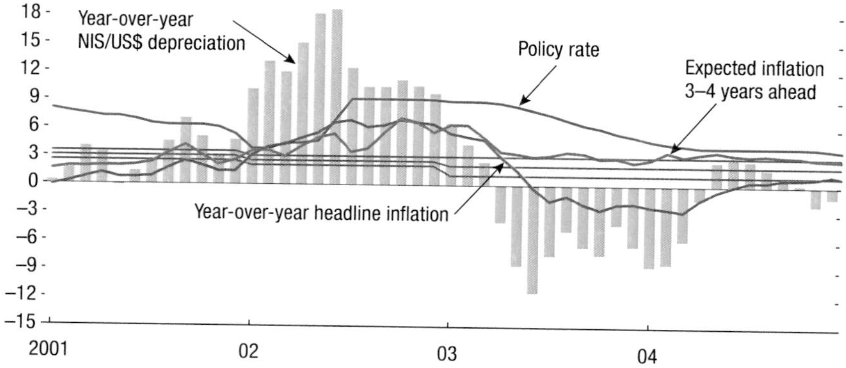

Sources: Argov and others 2007; Bank of Israel; Central Bureau of Statistics; and IMF staff estimates.
Note: NIS = new sheqel.

Israel 2001–07

In late 2001, responding to weakness in output after the collapse of the dot.com bubble and a steep rise in unemployment, the Bank of Israel cut the policy rate 200 basis points (Argov and others 2007). The new sheqel depreciated. Headline inflation rose to 7 percent by July 2002, much more than the 3 percent top of the target band (Figure 3.4). In response, the Bank of Israel raised the policy rate by 450 basis points in three steps and then held it at around 9 percent until mid-2003, even though the economy was still in recession.

Inflation dropped below zero in the second half of 2003 and the first half of 2004, yet inflation expectations were consistently above the 1–3 percent band. The real policy rate—the nominal rate less expected inflation one year ahead—rose to 6 percent during the second half of 2002 and remained around there through mid-2003, when the economy was still struggling to recover from recession. The abrupt changes in the policy rate in response to changes in current economic conditions at that time destabilized inflation expectations and economic activity.

These events contrasted with the more forward-looking approach to inflation targeting that the Bank of Israel later adopted. In 2006, headline inflation overshot the upper band (Figure 3.5). Much of this was due to one-time pass-through effects of exchange rate depreciation and a steep increase in oil prices. But some monetary policy response was required because spare capacity in the economy was limited. The central bank interest rate increase was measured, yet it did succeed in stabilizing inflation expectations.

These episodes illustrate that credibility is put at risk when the actual policy appears to be at odds with the announced objective. More positively, they also

Figure 3.5. Israel: Interest Rates, Inflation, and Exchange Rates, 2005–07
(Percent)

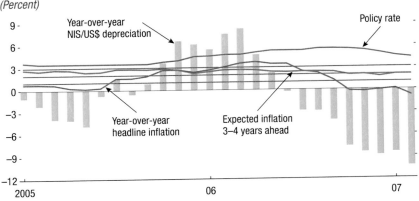

Sources: Argov and others 2007; Bank of Israel; Central Bureau of Statistics; and IMF staff estimates.
Note: NIS = new sheqel.

show that external shocks do not undermine credibility as long as the central bank's reaction is consistent with the objective.

A Multicountry Sample 2015–17

Each dot in the scatter diagram in Figure 3.6 relates the Consensus forecast of inflation three years ahead (vertical axis) to a given year's inflation rate (horizontal axis). Inflation is measured as the deviation from the official target. The data shown are from the 12 Consensus long-term forecasts conducted during 2015–17.

The diamonds for most inflation-forecast-targeting countries are grouped close to the horizontal axis. This implies that inflation expectations in these countries have been close to the inflation target, regardless of the current rate of inflation. Most other inflation-forecast-targeting countries are in the upper-left quadrant: that is, although their current inflation has been below target, forecasters expect future inflation to be above target. For stabilizing the economy, this is a good outcome, especially with the policy rate near zero, as the expected inflation overshoot reduces real interest rates and therefore stimulates output and pushes inflation back toward target.

The scatter of points for those countries not following inflation-forecast targeting all fall in the lower-left quadrant. That is, inflation has been below target, and forecasters expect this to continue: expectations have drifted with the current rate of inflation. This is a terrible outcome because the below-target expectations raise real interest rates and compound the low-inflation problem. These data therefore provide strong evidence that expectations have been better anchored in economies where monetary policy follows inflation-forecast-targeting principles.

Figure 3.6. Deviation of Consensus Headline Inflation Forecasts from Target
(Percentage point)

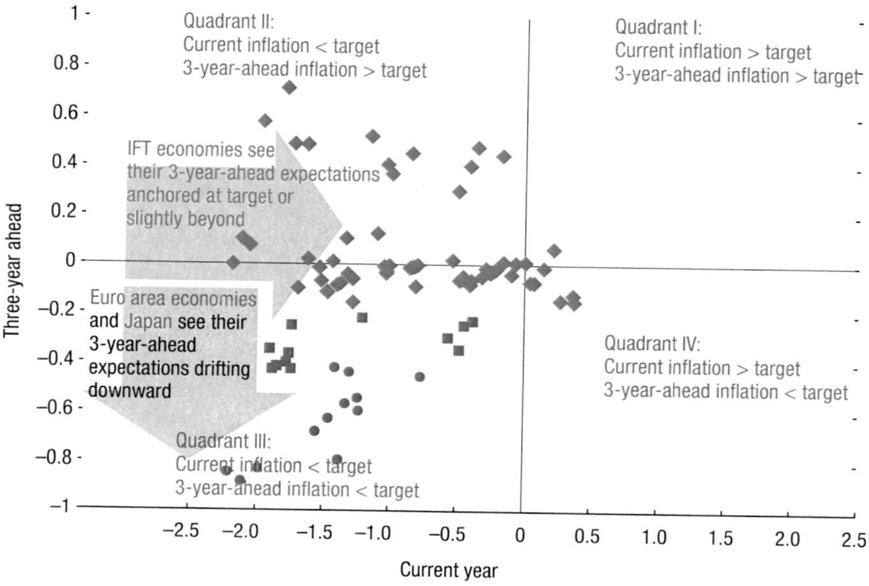

Source: Consensus Economics 2015–17.
Notes: Inflation-forecast-targeting (IFT) economies are indicated by green diamonds and include Canada, the Czech Republic, New Zealand, Sweden, and the United States. Euro area economies are indicated by blue squares. Japan is indicated by red dots.

RISK AVOIDANCE

Preventing a bad quasi-equilibrium is much better than having to find an effective cure. Therefore, the most appropriate policy response is one that is increasingly strong and increasingly risk-avoiding as an economy approaches a bad monetary equilibrium. Conventional rules that suggest a measured, linear response are no longer a useful characterization of policy under these circumstances.[5] A reaction function based on a quadratic loss function better captures an appropriate risk-avoidance strategy. The loss function implies an increasing response at the margin as negative deviations from the target grow and as economic slack increases. Model simulations show that, in response to a negative shock at the effective lower bound, with inflation already below target, and with a negative output gap, the optimal strategy holds the policy rate at the lower bound for a lengthy period (examples are provided in Chapter 9 for Canada and Chapter 10 for the Czech Republic). Publishing this outlook in a central bank forecast would lower expectations for interest rates over the medium term and reduce the exchange value for

---

[5]This includes the Taylor rule, which posits that the nominal interest rate should respond to divergences of actual inflation rates from target inflation rates in the short term.

the currency. This would boost demand and inflation—indeed, inflation may temporarily overshoot the target in the medium term. Under these circumstances, the overshoot would be welcome. It helps to offset the negative influence of the starting point on long-term inflation expectations, reinforcing the nominal anchor. At the same time, with the nominal policy rate stuck at the floor, the increased medium-term inflation lowers real interest rates, reinforcing the transmission of the policy action.

This highlights a practical advantage of the systematic approach to policy formulation and communication under a transparent inflation-forecast-targeting regime: the central bank does not have to announce the time horizon of the guidance nor list the data-dependent threshold conditions that would switch it off. These thresholds, particularly relating to the unemployment rate, have in practice proved unreliable. For example, the Fed has had to change its forward guidance policy several times in these respects since 2008. This gave the impression of improvisation, rather than a predictable policy.[6] The difficulty would be magnified if, as discussed above, the central bank deliberately plans a temporary overshoot of the long-term inflation target in an assertive anti-deflation strategy. If this outcome were realized without full publication of the central bank forecast, people might think the switch was left on too long and question the central bank's commitment to inflation control.

REFERENCES

Alichi, A., K. Clinton, C. Freedman, M. Juillard, O. Kamenik, D. Laxton, J. Turunen, and H. Wang. 2015. "Avoiding Dark Corners: A Robust Monetary Policy Framework for the United States." IMF Working Paper 15/134, International Monetary Fund, Washington, DC.

Argov, E., N. Epstein, P. Karam, D. Laxton, and D. Rose. 2007. "Endogenous Monetary Policy Credibility in a Small Macro Model of Israel." IMF Working Paper 07/207, International Monetary Fund, Washington, DC.

Batini, N., K. Kuttner, and D. Laxton. 2005. "Does Inflation Targeting Work in Emerging Markets?" Chapter IV, *World Economic Outlook*, September, International Monetary Fund, Washington, DC.

Bernanke, B.S. 2013. "Communication and Monetary Policy." Herbert Stein Memorial Lecture, Washington, DC, November.

Blanchard, O., and J. Galí. 2007. "The Macroeconomic Effects of Oil Shocks: Why Are the 2000s So Different from the 1970s?" NBER Working Paper 13368, National Bureau of Economic Research, Cambridge, MA.

Debelle, G., and D. Laxton. 1997. "Is the Phillips Curve Really a Curve? Some Evidence for Canada, the United Kingdom, and the United States." *IMF Staff Papers* 44 (2): 249–82.

Escolano, J., B. Aitken, P. Swagel, and D. Laxton. 2000. "Selected Issues: United Kingdom." IMF Staff Country Report 00/106, International Monetary Fund, Washington, DC.

Freedman, C., and D. Laxton. 2009. "Inflation Targeting Pillars: Transparency and Accountability." IMF Working Paper 09/262, International Monetary Fund, Washington, DC.

Gaspar, V., M. Obstfeld, R. Sahay, D. Laxton, D. Botman, K. Clinton, R. Duval, K. Ishi, Z. Jakab, L. Jaramillo Mayor, C. Lonkeng Ngouana, T. Mancini-Griffoli, J. Mongardini, S. Mursula, E. Nier, Y. Ustyugova, H. Wang, and O Wuensch. 2016. "Macroeconomic Management When Policy Space Is Constrained: A Comprehensive, Consistent and

---

[6]For a discussion of the US experience, see Alichi and others (2015).

Coordinated Approach to Economic Policy." IMF Staff Discussion Note 16/09, International Monetary Fund, Washington, DC.

Laxton, D., and P. N'Diaye. 2002. "Monetary Policy Credibility and the Unemployment-Inflation Nexus: Some Evidence from Seventeen OECD Countries." IMF Working Paper 02/220, International Monetary Fund, Washington, DC.

Summers, L. 1991. "Panel Discussion: Price Stability: How Should Long-Term Monetary Policy Be Determined?" *Journal of Money, Credit and Banking* 23 (3), Part 2, August.

Woodford, M. 2005. "Central-Bank Communication and Policy Effectiveness." Proceedings, Economic Policy Symposium, Federal Reserve Bank of Kansas City, August.

CHAPTER 4

Nuts and Bolts of a Forecasting and Policy Analysis System

RANIA AL-MASHAT, KEVIN CLINTON, DOUGLAS LAXTON, AND HOU WANG

> *Inflation-forecast targeting involves using a wide range of information in order to obtain the best forecasts for inflation and the economy. The staff must extract the underlying pressures on inflation and the economy from data that may be conflicting and noisy.*
> —D. Laxton, D. Rose, and A. Scott (2009)

Central bank staff need to be able to organize the efficient and thorough provision of economic information to enable monetary policy committees to make good decisions. That is the purpose of the Forecasting and Policy Analysis System (FPAS). It is intended to help monetary policy committee meetings focus squarely on the strategic, medium-term outlook. Forecast meetings with policymakers run the risk of getting sidetracked into technical details or wiggle in the latest numbers that have little importance in the grander scheme. The FPAS facilitates the big picture, employing a macroeconomic model with standard properties that broadly accord with the view of the monetary policy committee on how the economy works.

The main purposes of the forecast output are these:

- *A model-based, macroeconomic forecast.* The forecast provides an economically coherent view of the short- to medium-term outlook, with a baseline and alternative scenarios. Whereas the main forecast exercise would be quarterly (the periodicity of the national accounts), there would be updates for each monetary policy committee meeting. The most crucial part of the forecast is an endogenous future path for the short-term interest rate.

- *Measures of uncertainty.* The baseline forecast includes model-consistent confidence intervals for key variables (shown as bands or fan charts). These reflect a normal range of variability of random shocks implied by the historical data as well as parameter uncertainty.

- *Risk assessments.* The output of the forecasting team includes risk assessments to the baseline forecast in the form of alternative scenarios for specific assumed shocks, and options for the policy rule.

In view of the complexity of the economy, the large volume of relevant data, and the need to draw on expertise across departmental lines, production of the forecast and the related analyses make substantial demands on resources. The FPAS works on a calendar determined by the announced policy-decision dates of a particular monetary policy committee. Speed and accuracy are crucial, so that policymakers may base decisions on the most up-to-date information available. This requires a streamlined, robust production system—even then, the forecast takes several weeks to produce.

THE FORECASTING AND POLICY ANALYSIS SYSTEM

An effective system has the following components:

- *Full-time forecast team.* The demands on staff are ongoing in practice. Policymakers often ask for quick model-based responses to questions arising from current developments or policy debates, in addition to scheduled forecasts and updates. All this can be handled efficiently only by a team with full-time responsibility. There are, however, advantages to rotating staff between the forecasting team and other groups—to avoid burnout, to broaden work experience, to develop human capital, and to improve workforce flexibility.

- *Core quarterly forecasting model.* This core model should be small enough that forecasts with updated or alternative assumptions can be quickly and efficiently produced. This core model contains a standard transmission mechanism for monetary policy, and the forecast path for the short-term interest rate is endogenous.

- *A suite of satellite and ancillary models.* Satellite models would take results generated by the core model as inputs to derive projections of sectoral detail of interest to policymakers. A central bank would normally employ many ancillary models, results from which may be used as inputs to shape the dynamics of the core model, or the assumptions that underlie baseline or alternative scenarios. For example, sectoral specialists often use single-equation indicator models in their near-term monitoring.

- *Schedule of deadlines and meetings for each forecast exercise.* An example would be this sequence:

  ○ Issues meeting with representation from senior management to define the main influences in the upcoming outlook and to clear up technical issues regarding data, models, and the like.

  ○ Near-term forecast meeting.

  ○ First round projection incorporates the most recent data and allows diagnosis of previous forecast errors.

  ○ Several iterative rounds incorporate new model modifications, new external assumptions, and new, monitored, near-term forecast.

- Forecast meeting presents baseline and risk assessments to monetary policy committee members—who may request alternative scenarios.
- Monetary policy committee policy decision meeting.
- Writing deadlines for the internal forecast report and for the published monetary policy report, which includes key variables from the forecast.
- A "postmortem" to assess the preceding process and discuss avenues for improvement.

- *Near-term (current and next quarter) forecasting subsystem.* Expert judgment easily outperforms simple model extrapolations of GDP components, for short-term forecast accuracy. Judgmental (that is, monitored) short-term forecasts exploit simple empirical correlations, for example, leading indicator models, as well as special factors and nonquantitative knowledge bearing on how current developments are likely to unfold. The forecasting team would use a monitored near-term forecast to set initial conditions for the model-based medium-term forecast. Over horizons longer than a year, model-based forecasts are more useful, because they include the effects of endogenous policy responses and other macroeconomic feedback.

- *Source of external assumptions about the international economy.* These might be taken from the published forecasts of the IMF or other international institutions. The international departments of some central banks, however, develop their own views of the external outlook—for example, the Bank of Canada closely watches the US economy and commodity prices because of their dominant importance for the Canadian outlook.

- *Reporting database and network.* The forecast team updates the database weekly. It circulates a brief reporting package that highlights revisions to previous data and the new numbers. The arriving data are incorporated into updates of the monitored near-term forecast. Everyone involved in the process, across all departments, has immediate access to the relevant information, including the monitoring of the near-term forecast.

- *Adequate information technology.* This would include software for model building and simulation, for database updates and automated reports, and for the archiving of vintage models and databases. In view of staff turnover and the risk of loss of institutional memory, archives of model documentation are also essential.

- *Explicit accounting for revisions from one forecasting exercise to another.* These allow decomposition of the revisions into the various contributing factors:
  - Modifications of the model
  - Revisions to historical data
  - Revised views about long-term equilibrium values of variables like potential output, the real interest rate, and the real exchange rate
  - Unexpected changes in exogenous variables

Internal gains from a well-structured system are substantial. Staff input directly affects policy advice (most directly, in the form of the forecast interest rate path). As a result, staff members are better motivated and, knowing the direction of policy, work more effectively to serve the needs of policymakers. This helps keep the focus on the strategic medium-term issues at meetings with policymakers. Moreover, as staff members become better attuned to policymaker thinking, over time they develop ways to improve the process (for example, through better presentation materials or improved models). The system implies frequent communications both horizontally (across divisions) and vertically (between staff and senior management).

THE CORE MODEL

The core forecasting model varies in size, complexity, and theoretical specification from one central bank to another. In addition, the structure and calibration reflect the different economic features of each country. One common requirement, however, is that under simulation the model must exhibit standard macroeconomic properties that are plausible to policymakers. A second is production efficiency. The model should not be so large or complex that maintenance absorbs a lot of resources or that the derivation of forecasts consumes a lot of time. This argues for a model of modest size, using readily available and easily updated data.

At a minimum, the model produces forecast paths for inflation (core and headline), for GDP growth, for the output gap (actual GDP minus potential or full-employment GDP), for the short-term interest rate (the policy instrument for the purposes of the model), and for the exchange rate.

The simplest core model is organized around four key behavioral equations: an aggregate demand function for output, an expectations-augmented Phillips curve for inflation, a modified form of uncovered interest parity—which allows for variable country risk premiums—for the exchange rate, and a monetary policy reaction function for the interest rate. Other equations include identities, definitions, auxiliary analytical and reporting equations, statistical processes for trend variables (potential output and trends in the real exchange rate, interest rate, and country risk premium), and equations for international variables.

The aggregate demand equation explains the cyclical movements in output as a function of the real interest rate, real exchange rate, and foreign demand fluctuations. Higher real interest rates make borrowing for current consumption and investment costlier; this results in reductions in private outlays and overall demand. World demand is a key external driver of open economies. Movements in the real exchange rate also affect demand (both domestic and foreign) for domestic output by changing the price of locally produced goods relative to the rest of the world.

The Phillips curve embodies the dynamics of core consumer price inflation. The latter refers to the average rate of increase in sticky prices, which move over time rather than jump immediately, in response to pressures of supply and demand. In practice, consumer price inflation is defined to exclude energy and unprocessed food items, whose prices are subject to high short-term volatility. Over the cycle, according to the Phillips curve, it is output gaps—excess demand or excess supply—that drive core inflation. But with a modern expectations-augmented curve there is no lasting trade-off between output and inflation. In the long term, under inflation targeting, a policy reaction function ensures that the inflation rate converges to the fixed official target. The equation would also capture certain short- to medium-term factors. These include intrinsic persistence in inflation deriving from rigidities in adjustments of wages and prices, pass-through from changes in the real exchange rate (which affect the prices of imported consumer goods directly), and in noncore components (energy and food prices).

Uncovered interest parity has the exchange rate adjust to current and expected interest rate differentials (that is, the differences between the short-term rate of interest at home and abroad) and to investor perceptions captured in a risk premium. The longer a given interest differential is expected to persist, the greater the effect on the current exchange rate. For short-term forecasts, the country risk premium may for simplicity be set exogenously, based on judgment and on considerations not incorporated directly in the model. However, for long-term simulations, the model should have an endogenous risk premium that responds to changes in external and government debt. For emerging market economies, the evolution of the real exchange rate would also be affected by differential productivity trends.

The monetary policy rule (or reaction function) describes the systematic behavior of policymakers. The policy instrument, which is to say the short-term interest rate, reacts to actual and anticipated deviations in the inflation forecast and to domestic excess demand or excess supply (the output gap). The policy rule embodies some degree of interest rate smoothing, such that changes in the rate are typically distributed over time and not executed suddenly in one step. This gradualism is a consequence of the uncertainty associated with economic analysis, economic forecasts, and the evaluation of economic cycles; it also helps clarify the intent of the central bank's policy actions.[1] Notwithstanding the smoothing, the policy rule guarantees that core inflation will return to the target rate in the medium term following any shock. It is therefore a crucial foundation for the nominal anchor to the economy.

One may distinguish several transmission channels for the effects on domestic output and core inflation in such a model. The real interest rate affects the output gap, with a distributed lag, both directly (the internal channel) and through its impact on the exchange rate (the external channel). The exchange rate channel in the model has three distinct aspects: (1) direct, through imported goods in the consumer price index basket; (2) indirect, through prices of intermediate imported goods; and (3) expenditure switching, where the real exchange rate redirects

---

[1]Woodford (2003) justifies interest rate smoothing on the grounds of improved signal extraction. Incremental changes spread over time allow the public to discern more easily the intent of policymakers. A given change in the policy rate would then result in more predictable changes in longer-term interest rates. In contrast, frequent large changes in the policy rate would create noise and would not reliably be followed by the desired changes in longer-term rates.

spending toward, or away from, domestic production and therefore affects the output gap. In turn, changes in the output gap imply medium-term variations in the core rate of inflation.

Expectations play an important role in all of this, as is evident from the discussion in the previous chapter. Variations in the expected medium-term inflation rate affect the real interest rates at which households and firms borrow and save, and the behavior of the exchange rate. In addition, the aggregate demand equation may contain a forward-looking element, relating current investment and durable consumption decisions to expectations of future output.

The core model can be adapted to inflation-targeting regimes that are in the process of establishing credibility following years of inflation drift. For monetary policy in this phase of development, a credibility-building process may be added to the standard model, allowing the central bank to earn credibility over time if it succeeds in achieving announced targets—or vice versa if targets are missed.

Typical models embody model-consistent forward-looking expectations such that current behavior anticipates the model's own predictions for future periods. This allows analysts to explore complicated interactions between the private sector and the authorities. For example, simulation experiments can illustrate in numerical terms the implications of a policy credibility problem or the results of alternative strategies in situations where the reaction of the public's expectations to a policy action play a key role in policy transmission.

Numerical calibration of the coefficients of a core FPAS model draws on a wide range of evidence and theory. Calibration methodology contrasts with the traditional econometric approach to macro modeling, which was to estimate each equation individually in an attempt to uncover the data-generating process.[2] The objective of calibrating the model is a structure that in simulation yields economically plausible results and corresponds broadly with the data.

A close fit to historical data is not a requirement. Theoretical priors may take precedence over empirical estimates in the calibration of an equation if the estimates imply untenable properties for the whole system. This is not a trivial risk in view of the well-known conceptual difficulties of identification and estimation for systems of equations, not to mention the vagaries of the available data series, which are often short and affected by structural changes (Berg, Karam, and Laxton 2006).

DYNAMIC STOCHASTIC GENERAL EQUILIBRIUM METHODOLOGY

A relatively small core model on the above lines has been used in many central banks to good effect, and it may still be adequate in most countries. However, there has been a trend in the more advanced inflation targeters toward more sophisticated, dynamic stochastic general equilibrium (DSGE) models, which are based on

---

[2]The two approaches are not irreconcilable. Bayesian methodology provides a synthesis.

explicit optimizing behavior. These models require a much heavier input of specialized resources, and policymakers may find that their complexity presents a problem. The approaches can be blended as there is no conceptual inconsistency in their design. For example, DSGE models can be used to explore the longer-term implications of changes to government budgets, taking into account the dynamics of the public debt. Or they may be applied to certain key sectors (a case in point is agriculture in India). DSGE models are also useful for studying trends in real exchange rates or other unobservable variables like potential output.[3] The results would go as inputs to shape the dynamics of forecasts and simulations in the core model.

While the core model might initially abstract from some important macro-financial linkages and nonlinearities, it will be important to incorporate these features over time. Standard DSGE models now include financial shocks as well as financial accelerators that provide much stronger propagation mechanisms.[4] Chapter 7, for example, emphasizes the importance of incorporating financial information in both the baseline forecast and confidence bands. Other models have been developed to include important nonlinearities for doing monetary policy analysis.[5]

Looking ahead, as technical resources improve and policymakers demand for rigorous analysis increases, one might expect increased use of DSGE methodology in core FPAS models. Simpler approaches will continue to be used for various purposes in the suite of models, including for the core model in some cases. The likelihood is that the implementation of inflation-forecast targeting will continue to rely on a pragmatic blend of approaches to modeling. Moreover, the core model, regardless of the exact methodology employed, will continue to embody macroeconomic principles that can be understood by a broad, informed audience.

REFERENCES

Alichi, A., R. Al-Mashat, H. Avetisyan, J. Benes, O. Bizimana, A. Butavyan, R. Ford, N. Ghazaryan, V. Grigoryan, M. Harutyunyan, A. Hovhannisyan, E. Hovhannisyan, H. Karapetyan, M. Kharaishvili, D. Laxton, A. Liqokeli, K. Matikyan, G. Minasyan, S. Mkhatrishvili, A. Nurbekyan, A. Orlov, B. Pashinyan, G. Petrosyan, Y. Rezepina, A. Shirkhanyan, T. Sopromadze, L. Torosyan, E. Vardanyan, H. Wang, and J. Yao. Forthcoming. "Estimates of Potential Output and the Neutral Rate for the U.S. Economy." IMF Working Paper, International Monetary Fund, Washington, DC.

[3]See Laxton and Pesenti (2003) for a model that can be used to study trends in the real exchange rate caused by productivity catch-up in the traded-goods sector. Alichi and others (forthcoming) provide a multivariate filter for estimating potential output and the neutral rate for the US economy.

[4]Freedman and others (2009) and Christiano, Motto, and Rostagno (2014) provide structural DSGE models with financial accelerators.

[5]See Clark, Laxton, and Rose (2001) for a model with capacity constraints, and Argov and others (2007) for a model with endogenous policy credibility. See Laxton, Rose, and Tetlow (1993) for a discussion of the implications of falsely presuming linearity in the Phillips curve.

Argov, E., N. Epstein, P. Karam, D. Laxton, and D. Rose. 2007. "Endogenous Monetary Policy Credibility in a Small Macro Model of Israel." IMF Working Paper 07/207, International Monetary Fund, Washington, DC.

Berg, A., P. Karam, and D. Laxton. 2006. "A Practical Model-Based Approach to Monetary Policy Analysis—Overview." IMF Working Paper 06/80, International Monetary Fund, Washington, DC.

Christiano, L.J., R. Motto, and M. Rostagno. 2014. "Risk Shocks." *American Economic Review* 104 (1): 27–65.

Clark, P., D. Laxton, and D. Rose. 2001. "An Evaluation of Alternative Monetary Policy Rules in a Model with Capacity Constraints." *Journal of Money, Credit and Banking* 33 (1): 42–64.

Freedman, C., M. Kumhof, D. Laxton, D. Muir, and S. Mursula. 2009. "Fiscal Stimulus to the Rescue? Short-Run Benefits and Potential Long-Run Costs of Fiscal Deficits." IMF Working Paper 09/255, International Monetary Fund, Washington, DC.

Laxton, D., and P. Pesenti. 2003. "Monetary Policy Rules for Small, Open, Emerging Economies." *Journal of Monetary Economics* 50 (5): 1109–46.

Laxton, D., D. Rose, and A. Scott. 2009. "Developing a Structured Forecasting and Policy Analysis System to Support Inflation-Forecast Targeting (IFT)." Bank of Canada Working Paper 09/65, Ottawa.

Laxton, D., D. Rose, and R. Tetlow. 1993. "Monetary Policy, Uncertainty and the Presumption of Linearity." Bank of Canada Technical Report No. 63, Ottawa.

Woodford, M. 2003. "Optimal Interest Rate Smoothing." *Review of Economic Studies* 70 (4): 861–86.

CHAPTER 5

Monetary Operations

DARRYL KING AND TOMMASO MANCINI-GRIFFOLI

Monetary operations that stabilize and align short-term market rates with the policy rate reduce liquidity risks, assisting banks with their liquidity management and pricing policies. When short-term rates are stable, discrete changes in the policy rate will have greater impact on banks' pricing behavior as they will have more confidence that changes in the structure of interest rates will be sustained. —IMF (2015).

Prior chapters have focused on the design of institutions, the policy-making process, the construction of a consistent macroeconomic forecast, and the actions and words used to buttress transparency and credibility. This chapter focuses on implementation—the daily actions taken to translate policy decisions into tangible changes in economic incentives that underpin the effectiveness of monetary policy.

The operational framework of monetary policy comprises the operating target and monetary instruments (Figure 5.1).[1] Its purpose is to do the following:

- Ensure that the operating target of monetary policy (for example, a short-term money market interest rate) is consistently achieved
- Strengthen the credibility of the policy signal
- Ensure predictable and consistent liquidity conditions to market players
- Support development of financial markets, thereby strengthening the transmission of policy signals.

THE BUILDING BLOCKS

The Operating Target

The operating target signals the central bank's monetary policy stance and can be specified in various ways: as an interest rate, an exchange rate, or the growth rate of reserve money. In countries where markets and the financial sector are well

---

The authors gratefully acknowledge comments from Chikako Baba, Ivan Luis de Oliveira Lima, Kelly Eckhold, Claney Lattie, Romain Veyrune, Mariam El Hamiani Khatat, and Nils Maehle.

[1]For the purposes of this section the term *instrument* means *monetary instrument* and is distinguished from the reference in other chapters where *instrument* refers to a *policy instrument* in a broader macroeconomic sense.

Figure 5.1. The Monetary Policy Framework

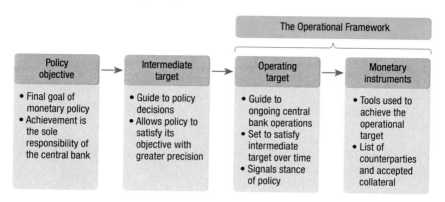

Source: Authors' construction.

developed, economies are sufficiently large and diversified, and central banks are independent from government, operational targets are usually defined in terms of interest rates. That is the focus of this chapter, in line with this book's overall purpose of exploring the frontiers of monetary policy. The alternative operating targets are briefly discussed in Box 5.1.

To continually align short-term interest rates with a desired policy stance, operational targets are generally specified in one of two ways:

- *Explicitly, on the basis of an announced target for a market rate* (or a combination of market rates). Traditionally, central banks have targeted an unsecured interbank rate because the interbank market was the most actively traded of the short-term money markets. However, unsecured interbank activity decreased since the global financial crisis with increased collateralization of short-term lending. Some central banks such as in Brazil target a secured rate, while others use a combination of rates—for example, repo and unsecured rates in Canada.

- *Implicitly, on the basis of the rate attached to a central bank instrument.* Some central banks define the marginal price of the liquidity that they offer or they accept as the policy rate. Transmission to short-term money market rates and beyond is usually ensured by arbitrage.

Operating targets are generally short-term rates—seven days or less—for four reasons.[2] First, central banks have more control over short-term rates, given their

---

[2]The Swiss National Bank is often cited as using an operating target longer than seven days. It sets a 1 percentage point range (currently –1.25 to –0.25) on the three-month Swiss-franc London interbank offered rate, and generally aims to keep the rate in the middle of the range. In managing this rate, the Swiss National Bank operates in the short-term repo market.

Box 5.1. Exchange Rate and Reserve Money Operating Targets

Most countries on the frontier of monetary policy have adopted some form of inflation-forecast targeting. In particular, most have a clear inflation target and a well-developed inflation forecast to guide policymaking. The operating target is commonly defined as an interest rate, managed with regular open market operations.

But in some cases, countries may adopt a different operational framework, while still targeting inflation. Two alternative frameworks stand out.

- **A managed exchange rate framework**. In some economies with exceptionally large shares of imports in the consumption basket, domestic inflation is heavily influenced by exchange rate shocks, or shocks to the price of foreign goods. In response, some countries have chosen to manage the exchange rate to stabilize prices. The Monetary Authority of Singapore (MAS), for instance, operates a managed float regime for the Singapore dollar. The operational target comprises a sloping band for the exchange rate, defined against a basket of currencies and reset periodically to ensure that it remains consistent with economic fundamentals and that it ultimately delivers price stability. The instrument of policy is foreign exchange intervention, although MAS acknowledges it does not control interest rates or the money supply. MAS has delivered consistently low and stable inflation (below 2 percent on average) since the framework's adoption in 1981, but there are few other successful examples of this type of arrangement. Few countries are as open to trade as Singapore (where the annual value of both exports and imports is well above 100 percent of GDP) or meet the other stringent conditions necessary for success: foreign reserves must be plentiful, fiscal policy must be especially predictable and responsible, shocks to capital flows must be relatively subdued, and business cycles must be well aligned with the country or countries against which the currency is managed.
- **Monetary targeting**. The operational target is the growth rate of reserve money, and the instrument is open market operations (commonly, the intermediate target is the growth rate of a broad monetary aggregate). Countries that adopt such a framework typically face one or two main constraints: very limited market development and financial sector penetration and a high degree of fiscal dominance (severe political pressure to keep interest rates low). The first constraint undermines the impact of an interest rate signal (although ensuring stable and predictable interest rates is likely an important catalyst for market development in the first place). And the second constraint limits the ability of the central bank to freely set interest rates. Often, however, frameworks targeting reserve money growth are transitory. As markets develop, changes in money velocity undermine control of inflation and the central bank establishes greater independence; as this occurs operational frameworks typically shift to targeting interest rates (see IMF [2015] for a discussion). The Bank of Tanzania, for instance, targets reserve money in its operations (and broad money as the intermediate target). It has achieved stable inflation between 2013 and 2017, close to its announced inflation objective of 5 percent. However, rigidly adhering to reserve money targets has resulted in volatile interest rates, and the Bank of Tanzania is now moving to an interest-rate-based operational framework with inflation forecasts as the intermediate target.

In the presence of other types of constraints central banks may rethink the entire monetary policy framework, including the objective and intermediate targets. For instance, countries with little institutional capacity may choose a pegged exchange rate regime, a choice that may be facilitated by a relatively closed capital account. Highly dollarized economies also face the choice between a currency board, an exchange rate peg, or, under some conditions, a strict inflation-targeting regime in the hope of rebuilding trust in the domestic currency. The presence of a high degree of administered prices does not necessarily call into question the appropriateness of inflation-forecast targeting, but it may reduce the effectiveness of monetary policy transmission.

Figure 5.2. A Stylized Central Bank Balance Sheet

Assets	Liabilities
Net international reserves	Currency in circulation
Government securities	Government deposits
Lending to banks (open market operations)	Bank reserves (required and/or excess)
Lending to banks (standing facilities)	Central bank securities and/or time deposits (open market operations)
	Capital and reserves

Source: Authors' construction.

monopoly over bank reserves. Second, longer rates require central banks to carry more duration or credit risk. Third, targeting longer rates may induce more short-term rate volatility due to shocks to term premiums. Fourth, holding longer-term rates fixed in between policy meetings could complicate communications and be financially costly when policy rate changes are needed and widely expected.

Monetary Policy Instruments

The traditional monetary policy instruments used outside of crisis situations are well known: reserve requirements, open market operations, and standing facilities.

Generally, a central bank's ability to guide market conditions comes from its monopoly over the supply of bank reserves, as illustrated in Figure 5.2, and, where relevant, its ability to influence the exchange rate by buying and selling foreign exchange with market participants.

That said, reserve requirements no longer play an important role in monetary policy implementation. This is true not only in most emerging market and advanced economies, but also in many low-income countries. Such requirements were previously used to help control monetary aggregates, as in the United States from the 1930s until the 1970s.[3] More recently, as operational frameworks shifted to target interest rates, reserve requirements have mostly been used—if at all—as microprudential or liquidity-management tools. Canada, New Zealand, and Norway, for instance, have removed reserve requirements altogether.

Open market operations involve the purchase or sale of marketable instruments either through outright or repurchase (repo) transactions or the issuance of deposits. The central bank seeks to adjust the supply or the price of bank reserves,

---

[3] In the United States, reserve requirements were initially used as a prudential tool to provide backing to the notes issued by private banks. Later refinements that permitted banks to meet reserve requirements on average over a given period (called the maintenance period) facilitated liquidity management in the face of liquidity shocks; see Gray (2011).

depending on the operating target, in response to forecasts of banking system liquidity.[4]

Standing facilities are instruments priced at fixed rates. They are available on demand at the discretion of central banks' counterparties that are used to set bounds on overnight interest rates because no bank would lend funds at a rate lower than the central bank's floor, whereas banks would not normally borrow at a higher rate than offered by the central bank's ceiling.[5] The width of the corridor matters, particularly when the operating target is set in the middle. If the corridor is too narrow, banks may have little incentive to trade; if it is too wide, rates may be more volatile.

Central banks must decide whether to set the policy rate in the middle or near the floor of the corridor. Having the rate in the middle often requires commercial banks to borrow, on net, from the central bank each day (a structural liquidity deficit), whereas setting the rate at the bottom is consistent with having banks investing, on net, with the central bank (a structural liquidity surplus). The central bank can structure its balance sheet to fit either environment by adjusting its longer-term assets (such as government securities and foreign assets) and liabilities (long-term, liquidity-absorbing repos and the reserve requirement, for example).

The rates at which the central bank conducts open market operations with its counterparties are transmitted to short-term money market rates. Counterparties are thus typically chosen because they are active in financial intermediation, usually banks and securities dealers. In economies with large and diverse financial sectors, it may be impossible to deal with all such entities; the central bank instead typically appoints a subset of the most active entities as counterparties, often called primary dealers. However, no one group of participants should have a distinct advantage over others, and primary dealers must be subjected to greater supervisory scrutiny to ensure that transmission of the rates is not impaired when shocks materialize.

The choice of counterparties must be adapted to the structure of the financial sector and the operational framework. For example, before the global financial crisis, the Federal Reserve Bank of New York—the implementation arm of the Federal Reserve System—dealt with about 20 primary dealers. After the global

---

[4]Open market operations also serve purposes other than the fine-tuning of liquidity conditions. Transactions of longer-term assets are used to manage trends in bank reserves arising from changes in the demand for currency in circulation, the amount of net foreign assets held, and other assets and liabilities on the central bank balance sheet.

[5]A central bank may not always be able to cap interbank rates at the ceiling of the interest rate corridor because banks may have insufficient eligible collateral or may fear stigma attached to borrowing from the central bank. In such cases, banks may prefer to pay higher rates to demonstrate continued market access, even though doing so may still send a negative signal. The situation in the United States is slightly different than described above; the federal funds rate does trade below the interest rate that the Federal Reserve pays depository institutions (namely, the interest on excess reserves—IOER) because not all entities that trade in the federal funds market are eligible to receive the IOER.

financial crisis, when structural liquidity in the banking system had increased dramatically, the Federal Reserve's list of counterparties expanded to include about 150. This happened because not all account holders were eligible to receive remuneration on their balances at the announced rate, the interest on excess reserves (commonly known as the IOER), thereby weakening the Federal Reserve's control over interest rates in the environment of abundant liquidity. To increase its control over interest rates, the Federal Reserve introduced a second rate attached to an overnight reverse repo facility (known as the ONRRP) and made it available to a broader range of entities upon application, subject to certain conditions. These entities were mainly money market mutual funds.

Policies governing the types of collateral accepted for open market operations and at the standing lending facility also vary across central banks and may affect monetary policy transmission. The choice of which collateral to accept may depend on the central bank's preference for liquid assets, the availability of various types of collateral, and development objectives. Some central banks accept only highly liquid securities, whereas others accept a very wide range of assets including loans. Risk-mitigation measures (haircuts and margining) are used to contain risks within prescribed limits and to keep price distortions across asset classes to a minimum.

Four Basic Designs

Interest-rate-based operational frameworks can be designed in four general ways: (1) a mid-corridor system targeting a market rate, (2) a mid-corridor system with the policy rate attached to a central bank instrument, (3) a floor system with bank reserves remunerated at the policy rate, and (4) a tiered-floor system with bank reserves remunerated at the policy rate up to a set limit, with the balance remunerated at a lower rate. There are, however, many variations and individual frameworks do not always fit neatly into any one of these categories.

Mid-Corridor System Targeting a Market Rate

Examples: Brazil, Canada, Chile, Czech Republic, Mexico, Sweden

This approach involves offering just enough liquidity to the banking system to satisfy the operational target, usually defined as a market rate (Figure 5.3). To achieve a rate in the middle of the corridor the probabilities of the system being *long* (downward pressure on rates) and *short* (upward pressure on rates) must be symmetrically distributed around zero. As a result, the system requires accurate high-frequency liquidity forecasts of the supply versus demand for bank reserves.[6] Forecasting reserve balances can be a difficult exercise. Shocks are often dominated by movements in the government's operating account (held at the central bank). Liquidity forecasting errors result in deviations of the market rate from target, especially when the demand curve is steeper, as toward the end of reserve

---

[6]The rationale here also applies when targeting a secured or composite rate.

Figure 5.3. Mid-Corridor System Targeting a Market Rate

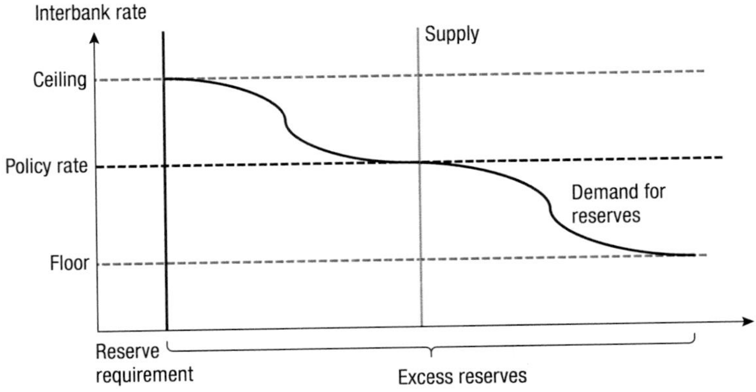

Source: Authors' construction.

maintenance periods.[7] Ideally, shocks can be minimized by having the government provide credible forecasts of its daily cash flows. And when shocks occur, mitigating action is possible, such as late-day fine-tuning operations.

The design of open market operations may also increase the chances of meeting the operating target. For example, setting the policy rate as the reserve price on such operations may help guide bidding.

This framework incentivizes banks to manage daily liquidity because being long or short incurs a penalty equal to half the width of the corridor. Interbank activity stimulates market development and monitoring, with some holding the view that transmission is strengthened.[8]

The Bank of Mexico's framework illustrates this option well. Through an agreement with the Ministry of Finance, all government receipts and payments are known one day in advance. This virtually eliminates liquidity shocks given that transactions in the foreign exchange market are also known in advance (usually because settlement occurs two days after the transaction is agreed) and that the demand for currency in circulation is stable although risk premium changes can still affect demand for reserves and thus overnight rates. The Bank of Mexico conducts two daily operations, with cut-off rates set at the policy rate. The last of

---

[7]Reserve averaging allows banks to meet their reserve target over the maintenance period rather than daily. Banks therefore do not need to respond immediately to liquidity shocks during the maintenance period thereby resulting in a flatter demand curve.

[8]Where markets do not function smoothly there may be a wide range in traded rates, with perhaps the central bank intermediating between surplus and deficit banks (through the standing facilities). Calibrating monetary operations in such circumstances is challenging.

these takes place at the end of the day to account for any error in the forecasted demand for currency. Because market participants are confident that the central bank will provide the necessary liquidity, bank excess reserves are almost always zero.

Mid-Corridor System with the Policy Rate Attached to a Central Bank Instrument

Examples: The euro area (before 2008), Indonesia

Central banks can attach the policy rate to a monetary policy instrument and then rely on arbitrage to pull other short-term rates close to it. The fixed-rate instrument is generally offered on a full allotment basis to avoid market distortions that may arise from trying to control both price and quantity (Figure 5.4).

Under one version of this system the central bank engineers a liquidity deficit (although it can also be used with a liquidity surplus) forcing banks to borrow from a seven-day repo facility each week. Banks must forecast their own liquidity needs, which they reveal at the weekly auction.

In some cases, if trading activity is low, market segmentation and coordination failures may result in overbidding and produce short-term volatility in the interest rate around the policy target.[9] Publishing liquidity forecasts and allowing banks to meet reserve requirements over sufficiently long periods (four to six weeks) can reduce the incentives to overbid and can encourage market activity. Furthermore, the central bank can conduct intraweek fine-tuning operations, although doing this frequently would resemble the mid-corridor system targeting a market rate, as discussed above.

Floor System with Excess Reserves Remunerated at the Policy Rate

Examples: United Kingdom and European Central Bank (after 2008)

Central banks can set the policy rate at the floor of the corridor and supply sufficient reserves to keep rates at or close to that floor (Figure 5.5).[10] This "floor system" became popular during the global financial crisis as central banks increased reserves much beyond what banks would require for payments and precautionary purposes.[11] Norges Bank first operated a floor system in the mid-1990s.

---

[9]See Veyrune, Della Valle, and Guo, forthcoming.

[10]Conceptually, the central bank can also operate a ceiling system under which there is a structural shortage of liquidity that forces banks to borrow from the lending facility each day. Such a system, once common, is rarely used now because it imposes liquidity risks that may undermine financial stability, given the possibility that banks may need to meet their payment obligations when high-quality collateral may be in short supply. One potential benefit of this system is that it may overcome the reluctance of banks to borrow from the central bank because of stigma, which can exacerbate problems in otherwise sound banks. Systematically forcing the banking system to borrow from the central bank each day may alleviate such stigma.

[11]The Federal Reserve was granted the legal right to remunerate reserves from October 2008 upon passage of the Financial Services Regulatory Relief Act of 2006. Initially this provision was to take effect in October 2011 but that date was brought forward to October 2008 as the global financial crisis unfolded.

Figure 5.4. Mid-Corridor System with the Policy Rate Attached to a Central Bank Instrument

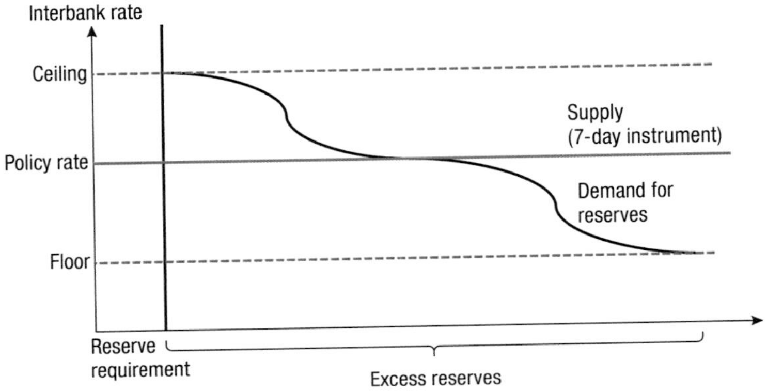

Source: Authors' construction.

The floor system breaks the link between the price and the quantity of bank reserves (for further discussion, see Goodfriend [2002]). Within the corridor and up to a certain amount, the demand for reserves is downward sloping; banks will agree to hold more reserves for precautionary reasons if the opportunity cost of holding them—the difference between the interbank rate and the rate on the deposit facility—is lower. However, when the interbank rate equals the deposit rate, the opportunity cost of holding reserves is zero.[12] The central bank can therefore increase the amount of reserves without the need to change the interest rate or cause it to move. The central bank thereby controls both the price and the quantity of reserves, as illustrated in Figure 5.5: the demand curve is flat to the right of where it meets the floor.

Ideally, the central bank would supply liquidity close to the point where the demand curve meets the floor in order to retain a degree of liquidity risk and thus spur some trading of reserve balances among banks. If supply is far to the right of this point (as when central banks engage in quantitative easing), there is little incentive to trade.

A Tiered-Floor System

Examples: Norway, New Zealand

Some central banks are concerned about the reduced level of interbank activity that results from floor systems. To attenuate such effects and to incentivize banks to manage their liquidity more actively, some central banks remunerate reserves

---

[12]In reality, the interbank rate may never quite reach the floor of the corridor given that deposits at the central bank are risk-free whereas placements with banks involve some credit and operational risks.

Figure 5.5. Floor System with Excess Reserves Remunerated at the Policy Rate

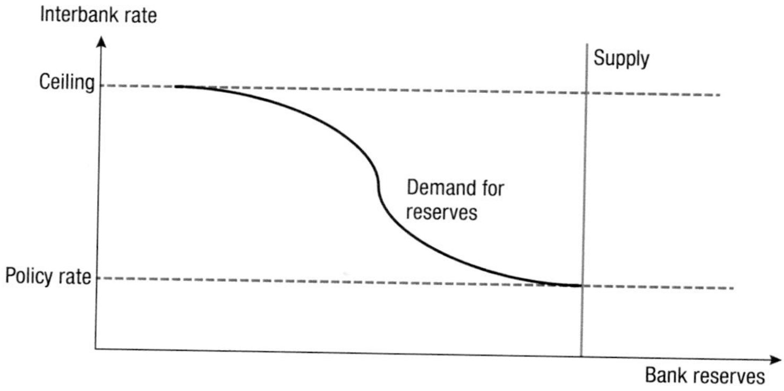

Source: Authors' construction.

at the policy rate up to a limit, while offering a lower rate on the balance (Figure 5.6). The limit is based on an assessment of each bank's precautionary demand for reserves. In New Zealand, the limit is based on payment flows, the volume of liquid assets, and other balance sheet metrics. Reserves exceeding the quota are remunerated at 100 basis points below the policy rate.[13] Furthermore, to implement this framework, the Reserve Bank of New Zealand had to ensure sufficient liquidity in the banking system. Because of a shortage of high-quality liquid assets, the central bank resorted to cross-currency swaps.

Assessing Operational Frameworks

Three categories of criteria help identify the strengths and weaknesses of the various operational frameworks: (1) clarity, robustness, and accuracy in satisfying the operational target; (2) transmission, market development, and activity; and (3) costs and capacity requirements, along with risks to the central bank.

Clarity, Robustness, and Accuracy in Satisfying the Operational Target

To maximize effective transmission, frameworks must be clearly understood by market participants and counterparties, and must be appropriately designed to reflect their levels of financial development.[14] The central bank should clearly communicate both the liquidity conditions it considers consistent with its operational target and the terms for participating in open market operations.

---

[13]Bindseil (2016) models this approach, showing that smaller quotas (smaller amounts remunerated at the policy rate) increase money market turnover and interest rate volatility.

[14]Central bank operations are generally straightforward, but on occasion financial options or algorithms have been used (for example, Bank of England collateralized operations).

Figure 5.6. A Tiered-Floor System

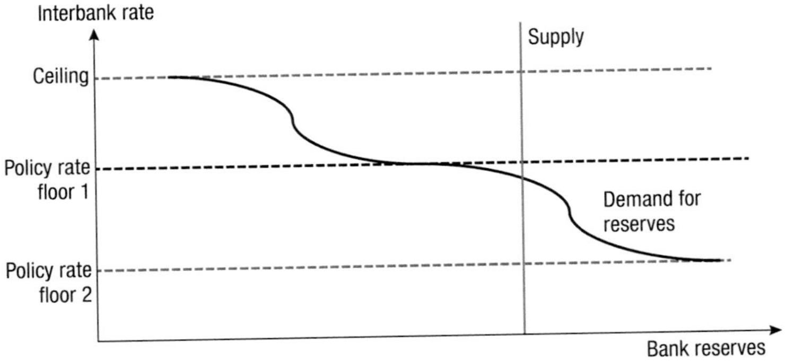

Source: Authors' construction.

Operational transparency reduces information asymmetries and aids pricing and transmission to longer rates.

Operational frameworks are generally clearer if they do not need to be adapted to changes in economic circumstances. Some designs may be more robust to changes in market conditions than others. Quantitative easing, for instance, forced a shift from mid-corridor systems to floor systems. But all systems allow for some flexibility through increasing the number of counterparties and broadening the range of eligible collateral if needed, without fundamentally changing the operational framework.

Transmission, Market Development, and Activity

The central bank is the heart of an economy's financial system. Its operations therefore shape the behavior and functioning of the market and influence policy transmission.

The choice of an operational framework will impact interbank activity. Increased risks and costs of excess or insufficient liquidity to meet end-of-day payment needs will motivate interbank trading. Instrument design also impacts the incentives to trade (for example, the width of the corridor) and the pricing of securities (such as through the supply of high-quality liquid assets). The operational framework may also affect the allocation of credit.[15] The smooth functioning of markets can be promoted by specific facilities (for example, securities

---

[15]For instance, the Federal Reserve focused on the allocation of credit. The Federal Open Market Committee's September 2014 Policy Normalization Principles and Plans said, "The Committee intends that the Federal Reserve will, in the longer run, hold no more securities than necessary to implement monetary policy efficiently and effectively, and that it will hold primarily Treasury securities, thereby minimizing the effect of Federal Reserve holdings on the allocation of credit across sectors of the economy."

lending). Last, counterparty and collateral policies can affect the pricing and distribution of liquidity and securities. The question, however, is the extent to which short-term interbank activity is needed for effective transmission.

Costs and Capacity Requirements and Risks to the Central Bank

Operational choices also have an impact on the costs to the central bank. High-frequency liquidity forecasts and daily operations require administrative resources and significant capacity. In addition, the choice of a framework may affect operating costs—for example, when sterilizing a large amount of liquidity.

Risks will also depend on the design of operations. Complex procedures increase operational risks, and larger balance sheets induce more interest rate risk, and perhaps credit risk as well. Except in a crisis, central banks generally limit credit risk by holding government securities against their currency liabilities.

CONCLUSIONS

The interest-rate-based frameworks discussed earlier can be broadly mapped against the above criteria. Four trends appear when moving from the frameworks on the left toward the frameworks on the right in Figure 5.7 (a more detailed assessment appears in Annex 5.1).

First, clarity, robustness, and accuracy increase. The floor system is the simplest framework, and it remains applicable in both normal and crisis times—even when hitting the effective lower bound and when needing to vastly expand reserves. Moreover, the policy rate can be achieved independent of market structure and conditions, because the central bank controls the remuneration of reserve balances. Conversely, the mid-corridor system targeting a market rate requires precise forecasting of liquidity conditions and calibration of operations to achieve the operating target, tasks that are beyond some central banks.

Second, incentives to trade diminish. Incentives for banks to actively manage liquidity are highest under mid-corridor systems targeting a market rate, when liquidity is scarce and the opportunity costs of being caught with an excess or shortage of liquidity are also high. In contrast, under floor systems, incentives for trading and monitoring in short-term money markets and liquidity risks are reduced.[16]

Third, operational costs diminish when moving away from the mid-corridor system targeting a market rate, especially because there is less need for liquidity forecasting. This is true even in mid-corridor systems attached to a central bank instrument and more so in floor systems, which do not require accurate liquidity forecasts, frequent operations, or well-functioning markets.

Finally, the larger balance sheet of floor and tiered systems impose higher risks to central banks. Asset price fluctuations affect central banks' equity positions,

---

[16]In addition to changes in operational frameworks, changes in banking regulation have undermined activity in short-term money markets. The liquidity coverage ratio requires banks to hold high-quality liquid assets against net outflows within a 30-day window; interbank borrowing falls into this category. A ratio limiting bank leverage (the supplementary leverage ratio) also discourages money market activity (CGFS 2015).

Figure 5.7. Comparing Operational Frameworks

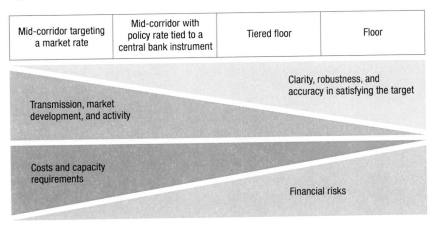

Source: Authors' construction.

and although most central banks do not mark their balance sheets to markets, perceived losses can bring about political scrutiny and undesirable pressures.

How central banks decide to balance these trade-offs depends on country circumstances and constraints. The importance of decisions about clarity and simplicity, for instance, are functions of the central bank's ability to communicate, and of the sophistication of counterparties.

The importance of trading incentives will likely depend on the relative priority of financial market development and the extent to which interbank activity matters for transmission (Potter 2016). Some views have changed since the global financial crisis, at least in countries where markets are well-developed. Active short-term interbank markets may be less important for transmission and interbank monitoring than previously thought.[17] However, further investigation is

---

[17]On monitoring, Bernhardsen and Kloster (2010) investigate the question of interbank monitoring, and note that most interbank activity is at very short maturities, so lenders only had incentives to consider counterparty solvency over a few days, while an assessment of solvency over a longer period is more relevant to financial stability. On transmission, evidence points to continued effectiveness, though estimates are subject to significant uncertainty. Federal Open Market Committee participants suggest the floor system run by the Federal Reserve since the global financial crisis is "effective in enabling interest rate control across a wide range of circumstances" (Federal Reserve 2016). However, Bech, Klee, and Stebunovs (2012) find some slippage in transmission; they conclude that "pass-through from the federal funds rate to the repo deteriorated somewhat during the zero lower bound period." Beaupain and Durre (2016) and Christensen and Gillan (2017) actually find that market liquidity increased in recent periods of excess liquidity, both in euro area money markets, and United States' bond markets, but only as a result of active large scale asset purchases by the central bank. As CGFS (2015) emphasizes, though, empirical work to date has had trouble dissociating the effects of excess liquidity on transmission from those of regulation, bank specific features, and risk premiums associated with the crisis.

necessary to reach firmer conclusions, and data are still being collected as central banks begin normalizing rates.

Market development is likely to be a relatively more important objective in lesser developed markets, favoring approaches that incentivize interbank activity, such as mid-corridor systems. An analogous situation is that when central banks step back from foreign exchange intervention, participants are incentivized to actively manage and distribute risks, including through product innovation, such as new hedging instruments.

There are competing views on the appropriate size of central banks' balance sheets. Buiter and others (2017) emphasize that the optimal size is "unknown and probably unknowable." Bindseil (2016) favors a small balance sheet to signal well-functioning markets but does not account for the possibility that markets may not function well or that balance sheets may be large for other policy or legacy reasons. Greenwood, Hanson, and Stein (2016) argue for retaining a large balance sheet to control financial stability risks outside of the banking system.[18] The political economy risks associated with a large balance sheet may also be a relevant consideration in some jurisdictions.

Other constraints will affect central banks' choice of framework. For example, central banks may be forbidden from remunerating reserve holdings of all entities or from issuing securities. There also could be legal restrictions on the use of other instruments (such as reserve requirements) that undermine central banks' ability to provide a buffer against liquidity shocks. And the availability of liquid government securities could limit the size of a central bank's balance sheet. Finally, weak transmission is not necessarily a reason for changing operational frameworks. Transmission may be affected by external factors, such as uncompetitive banking systems with high nonperforming-loan ratios and poor creditor rights, or information asymmetries leading to segmented money markets. Nevertheless, appropriate design, communication, and conduct of monetary operations are prerequisites for effective policy transmission.

---

[18]Greenwood, Hanson, and Stein (2016) argue for the Fed to use its balance sheet by supplying safe assets (that is, overnight reverse repurchase transactions) to lean against private sector maturity transformation. Reducing the scarcity of safe assets also reduces the incentives for financial intermediaries to fund on a short-term basis. They note that by impacting market-determined spreads on interest rates, regulated banks and unregulated shadow banks are affected. Such a measure they say, "gets into all the cracks."

ANNEX 5.1

TABLE 5.1.1.

Assessing the Operational Frameworks

Other Operational Features	Mid-Corridor Targeting a Market Rate / Averaged Reserve Requirement (daily operations)	Mid-Corridor Policy Rate Attached to a CB Instrument (such as a seven-day repo) / Averaged Reserve Requirement (ad hoc intraweek operations)	Tiered Floor / Quotas Set on Payments Activity and Balance Sheet Metrics	Floor / Liquidity Supplied Close to the Amount Required to Keep Rates at the Floor
Clarity, Robustness, and Accuracy in Satisfying the Operational Target				
Achieves the operational target (where liquidity forecasting is difficult or markets do not function smoothly)	1	2	3	3
Is durable across different financial states of the world	1	1	2	3
Transmission, Market Development, and Activity				
Provides incentives to trade in the short-term money market	3	2	2	1
Has minimal impact on credit allocation	3	3	2	1
Costs and Capacity Constraints, and Risks to the Central Bank				
Minimizes the operational costs (liquidity forecasts and frequency of operations)	1	2	2	3
Minimizes financial risks (credit and interest rate risks)	3	3	2	1

Source: Authors' construction.
Notes: 1 = not supportive, 2 = neutral or unclear, and 3 = broadly supportive. CB = central bank.

REFERENCES

Beaupain, Renaud and Alain Durré. 2016. "Excess Liquidity and the Money Market in the Euro Area." *Journal of Macroeconomics* 47 (2016) 33–44.

Bech, Morten L., Elizabeth Klee, and Viktors Stebunovs. 2012. "Arbitrage, Liquidity and Exit: The Repo and Federal Funds Markets Before, During, and Emerging from the Financial Crisis." Finance and Economics Discussion Series 2012–21. Board of Governors of the Federal Reserve System.

Bernhardsen, Tom, and Arne Kloster. 2010. "Liquidity Management System: Floor or Corridor?" *Norges Bank Staff Memo* 4/2010, Oslo.

Bindseil, Ulrich. 2016. "Evaluating Monetary Policy Operational Frameworks." Paper prepared for the Federal Reserve Bank of Kansas City's Jackson Hole Conference.

Buiter, Willem, Ebrahim Rahbari, Kim D. Jensen, and Cesar Rojas. 2017. "Why Does the Fed (or any Central Bank) Wish to Shrink Its Balance Sheet?" *Citi Research, Multi-Asset, Global, Global Economics View*, August 9, 2017.

Christensen, Jens H. E., and James M. Gillan. 2017. "Does Quantitative Easing Affect Market Liquidity?" Federal Reserve Bank of San Francisco Working Paper.

Committee on the Global Financial System Markets Committee (CGFS). 2015. "Regulatory Change and Monetary Policy." *CGFS Papers* 54.

Federal Reserve. 2016. "Minutes of the Federal Open Market Committee November 1–2, 2016." Board of Governors of the Federal Reserve System.

Goodfriend, Marvin. 2002. "Interest on Reserves and Monetary Policy." *FRBNY Economic Policy Review* (May).

Gray, Simon. 2011. "Central Bank Balances and Reserve Requirements." IMF Working Paper 11/36, International Monetary Fund, Washington, DC.

Greenwood, Robin, Samuel G. Hanson, and Jeremy C. Stein. 2016. "The Federal Reserve's Balance Sheet as a Financial-Stability Tool." *2016 Economic Policy Symposium Proceedings*. Jackson Hole: Federal Reserve Bank of Kansas City.

International Monetary Fund (IMF). 2015. "Evolving Monetary Policy Frameworks in Low-Income and Other Developing Countries." *IMF Policy Paper*, October.

Potter, Simon. 2016. "Discussion of 'Evaluating Monetary Policy Operational Frameworks by Ulric Bindseil'." Remarks at the Economic Symposium at Jackson Hole, Wyoming.

Veyrune, Romain, Guido Della Valle, and Shaoyu Guo. Forthcoming. "Relationship between Short-term Interest Rates and Excess Reserves in the Euro-system: A Logistic Approach." IMF Working Paper, International Monetary Fund, Washington, DC.

Monetary Policy and Financial Stability

TOBIAS ADRIAN, GIOVANNI DELL'ARICCIA, VIKRAM HAKSAR, AND
TOMMASO MANCINI-GRIFFOLI

Monetary policy faces significant limitations as a tool to promote financial stability . . .
[However,] it may be appropriate to adjust monetary policy to "get in the cracks" that
persist in the macroprudential framework —J. Yellen (2014)

Should monetary policy have an objective besides price and output stability—
namely, to minimize the risks of costly financial crises? Although such crises are
rare events, the fact that they bring significant economic hardship means that
preventing or minimizing the potential damage should be a first-order policy
priority. Micro- and macroprudential policies would seem the most appropriate
tools because they are designed to tackle specific financial vulnerabilities and
thereby mitigate the probability of financial crises. However, their effectiveness
remains somewhat uncertain, as does the willingness of politicians to adopt them.
As a result, the spotlight turns naturally to monetary policy.

Weighing the possible role of monetary policy in reducing the risk of crises
involves assessing whether interest rates should be raised more than required by
medium-term price stability and full employment mandates. This involves three
broad steps: first, estimating the link between policy rates and crisis probabilities;
second, gauging the potential trade-off between meeting traditional policy mandates and containing the risks of a crisis; and third, determining whether the
trade-off is worth it—namely, whether the welfare benefits are higher than costs.

To preview our results: First, interest-rate hikes during phases of economic
expansion seem to reduce the probability of severe crises by influencing key macroeconomic variables such as credit growth. But the estimated effects tend to be
small and to occur with a lag, after initially weakening private sector balance
sheets. Second, the trade-off between financial stability and medium-term price
and output stability objectives does not always seem severe. Most often, crisis risks
build as economies grow strongly; higher interest rates are therefore warranted
solely on the basis of traditional monetary policy objectives. As the 2008 global
financial crisis showed, however, risks can still accumulate when inflation is close

to target and the output gap appears to be closed.[1] Finally, based on historical data, it appears that raising interest rates more than warranted by the price stability mandate in an attempt to preempt risks of occasional major crises generally implies costs that outweigh the potential benefits.[2] Hence, adding financial stability as a separate objective for monetary policy besides inflation and output goals seems ill-advised.

However, that is not to say that monetary policymakers should remain oblivious to financial sector frictions and vulnerabilities. As argued in Chapter 7, these are particularly important in determining continuously evolving downside risks to economic activity, which should be distinguished from risks of devastating one-off crises (the focus of this chapter). Adrian, Boyarchenko, and Giannone (2016) suggest that financial conditions—an aggregate index of market prices such as credit spreads, loosely capturing the price of risk—provide policymakers with insights into how these continuously evolving downside risks to growth are likely to evolve. Responding to financial conditions when setting monetary policy is welfare-improving over the short to medium term for optimally behaving inflation-targeting central banks, even if doing so may involve some trade-off with current economic conditions (Adrian and Duarte 2016). This approach is consistent with "flexible inflation targeting" (Svensson 1997a, 1997b).

MACROPRUDENTIAL POLICY, AN EFFECTIVE WAY TO TACKLE VULNERABILITIES?

Financial crises are typically deeper and more persistent than normal recessions. In advanced and emerging market economies after World War II, real GDP per capita following financial crises has lagged behind its average recovery path after normal recessions by about 4 to 5 percent after five years.[3] Moreover, crises typically undermine countries' fiscal positions, as well as social and political stability and cohesion.

---

[1]See IMF (2015a) for a further discussion of trade-offs otherwise left out of this chapter.

[2]See Smets (2014) for an overview of the literature weighing the costs and benefits of using monetary policy to support financial stability. Smets largely sides with resorting to prudential supervision and regulation, as opposed to monetary policy. IMF (2015a) takes a similar view after broadly surveying the literature and undertaking independent analysis, while Svensson (2017) argues that higher policy interest rates could actually undermine financial stability. Caruana (2011) and Borio (2014) instead suggest that monetary policy should on average be tighter to support financial stability. Model evidence, as discussed later in this chapter, is somewhat more mixed.

[3]See Jordà, Schularick, and Taylor (2015). These are average numbers, and individual crises can lead to larger losses. See also Calvo and Mendoza (1996), Kaminsky and Reinhart (1999), Allen and Gale (2000), Cerra and Saxena (2008), Reinhart and Rogoff (2009), and more recently, Taylor (2015). Taylor suggests that evidence for advanced and emerging market economies is quite similar. Such works on crises were highly influential in emerging markets, even when published before the global financial crisis, but remained at the periphery of policymaking in most advanced economies. Blanchard, Cerutti, and Summers (2015) as well as Martin, Munyan, and Wilson (2015) document more persistent effects of financial crises on output, potentially affecting productivity growth.

Emphasis has therefore shifted to containing systemic risks, as opposed to waiting to clean up after a crisis hits, by complementing traditional microprudential policies aimed at individual institutions with macroprudential policy frameworks, as recommended in IMF (2013, 2014). Examples of the latter include both cyclical instruments such as countercyclical capital buffers, loan-to-value limits, or dynamic loss provisioning, and permanent measures to strengthen the structural resilience of the financial system (for example, minimum capital and liquidity ratios and improvements in supervision and financial infrastructures). A distinction can also be made between demand-side policies limiting risks taken by borrowers and those supply-side policies that aim to restrain lenders' exposures.

Macroprudential policies offer the hope of targeting specific sources of vulnerability or financial frictions that affect one or more sectors at a lower cost than would be incurred using monetary policy. Such distortions include, for instance, the relationship between asset prices and credit growth, where higher asset prices allow borrowers to pledge more collateral and thus increase debt, until a shock forces them to deleverage rapidly, with potential externalities on other debtors.[4]

As discussed in IMF (2013) and Blanchard, Dell'Ariccia, and Mauro (2010, 2013), the policy burden of minimizing crisis risks should fall primarily on macroprudential policies, should they prove well targeted and effective. For now, empirical evidence on the effectiveness of macroprudential policies remains relatively thin and scattered, although it is growing quickly and, in areas, is encouraging.[5]

In addition, macroprudential policy has several advantages over monetary policy for containing financial stability risks (as discussed in Adrian 2017). First, monetary policy may be less effective in building a resilient financial sector

---

[4]As initially framed in Bernanke, Gertler, and Gilchrist (1999). See Brunnermeier, Eisenbach, and Sannikov (2012) and Leeper and Nason (2014) for a survey of financial frictions. Other distortions include incomplete or asymmetric information, liquidity constraints, funding constraints, moral hazard stemming from policy actions like bailouts, monitoring costs or costly state verification, incentives and principal-agent problems, and regulatory arbitrage.

[5]Gaspar and others (2016) makes the same argument. See IMF (2014) for guidance on the use of macroprudential policy. For cross country analysis, see Altunbas, Binici, and Gambacorta (2017), Akinci and Olmstead-Rumsey (2015), Cerutti, Claessens, and Laeven (2015), Freixas, Laeven, and Peydró (2015), McDonald (2015), Claessens (2014), Galati and Moessner (2014), Bakker and others (2012), and Lim and others (2011). Zhang and Zoli (2014) and Bruno and Shin (2014) offer a review of macroprudential policies in Asia; Cerutti, Claessens, and Laeven (2015), Kuttner and Shim (2013), and Crowe and others (2011) focus on instruments geared toward the real estate market; He (2013) surveys Hong Kong SAR's approach to financial stability; Tressel and Zhang (2016) review the euro area; Jacome and Mitra (2015) and Christensen (2011) review debt-to-income and loan-to-value (LTV) limits; Benes, Laxton, and Mongardini (2016) and Benes, Kumhof, and Laxton (2014a, 2014b) develop models to study the benefits of LTV limits and countercyclical buffers; Shin (2011) considers a levy on banks' noncore liabilities; and Epure and others (2018), Dassatti Camors and Peydro (2014), Aiyar, Calomiris, and Wieladek (2012), Jimenez and others (2012), Igan and Kang (2011), Wong and others (2011), and Saurina (2009) study sectoral, firm-level, or credit registry data. The IMF's Global Macroprudential Policy Index offers a database of macroprudential instruments for research purposes.

because it would be used only occasionally, in response to mounting, observable risks to financial stability.[6] In contrast. macroprudential policy, such as counter-cyclical capital requirements, can be made to bind for extended periods and, once implemented, can operate without any transmission lag. Second, monetary policy is not targeted enough to address differential financial vulnerabilities across various sectors of the economy and may constrain growth in all sectors—in that sense it is a "blunt" instrument. For instance, a residential or commercial real estate boom may develop because of the behavior of lenders and borrowers active in that particular sector and occur at times when financial conditions are not particularly easy across the whole economy.

However, even the stronger combination of micro- and macroprudential policies that is emerging may not suffice to contain financial stability risks. Viñals (2013), for instance, points to a strong bias toward inaction in the implementation of macroprudential policies due to political constraints and the fact that policy objectives are difficult to gauge in real time until a crisis actually materializes. Adrian and others (2017) report that US policymakers are hesitant to resort to macroprudential policies due to implementation lags and limited scope. Moreover, the well-targeted nature of prudential policies, even if effective, could be a detriment to countering unknown risks. As Stein (2014) points out, monetary policy "gets into all cracks," whereas macroprudential policy can be arbitraged across jurisdictions, markets, and institutions.

THE LINK BETWEEN INTEREST RATES AND CRISIS RISK

Interest rates can affect key macroeconomic and financial variables that in turn affect the probability of crises. But these effects tend to be small, and estimates of them greatly depend on the time horizon and the state of the financial system.

In the short to medium term, before agents are able to adjust their balance sheets, theory suggests that higher interest rates work against financial stability, although the extent is likely contingent on existing conditions and thus remains an empirical question. First, by reducing aggregate demand, monetary tightening reduces household earnings and firms' profitability. Second, monetary tightening leads to an increase in the interest rate burden, especially if liabilities are at variable rates and have short maturities. Third, higher interest rates tend to reduce asset prices and the value of legacy assets held by financial institutions. Finally, higher policy rates typically flatten the yield curve and—to the extent that they compress term premiums—tend to reduce bank profits at the outset.

---

[6]It is not plausible for monetary policy to keep interest rates persistently higher than warranted by price and output stability. Higher rates would create persistently lower inflation. This would eventually decrease inflation expectations and in the end leave real rates—and thus financial risks—unchanged, while aggravating risks of hitting the zero lower bound.

In theory, the effects should reverse over the medium to longer term, as households, firms, and financial institutions readjust their balance sheets and adapt their behavior. In particular, higher borrowing costs should induce households and firms to gradually reduce leverage through the conventional intertemporal substitution effect. Tighter monetary conditions are also likely to gradually reduce leverage in the banking sector—as shown in Dell'Ariccia, Laeven, and Marquez (2014)—due to stronger monitoring incentives. By reducing the motivation to search for yield, higher rates should reduce risk-taking by financial intermediaries that have fixed long-term liabilities, such as insurers and pension funds.

Empirical results broadly support these theoretical predictions. In the short term, the ratio of real debt to GDP seems to rise, because nominal GDP responds faster than nominal debt to an interest rate hike, especially with lengthy loan amortization periods (Alpanda and Zubairy 2014; Gelain, Lansing, and Natvik 2015). Because real debt and debt-servicing costs increase with higher interest rates, default rates rise in the quarters following an interest rate shock (IMF 2015a). In the longer term, real debt levels tend to decrease, though the magnitude of the change varies across estimation methods and samples.[7]

Banks and nonbanks generally respond to higher interest rates by reducing their leverage.[8] In the initial quarters, however, leverage tends to rise across financial firms. Banks typically tighten their lending standards, grant fewer loans to risky firms, and extend fewer risky new loans.[9] Some research indicates that distance to default—a measure of banks' riskiness—eventually increases (indicating lower risk) following rate hikes, even though it initially drops (see IMF [2015a] for a discussion).

These effects underscore that there is a link between policy interest rates and the probability of crises. The most stable link hinges on credit growth. Using annual data from 1870 to 2008 for 14 advanced economies, Schularick and Taylor (2012) document that faster credit growth over the previous five years is associated with a higher probability of a financial crisis. IMF (2015a) finds similar results using a larger set of 35 advanced economies and quarterly data from 1960 onward.

---

[7]A temporary monetary policy tightening of 100 basis points is found to decrease real debt levels by up to 0.3 percent and 2 percent, after 4 to 16 quarters, depending on the model. See Sveriges Riksbank (2014) for a middle-of-the-road result, showing that debt contracts by 1 percent at the peak, after 8 quarters. IMF (2015a) surveys other related papers.

[8]See Cecchetti, Mancini-Griffoli, and Narita (2017) and Bruno and Shin (2014). The first also finds that leverage decreases abroad when US monetary policy tightens, as does Miranda-Agrippino and Rey (2014).

[9]See Maddaloni and Peydro (2011), Jimenez and others (2012), Dell'Ariccia, Laeven, and Suarez (2013), De Nicolo and others (2010), Adrian and Shin (2009), Freixas, Martin, and Skeie (2011), Diamond and Rajan (2012), Borio and Zhu (2012), and Acharya and Naqvi (2012). Most papers are based on survey data. Cecchetti, Mancini-Griffoli, and Narita (2017) find that Sharpe ratios decrease following protracted rate cuts. Demirgüç-Kunt and Detragiache (1998, 2005) find that bank profits drop due to higher real interest rates and undermine banking sector stability in the short to medium term.

According to this evidence, higher interest rates should reduce the probability of a crisis over the medium to long term. The probability of a crisis first increases, then decreases to its trough after three to five years following an interest rate increase. At that point, the probability has been reduced by between 0.04 and 0.3 percentage points following a 100-basis-point interest rate hike for a year, given the range of effects found in the literature.[10] These are relatively small numbers and suggest that significantly reducing the probability of a crisis would likely require substantial hikes in interest rates since the nexus of credit growth and asset price spirals does not seem to be very sensitive to interest rates. However, Adrian and Liang (2018) argue that such estimates are subject to substantial uncertainty. In addition, much more research is needed to enable robust estimates of the linkages from monetary policy to household and business credit—and ultimately from credit growth—not only to the probability of a subsequent recession but also to its severity. Furthermore, there are channels besides credit growth that the literature is only starting to quantify.

THE COSTS OF A FINANCIAL STABILITY MANDATE GENERALLY OUTWEIGH THE BENEFITS

The welfare effects from pursuing an additional financial stability mandate for monetary policy should be evaluated in a full-blown model because only a model that captures financial frictions and risk-taking behavior can account for the endogeneity of agents' response to a change in the monetary policy rule. More concretely, if monetary policy were credibly and openly to pursue an additional financial stability mandate, households and firms might take fewer risks from the start. As a result, there may be less need to raise rates than if monetary policy were conducted in a more unpredictable and ad hoc fashion.

Modeling crises and risk-taking behavior is complex. Any such models need to incorporate heterogeneous agents to generate lending, as well as some form of financial friction so that shocks to financial variables have real consequences. In addition, such models need to allow for global nonlinearities, so that economies can fluctuate between a normal state and a crisis state. Ideally, the probability of changing states should depend on a state variable that is endogenous to the model, and risk-taking behavior, including relevant externalities, should be built on minimal assumptions and optimal—though not necessary fully rational—behavior.

There are some models that quantify the welfare effects of pursuing the additional goal of financial stability, but few exhibit all the features described above. Ajello and others (2016) develop a linearized New Keynesian model calibrated to match historical data in which the economy risks jumping from a normal state to a crisis state depending on credit growth. They find that even when crises have

---

[10]See IMF (2015a) for a further discussion, including of somewhat larger effects when hikes coincide with periods of rapid credit growth, but also of the potential for credit growth to pick up more strongly after the initial rate hike, thereby reducing or reversing the drop in crisis probability, as in Svensson (2017).

relatively large costs, optimal policy differs only very slightly from a traditional response that is oblivious to crisis risks. (Of course, the fact that the model itself is linearized does present problems for modeling crises.) Gourio, Kashyap, and Sim (2016) and Filardo and Rungcharoenkitkul (2016) study similar but somewhat richer frameworks and find more substantial gains from using monetary policy to contain crisis risks. The former assume that crises permanently depress productivity and that a relaxation of the financial constraint (positive financial shocks) increases the probability of crises while lowering inflation, thereby inducing a stark trade-off between managing crises and stabilizing prices (Gourio, Kashyap, and Sim 2016).

A more recent class of promising models features global nonlinearities; one of these is discussed and calibrated in Chapter 7. This literature is very young and it is premature to draw definitive conclusions,[11] but results so far suggest that optimal monetary policy should take financial conditions into account, even without a separate objective related to financial stability or the prevention of financial crises. Intuitively, financial conditions provide information on risks to GDP growth and inflation, and so should enter the optimal monetary policy rule in a forward-looking, inflation-forecast-targeting framework.

A separate literature assesses the costs and benefits of using interest rates to pursue the additional goal of financial stability using a simpler framework, following Svensson (2015) and IMF (2015a). The empirical relationships discussed previously offer a rough estimate of the effects of monetary policy, albeit in partial equilibrium.

Costs of raising rates more—or keeping rates higher—than warranted to satisfy medium-term price and output stability mandates are well understood. Output decreases while unemployment increases. And inflation remains below target for longer, possibly undermining the stability of inflation expectations and thereby raising the trade-off between price and output stability, as mentioned throughout this book.

The IMF's Global Integrated Monetary and Fiscal model, which is also used by many central banks, implies that unemployment would rise by somewhat less than ½ percentage point because of a 100-basis-point increase in short-term interest rates for a year. This estimate is broadly consistent with those obtained using vector autoregression (VAR) models to estimate the transmission of monetary policy.[12]

Benefits instead usually seem smaller. To be comparable, these can be expressed as expected gains in employment—given the lower longer-term probability of a crisis—and assumed rises in unemployment if a crisis occurs. However, even if one overlooks the shorter-term increases in the probability of a crisis produced by the higher rates, the benefits seem relatively small. To justify using monetary policy to mitigate the risk of a crisis, the severity of the potential crisis and the link between interest rates and the crisis probability need to be at the upper range of existing empirical estimates. IMF (2015a) discusses these results in further

---

[11]For examples of models exhibiting global nonlinearities, see Benes, Kumhof, and Laxton (2014a, 2014b) and Benes, Laxton, and Mongardini (2016).

[12]See Altavilla and Ciccarelli (2009) for a survey.

detail, based on a simplified two-period model and a Bayesian VAR model responding to an interest rate shock. However, as discussed, these models do not fully capture all the channels through which interest rates impact the buildup of financial vulnerabilities.

OTHER CONSIDERATIONS

The above discussion offers a stake in the ground, largely defining what can be quantified. But other considerations are relevant, and these relate to the costs of clouded communications, spillovers, and effects specific to small open economies—typically emerging markets.

The use of policy rates to reduce the risks of a crisis could undermine the credibility and effectiveness of monetary policy, including by unanchoring inflation expectations. Credibility and policy effectiveness largely stem from transparency, predictability, and observable success, which are key underpinnings of the flexible-inflation-targeting framework. By contrast, pursuing the objective of financial stability requires policy action to be justified on the basis of distant events that are rarely observable, difficult to forecast, and even difficult to define precisely. What, for instance, is the socially acceptable level of financial stability? The IMF's October 2017 *Global Financial Stability Report* proposes a new metric for financial stability, namely, growth at risk (GaR)—defined as the value at risk of future GDP growth as a function of financial vulnerability. Systematically evaluating GaR and reporting on GaR should help clarify central banks' expectations for and communication about financial stability. The credibility of monetary policy can be put further at risk by the pursuit of a financial stability objective, both because crises are bound to still occur occasionally and because the central bank might at times underdeliver on the inflation objective.

For large economies with strong cross-border financial links, both the benefits and the costs of adding a financial stability objective to monetary policy may be larger because of the potential spillovers. Financial crises in large countries can have strong effects across borders due to financial linkages, as discussed in the *IMF Spillover Report* (IMF 2015c). Thus, if monetary policy in a large country were to decrease the probability of a crisis, it would avoid not only higher domestic costs but also higher international costs. This would be a positive effect from a global welfare perspective. However, higher interest rates in the large country could also have negative effects on smaller countries through trade linkages (more sluggish demand from the large country, compensated for in part by a stronger currency). So it seems that on balance global cost-benefit effects are ambiguous.

For small open economies, the case for pursuing an additional financial stability objective appears even weaker. First, financial stability concerns in such economies often stem from strong capital inflows that drive up asset prices and compress credit spreads (Sahay and others 2014). In such circumstances, increasing domestic interest rates by more than warranted to stabilize prices may be counterproductive and may actually exacerbate instability by attracting further capital inflows.[13] Second, whatever the source of financial vulnerability, higher rates would tend to appreciate the domestic currency and strengthen balance sheets for those with debts in foreign currency. In this regard, the IMF's October 2015 *Global Financial Stability Report* (IMF 2015b) highlights the extent to which firms in emerging markets are exposed to foreign currency debt. In fact, higher rates could even increase the share of foreign currency debt, a common problem in economies that are highly dollarized. As a result, debt levels may actually increase instead of decrease (Ozkan and Unsal 2014). Other policies may be more appropriate for managing the financial stability risks that stem from capital inflows (IMF 2012).

CONCLUSIONS

Severe financial crises impose enormous costs on society. Their occurrence therefore must be preempted, but with which policy? The analysis in this chapter indicates monetary policy is generally not the appropriate tool. Raising interest rates more than warranted by medium-term price and output stability objectives seems to increase the overall costs to society by raising unemployment and lowering real activity. These generally exceed the gains achieved from reducing the risks of a financial crisis. Moreover, an additional financial stability objective may cloud communications and undermine the credibility, and therefore the effectiveness, of monetary policy.[14]

Micro- and macroprudential policies seem most appropriate for mitigating the risks of a financial crisis. These policies are designed to target risks at their source with minimal distortions on other sectors and to strengthen the resilience of the financial system to potential shocks. However, the effectiveness of macroprudential policy is not yet firmly established, though early evidence seems promising. And the ultimate effectiveness of such policies could suffer from inaction bias, implementation lags, and a scope that is too narrow to affect newly emerging risks. As a priority, prudential policies (both micro and macro) should be designed and improved to overcome, or at least minimize, these hurdles.

Even if the policy hurdles are minimized, there remains the question raised in Federal Reserve Chair Janet Yellen's quote that tops this chapter: should monetary policy be used occasionally to complement prudential measures? More work is certainly needed to deepen the analysis summarized in this chapter. One need is for more accurate models of risk-taking behavior and its contribution to the risk

---

[13]See Ahmed and Zlate (2014), Forbes and Warnock (2011), Fratzscher (2011), and Ghosh and others (2012) for a discussion of how interest rate differentials drive capital flows.

[14]Similar arguments apply to the question of whether foreign exchange stability should be an additional objective of monetary policy. Chapter 10, for example, discusses the Czech experience, highlighting how the central bank was forced to abandon a pegged exchange rate in 1998 because it interfered with its ability to stabilize prices (Holub and Hurník 2008). However, the chapter also shows that foreign exchange interventions aiming to satisfy output and inflation objectives in an internally consistent framework can be powerful tools when central banks lose their interest rate instrument at the effective lower bound.

of a financial crisis, as well as the behaviors taken in response to monetary policy. There is also a need to uncover the links between credit growth and the severity of a recession or crisis, not just the probability of such an event. Finally, exploration is needed of other channels that lead to systemic risks.

The message of this chapter—that inflation-forecast-targeting central banks should not generally pursue the additional mandate of mitigating the risks of major financial crises—should be distinguished from that of Chapter 7, which argues that monetary policy should respond to financial conditions. Monitoring financial conditions provides valuable information on the continuously evolving downside risks to inflation and growth over the short-to-medium-term policy horizon that stem from vulnerabilities in the financial sector. Responding to financial conditions thus improves welfare even with a monetary policy mandate that remains focused on medium-term price and output stability.

REFERENCES

Acharya, Viral V., and Hassan Naqvi. 2012. "The Seeds of a Crisis: A Theory of Bank Liquidity and Risk-Taking over the Business Cycle." CEPR Discussion Paper 8851, Centre for Economic Policy Research, London.

Adrian, Tobias. 2017. "Macroprudential Policy and Financial Vulnerabilities." Speech given at the European Systemic Risk Board Annual Conference, European Central Bank, Frankfurt, September 22. http://www.imf.org/en/News/Articles/2017/09/22/sp092217-macroprudential-policy-and-financial-vulnerabilities

———, Nina Boyarchenko, and Domenico Giannone. 2016. "Vulnerable Growth." Federal Reserve Bank of New York Staff Report 794, New York.

Adrian, Tobias, and Fernando Duarte. 2016. "Financial Vulnerability and Monetary Policy." Federal Reserve Bank of New York Staff Report 804, New York.

Adrian, Tobias, Patrick de Fontnouvelle, Emily Yang, and Andrei Zlate. 2017. "Macroprudential Policy: A Case Study from a Tabletop Exercise." *Economic Policy Review* 23 (1): 1–30.

Adrian, Tobias, and Nellie Liang. 2018. "Monetary Policy, Financial Conditions, and Financial Stability." *International Journal of Central Banking* 14 (1): 73–131.

Adrian, Tobias, and Hyun Song Shin. 2018. "Procyclical Leverage and Value-at-Risk." *Review of Financial Studies* 27 (2): 373–403.

Ahmed, Shaghil, and Andrei Zlate. 2014. "Capital Flows to Emerging Market Economies: A Brave New World?" *Journal of International Money and Finance* 48 (PB): 221–48.

Aiyar, Shekhar, Charles W. Calomiris, and Tomasz Wieladek. 2012. "Does Macro-Pru Leak? Evidence from a UK Policy Experiment." NBER Working Paper 17822, National Bureau of Economic Research, Cambridge, MA.

Ajello, Andrea, Thomas Laubach, J. David Lopez-Salido, and Taisuke Nakata. 2016. "Financial Stability and Optimal Interest-Rate Policy." Finance and Economics Discussion Series 2016–067, Board of Governors of the Federal Reserve System, Washington, DC.

Akinci, Ozge, and Jane Olmstead-Rumsey. 2015. "How Effective Are Macroprudential Policies? An Empirical Investigation." International Finance Discussion Paper 1136, Board of Governors of the Federal Reserve System, Washington, DC.

Allen, Franklin, and Douglas Gale. 2000. "Asset Price Bubbles and Monetary Policy." Center for Financial Institutions Working Paper 01–26, Wharton School Center for Financial Institutions, University of Pennsylvania, Philadelphia, PA.

Alpanda, Sami, and Sarah Zubairy. 2014. "Addressing Household Indebtedness: Monetary, Fiscal or Macroprudential Policy?" Working Paper 14–58, Bank of Canada, Ottawa.

Altavilla, Carlo, and Matteo Ciccarelli. 2009. "The Effects of Monetary Policy on Unemployment Dynamics under Model Uncertainty—Evidence from the US and the Euro Area." CESifo Working Paper Series 2575, CESifo Group, Munich.

Altunbas, Yener, Mahir Binici, and Leonardo Gambacorta. 2017. "Macroprudential Policy and Bank Risk." BIS Working Paper 646, Bank for International Settlements, Basel.

Bakker, Bas B., Giovanni Dell'Ariccia, Deniz Igan, Luc Laeven, Hui Tong, and Jerome Vandenbussche. 2012. "Policies for Macrofinancial Stability: How to Deal with Credit Booms." IMF Staff Discussion Note (June), International Monetary Fund, Washington, DC.

Benes, J., M. Kumhof, and D. Laxton. 2014a. "Financial Crises in DSGE Models: Selected Applications of MAPMOD." IMF Working Paper 14/56, International Monetary Fund, Washington, DC.

———. 2014b. "Financial Crises in DSGE Models: A Prototype Model." IMF Working Paper 14/57, International Monetary Fund, Washington, DC.

Benes, J., D. Laxton, and J. Mongardini. 2016. "Mitigating the Deadly Embrace in Financial Cycles: Countercyclical Buffers and Loan-to-Value Limits." IMF Working Paper 16/87, International Monetary Fund, Washington, DC.

Bernanke, Benjamin, Mark Gertler, and Simon Gilchrist. 1999. "The Financial Accelerator in a Quantitative Business Cycle Framework." In *Handbook of Macroeconomics*, Edition 1, Volume 1, Chapter 21: 1341–93, edited by J. B. Taylor and M. Woodford. Amsterdam: Elsevier.

Blanchard, Olivier, Eugenio Cerutti, and Lawrence Summers. 2015. "Inflation and Activity: Two Explorations and Their Monetary Policy Implications." NBER Working Paper 21726, National Bureau of Economic Research, Cambridge, MA.

Blanchard, Olivier, Giovanni Dell'Ariccia, and Paolo Mauro. 2013. "Rethinking Macro Policy II." IMF Staff Discussion Note (April), International Monetary Fund, Washington, DC.

———. 2010. "Rethinking Macroeconomic Policy." IMF Staff Position Note, February, International Monetary Fund, Washington, DC.

Borio, C. 2014. "Monetary Policy and Financial Stability: What Role in Prevention and Recovery?" BIS Working Paper 440, Bank for International Settlements, Basel.

———, and Haibin Zhu. 2012. "Capital Regulation, Risk-Taking and Monetary Policy: A Missing Link in the Transmission Mechanism?" *Journal of Financial Stability* 8 (4) 236–51.

Brunnermeier, Markus K., Thomas M. Eisenbach, and Yuliy Sannikov. 2012. "Macroeconomics with Financial Frictions: A Survey." NBER Working Paper 18102, National Bureau of Economic Research, Cambridge, MA.

Bruno, Valentina, and Hyun Song Shin. 2014. "Assessing Macroprudential Policies: Case of South Korea." *Scandinavian Journal of Economics* 116 (1): 128–57.

Calvo, Guillermo A., and Enrique G. Mendoza. 1996. "Mexico's Balance-of-Payments Crisis: A Chronicle of a Death Foretold." *Journal of International Economics* 41(3–4): 235–64.

Caruana, J. 2011. "Central Banking between Past and Future: Which Way Forward after the Crisis?" Speech to the South African Reserve Bank, 90th Anniversary Seminar, Pretoria, July.

Cecchetti, Stephen, Tommaso Mancini-Griffoli, and Machiko Narita. 2017. "Does Persistently Loose Monetary Policy Brew Financial Risks?" IMF Working Paper 17/65, International Monetary Fund, Washington, DC.

Cerra, Valerie, and Sweta C. Saxena. 2008. "Growth Dynamics: The Myth of Economic Recovery." *American Economic Review* 98 (1): 439–57.

Cerutti, Eugenio, Stijn Claessens, and Luc Laeven. 2015. "The Use and Effectiveness of Macroprudential Policies: New Evidence." IMF Working Paper 15/61, International Monetary Fund, Washington, DC.

Christensen, I. 2011. "Mortgage Debt and Procyclicality in the Housing Market." *Bank of Canada Review* (Summer). Ottawa: Bank of Canada.

Claessens, Stijn. 2014. "An Overview of Macroprudential Policy Tools." IMF Working Paper 14/214, International Monetary Fund, Washington, DC.

Crowe, Christopher W., Giovanni Dell'Ariccia, Deniz Igan, and Pau Rabanal. 2011. "Policies for Macrofinancial Stability; Options to Deal with Real Estate Booms." IMF Staff Discussion Note (February), International Monetary Fund, Washington, DC.

Dassati Camors, Cecilia and Jose-Luis Peydro. 2014. "Macroprudential and Monetary Policy: LoanLevel Evidence from Reserve Requirements." Unpublished, Universitat Pompeu Fabra, Spain.

Dell'Ariccia, Giovanni, Luc Laeven, and Gustavo Suarez. 2013. "Bank Leverage and Monetary Policy's Risk-Taking Channel; Evidence from the United States." IMF Working Paper 13/143, International Monetary Fund, Washington, DC.

Dell'Ariccia, Giovanni, Luc Laeven, and Robert Marquez. 2014. "Real Interest Rates, Leverage and Bank Risk-Taking." *Journal of Economic Theory* 149: 65–99.

Demirguc-Kunt. 1998. "Financial Liberalization and Financial Fragility." IMF Working Paper 98/83, International Monetary Fund, Washington, DC.

———, Asli, and Enrica Detragiache. 2005. "Cross-Country Empirical Studies of Systemic Bank Distress: A Survey." National Institute of Economic and Social Research, *National Institute Economic Review* 192 (1): 68–83.

De Nicolo, Gianni, Giovanni Dell'Ariccia, Luc Laeven, and Fabian Valencia. 2010. "Monetary Policy and Bank Risk Taking." IMF Staff Position Note 10/09, International Monetary Fund, Washington, DC.

Diamond, Douglas W., and Raghuram G. Rajan. 2012. "Illiquid Banks, Financial Stability, and Interest Rate Policy." *Journal of Political Economy* 120 (3): 552–91.

Epure, Mircea, Irina Mihai, Camelia Minoiu, and Jose-Luis Peydro. 2018. "Household Credit, Global Financial Cycle, and Macroprudential Policies: Credit Register Evidence from an Emerging Country." IMF Working Paper 18/13. International Monetary Fund, Washington, DC.

Filardo, Andrew, and Phurichai Rungcharoenkitkul. 2016. "A Quantitative Case for Leaning against the Wind." BIS Working Paper 594, Bank for International Settlements, Basel.

Forbes, Kristin J., and Francis E. Warnock. 2011. "Capital Flow Waves: Surges, Stops, Flight, and Retrenchment." NBER Working Paper 17351, National Bureau of Economic Research, Cambridge, MA.

Fratzscher, Marcel. 2011. "Capital Flows, Push versus Pull Factors and the Global Financial Crisis." NBER Working Paper 17357, National Bureau of Economic Research, Cambridge, MA.

Freixas, Xavier, Luc Laeven, and Jose-Luis Peydró. 2015. *Systemic Risk, Crises and Macroprudential Policy*. Boston, MA: MIT Press.

Freixas, Xavier, Antoine Martin, and David Skeie. 2011. "Bank Liquidity, Interbank Markets, and Monetary Policy." *Review of Financial Studies* 24 (8): 2656–92.

Galati, Gabriele, and Richhild Moessner. 2014. "What Do We Know about the Effects of Macroprudential Policy?" DNB Working Paper 440, Netherlands Central Bank Research Department, De Nederlandsche Bank, Amsterdam.

Gaspar, V., M. Obstfeld, R. Sahay, D. Laxton, D. Botman, K. Clinton, R. Duval, K. Ishi, Z. Jakab, L. Jaramillo Mayor, C. Lonkeng Ngouana, T. Mancini-Griffoli, J. Mongardini, S. Mursula, E. Nier, Y. Ustyugova, H. Wang, and O. Wuensch. 2016. "Macroeconomic Management When Policy Space Is Constrained: A Comprehensive, Consistent and Coordinated Approach to Economic Policy." IMF Staff Discussion Note 16/09, International Monetary Fund, Washington, DC.

Gelain, Paolo, Kevin J. Lansing, and Gisle J. Natvik. 2015. "Leaning against the Credit Cycle." Norges Bank Working Paper 2015/04, Norges Bank, Oslo.

Ghosh, Atish R., Jun Kim, Mahvash S. Qureshi, and Juan Zalduendo. 2012. "Surges." IMF Working Paper 12/22, International Monetary Fund, Washington, DC.

Gourio, Francois, Anil Kashyap, and Jae Sim. 2016. "The Tradeoffs in Leaning against the Wind." Unpublished.

He, Dong. 2013. "Hong Kong's Approach to Financial Stability." *International Journal of Central Banking* 9 (1): 299–313.

Holub, T., and J. Hurník. 2008. "Ten Years of Czech Inflation Targeting: Missed Targets and Anchored Expectations." *Emerging Markets Finance and Trade* 44 (6): 67–86.

Igan, Deniz, and Heedon Kang. 2011. "Do Loan-to-Value and Debt-to-Income Limits Work? Evidence from Korea." IMF Working Paper 11/297, International Monetary Fund, Washington, DC.

International Monetary Fund (IMF). 2012. "The Liberalization and Management of Capital Flows, an Institutional View." IMF Policy Paper (November), Washington, DC.

———. 2013. "Key Aspects of Macroprudential Policies." IMF Policy Paper (June), Washington, DC.

———. 2014. "Staff Guidance Note on Macroprudential Policy." IMF Policy Paper (November), Washington, DC.

———. 2015a. "Monetary Policy and Financial Stability." IMF Policy Paper August. Washington, DC.

———. 2015b. *Global Financial Stability Report.* Washington, DC, April.

———. 2015c. *Spillover Report.* Washington, DC, June.

———. 2017. *Global Financial Stability Report.* Washington, DC, October.

Jacome, Luis, and Srobona Mitra. 2015. "LTV and DTI Limits—Going Granular." IMF Working Paper 15/154, International Monetary Fund, Washington, DC.

Jiménez, Gabriel, Steven Ongena, José-Luis Peydró, and Jesús Saurina. 2012. "Macroprudential Policy, Countercyclical Bank Capital Buffers and Credit Supply: Evidence from the Spanish Dynamic Provisioning Experiments." Working Paper 628, Barcelona Graduate School of Economics.

Jordà, Òscar, Moritz Schularick, and Alan M. Taylor. 2015. "Betting the House." *Journal of International Economics* 96 (S1): S2–S18.

Kaminsky, Graciela L., and Carmen M. Reinhart. 1999. "The Twin Crises: The Causes of Banking and Balance-of-Payments Problems." *American Economic Review* 89 (3): 473–500.

Kuttner, Kenneth N., and Ilhyock Shim. 2013. "Can Non-Interest Rate Policies Stabilise Housing Markets? Evidence from a Panel of 57 Economies." BIS Working Paper 433, Bank for International Settlements, Basel.

Leeper, Eric M., and James M. Nason. 2014. "Bringing Financial Stability into Monetary Policy." CAMA Working Paper 2014–72, Centre for Applied Macroeconomic Analysis, Crawford School of Public Policy, The Australian National University, Canberra.

Lim, C., F. Columba, A. Costa, P. Kongsamut, A. Otani, M. Saiyid, T. Wezel, and X. Wu. 2011. "Macroprudential Policy: What Instruments and How to Use Them?" IMF Working Paper 11/238, International Monetary Fund, Washington, DC.

Maddaloni, Angela, and Jose-Luis Peydro. 2011. "Bank Risk-Taking, Securitization, Supervision, and Low Interest Rates: Evidence from the Euro-area and the U.S. Lending Standards." *Review of Financial Studies* 24 (6): 2121–65.

Martin, R., T. Munyan, and B. A. Wilson. 2015. "Potential Output and Recessions: Are We Fooling Ourselves?" International Finance Discussion Paper 1145, Board of Governors of the Federal Reserve System, Washington, DC.

McDonald, Chris. 2015. "When Is Macroprudential Policy Effective?" BIS Working Paper 496, Bank for International Settlements, Basel.

Miranda-Agrippino, Silvia, and Hélène Rey. 2015. "World Asset Markets and the Global Financial Cycle." CEPR Discussion Paper 10936, Centre for Economic Policy Research, London.

Ozkan, Gulcin, and Filiz Unsal. 2014. "On the Use of Monetary and Macroprudential Policies for Small Open Economies." IMF Working Paper 14/112, International Monetary Fund, Washington, DC.

Reinhart, C.M., and K.S. Rogoff. 2009. "The Aftermath of Financial Crises." *American Economic Review* 99 (2): 466–72.

Sahay, Ratna, Vivek B. Arora, Athanasios V. Arvanatis, Hamid Faruqee, Papa N'Diaye, and Tommaso Mancini-Griffoli. 2014. "Emerging Market Volatility: Lessons from the Taper

Tantrum." IMF Staff Discussion Note (October), International Monetary Fund, Washington, DC.

Saurina, J. 2009. "Dynamic Provisioning: The Experience of Spain." In *Crisis Response Note 7*, The World Bank Group, Washington, DC.

Schularick, Moritz, and Alan M. Taylor. 2012. "Credit Booms Gone Bust: Monetary Policy, Leverage Cycles, and Financial Crises, 1870–2008." *American Economic Review* 102 (2): 1029–61.

Shin, H.S. 2011. "Macroprudential Policies beyond Basel III." Macroprudential Regulation and Policy, BIS Seoul Conference volume, BIS Papers 60, Bank for International Settlements, Basel.

Smets, Frank. 2014. "Financial Stability and Monetary Policy: How Closely Interlinked?" *International Journal of Central Banking* 10 (2): 263–300.

Stein, Jeremy C. 2014. "Incorporating Financial Stability Considerations into a Monetary Policy Framework." Speech delivered at the International Research Forum on Monetary Policy, Washington, DC, March 21.

Svensson, Lars E. O. 1997a. "Inflation Forecast Targeting: Implementing and Monitoring Inflation Targets." *European Economic Review* 41 (6): 1111–46.

———. 1997b. "Inflation Targeting in an Open Economy: Strict or Flexible Inflation Targeting?" Reserve Bank of New Zealand Working Paper G97/8.

———. 2015. "Inflation Targeting and Leaning against the Wind." Forthcoming in South African Reserve Bank, Fourteen Years of Inflation Targeting in South Africa and the Challenge of a Changing Mandate: South African Reserve Bank Conference Proceedings 2014. Pretoria: South African Reserve Bank.

———. 2017. "Cost-Benefit Analysis of Leaning against the Wind." *Journal of Monetary Economics* 90 (2017): 193–213.

Sveriges Riksbank. 2014. "The Effects of Monetary Policy on Household Debt." Box in the Monetary Policy Report.

Taylor, Alan M. 2015. "Credit, Financial Stability, and the Macroeconomy." NBER Working Paper 21039, National Bureau of Economic Research, Cambridge, MA.

Tressel, Thierry, and Sophia Zhang. 2016. "Effectiveness and Channels of Macroprudential Instruments." IMF Working Paper 16/4, International Monetary Fund, Washington, DC.

Viñals, José. 2013. "Making Macroprudential Policy Work." Speech delivered at the Brookings Institution, Washington, DC, September 16.

Wong, T. C., Tom Fong, Ka-Fai Li, and Henry Choi. 2011. "Loan-to-Value Ratio as a Macroprudential Tool—Hong Kong's Experience and Cross-Country Evidence." Systemic Risk, Basel III, Financial Stability and Regulation 2011.

Yellen, Janet L. 2014. "Monetary Policy and Financial Stability." Speech delivered at the 2014 Michel Camdessus Central Banking Lecture, International Monetary Fund, Washington, DC, July 2.

Zhang, Longmei, and Edda Zoli. 2014. "Leaning against the Wind: Macroprudential Policy in Asia." IMF Working Paper 14/22, International Monetary Fund, Washington, DC.

CHAPTER 7

Financial Conditions

Tobias Adrian, Fernando Duarte, Federico Grinberg, Tommaso Mancini-Griffoli

Financial conditions are important. They matter enormously to monetary policy because their movements can often diverge from the trajectory of short-term rates, and because they affect economic activity and the economic outlook. While it is essential to account for financial conditions appropriately in conducting monetary policy, it is also important not to overreact to every short-term wiggle in financial markets. In addition, it is important to remember that the policy goal is not the level of financial conditions per se, but the achievement of the Federal Reserve's dual mandate objectives.—W. Dudley (2017)

Financial conditions play an important role in monetary policy. In general, indices of financial conditions gauge how easily money and credit flow through the economy via financial markets by examining indicators such as borrowing costs, risk spreads, asset price volatility, exchange rates, inflation rates, and commodity prices. Central banks commonly adjust their policy stances and their forward guidance as a function of shocks to financial conditions. For example, the asset purchase programs that major central banks undertook after the global financial crisis were aimed at influencing financial conditions in risky asset markets, such as longer-term sovereign debt markets through term premiums, mortgage markets through mortgage spreads, and even credit markets in some jurisdictions.

Financial conditions are therefore highly significant forecasting variables for the conditional distribution of the output gap. This chapter extends recent work by Adrian, Boyarchenko, and Giannone (2016) to a multicountry setting. We document that loose financial conditions forecast a high output gap and low output gap volatility, a finding that is robust to variations in the indicators of financial conditions, countries, and time samples used.

We summarize the downside risk to GDP using the notion of growth at risk (GaR), which was developed by the IMF and explained in the October 2017 *Global Financial Stability Report* (IMF 2017). GaR(τ) is the value at risk (VaR) of

The authors would like to thank Doug Laxton, Benjamin Marrow, Maury Obstfeld, Vitor Gaspar, and Shujaat Khan for helpful comments.

the GDP gap τ quarters into the future. GaR is shown to vary primarily as a function of financial conditions but not as a function of other nonfinancial economic conditions (such as inflation or unemployment), as discussed in IMF (2017). Financial conditions should be a key variable for the conduct of monetary policy, even if they do not enter the central bank's objective (or loss) function, because they significantly determine GaR.

To study the quantitative importance of GaR for monetary policymaking, we calibrate an optimal monetary policy rule in a reduced form macro-financial model. The model features a standard New Keynesian setup with a Phillips curve that is determined by producers with staggered price setting. A financial intermediation sector is added on to the standard New Keynesian model of Woodford (2001) and Galí (2015) and is subject to a VaR constraint, as in Adrian and Duarte (2016). The price of risk varies as a function of the tightness of the VaR constraint of intermediaries, shifting the household consumption Euler equation (the investment/saving (IS) curve). Notably, the state variables that impact the second moment of consumption also impact its first moment. Hence, monetary policy moves both first and second moments. This is important to link monetary policy to the volatility of output.

The optimal monetary policy rule in this reduced form setting depends not only on the output gap and inflation, but also on financial conditions. We calibrate the optimal monetary policy rule across countries, and find that optimal monetary policy deviates significantly from a classic Taylor rule.[1] This is because financial conditions carry important information about the evolution of the variance of output gaps. In other words, financial conditions help policymakers better take into account the distribution of output gaps, including downside risks.

There are sizable welfare gains from using an augmented Taylor rule that includes financial conditions over a classic Taylor rule. In the augmented Taylor rule, monetary policy is allowed to respond to financial conditions, whereas it is constrained from doing so when following a classic Taylor rule. Results are robust to the choice of country and time sample, and to whether or not we include the global financial crisis. Welfare gains are approximately equal for advanced and emerging market economies, although the trade-off between the mean and variance of the output gap appears somewhat more attenuated in emerging markets. In all cases, however, optimal monetary policy responds to financial conditions.

These findings contribute to the recent debate about the role of financial stability in monetary policy. To date, the debate has essentially focused on whether monetary policy should pursue an additional mandate—that of minimizing the risks of costly financial crises. The literature, summarized in Smets (2014) and expanded in IMF (2015) and Svensson (2015), focuses on the costs and benefits of increasing policy rates above what is warranted to satisfy inflation and output

[1]The Taylor rule, named after Taylor (1993), is taken here to be a simple rule used to set monetary policy in response to the output gap and deviations of inflation from target.

objectives so as to diminish the risks of occasional crises. As explained in Chapter 6, in general and under plausible calibrations, the costs of doing so tend to outweigh the benefits. In addition, macroprudential policy appears better suited to directly target the imperfections that undermine financial stability, with the implication that monetary policy should remain focused on its output and price stability mandates. We maintain that assumption in this chapter—with the innovation that to do so optimally, monetary policymakers should use financial conditions to forecast not only the mean (as in standard analyses), but also the variance of output.

Our findings are closely related to the recent literature on the role of financial intermediation in monetary policy. Curdia and Woodford (2010), Gertler and Karadi (2011), and Gambacorta and Signoretti (2014) consider the welfare gains of monetary policy responding to credit spreads. They generally find that such a response is preferable following financial sector shocks but not necessarily in response to others, such as productivity shocks. This chapter studies instead a nonlinear model better suited to emphasize second moments—namely, the variance of GDP—because of the capacity of financial conditions to forecast downside risks to GDP.

FINANCIAL CONDITIONS AND GROWTH AT RISK

We investigate the conditional distribution of the GDP gap as a function of financial conditions by modeling the mean and variance of the output gap as functions of financial conditions for a sample of advanced and emerging market economies. We run panel regressions to gauge average behavior across countries.

The goal in this initial analysis is to quantify the trade-off between the mean and variance of the output gap. This trade-off is a key ingredient in monetary policy decisions, because output and inflation stabilization crucially depend on the conditional mean and variance of the output gap.

We find a clear negative relationship between the mean and variance of the output gap. When financial conditions become tighter (higher credit spreads or higher price of risk), the output gap falls and its variance grows. This emphasizes a key trade-off for policymakers. These results are robust to the sample and period of study, although there is heterogeneity across countries. If anything, the trade-off has become less pronounced more recently and is somewhat smaller in emerging market economies than in advanced economies.

We use quarterly data throughout. Consumer price indices (CPIs) and real GDP are obtained from the IMF's International Financial Statistics database. The output gap is computed by applying to the GDP data a Hodrick-Prescott filter with coefficient $\lambda = 1600$. The inflation rate is defined as the year-over-year percentage change in consumer prices. The financial conditions indices (FCIs) employed in the analysis are from the IMF's *Global Financial Stability Report* (IMF 2017). Univariate FCIs offer a parsimonious way of summarizing the

TABLE 7.1.

Country Coverage	
Advanced Economies	**Emerging Markets**
Australia (AUS)	Brazil (BRA)
Canada (CAN)	Chile (CHL)
France (FRA)	China (CHN)
Germany (DEU)	India (IND)
Italy (ITA)	Indonesia (IDN)
Japan (JPN)	Korea (KOR)
Sweden (SWE)	Mexico (MEX)
United Kingdom (GBR)	Russia (RUS)
United States (USA)	South Africa (ZAF)
	Turkey (TUR)

Note: Three-letter country codes are from the International Organization for Standardization.

information contained in asset prices and credit aggregates from broad sets of domestic and global financial variables.[2] Higher FCI values correspond to tighter financial conditions or a higher price of risk. All estimations use the logarithm of the FCIs.[3] The panels are unbalanced, with data for advanced economies starting in 1973 and for emerging market economies starting in 1990. Country coverage is presented in Table 7.1.

Estimation

For the panel estimation, we apply a two-step procedure.

$$\Delta y_{i,t} = \alpha_0 + \alpha_{i,1} + \alpha_{21} s_{i,t-1} + \alpha_{23} y_{i,t-1} + \alpha_{34} \pi_{i,t-1} + \epsilon_{i,t}, \tag{7.1}$$

where $y_{i,t}$ is the output gap for country i and $\Delta y_{i,t}$ is its change between periods $t-1$ and t, $\pi_{i,t-1}$ is the lagged inflation rate, $s_{i,t-1}$ is the lagged FCI, and $\epsilon_{i,t}$ is a heteroscedastic error term.

In the second step, we model the heteroscedasticity in $\Delta y_{i,t}$ by taking the estimated residuals $\widehat{\epsilon}_{i,t}$ and we calculating $ln(\widehat{\epsilon}_{i,t}^2)$. We interpret these log-squared residuals as the realized volatility of the output gap and we regress them on the same variables used in equation (7.1):

$$ln(\widehat{\epsilon}_{i,t}^2) = \beta_0 + \beta_{i,1} + \beta_{12} s_{i,t-1} + \beta_{23} y_{i,t-1} + \beta_{34} \pi_{i,t-1} + \nu_{i,t} \tag{7.2}$$

Both panel regressions are estimated by ordinary least squares (OLS) with fixed effects and robust standard errors. Results for regressions 7.1 and 7.2 are presented in Table 7.2.

---

[2]See IMF (2017) for more details on the underlying data and estimation methods.

[3]As FCIs are standardized, a country-common positive constant for the FCIs is added first to have strictly positive domain and then standardize the resulting logarithm. Results are robust to the choice of the constant.

TABLE 7.2.

Output Gap Conditional Mean and Volatility from Panel Estimates

	Advanced Economies		Emerging Markets	
	(1)	(2)	(1)	(2)
	$\Delta y_{i,t}$	$\ln(\hat{\epsilon}_{i,t}^2)$	$\Delta y_{i,t}$	$\ln(\hat{\epsilon}_{i,t}^2)$
$S_{i,t-1}$	−0.57*	0.65*	−1.28*	0.93**
$y_{i,t}$	−0.18*	0.05	−0.30*	0.14*
$\pi_{i,t}$	0.01	0.09*	−0.00	0.01
Constant	0.64*	−3.32*	0.41*	−1.84*
Observations	1,602	1,602	918	918
R^2	0.13	0.04	0.18	0.03
Number of countries	10	10	10	10

Sources: Data for Real GDP and consumer price index inflation come the IMF's International Financial Statistics database. Data for financial conditions indices come from IMF (2017). Sample for advanced economies covers 1973:Q1 to 2016:Q4, while emerging markets' sample covers 1990:Q1 to 2016:Q4.

Notes: $S_{i,t}$ = financial conditions index; $y_{i,t}$ = output gap; $\pi_{i,t}$ = consumer price index inflation rate; $\hat{\epsilon}_{i,t}$ = residuals from equation (7.1) *p<0.01, **p<0.05.

The estimates from regressions (7.1) and (7.2) show that financial conditions are significant in explaining the first and second moments of the output gap, both for advanced economy and emerging market economy samples. This is in line with Adrian and Duarte (2016) and IMF (2017). The output gap depends negatively on financial conditions (a higher FCI, namely higher spreads, induces a lower output gap), whereas the correlation is positive for the variance of the output gap. As a result, the unconditional distribution of the output gap is skewed, even if shocks are normal. This is as in Adrian, Boyarchenko, and Giannone (2016).

To show the negative conditional relationship between the mean and variance of the output gap, we regress the fitted values of the dependent variable in Equation 7.1 on the fitted values of the dependent variable in equation (7.2). Figure 7.1 shows the scatter plots and fitted OLS line.

The negative relationship underscores the intratemporal trade-off faced by policymakers. A closed output gap (an output gap of zero) is consistent with a positive variance, a result of the positive intercept. The trade-off that arises is captured by the slope of the best-fit line. Reducing the output gap from a positive level to zero, for instance, comes with an increase in variance. The steeper the line, the shallower the trade-off. In the limiting case of a vertical line, the trade-off disappears. Variance would be constant (homoscedastic), and the central bank would be able to adjust the output gap with no cost to volatility.

This trade-off seems to have diminished in recent years. The absolute values of both the intercept and the slope have increased over time; that is, curves have become steeper. Figure 7.2 shows the scatter plot and fitted OLS regression lines for two subsamples. For advanced economies, the sample is divided into two periods, from 1973 to the end of 1990 and from 1991 to the end of 2016. For emerging market economies, the sample is divided into the periods between 1990 and 1995, and 1996 to the end of 2016. If anything, the trade-off between the mean and the variance of the output gap appears somewhat stronger for advanced economies than for emerging market economies.

Figure 7.1. Estimated Mean and Volatility from Panel Estimation

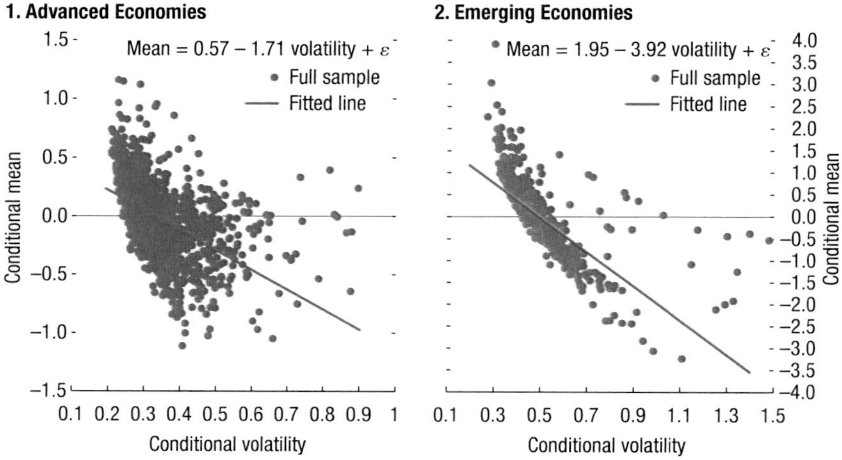

1. Advanced Economies

Mean = 0.57 − 1.71 volatility + ε^-

- Full sample
— Fitted line

(y-axis: Conditional mean, values 1.5, 1.0, 0.5, 0.0, −0.5, −1.0, −1.5)

(x-axis: Conditional volatility, values 0.1 0.2 0.3 0.4 0.5 0.6 0.7 0.8 0.9 1)

2. Emerging Economies

Mean = 1.95 − 3.92 volatility + ε^-

- Full sample
— Fitted line

(y-axis: Conditional mean, values 4.0, 3.5, 3.0, 2.5, 2.0, 1.5, 1.0, 0.5, 0.0, −0.5, −1.0, −1.5, −2.0, −2.5, −3.0, −3.5, −4.0)

(x-axis: Conditional volatility, values 0.1 0.3 0.5 0.7 0.9 1.1 1.3 1.5)

Source: Authors' calculations.

The Model

The model, taken from Adrian and Duarte (2016), is a microfounded nonlinear New Keynesian model augmented by a financial intermediation sector with vulnerabilities, but otherwise standard.

There are four types of agents in the economy: a representative household, firms that produce consumption goods, banks that intermediate household savings and finance producers, and a central bank.

Firms are exactly as in the standard New Keynesian model. They produce a continuum of differentiated goods in a monopolistically competitive way with sticky (Calvo-style, assuming a fixed probability of being able to reset prices at any given time) prices using a production technology that is linear in labor. There is no physical capital and productivity is constant.

The representative household maximizes its utility of consumption and leisure subject to its budget constraint. Unlike the standard New Keynesian model, the household cannot directly finance the firms that produce consumption goods in the economy. Instead, it can only invest in the intermediary sector by trading a complete set of zero-net-supply Arrow-Debreu securities with intermediaries (which can replicate, among other payoffs, the payoff of riskless deposits).

The intermediary sector invests the resources obtained from households and its previously accumulated net worth in a portfolio of assets. Intermediaries have the necessary information, expertise, or relationships to directly finance goods producers. Therefore, intermediaries can hold in their portfolios the stocks and bonds of the goods-producing firms. Each intermediary can also hold stocks and

Figure 7.2. Estimated Mean and Volatility from Panel Estimation on Subsamples

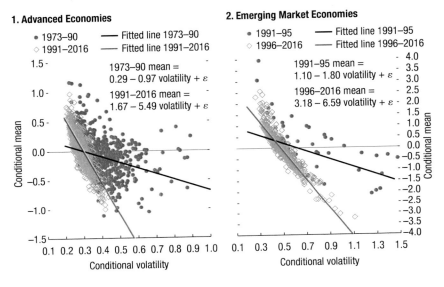

Source: Authors' calculations.

bonds of other intermediaries and trade a complete set of Arrow-Debreu securities with the household and with other intermediaries. There are two frictions in the intermediary sector. First, intermediaries are subject to exogenous preference shocks, which are the only shocks in the economy. These preference shocks can be interpreted as shocks that shift intermediaries' effective risk aversion or their beliefs. Second, when picking their optimal portfolio to maximize the expected net present value of dividends (shareholder value), intermediaries are subject to a VaR constraint that limits the amount of tail risk they can take.[4]

The *central bank* has a dual mandate to minimize the present value of mean square deviations of inflation and the output gap from target.

Policy can achieve neither the first- nor the second-best equilibrium. The first-best is the allocation that coincides with the one obtained in the decentralized equilibrium in which firm prices are fully flexible and households can finance firms without any frictions (without the need for an intermediary). The second-best can be obtained when retaining sticky prices but removing the friction that households cannot invest in firms without an intermediary. For both the first- and second-best equilibriums, all endogenous variables are constant since the only shock in the economy is to the preferences of intermediaries, and they

---

[4]Adrian and Shin (2010) provide extensive motivation.

are bypassed completely.[5] In the presence of the three introduced frictions—the inability of the household to finance firms directly, the preference shocks to intermediaries, and the VaR constraint—the decentralized equilibrium always results in allocations with lower welfare than in the second-best case.[6] This holds true independent of monetary policy. From the point of view of the central bank, the frictions are taken as given and cannot be eliminated by monetary policy. The best the central bank can achieve is a third-best equilibrium.

The reduced-form version of the model is given by

$$dy_t = \frac{1}{\gamma}(i_t - \pi_t - r)dt + d(rp_t), \tag{7.3}$$

$$d\pi_t = (\beta\pi_t - \kappa y_t)dt, \tag{7.4}$$

$$i_t = \Psi_0 + \Psi_\pi \pi_t + \Psi_y y_t + \Psi_v V_t, \tag{7.5}$$

$$V_t = -\mathbb{E}_t[dy_t]\tau - \alpha\mathbb{V}_t[dy_t]\sqrt{\tau}, \tag{7.6}$$

$$d(rp_t) = \xi(V_t - s_t)dZ_t, \tag{7.7}$$

$$ds_t = -\rho_s(s_t - \bar{s}) + \sigma_s dZ_s. \tag{7.8}$$

The core of the model consists of traditional IS and Phillips curves, although the former is expanded to include the risk premium. Equation (7.3) is the dynamic IS equation, the linearized first-order condition[7] of the representative household. The constant $\gamma - 1 > 0$ is the elasticity of intertemporal substitution,[8] and the constant r is the natural rate of interest. The endogenous variables in the dynamic IS equation are the output gap, y_t, the nominal interest rate, i_t, inflation, π_t and the risk premium rp_t. Equation (7.4) is the New Keynesian Phillips curve, the firms' linearized first-order conditions when they maximize profits by picking the price of differentiated consumption goods under monopolistic competition while subject to consumers' demand and Calvo pricing. The constant $\beta > 0$ is the representative household's discount rate and $\kappa > 0$ is related to the amount of price stickiness in the economy. As $\kappa \to \infty$, prices become fully flexible, while as $\kappa \to 0$, prices become fixed.

---

[5]There is also an inefficiency associated with the monopoly power of firms, which we reduce to zero in steady-state by means of an appropriate tax.

[6]If the decentralized economy with all three frictions were to replicate the first or second best, it would have to feature constant consumption for the household. The trading between the household and the intermediaries would have to be such that intermediaries provide full insurance to the household against all shocks. If that were the case, intermediaries would bear all the risk in the economy, which always implies that, eventually, intermediaries must violate their VaR constraint, showing that no equilibriums exist with constant consumption for the household.

[7]For all stochastic processes, linearization means linearizing the drift and stochastic parts of the true nonlinear process around the deterministic steady-state.

[8]The representative agent has constant relative risk aversion (CRRA) utility, and hence γ is its coefficient of relative risk aversion.

Equation (7.5) is the central bank's policy rule, where ψ_0, ψ_π, ψ_y and ψ_v are constants picked by the central bank. In addition to responding to inflation and the output gap, as is typical in a traditional Taylor rule, the central bank can also respond to output gap vulnerability, V_t.

Output gap vulnerability is defined in equation (7.6) as the VaR of the growth rate of the output gap projected at horizon $\tau > 0$ and level $\mathcal{N}(-\alpha)$, where $\mathcal{N}$ is the cumulative distribution function of a standard normal distribution. This means that V_t is the $\mathcal{N}(-\alpha)$ quantile of the projected distribution of $dy_{t+\tau}$ conditional on time t information. For example, if $\tau = 1$ and $\alpha = \mathcal{N}^{-1}(0.05) = -1.96$, V_t is the 5th percentile of the one-year-ahead output gap growth distribution.

The central bank may want to respond to vulnerability because, as shown in equation (7.7), it is the key endogenous determinant of the risk premium rp_t that, in turn, directly contributes to the output gap dynamics in the IS equation. The parameter ξ in equation (7.7) is a reduced-form parameter that captures the strength of the frictions—preference shocks and VaR constraint—in the intermediation sector. When $\xi = 0$, the risk premium is constant (in particular, it is constant with a value of 0) and the model collapses to a standard deterministic New Keynesian model in continuous time identical to that studied in Werning (2011) and Cochrane (2017). When $\xi \neq 0$, on the other hand, fluctuations in risk premiums induce changes in the conditional volatility of the output gap through equation (7.3).

Output gap vulnerability is a consequence of intermediaries' VaR constraint combined with the trading between the household and intermediaries of a complete set of Arrow-Debreu securities. The VaR constraint creates vulnerability in the intermediaries' net worth; the trading between the household and intermediaries equalizes their marginal utilities, transmitting the vulnerability from intermediaries to households. Of course, without any risk in the economy, the VaR constraint would never bind, so it is crucial to have some uncertainty for vulnerability to arise.

Uncertainty comes from exogenous shocks to vulnerability given by s_t, which also affect the risk premium as shown in equation (7.7). The process for s_t is a simple autoregressive process given by equation (7.8). The constant s is the long-term mean of s_t, $\sigma_s > 0$ is its instantaneous volatility and $\rho_s > 0$ controls its rate of mean reversion.

This model exhibits a key amplification mechanism. Fluctuations in risk premiums induce changes in the conditional volatility of the output gap, as discussed earlier. Changes in the output gap feed into vulnerability through equation (7.6). As vulnerability changes, so do risk premiums, and this again affects the output gap, vulnerability, and so on. The endogenous feedback between risk premiums, vulnerability, and the output gap is the result of the amplification mechanisms in the intermediation sector that arise due to financial frictions.[9]

---

[9] See Adrian and Shin (2009) for an illustration of how a VaR constraint can generate amplification.

As a result, when considering how to conduct monetary policy, the central bank must consider vulnerability not only because it is informative about the state of the economy but also because changes in policy endogenously change V_t, and changes in V_t feed back into inflation and the output gap. Note that even if the central bank set $\psi_v = 0$, it would still have an important impact on V_t through its influence on π_t and y_t.

CALIBRATION

For simplicity, we now consider a simplified version of the model in which prices are fully rigid. This implies inflation is identically equal to zero at all times. Plugging equation (7.7) into equation (7.3), the dynamics of the economy reduce to

$$dy_t = \frac{1}{\gamma}\left(i_t - r + \gamma\hat{\eta}\xi\left(V_t - s_t - \frac{1}{2}\frac{\hat{\eta}}{\xi\gamma}\right)\right)dt + \xi(V_t - s_t)dZ_t \tag{7.9}$$

$$V_t = -\mathbb{E}_t[dy_t]\tau - \alpha\mathbb{V}_t[dy_t]\sqrt{\tau} \tag{7.10}$$

$$ds_t = -\rho_s(s_t - \bar{s}) + \sigma_s dZ_t \tag{7.11}$$

where y_t is the output gap, i_t is the nominal (and real, since inflation is zero) risk-free rate, V_t is vulnerability, as defined by equation (7.10), s_t is an exogenous shock, and Z_t is a standard Brownian motion. As for the constants, $\gamma - 1$ is the elasticity of intertemporal substitution, r is the natural rate, and $\hat{\eta}$, ξ, α, τ, ρs, $\bar{s}$, σs are parameters related to vulnerability that have to be calibrated.

To calibrate, we use the time series for the conditional mean, $\mathbb{E}_t[dy_t]$, and conditional volatility, $\mathbb{V}_t[dy_t]$, of output gap growth that we obtained above. In the model, these are given by

$$\mathbb{E}_t[dy_t] = \frac{1}{\gamma}\left(i_t - r + \gamma\hat{\eta}\xi\left(V_t - s_t - \frac{1}{2}\frac{\hat{\eta}}{\xi\gamma}\right)\right) \tag{7.12}$$

$$\mathbb{V}_t[dy_t] = \xi(V_t - s_t) \tag{7.13}$$

Using equations (7.9), (7.10), (7.12), and (7.13), we get

$$\mathbb{E}_t[dy_t] = -\frac{1 + \alpha\sqrt{\tau}\xi}{\tau\xi}\mathbb{V}_t[dy_t] - \frac{1}{\tau}s_t. \tag{7.14}$$

This equation shows that the model can generate the same linear relation between the conditional mean and conditional volatility of the output gap that we observe in the data, displayed in Figure 7.1. In addition, as in the data, the model can generate dispersion around the mean-volatility line. In the model, the variation in the mean and volatility of the output gap occurs through the vulnerability shock s_t. Shocks to vulnerability shift the mean-volatility line up and down in parallel fashion (by changing the value of its intercept).

To estimate the parameters of the model, we run a regression of $\mathbb{E}_t[dy_t]$ on $\mathbb{V}_t[dy_t]$

$$\mathbb{E}_t[dy_t] = A \times \mathbb{V}_t[dy_t] + B + \varepsilon_t \tag{7.15}$$

and obtain OLS estimates for $\hat{A}$ and $\hat{B}$. We compare equations (7.14) and (7.15) to identify

$$\hat{A} = -\frac{1 + \alpha\sqrt{\tau}\,\xi}{\tau\xi}$$

$$\hat{B} = -\frac{1}{\tau}\bar{s}$$

$$\hat{\varepsilon}_t = -\frac{1}{\tau}(s_t - \bar{s})$$

We set by hand

$$\alpha = -1.645$$

$$\sqrt{\tau} = 1$$

to have a one-year horizon ($\tau = 1$) VaR at around the 5 percent level ($\alpha = -1.645$). It then follows that

$$\bar{s} = -\hat{B}\tau$$

$$\xi = -\frac{1}{\hat{A}\tau + \alpha\sqrt{\tau}}$$

$$\rho_s = -\log\left(\frac{Cov(\hat{\varepsilon}_{t+1}, \hat{\varepsilon}_t)}{Var(\hat{\varepsilon}_t)}\right)$$

$$\sigma_s = \frac{Std(\hat{\varepsilon}_t)}{\sqrt{\Delta t}}$$

where σ_s is adjusted by $1/\sqrt{\Delta t}$ so that it represents an annual volatility (Δt is the frequency of the data used in regression (7.15); for example, if the data are quarterly, then $\Delta t = 1/4$).

Table 7.3 shows the calibrated parameter values from estimating the conditional mean and conditional volatility obtained with the panel data regressions.

In the next section, when calculating welfare, we reintroduce the Phillips curve. We calibrate κ by choosing $\beta = 0.01$, and then estimating the model's Phillips curve country-by-country and averaging the values.

TABLE 7.3.

Calibration Values from Panel Estimates			
	AE (1973–2016)	AE (1973–90)	AE (1991–2016)	EME (1996–2016)
$\bar{s}$	−0.57	−0.29	−1.67	−3.18
ξ	0.30	0.38	0.14	0.12
ρ_s	0.14	0.21	0.12	0.15
σ_s	0.27	0.29	0.19	0.25
κ	0.18	−0.04	0.20	−0.36

Source: Authors' calculations.
Notes: AE = advanced economies; EME = emerging market economies. Coefficients are drawn from equations (7.3) to (7.8).

Figure 7.3. Changes in the Mean and Variance of Output Gap Growth after Looser Financial Conditions, an Illustration

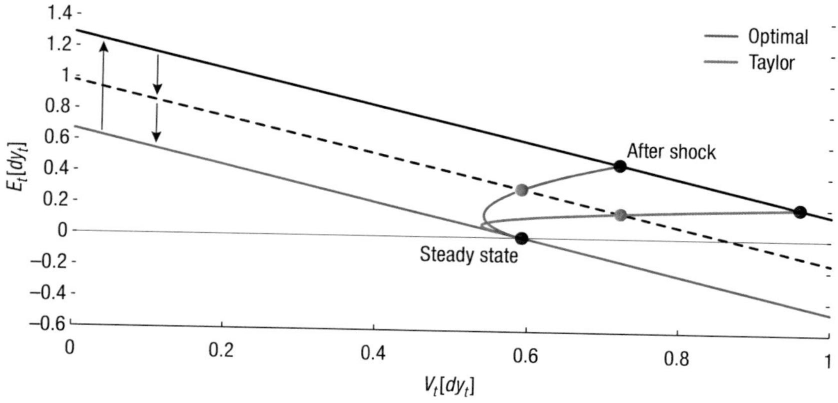

Source: Authors' calculations.

WELFARE GAINS

To investigate the welfare gains from responding to financial conditions, we consider both a classic Taylor rule, under which central banks are constrained to respond only to changes in output gaps and inflation, and an augmented rule, under which central banks can also respond to changes in financial conditions. In all cases, central banks pick coefficients in the Taylor rule to minimize the net present value of the same loss function.

To develop intuition, Figure 7.3 shows how the mean and volatility of output gap growth change after a shock that loosens financial conditions.[10] We assume the economy is initially at the deterministic steady state (the black dot on the horizontal axis). The red line is the mean-volatility line described by equation (7.14) evaluated at the steady-state level of s_t. After a shock that loosens financial conditions, the mean-volatility line jumps up (black line). The economy must always be on this line. Depending on what monetary policy rule the central bank implements, the economy can jump to any point in the new mean-volatility line. For the two rules we consider, both the mean and volatility of output gap growth initially increase. However, the optimal rule places a higher weight than the Taylor rule on the stabilization of volatility. As the economy adjusts back toward steady state, the line reverts continuously to its initial position, with the economy moving along with it. The slope of the line is the same throughout, as it is

---

[10]For this illustrative example, we use the parameters from Adrian and Duarte (2016) ($\bar{s}$ = –0.67, ξ = 0.36, ρ_i = –log(0.12), σ_s = 0.31, r = 0.04, $\hat{\eta}$ = 0.05, γ = 2) and consider a two standard deviation shock to s_t.

TABLE 7.4.

Monetary Policy Rule Coefficients						
	Optimal rule			**Taylor rule**		
	y_t	π_t	s_t	y_t	π_t	s_t
AE 1973–2016	−3.54	3.13	−0.14	−3.46	3.06	0.00
AE 1973–1990	−2.86	2.59	−0.64	−2.65	2.49	0.00
AE 1991–2016	−3.86	3.38	−0.01	−3.85	3.38	0.00
EME 1990–2016	−3.82	3.36	−0.03	−3.80	3.34	0.00
EME 1990–1995	−3.57	3.16	−0.50	−3.21	3.04	0.00
EME 1995–2016	−3.87	3.39	−0.01	−3.86	3.38	0.00

Source: Authors' calculations.
Notes: AE = Advanced economies; EME = Emerging market economies. s_t: FCI, y_t: Real GDP, π_t CPI inflation rate.

determined by α, τ, and ξ, the parameters that determine the strength of the frictions—and the amplification—in the intermediation sector. Monetary policy determines where in the line the economy is at each point in time but takes the line and its dynamics as given.

For the two interest rate rules we consider, central banks chose to increase interest rates in response to looser financial conditions. Looser financial conditions are accompanied by a higher output gap and higher inflation. The coefficients reported in Table 7.4 show that the optimal rule responds to the higher output gap by lowering interest rates, but to higher inflation and the lower vulnerability shock by increasing interest rates. Quantitatively, the net effect is positive, so interest rates end up increasing. For the classic Taylor rule, the responses to the output gap and inflation are more attenuated when compared with the optimal rule (coefficients tend to be closer to zero), while the response to the vulnerability shock s_t is zero by assumption. The end result is that interest rates also increase in response to looser financial conditions but by less than in the optimal rule.[11] Figure 7.4 shows the initial increase in interest rates implied by our calibrations after a one-standard-deviation shock to financial conditions.

The results are robust to the choice of country and time samples, despite some heterogeneity. Coefficients on output and inflation are relatively stable across rules and samples.

Coefficients on financial conditions may appear small, but this does not mean central banks put little emphasis on financial conditions in their optimal responses. A shock to financial conditions also affects the output gap and inflation. Thus, by optimally choosing high weights on these variables, the central bank is in practice already responding to financial conditions.

---

[11]For this analysis, it is important to recall that there is a single shock that simultaneously affects vulnerability, the output gap, and inflation. Instead of the linear interest rate rules that we consider, which are a function of two or three variables, they can also be thought of as nonlinear rules in a single variable (which can be taken to be vulnerability or the output gap). In addition, because our model does not have the usual demand and supply shocks that are standard in the New Keynesian model, the sign and magnitude of the coefficients in Table 7.4 need not resemble the usual coefficients (of about 2 for inflation and about 1 for the output gap).

Figure 7.4. First Period Response of Policy Rates to Looser Financial Conditions

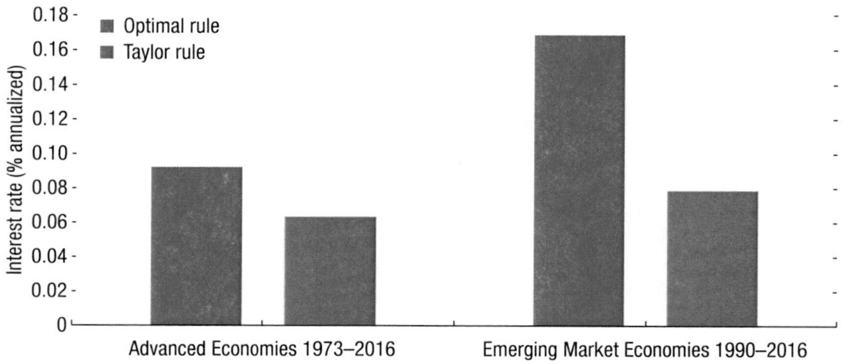

Source: Authors' calculations.

The fact that optimal policy responds at all to financial conditions, over and above its decisive reaction to output and inflation, is a notable feature of the model. Financial conditions contain information about the variance of output, which enters the central bank's loss function through the expected squared deviation of the output gap from target. Importantly, the strong relationship between the mean and variance of output, as documented earlier, holds conditional on financial variables. Thus, if the central bank does not respond to, or is oblivious to, the financial conditions shock, it will not be able to anticipate changes to the variance of the output gap. From the standpoint of the data, this is equivalent to saying that the unconditional relationship between the mean and variance of output gaps is nonlinear; knowing the realization of one, at any given time, is not especially informative for the level of the other. In addition to using financial conditions as a signal about the state of the economy, monetary policy also takes into account the fact that it can endogenously affect them. Optimal policy understands there is feedback between interest rates and the conditional mean and the conditional volatility of the output gap.

Consequently, the welfare gains from responding to financial conditions are significant. Table 7.5 shows welfare in consumption-equivalent units. In most cases, they are on the order of 10 percent. Again, results are robust to the choice of sample, as shown in Table 7.5. Interestingly, welfare gains have decreased in the more recent sample. This is consistent with the lower trade-offs between mean and variance of output gaps in recent years (as documented and discussed in the section on Financial Conditions and Growth at Risk). On the whole, welfare gains are approximately equal among advanced and emerging market economies.

In reality, welfare differences between the classic and augmented Taylor rules are likely to be greater than suggested by this stylized model. For instance, in the data the effect of a financial conditions shock on output is not immediate. Thus,

TABLE 7.5.

Welfare under Optimal and Classic Taylor Monetary Policy Rules				
	Optimal rule	Taylor rule	Difference in welfare	Welfare gain (in percent)
AE 1973–2016	3.03	2.72	0.32	0.12
AE 1973–1990	3.53	2.58	0.95	0.37
AE 1991–2016	2.34	2.22	0.12	0.06
EME 1990–2016	5.64	5.21	0.43	0.08
EME 1990–1995	4.53	2.23	2.30	1.03
EME 1995–2016	5.15	4.73	0.42	0.09

Source: Authors' calculations.
Notes: AE = advanced economies; EME = emerging market economies.

responding to changes in financial conditions allows monetary policy to be more forward looking, as opposed to responding only after the output gap appears. Also, a richer model with capital and investment could produce a drop in inflation following a compression of financial conditions; lower credit spreads would decrease the cost of capital and thus the marginal costs of production, as in Gourio, Kashyap, and Sim (2017). In such a model, the classic Taylor rule might respond by cutting rates due to lower inflation. However, an augmented rule that takes spreads into account might instead recommend a lower cut. In this model, a financial conditions shock is similar to a demand shock in that it increases output and inflation and therefore requires an unequivocal hike without a stark trade-off between output and inflation stabilization.[12]

RELATED LITERATURE

In exploring the role of financial conditions in the relation between policy interest rates and the mean and variance of output gaps for a cross-section of countries two steps are relevant: linking policy rates to financial conditions, and linking financial conditions to output. Both steps are underpinned by a rich literature—empirical and theoretical—emphasizing financial frictions.

The link between policy rates and financial conditions rests on the risk-taking capacity of intermediaries. As this capacity evolves over time, in part due to changes in policy rates, so does the compensation intermediaries require to hold risk—the risk premium. In segmented markets, this determines credit spreads as well as asset prices. Risk-taking capacity is typically limited by intermediaries' balance sheets—their size, value of collateral, net worth, value at risk, or other such measures—in what is referred to as a financial friction. Examples are Adrian, Moench, and Shin (2010), and Adrian, Etula, and Muir (2014), in which broker-dealers price assets according to their balance sheets; if these are strong and the marginal value of wealth is low, expected returns on risky assets can also afford

---

[12]The similarity is all the more striking when digging into the model; as explained earlier, the financial conditions shock is modeled as a shock to the preferences of bankers that is transmitted to households' marginal utilities through trade.

to be low. This chapter's model shares these mechanisms, insofar as policy rates affect the VaR constraint of intermediaries.

A growing empirical literature documents the link between policy rates and financial conditions. Gilchrist and Zakrajšek (2012) provide a hint: shocks to profits of broker-dealers—presumably coming in part from monetary policy—affect their credit default swap rates and the excess bond premiums (a measure of credit spreads). Gertler and Karadi (2015), and Boyarchenko, Haddad, and Plosser (2016) examine the issue directly, while carefully identifying monetary policy shocks using high-frequency analysis. In both cases, higher policy rates increase credit spreads.

The link between financial conditions and output has been explored by, among others, Philippon (2009), Gilchrist and Zakrajšek (2012), Krishnamurthy and Muir (2016), and López-Salido, Stein, and Zakrajšek (2017). A common result emerges despite the differences in methods and samples: higher credit spreads—or tighter financial conditions—coincide with a contraction in output. The forecasting power of spreads varies somewhat among papers. Krishnamurthy and Muir (2016) document that before financial crises spreads remain particularly tight despite strong credit growth. Similarly, López-Salido, Stein, and Zakrajšek (2017) suggest that spreads are mean-reverting so that a period of tight spreads forecasts one of wider spreads and lower growth.

Some empirical papers extend the analysis from the mean to the variance of output. Notably, Adrian, Boyarchenko, and Giannone (2016) emphasize that deteriorating financial conditions (wider spreads) are associated with an increase in the conditional volatility of GDP growth and a decrease in its conditional mean. Together, these results increase downside risks to GDP growth, and emphasize the importance of financial conditions for forecasting downside risks—or vulnerabilities—to growth. These same findings emerge from this chapter's model and are corroborated by its empirical investigation.

The relationship between financial conditions and output finds root in an older theoretical literature. Seminal contributions of Bernanke and Gertler (1989), Kiyotaki and Moore (1997), and Bernanke, Gertler, and Gilchrist (1999) emphasize the role of the financial sector in amplifying the effects of monetary policy shocks. These models exhibit borrowing and lending (between households and firms; later models introduce heterogeneous households). But equity issuance is constrained due to agency costs, and debt issuance is subject to frictions that are either exogenous or depend endogenously on collateral values or levels of debt. As a result, monetary policy shocks have a larger effect on output than shown in representative agent models that abstract from the financial sector.

The more recent theoretical literature has evolved in two ways: one explaining, and the other expanding upon, basic dynamics. A first strand has rationalized why agents take on excessive debt or leverage if doing so undermines economic stability. The answer lies in overlooking the macro implications of individual actions—a phenomenon called externalities (see, for instance, Stein 2012; Dàvila and Korinek 2016; Farhi and Werning 2016; as well as Korinek and Simsek 2016).

A second strand has emphasized nonlinear effects of financial frictions on intermediaries' balance sheets, as in He and Krishnamurthy (2014) and Brunnermeier and Sannikov (2014). Doing so allows for stronger amplification effects—closer to those observed in the data. The new models study global dynamics since they are not linearized around a steady state. And as constraints on the balance sheets of intermediaries bind only occasionally (and following negative rather than positive shocks), the models allow for more realistic dynamics: asymmetric amplification of shocks and periods of crisis following others of more normal growth. He and Krishnamurthy (2014) show that such dynamics help explain asset prices. Brunnermeier and Sannikov (2014) also show important implications for regulation; the model economy can remain in a crisis state for a prolonged time if initial capital cushions are too slim. This chapter's underlying model shares these same characteristics, as needed to explicitly study output volatility.

While this newer class of models does not dwell on monetary policy—unlike this chapter—somewhat older papers do. Curdia and Woodford (2010), spurred by the global financial crisis, consider whether monetary policy should respond to financial conditions—credit spreads in particular—following the recommendations of McCulley and Toloui (2008) and Taylor (2008), while Christiano and others (2010) favor a response to aggregate credit growth. Gambacorta and Signoretti (2014) build on Curdia and Woodford (2010) by adding further frictions, and Gertler and Karadi (2011) advance a model where central banks can complement the private sector's intermediation function, carving out a role for asset purchases.

In these models, the welfare gains from monetary policy responding to financial conditions are not clear cut (especially in Curdia and Woodford [2010]). Gains are greater following a shock to credit spreads, but not in response to other shocks. A productivity shock, for instance, will increase output and encourage lending, thereby raising credit spreads. But a cut in interest rates to stabilize spreads would lead to inefficient inflation. In the end, welfare gains from responding to financial conditions are shock dependent. This chapter instead remains focused on the effects of a single shock to financial conditions.

CONCLUSIONS

Economists and policymakers have debated for some time the degree to which financial conditions should or should not enter monetary policy rules. Some, including Bernanke, Gertler, and Gilchrist (1999), Bernanke and Gertler (2001), and Svensson (2017), have argued that monetary policy should take financial conditions into account only to the extent that they change the forecast of inflation or output. We extend that logic by arguing that monetary policymakers should care not just about the conditional mean forecasts of inflation and output, but also about the downside risks of those quantities. A monetary policymaker who aims to minimize the expected present discounted value of squared output losses and squared inflation deviations would naturally care about the conditional variance of output and inflation, and not just the conditional mean.

Empirically, this analysis shows that both the conditional mean and the conditional volatility of the output gap are significantly related to financial conditions. This builds on a robust literature on the forecasting power of term spreads, credit spreads, and market volatility for downside risks to output. Notably, the conditional means and conditional volatilities of the output gap are negatively correlated: when financial conditions deteriorate, the conditional mean declines and the conditional volatility increases. This negative correlation between the conditional mean and the conditional volatility of GDP gives rise to a strongly negatively skewed unconditional distribution of GDP. These findings are present in advanced economies and emerging markets alike.

In calibrating a reduced-form New Keynesian model with financial frictions to the empirical relationship between financial conditions and the time-varying moments of the output gap distribution, we demonstrate the importance of financial vulnerability in central bank considerations. The micro foundation of that model is provided by Adrian and Duarte (2016). Using the optimal monetary policy rule, we find that monetary policy should be conditioned on financial vulnerability in addition to the output gap and inflation. The welfare gains from doing so are significant. Intuitively, monetary policy that takes financial conditions into account mitigates GDP risk.

The results are particularly robust across time periods (before and after the global financial crisis) and types of countries. Welfare gains from responding to financial conditions are broadly equal for advanced and emerging market economies. Our results suggest the need to reformulate the policy approach to the relationship between financial stability and monetary policy. Clearly, monetary policy should take financial conditions into account, even if macroprudential policy is the appropriate tool to lean against the buildup of significant financial imbalances. Indeed, Peek, Rosengren, and Tootell (2016) document that references to financial conditions are increasingly common in monetary policy statements.

ANNEX 7.1. OPTIMAL MONETARY POLICY

The central bank solves

$$L(y_t, \pi_t, s_t) = \min_{\{i_s\}_{s=t}^\infty} \mathbb{E}_t \int_t^\infty e^{-\beta s} (y_s^2 + \pi_s^2) ds$$

subject to equations (7.3)–(7.8). Using equations (7.25) and (7.26) from Annex 7.2, the central bank's problem can be written as

$$L(y_t, \pi_t, s_t) = \min_{\{V_s\}_{s=t}^\infty} \mathbb{E}_t \int_t^\infty e^{-\beta s} (y_s^2 + \pi_s^2) ds$$

such that

$$dy_t = -\xi \left(\frac{1 + \alpha \xi \sqrt{\tau}}{\xi \tau} V_t - \frac{\alpha}{\sqrt{\tau}} s_t \right) dt + \xi (V_t - s_t) dZ_t$$

$$d\pi_t = (\beta \pi_t - \kappa y_t) dt$$

$$ds_t = -\kappa(s_t - \bar{s}) + \sigma_s dZ_t.$$

The Hamilton-Jacobi-Bellman (HJB) equation is

$$0 = \min_V \left\{ \xi\left(\sigma_s L_{ys} - ML_y\right)V + \frac{\xi^2}{2}(V - s)^2 L_{yy} \right\}$$

$$+y^2 + \pi^2 - \beta L + \frac{\xi\alpha}{\sqrt{\tau}} L_y s - \kappa(s - \bar{s}) L_s + (\beta\pi - \kappa y) L_\pi + \frac{\sigma_s^2}{2} L_{ss} - \sigma_s \xi L_{ys} s.$$

The first order condition (FOC) is

$$V = s + \frac{M}{\xi} \frac{L_y}{L_{yy}} - \frac{\sigma_s}{\xi} \frac{L_{ys}}{L_{yy}}.$$

Plugging the optimal V into the HJB gets

$$0 = 3M\sigma_s \frac{L_{ys} L_y}{L_{yy}} - \frac{\sigma_s^2}{2} \frac{L_{ys}^2}{L_{yy}} - \frac{M^2}{2} \frac{L_y^2}{L_{yy}} + y^2 + \pi^2 - \beta L$$

$$+\xi\left(\frac{\alpha}{\sqrt{\tau}} - M\right) L_y s - \kappa(s - \bar{s}) L_s + (\beta\pi - \kappa y) L_\pi + \frac{\sigma_s^2}{2} L_{ss}.$$

A solution is needed for the form

$$L(y, \pi, s) = c_0 + c_1 y + c_2 y^2 + c_3 s + c_4 s^2 + c_5 ys + c_6 \pi + c_7 \pi^2 + c_8 y\pi + c_9 \pi s.$$

Plugging into the HJB, using

$$L_y = c_1 + 2c_2 y + c_5 s + c_8 \pi$$

$$L_{yy} = 2c_2$$

$$L_\pi = c_6 + 2c_7 \pi + c_8 y + c_9 s$$

$$L_s = c_3 + 2c_4 s + c_5 y + c_9 \pi$$

$$L_{ss} = 2c_4$$

$$L_{ys} = c_5$$

and setting the coefficients in front of combinations of the state variables to zero, produces the following system of equations in c0, ..., c9:

$$[y^2]:0 = \left(1 - \beta c_2 - \kappa c_8 - c_2 M^2\right)$$

$$[y\pi]:0 = \left(-c_8 M^2 - 2\kappa c_7\right)$$

$$[ys]:0 = \left(2c_2 \xi\left(\frac{\alpha}{\sqrt{\tau}} - M\right) - \kappa c_9 - \beta c_5 - M^2 c_5\right)$$

$$[y]:0 = \left(3\sigma_s c_5 M - c_1 M^2 - \beta c_1 - \kappa c_6\right)$$

$$[\pi^2]:0 = \left(\beta c_7 - \frac{1}{4}\frac{M^2}{c_2} c_8^2 + 1\right)$$

$$[\pi s]:0 = \left(c_8 \xi\left(\frac{\alpha}{\sqrt{\tau}} - M\right) - \frac{1}{2}\frac{M^2}{c_2} c_5 c_8\right)$$

$$[\pi]:0 = \left(\frac{3}{2}M\frac{\sigma_s}{c_2}c_5 c_8 - \frac{1}{2}M^2\frac{c_1}{c_2}c_8\right)$$

$$[s^2]:0 = \left(c_5\xi\left(\frac{\alpha}{\sqrt{\tau}} - M\right) - \beta c_4 - \frac{1}{4}\frac{M^2}{c_2}c_5^2\right)$$

$$[s]:0 = \left(c_1\xi\left(\frac{\alpha}{\sqrt{\tau}} - M\right) - \beta c_3 + \frac{3}{2}M\frac{\sigma_s}{c_2}c_5^2 - \frac{1}{2}M^2\frac{c_1}{c_2}c_5\right)$$

$$[const]:0 = \left(\sigma_s^2 c_4 - \beta c_0 - \frac{1}{4}\frac{\sigma_s^2}{c_2}c_5^2 - \frac{1}{4}M^2\frac{c_1^2}{c_2} + \frac{3}{2}M\sigma_s\frac{c_1}{c_2}c_5\right)$$

with solution

$$c_8: \begin{cases} \dfrac{2\kappa(\beta + M^2)}{M^2\beta} & , \text{ if } M^2 = \beta \\[2ex] \dfrac{1}{M^2 - \beta}\left(-\dfrac{\beta}{\kappa} \pm \kappa\sqrt{\beta^2 + 4\kappa^2\left(M^2 - \left(\dfrac{\beta}{M}\right)^2\right)}\right) & , \text{ if } M^2 \neq \beta \end{cases}$$

$$c_1: \frac{3\sigma_s}{M}\frac{2\xi}{M^2}\left(\frac{\alpha}{\sqrt{\tau}} - M\right)\left(\frac{1}{\beta + M^2} - \frac{\kappa}{\beta + M^2}c_8\right)$$

$$c_2: -\frac{1}{M^2 + \beta}(\kappa c_8 - 1)$$

$$c_3: -\frac{6\sigma_s\xi^2(\alpha - M\sqrt{\tau})^2}{M^3\beta\tau(M^2 + \beta)}(\kappa c_8 - 1)$$

$$c_4: -\frac{\xi^2(\alpha - M\sqrt{\tau})^2}{M^2\beta\tau(M^2 + \beta)}(\kappa c_8 - 1)$$

$$c_5: -\frac{2\xi(\alpha - M\sqrt{\tau})}{M^2(M^2 + \beta)\sqrt{\tau}}(\kappa c_8 - 1)$$

$$c_6: \frac{6\beta\sigma_s\xi(\alpha - M\sqrt{\tau})}{M^3\kappa(M^2 + \beta)\sqrt{\tau}}(\kappa c_8 - 1)$$

$$c_7: -\frac{M^2}{2\kappa}c_8$$

$$c_9: \frac{2\xi\beta(\alpha - M\sqrt{\tau})}{M^2\kappa(M^2 + \beta)\sqrt{\tau}}(\kappa c_8 - 1)$$

$$c_0: \frac{1}{\beta}\left(\sigma_s^2 c_4 - \frac{\sigma_s^2}{4}\frac{c_5^2}{c_2} - \frac{M^2}{4}\frac{c_1^2}{c_2} + \frac{3M\sigma_s}{2}\frac{c_1 c_5}{c_2}\right).$$

ANNEX 7.2. DERIVATION OF THE SOLUTION

Plugging equation (7.7) into equation (7.3) it can be seen that

$$\mathbb{E}_t[dy_t] = \tfrac{1}{\gamma}(i_t - \pi_t - r) \tag{7.16}$$

$$\mathbb{V}_t[dy_t] = \xi(V_t - s_t) \tag{7.17}$$

so that equation (7.6) can be written as

$$V_t = -\tfrac{1}{\gamma}(i_t - \pi_t - r)\tau - \alpha\xi(V_t - s_t)\sqrt{\tau}. \tag{7.18}$$

Solving equation (7.18) for i_t gives

$$i_t = \pi_t + r - \frac{\gamma(\alpha\xi\sqrt{\tau} + 1)}{\tau}V_t + \frac{\gamma\alpha\xi}{\sqrt{\tau}}s_t. \tag{7.19}$$

Using equation (7.19) in equation (7.3) gives

$$dy_t = -\xi\left(\frac{1 + \alpha\xi\sqrt{\tau}}{\xi\tau}V_t - \frac{\alpha}{\sqrt{\tau}}s_t\right)dt + \xi(V_t - s_t)dZ_t. \tag{7.20}$$

And again it can be identified that

$$\mathbb{E}_t[dy_t] = -\xi\left(\frac{1 + \alpha\xi\sqrt{\tau}}{\xi\tau}V_t - \frac{\alpha}{\sqrt{\tau}}s_t\right) \tag{7.21}$$

$$\mathbb{V}_t[dy_t] = \xi(V_t - s_t). \tag{7.22}$$

Eliminating V_t from equations (7.21) and (7.22) gets

$$\mathbb{E}_t[dy_t] = M \times \mathbb{V}_t[dy_t] - \tfrac{1}{\tau}s_t \tag{7.23}$$

where the definition of M is

$$M \equiv -\frac{1 + \alpha\xi\sqrt{\tau}}{\xi\tau}.$$

Plugging equation (7.5) into equation (7.18) and solving for V_t gives

$$V_t = -\frac{1}{\psi_v - M\gamma\xi}\left(\psi_0 - r + (\psi_\pi - 1)\pi_t + \psi_y y_t\right) + \frac{\alpha\gamma\xi}{\sqrt{\tau}(\psi_v - M\gamma\xi)}s_t. \tag{7.24}$$

Finally, plugging equation (7.24) into equation (7.20) and rearranging produces

$$dy_t = \frac{\xi M}{\psi_v - \xi M\gamma}\left(r - \psi_0 + (1 - \psi_\pi)\pi_t - \psi_y y_t + \frac{\alpha}{\sqrt{\tau}}\frac{\psi_v}{M}s_t\right)dt \tag{7.25}$$

$$+\frac{\xi}{\psi_v - \xi M\gamma}\left(r - \psi_0 + (1 - \psi_\pi)\pi_t - \psi_y y_t + \left(M\gamma\xi + \frac{\alpha}{\sqrt{\tau}}\frac{\gamma}{\xi} - \psi_v\right)s_t\right)dZ_t$$

$$d\pi_t = (\beta\pi_t - \kappa y_t)dt. \tag{7.26}$$

Equations (7.25) and (7.26) determine y_t and π_t as a function of the exogenous variables s_t and Z_t. Given y_t, π_t and the exogenous variables s_t and Z_t, equation (7.24) determines V_t. Once V_t has been found, equation (7.5) determines i_t.

REFERENCES

Adrian, T., N. Boyarchenko, and D. Giannone. 2016. "Vulnerable Growth." CEPR Discussion Paper 11583, Centre for Economic Policy Research, London.

Adrian, T., and F. Duarte. 2016."Financial Vulnerability and Monetary Policy," Staff Report 804, Federal Reserve Bank of New York, revised 01 Sep 2017.

Adrian, T., E. Etula, and T. Muir. 2014. "Financial Intermediaries and the Cross-Section of Asset Returns." *Journal of Finance* 69 (6): 2557–96.

Adrian, T., E. Moench, and H.S. Shin. 2010. "Macro Risk Premium and Intermediary Balance Sheet Quantities." *IMF Economic Review* 58 (1): 179–207.

Adrian, T., and H.S. Shin. 2010. "Financial Intermediaries and Monetary Economics." In *Handbook of Monetary Economics* 3: 601–50, edited by Benjamin M. Friedman and Michael Woodford. Amsterdam: Elsevier.

———. 2009. "Money, Liquidity, and Monetary Policy." *American Economic Review* 99: 600–05.

Bernanke, B.S., and M. Gertler. 1989. "Agency Costs, Net Worth, and Business Fluctuations." *The American Economic Review* 79 (1): 14–31.

———. 2001. "Should Central Banks Respond to Movements in Asset Prices?" *The American Economic Review* 91 (2): 253–57.

———, and S. Gilchrist. 1999. "The Financial Accelerator in a Quantitative Business Cycle Framework." In *Handbook of Macroeconomics* 1: 1341–93, edited by J. B. Taylor and M. Woodford. Amsterdam: Elsevier.

Boyarchenko, N., V. Haddad, and M.C. Plosser. 2016. "The Federal Reserve and Market Confidence." Federal Reserve Bank of New York Staff Report 773, New York.

Brunnermeier, M. K., and Y. Sannikov. 2014. "A Macroeconomic Model with a Financial Sector." *The American Economic Review* 104 (2): 379–421.

Christiano, L. J., C. Ilut, R. Motto, and M. Rostagno. 2010. "Monetary Policy and Stock Market Booms." Proceedings—Economic Policy Symposium—Jackson Hole, Federal Reserve Bank of Kansas City, 85–145.

Cochrane, J. H. 2017. "The New-Keynesian Liquidity Trap." *Journal of Monetary Economics* 92: 47–63.

Curdia, V., and M. Woodford. 2010. "Credit Spreads and Monetary Policy." *Journal of Money, Credit and Banking* 42 (s1): 3–35.

Dàvila, E., and A. Korinek. 2016. "Fire-Sale Externalities." NBER Working Paper 22444, National Bureau of Economic Research, Cambridge, MA.

Dudley, William C. 2017. "The Importance of Financial Conditions in the Conduct of Monetary Policy." Remarks at the University of South Florida Sarasota-Manatee, Sarasota, Florida (March 30).

Farhi, E., and I. Werning. 2016. "A Theory of Macroprudential Policies in the Presence of Nominal Rigidities." *Econometrica* 84 (5): 1645–704.

Galí, J. 2015. *Monetary Policy, Inflation, and the Business Cycle: An Introduction to the New Keynesian Framework and Its Applications.* Princeton, NJ: Princeton University Press.

Gambacorta, L., and F.M. Signoretti. 2014. "Should Monetary Policy Lean against the Wind? An Analysis Based on a DSGE Model with Banking." *Journal of Economic Dynamics and Control* 43 (June): 146–74.

Gertler, M., and P. Karadi. 2011. "A Model of Unconventional Monetary Policy." *Journal of Monetary Economics* 58 (1): 17–34.

———. 2015. "Monetary Policy Surprises, Credit Costs, and Economic Activity." *American Economic Journal: Macroeconomics* 7 (1): 44–76.

Gilchrist, S., and E. Zakrajšek. 2012. "Credit Spreads and Business Cycle Fluctuations." *The American Economic Review* 102 (4): 1692–720.

Gourio, F., A.K. Kashyap, and J. Sim. 2017. "The Tradeoffs in Leaning against the Wind." NBER Working Paper 23658, National Bureau of Economic Research, Cambridge, MA.

He, Z., and A. Krishnamurthy. 2014. "A Macroeconomic Framework for Quantifying Systemic Risk." NBER Working Paper 19885, National Bureau of Economic Research Cambridge, MA.

International Monetary Fund (IMF). 2017. "Growth at Risk: A Macroeconomic Measure of Financial Stability." In *Global Financial Stability Report*, October, Washington, DC.

———. 2015. "Monetary Policy and Financial Stability." IMF Policy Paper, August, Washington, DC.

Kiyotaki, N., and J. Moore. 1997. "Credit Cycles." *Journal of Political Economy* 105 (2): 211–48.

Korinek, A., and A. Simsek. 2016. "Liquidity Trap and Excessive Leverage." *The American Economic Review* 106 (3): 699–738.

Krishnamurthy, A., and T. Muir. 2016. "How Credit Cycles across a Financial Crisis." Unpublished, Stanford University, June.

López-Salido, D., J.C. Stein, and E. Zakrajšek. 2017. "Credit-Market Sentiment and the Business Cycle." *The Quarterly Journal of Economics*, 132 (3): 1373–426.

McCulley, P., and R. Toloui. 2008. "Chasing the Neutral Rate Down: Financial Conditions, Monetary Policy, and the Taylor Rule." Global Central Bank Focus, Pacific Investment Management Company (PIMCO), February 21.

Peek, J., E.S. Rosengren, and G. Tootell. 2016. "Does Fed Policy Reveal a Ternary Mandate?" FRBB Working Paper 16–11, Federal Reserve Bank of Boston, Boston, MA.

Philippon, T. 2009. "The Bond Market's Q." *The Quarterly Journal of Economics* 124 (3): 1011–56.

Smets, F. 2014. "Financial Stability and Monetary Policy: How Closely Interlinked?" *International Journal of Central Banking* 10 (2): 263–300.

Stein, J. C. 2012. "Monetary Policy as Financial Stability Regulation." *The Quarterly Journal of Economics* 127 (1): 57–95.

Svensson, L. E. O. 2015. "Inflation Targeting and Leaning against the Wind." In *South African Reserve Bank, Fourteen Years of Inflation Targeting in South Africa and the Challenge of a Changing Mandate: South African Reserve Bank Conference Proceedings 2014*. Pretoria: South African Reserve Bank.

———. 2017. "Cost-Benefit Analysis of Leaning against the Wind." *Journal of Monetary Economics* 90 (October): 193–213.

Taylor, John B. 1993. "Discretion versus Policy Rules in Practice." Carnegie-Rochester Conference Series on Public Policy 39. North-Holland, 1993.

———. 2008. "Monetary Policy and the State of the Economy." Testimony before the Committee on Financial Services, U.S. House of Representatives, February 12.

Werning, I. 2011. "Managing a Liquidity Trap: Monetary and Fiscal Policy." NBER Working Paper 17344, National Bureau of Economic Research, Cambridge, MA.

Woodford, M. 2001. "The Taylor Rule and Optimal Monetary Policy." *The American Economic Review* 91 (2): 232–37.

CHAPTER 8

Transparency and Communications

Rania Al-Mashat, Kevin Clinton, Douglas
Laxton, and Hou Wang

> *There are two key factors behind the move to increased transparency on the part of central banks. The first is the relationship between transparency and the effectiveness of monetary policy. The second is the link between transparency and accountability.—C. Freedman and D. Laxton (2009).*

Proactive and well-planned communications can improve the effectiveness of monetary policy. Increased recognition of this principle since the inception of inflation targeting has led central banks to devote considerable resources and effort to their communications strategies.[1] One of the key pieces of information published by central banks that implement inflation-forecast targeting is the macroeconomic forecast on which policy decisions are based. Central bank websites provide rapid access to this forecast, to the latest relevant information and policy statements, and to staff research. The checklist in Box 8.1 provides a useful guide to the monetary policy items that central banks release and gives a short summary of the types of publication involved.

COMMUNICATIONS IN SUPPORT OF INFLATION TARGETING

When a central bank first implements inflation targeting, an important message to convey is that uncontrolled inflation is not conducive to a well-functioning economy. Low and stable inflation is a means to the end of a healthy, growing economy that provides jobs and higher living standards in an environment of relative stability. A parallel message concerns the limits of monetary policy. Sound monetary policy is necessary for achieving economic goals but insufficient by itself. Fiscal policy, structural policies, and the framework of regulations are also crucial. Moreover, economic activity is prone to fluctuations; periods of recovery and growth are followed by shorter periods of recession. And while monetary policy aimed at controlling inflation may moderate the business cycle, it cannot eliminate it.

---

[1]This chapter draws freely from Freedman and Laxton (2009).

The evolution of flexible inflation targeting has subtly altered central bank messaging. The primary goal remains the same: instilling firm expectations that policy will over time maintain price stability as defined by the inflation target. But instead of insisting on the need to keep inflation low, inflation-forecast targeters have shifted to stressing the symmetry of their reaction to deviations above and below the official target and their dual objective of maintaining high output (Clinton and others 2015). In the wake of the global financial crisis, when the main risk to inflation control has been on the downside and long-term inflation expectations have slipped below target levels, the message that monetary policy will act with due speed to raise inflation has been important for maintaining the stability of the nominal anchor. And inflation-forecast-targeting central banks, in explicit recognition of the trade-off between their dual goals, devote much space in their public materials to assessments of current and projected output gaps.

Inflation targeters try to communicate how the regime will be implemented. As noted in Dooley, Dornbusch, and Park (2002,12), "Credibility comes from the demonstration that the government has a consistent policy framework and can explain and learn from past errors in the context of that framework." This means that technical and nontechnical discussions of the goals need to be communicated, along with the central bank's understanding of the transmission mechanism (and its uncertainties), and an explanation of its chosen target. Dooley, Dornbusch, and Park (2002) emphasize that the approach seeks to appropriately balance stabilizing strong output and keeping inflation on target. This implies a medium-term horizon, with inflation returning gradually to target, since a short horizon would imply sharp policy interest rate responses and volatile output. Thus, while people should expect that in any given month inflation will be off target, they should be persuaded that the central bank's policy actions will return inflation to target over the medium term. The nominal anchor is the expectation, in all eventualities, that the long-term rate of inflation will be on target. While a consistent pattern of policy responses provides the ultimate basis for a credible regime, clear communications from the central bank on the intent of current policy actions accelerate the credibility-building process.

Under an inflation-forecast-targeting regime, the release of the central bank's forecast for output and inflation is essential news for the business and financial media. The forecast changes over time because of new information and changes in the interpretation of economic developments. In turn, the central bank's evolving views on the economic outlook are a central element in the analyses and discussions of academics, financial market participants, and commentators in the business media (including the experts that journalists rely on for comments), who are the main conduit of information to the public. The central bank's message must be tailored to multiple audiences. These include the public at large, financial markets, the media, parliamentary bodies, and the government.

The central bank's statement of record is a monetary policy report (sometimes called an inflation report), usually published quarterly, shortly after a policy decision meeting. The monetary policy report sets out recent global and domestic output and inflation developments, an updated outlook, and the implications for the setting of the policy interest rate. The report describes the central bank's view of the major forces driving the economy and highlights the risks to the outlook and to the projected interest rate path. It also presents confidence bands around the baseline forecast paths and alternative forecast scenarios based on different assumptions about the driving forces. Transparency requires that the information released in the monetary policy report, including the forecast, corresponds to the information that a monetary policy committee used to make its decision. To amplify the impact of the report, members of senior management meet with interested groups, appear before parliamentary bodies, and deliver speeches and lectures.

The normal convention after a monetary policy committee decision is for the central bank to announce immediately the policy interest rate that will be in place until the next meeting. Soon afterward, press releases provide a brief rationale. Policies toward release of minutes released by a monetary policy committee vary with respect to the details released and time elapsed between the meeting and the time of the release of the minutes. But all inflation-targeting central banks provide a timely description of the range of views among members. This conveys the central tendency of opinion and, just as important, the range of dispersion provides an indicator of the size of the uncertainties confronting monetary policy. This gives the markets an understanding of which developments will be central to the bank's thinking on interest rate decisions over a certain time frame, and how it might react to new information in the areas where it expresses most uncertainty.

Modern communication technology provides numerous platforms for reaching the public—websites, blogs, Twitter, Facebook, and so on. Ideally, use of these should be integrated and complement each other. Otherwise, there is a risk of over-communicating, and transmitting mixed messages through the various channels.

Publishing the Central Bank Forecast

The model-based staff forecast presented to the monetary policy committee meetings of inflation-forecast-targeting central banks provides a coherent macroeconomic narrative, linking the current and forecast settings of the interest rate instrument to the inflation and output objectives. As discussed in Chapter 3, all inflation-forecast-targeting central banks publish explicit forecasts for medium-term inflation and output growth, as well as information on the projected policy interest rate in their baseline forecast. A key reason for transparency about the forecast is that it helps guide expectations, among the public and in financial markets, in support of the objectives of policy.

In all cases, the central bank's communications indicate not just a possible path for the future policy rate, but also a sense of how it might change in response to a variety of developments. Most central banks publish just a verbal, qualitative, description of the forecast rate path. For example, the December 2017 Monetary Policy Report for Chile indicates that the policy rate "remaining fairly stable to start approaching its neutral level only once the economy begins to close the gap."

Box 8.1. Communicating about Monetary Policy

What to Communicate?

A hierarchy of required content might go as follows:
- Mandate
- Numerical inflation objective
- General strategy that guides central bank decisions
- Reasons for actual decisions in the period under review
- Assessment of current economic conditions and output gap
- Forward-looking assessment of inflation pressures
- Macroeconomic forecast highlighting output and inflation (that is, policy objectives)
- Main risks around the forecast and their distribution (for example, weighted to one side, or balanced)
- Description of relevant actual policy trade-offs in the context of the forecast
- Endogenous future path of the policy interest rate (the instrument)

The first three points are usually covered in a "boilerplate" statement, repeated at the start of each monetary policy report.

Practices vary across institutions with respect to communicating quantitative information such as explicit numerical forecasts versus qualitative communications such as descriptions of the forecast. Most inflation-targeting central banks publish forecasts of inflation and GDP growth and estimates of the output gap in their monetary policy reports. Only a small *avant-garde* group publishes interest rate forecasts.

Common Media

- Quarterly monetary policy report, sometimes known as the inflation report, containing all the above content
- Press conferences to explain and answer questions about objectives, decisions, and the forecast assumptions
- Minutes of monetary policy committee meetings describing the range of views expressed

Their view is that the monetary policy committee must be free to adjust policy rates to all possible contingencies, and that they do not want to confuse the public by appearing to have a commitment toward the interest rate (Freedman and Laxton 2009). However, a group of central banks in the *avant-garde* on inflation targeting (including the Reserve Bank of New Zealand, the Czech National Bank, Sverige Riksbank, and Norges Bank) release the full forecast, including the projected numerical path of the policy rate. The publication of confidence bands and alternative scenarios embodying different sets of assumptions underlines the uncertainties that attend the forecast and the conditionality of the interest rate path.

Publishing the forecast rate path—which in this book is called conventional forward guidance—strengthens the transmission of policy actions. The evidence shows that financial market participants quickly adapt to the conditionality of the rate forecast and do not take it as a commitment from the central bank. For example, Ferrero and Secchi (2007), in a cross-country study, find that the announcement of policy intentions improves the ability of market operators to

Figure 8.1. Change in Norway's 12-Month Rate after Revision in Norges Bank's Policy Rate, 2001–16
(Percent)

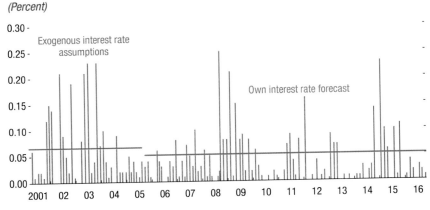

Sources: Thomson Reuters; and Norges Bank.
Notes: 2001–Oct. 2013, NIBOR 12 months; since 2014, NIBOR 6 months (12-month data do not exist after 2014). NIBOR = Norwegian Interbank Offered Rate.

predict monetary policy decisions. In New Zealand, the short-term yield curve responds to surprises in the release of the path, indicating that market participants take the forecast seriously.

The experience of Norges Bank before and after November 2005, when it began to publish its forecast interest rate path, is similar. Figure 8.1 shows the change in the 12-month interest rate that followed the bank's announcement of a revision in the policy rate. The size of the change was lower after Norges Bank started to publish the explicit forecast. Financial markets evidently got a better idea of its monetary policy intentions, and the element of surprise in the actual policy rate change was reduced.

Moreover, conventional forward guidance may avoid the awkwardness associated with ad hoc forward guidance, as practiced by the Federal Reserve and many other central banks after the global financial crisis, since it supplies the market with a regular flow of quantitative information on the central bank's intentions for policy instruments (Alichi and others 2015). In contrast, an ad hoc flow of verbal communication on forward guidance may provoke varying interpretations, and financial markets might misunderstand its implications. For example, during the 2013 "taper tantrum," bond yields rose far more sharply than warranted by the Federal Open Market Committee statement about a gradual reduction in quantitative easing (Bernanke 2013). As policy moves from a prolonged period of ease with rock-bottom interest rates, the publication of the expected gradually tightening path for the interest rate and for quantitative easing, in precise numerical terms that are free of ambiguity, would allay the risk of an unwarranted snap-back in bond yields much more effectively than verbal descriptions of likely changes in the instruments.

Institutional Modalities for the Forecast

Ownership of a published central bank forecast package may be an issue: are the forecasts owned by staff forecasters or policymakers? It seems better in many advanced economies with established histories of credible inflation targeting to regard the central bank forecast as belonging to staff rather than senior management, but this is a pragmatic judgment and would not apply to all circumstances.

The technical complexities—deriving model-based baseline forecasts, confidence intervals, and alternative scenarios—inevitably involve input from highly specialized staff. Senior managers of the institution would be expected to make sure that these resources were adequate to the job, and to have confidence in the technical quality of the forecast and associated analysis. Their role should also be to make sure that the forecasting team takes account of policymakers' views on the major issues. With a properly functioning forecasting and policy analysis system, the range of opinions within the monetary policy committee concerning the outlook would generally be reflected in alternative scenarios prepared by the staff, if not in the baseline, and in their analysis of uncertainties.

In other words, in a broad sense, the monetary policy committee bears responsibility in the public view of the institution. Its members defend the system that produces the forecast and the overall quality of the forecasts as inputs to decision making. However, regarding the contents of a given forecast, monetary policy committee members should focus on broad, strategic questions. They need not be closely connected to the production process, and probably should not be, considering the high-profile tasks that demand their time and attention. In public, they need not necessarily defend any aspect of a single forecast package.

As input to decision-making, the forecast—including the alternative scenarios and risk analyses—is one among the many inputs policymakers consider, though normally it is the most important one. However, it is vital that members of the monetary policy committee do have solid economic arguments for their views in circumstances when they differ from those of central bank staff. For example, at times it may be uncertain whether recent inflation pressures are persistent or transitory. In the former case, central bank action may well be required to counter the pressures, while in the latter, the problem unwinds itself without any central bank action. Another example would be where the baseline projection is for a slowdown, and hence a reduction in the rate of inflation, but the projected slowdown is not yet reflected in the data. Whether the central bank should ease immediately, or take a wait-and-see stance, can be the subject of legitimate disagreement.

Communications may be simpler when the forecast is presented as a staff input. The alternative approach, in which the monetary policy committee takes ownership of the projection, may be more difficult at a central bank where decisions are made by vote, not by consensus (or by the central bank governor alone). Voting members may have divergent views that cannot be represented in a single forecast. Because of more limited data, more rapid structural changes, and greater external exposures and uncertainties, monetary policy committee members in emerging market economies are more likely than those in advanced economies to have different views on how the economy functions, and on the depth and duration of disturbances. Where there is no consensus, a central bank with seven voting members might have to publish as many as seven projections in the monetary policy report. And how would all this be accommodated in the write-up that explains policy? Such an approach would likely be inefficient internally and confusing to the public. Instead, a published staff forecast would be a point of reference with which individual members could compare their own views. Clear and transparent explanations of such differences in the monetary policy report would help financial-market participants to understand the central bank's action (or absence of action). It might even increase the credibility of the central bank, since the debate would shed light on how it would react when future data reveal which of the opposing views was more valid. (The extent to which individual views in monetary policy committee policy debates should be published is a separate issue that is not examined here.)

As one example, the following statement is taken from the Czech National Bank's *Inflation Report*.

> The forecast is the key, but not the only, input to our monetary policy decision-making. Unless the economic situation requires an extraordinary monetary policy meeting, the Bank Board meets eight times a year to discuss monetary policy issues. At four of the meetings (in February, May, August and November) we discuss a new forecast, while at the other four (in March, June, September and December) we discuss the risks and uncertainties of the most recent forecast in the light of newly available information on domestic and foreign economic developments. Due to the arrival of new information since the forecast was drawn up and to the possibility of the Bank Board members assessing its risks differently, the decision we adopt may not fully correspond to the message of the forecast prepared by our experts. (CNB Inflation Report, IV/2017)

There are, however, caveats to this approach. In some countries, the central bank governor, rather than a committee, is accountable for the conduct of monetary policy. New Zealand is an example. Since the governor may well set the main themes of the forecast, she or he must therefore defend it in justifying the policy actions. In many emerging market economies, or ones that do not have a long history of inflation targeting, monetary policy committee members are expected to engage thoroughly in setting the assumptions. As the central bank builds its credibility, the governor and other members may provide extensive information about the forecast, explaining the reasons behind deviations as new data are released, or any changes in model assumptions. Since they share responsibility for the forecast, they must be prepared to defend it in public. In some countries, the overriding communications priority may be to promote a commitment to the inflation target without confusing the issue. Nuances that may be appropriate in countries where the public is accustomed to receiving a large daily volume of information on economic and financial developments may not be appropriate in others.

IMPROVED ACCOUNTABILITY

In addition to improving monetary policy effectiveness, the trend to greater transparency helps improve accountability. This is a necessary counterpart to operational independence of a public agency in a democracy. Increasingly, central banks around the world are given responsibility for monetary policy in the context of objectives defined in legislation or treaty, or in agreements between the government and central bank. A formal process holds central banks, as unelected bodies, accountable for their stewardship of policy, and they answer by a formal process to government or parliament and, in a more general way, to the public at large. For the process to be effective, the oversight body must have sufficient information to evaluate the conduct of monetary policy. As such, increased accountability and increased transparency take the same path.

Accountability requires the central bank to regularly provide information on (1) where inflation is in respect to the target, and why the outcome differs from what had been expected; (2) what the outlook for inflation is in the changed circumstances; and (3) what can be done under these circumstances to bring inflation back to target. This type of explanation is typically provided in the monetary policy report. Another element of accountability is the required appearances of the governor and members of the monetary policy committee before parliamentary committees to explain the policy framework and the central bank's views on current economic developments, and to justify any recent interest rate actions. Speeches by the governor and other members of the monetary policy committee at a wide range of events provide other avenues of accountability to a broader public audience.

It is not required that inflation-targeting errors be small. Accountability does not mean that the central bank must score success after success in having outcomes within a prespecified band. More important is that the shocks causing the inflation rate to fall outside the band can be explained, along with why they could not have been foreseen and prevented, and what policy interest rate path is likely to bring inflation back to the target over the medium term. What this may imply for output and employment should also feature in announcements. Indeed, deviations from target provide the central bank with a public communications opportunity to explain the nature of its systematic policy response for returning inflation to target.

Longer-term assessments of policy conduct are appropriate at times when the existing target is up for review. For example, the statement of objectives in the agreement between the Bank of Canada and the government of Canada has a five-year term. A thorough review of the preceding term precedes each renewal and features the new developments and difficulties that policy has had to confront, alongside examination of possible modifications to the inflation-control-target renewal agreement (Bank of Canada 2016). Academics, journalists, and other outside policy analysts air their judgments of the monetary policy record and their opinions on whether the framework should remain as is or be changed.

COMMUNICATING UNCERTAINTY

An issue with which central banks struggle is how best to characterize and communicate the risks around their baseline forecasts. Monetary policy reports often present confidence bands, or fan charts, around the forecast paths for inflation and the output gap, and so on. These are useful in describing the normal range of risks surrounding the baseline forecast. Likewise, discussions in the monetary policy report provide a verbal description of the main risks perceived by the monetary policy committee, and whether they are likely biased in one direction or the other. Alternative scenarios illustrate the uncertainties implied by shocks that committee members judge as relevant and beyond the normal range of random variability. Importantly, a central bank would indicate how the policy rate might respond should any of the suggested shocks eventuate. That is a concrete and effective method of communicating to the financial markets the nature of the perceived risks and of the systematic policy reaction function.

Published minutes of monetary policy committee meetings are another channel for communicating uncertainties. They may provide a different, livelier perspective of the range of members' views than charts of confidence bands and alternative scenarios. However, if minutes are published, the discussion of the differences in views of members must be framed to promote increased understanding of the issues confronting the committee and to avoid confusion. Blinder (2009) warns that communicating a diversity of views may give an accurate picture of uncertainty, but at the expense of clarity of message. In a system with decision by majority vote, not all members of the monetary policy committee will be able to use only the consensus outlook in their presentations. Commentators and markets would expect members to air their different views when there is a split vote.

COMPLICATIONS ASSOCIATED WITH A FINANCIAL STABILITY MANDATE

Modifying the inflation-targeting mandate to recognize a financial stability objective for monetary policy raises awkward communications issues for monetary policymakers. Such a mandate would involve diverting from the policy interest rate path that would, according to the central bank's forecast, best achieve the inflation target, with the purpose of that diversion being to moderate financial sector disturbances. The communications strategy of the financial regulator regarding macroprudential instruments is less problematic. In the discussion that follows, for simplicity's sake, the monetary policy function and the regulatory function are regarded as separate—even though they may both be under the central bank, as they are in many jurisdictions.

The primary goal of monetary policy communications is to promote positive outcomes—namely, to anchor expectations on the inflation target. In contrast, macroprudential policy communications aim at avoiding negative outcomes—and their focus tends to change over time. During normal times, effective communication discourages excessive optimism about asset prices and credit risks. Thus, macroprudential communications paint downside-risk scenarios, highlighting perceived vulnerabilities in the financial system and the risk of bad events that might cause system-wide failures, drawing attention to tail events. During crises, the messaging from the central bank switches to assurances that the banking system has an ample supply of liquidity, encouraging calm, and statements of confidence that normalcy will be restored in a timely manner.

The communication challenge may be immense when monetary policy "leans" to subdue sustained credit growth or asset price movements, the two main indicators for macro-financial stability (Borio 2014). Monetary policy and financial stability actions then merge. If asset prices and credit growth are not deemed to be excessive, the policy rate setting may aim exclusively at achieving a desirable path to the inflation target, for example, that described by the central bank's macroeconomic forecasting model. If asset prices and credit growth are judged to be out of line, the policy rate path would change, as would the forecasts for inflation and output. In addition to reporting on the expected future paths of output, inflation, and the policy interest rate, a central bank with an integrated inflation target–financial stability mandate would report on the projected paths of credit conditions and asset prices, and on the risk of a serious financial shock. Since the business cycle and the credit cycle are not synchronous, they may point in different directions with regard to an appropriate stance for monetary policy.

REFERENCES

Alichi, A., K. Clinton, C. Freedman, O. Kamenik, M. Juillard, D. Laxton, J. Turunen, and H. Wang. 2015. "Avoiding Dark Corners: A Robust Monetary Policy Framework for the United States." IMF Working Paper 15/134, International Monetary Fund, Washington, DC.

Bank of Canada. 2016. "Renewing Canada's Inflation-Control Agreement." http://www.bankofcanada.ca/core-functions/monetary-policy/renewing-canadas-inflation-control-agreement/.

Bernanke, B.S. 2013. "Communication and Monetary Policy." Herbert Stein Memorial Lecture, Washington, DC, November.

Blinder, A.S. 2009. "Talking about Monetary Policy: The Virtues (and Vices?) of Central Bank Communication." BIS Working Paper 274, Bank for International Settlements, Basel.

Borio, C. 2014. "Monetary Policy and Financial Stability: What Role in Prevention and Recovery?" BIS Working Paper 440, Bank for International Settlements, Basel.

Clinton, K., C. Freedman, M. Juillard, O. Kameník, D. Laxton, and H. Wang. 2015. "Inflation-Forecast Targeting: Applying the Principle of Transparency." IMF Working Paper 15/132, International Monetary Fund, Washington, DC.

Czech National Bank. 2017. *Inflation Report* IV/2017.

Dooley, M., R. Dornbusch, and Y.C. Park. 2002. "A Framework for Exchange Rate Policy in Korea." Korea Institute for International Economic Policy, Working Paper 02–02.

Ferrero, G., and A. Secchi. 2007. "The Announcement of Future Policy Intentions." Bank of Italy Working Paper, May.

Freedman, C., and D. Laxton. 2009. "Inflation Targeting Pillars: Transparency and Accountability." IMF Working Paper 09/62, International Monetary Fund, Washington, DC.

PART III

Inflation-Forecast Targeting in Four Countries

CHAPTER 9

Canada: A Well-Established System

RANIA AL-MASHAT, KEVIN CLINTON, DOUGLAS
LAXTON, AND HOU WANG

> *WHEREAS it is desirable to establish a central bank in Canada to regulate credit and currency in the best interests of the economic life of the nation, to control and protect the external value of the national monetary unit and to mitigate by its influence fluctuations in the general level of production, trade, prices and employment, so far as may be possible within the scope of monetary action, and generally to promote the economic and financial welfare of Canada. —Preamble to the Bank of Canada Act*

For a quarter-century, the Bank of Canada has pursued flexible inflation targeting.[1] The inflation-control targets, defined in agreements between the bank and the government of Canada, put the broad, multiple objectives defined by the preamble to the Bank of Canada Act into operational form. The mandate includes objectives for stabilizing output and inflation. Flexible inflation targeting, which accounts for the lagged effects of monetary policy on inflation and output and the short-term trade-offs between these goal variables, is squarely in line with this mandate.

The Canadian monetary framework is well tested and, without question, sound.[2] And like any good arrangement for economic policy, the inflation-control-target agreements between the government and the central bank have a process for periodic review, assessment, and possible revision. This occurs every five years, and the current agreement is up for renewal in 2021.

Without questioning the success of the existing regime, the framework could be improved with greater transparency about the expected path of the policy rate—a step that in this book is called conventional forward guidance. Conventional forward guidance would involve routine publication of the forecast path of the policy rate and other relevant macroeconomic variables (such as the output gap and inflation) following the central bank's policy decision meetings.

Before going further, it is worth drawing attention to the outstanding record of inflation control. Since 1994, headline consumer price index (CPI) inflation has averaged just under the 2 percent target. Expectations have been firmly anchored through the ups and downs of the business cycle and the exogenous

---

[1]See Bank of Canada (2012).

[2]For a discussion of the history of inflation targeting in Canada, see Lane (2015).

Figure 9.1. Inflation and Consensus Inflation Expectations for Canada, 1979–2017
(Percent)

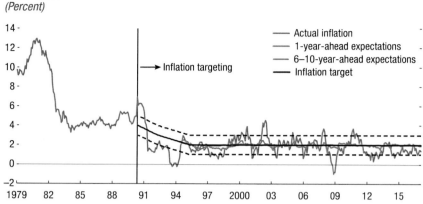

Source: Consensus Economics.

price shocks that have occasionally driven the actual inflation rate off target. Thus, in 2016 the outlook for inflation remained remarkably stable despite the large impact of the recent oil price shock (Figure 9.1 and Table 9.1).

The most transparent inflation-targeting central banks have adopted inflation-forecast targeting. The central bank's forecast represents an ideal intermediate target that is used to communicate how it is managing the short-term output-inflation trade-off (Svensson 1997). That is, monetary policy targets the path of the central bank's inflation forecast, which gradually converges to the 2 percent long-term target. The rationale is that this forecast embodies all relevant factors known to the central bank that may affect the future course of inflation. These factors include policymakers' own preferences for the output-inflation trade-off, their assessments of the state of the economy, and their views on the transmission of monetary policy to output and inflation. Thus, the forecast embodies policymakers' views of the best feasible path for the inflation rate from its current level to the long-term target rate. From this perspective, the central bank's inflation forecast is itself an ideal operational target for monetary policy, over the medium and long term. Table 9.1 indicates, in an international comparison, that the inflation-forecast-targeting approach has had superior results in anchoring long-term inflation expectations to the announced targets.

Inflation-forecast-targeting central banks, Sveriges Riksbank, the Czech National Bank, and the Reserve Bank of New Zealand, ranked as the top three in the Dincer-Eichengreen index of central bank transparency (Figure 9.2). On this measure, they have overtaken the Bank of Canada, which was an early pioneer of inflation targeting and which, in conjunction with the IMF, provided advice on implementing the regime to several of them.

TABLE 9.1.

Inflation Expectations Are Better Anchored in Inflation-Forecast-Targeting Countries

	2016	2017	2018	Cumulative Deviations from Inflation Objectives (2017–18) (Percentage points)	IFT Central Bank[1]
Canada	1.7	2.1 (0.1)	2.0 (0.0)	0.1	Yes (1994)
Czech Republic	0.6	1.7 (−0.3)	2.1 (0.1)	−0.2	Yes (2002)
New Zealand	0.7	1.7 (−0.3)	2.0 (0.0)	−0.3	Yes (1997)
Sweden	1.0	1.5 (−0.5)	2.2 (0.2)	−0.3	Yes (2007)
United States[2]	1.3	2.3 (0.0)	2.3 (0.0)	0.0	Yes (2012)
Euro Area	0.3	1.3 (−0.7)	1.5 (−0.5)	−1.2	No
Japan	−0.1	0.6 (−1.4)	0.9 (−1.1)	−2.5	No

Source: Consensus Economics, July 2016.
Note: The numbers in parentheses represent percentage point deviations from the inflation targets.
[1]Inflation-forecast-targeting (IFT) central banks use consistent macro forecasts to explain how they adjust their instruments to achieve their output-inflation objectives.
[2]The implicit consumer price index (CPI) inflation objective for the United States is estimated by the authors at about 0.3 percentage point above the Fed's official personal consumption expenditures (PCE) inflation objective of 2.0 percent. This is based on the difference in long-term CPI and PCE inflation forecasts from the Philadelphia Fed's Survey of Professional Forecasters.

Figure 9.2. Dincer-Eichengreen Central Bank Transparency Index, 1998–2014

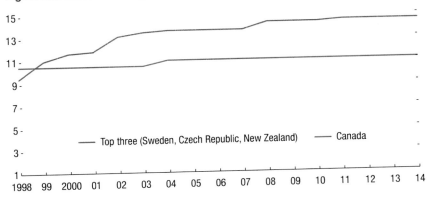

Source: Dincer and Eichengreen 2014.

Figure 9.3. Oil Price and Canadian Exchange Rate, 2002–17

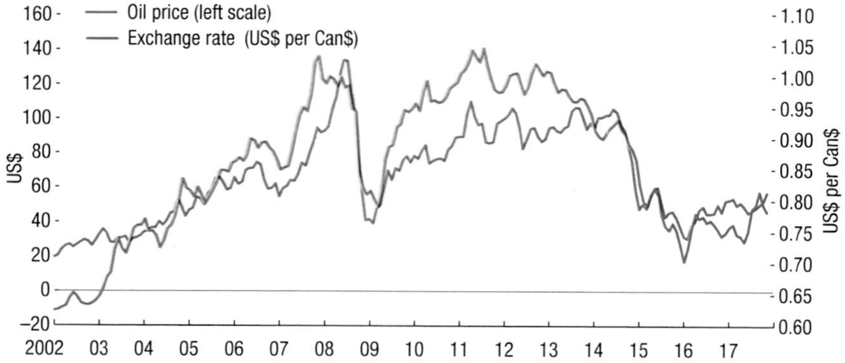

Source: Haver Analytics.

Several factors have contributed to the marked success of the framework in Canada. First, the exchange rate against the US dollar has been allowed to vary over a wide range, absorbing large shocks to the terms of trade and thereby buffering their impact on domestic output and inflation (Figure 9.3).

Second, fiscal policy has mainly played a supportive role, with surpluses during the pre-2008 expansion switching to large deficits after the global financial crisis, which reflect endogenous effects of the recession, and the 2009–10 fiscal stimulus. The budgetary consolidation during 2012–15, with smaller deficits, eventually restored a declining government-debt-to-GDP ratio.

After 2016, fiscal policy has been stimulative—appropriately in view of the macroeconomic circumstances.

Third, during 2010–13, Canada benefited from booming demand for oil and other commodities, driven by the expansion in China and other emerging markets, which stimulated domestic investment and output. This fortuitous development largely shielded Canada from the negative effects of the large drop of the global equilibrium real interest rate in the wake of the 2008 global financial crisis. In many advanced economies, chronic excess capacity and unduly low inflation rates have persisted despite extremely low interest rates. The global level of nominal rates consistent with maintaining output at potential is well below the pre-2008 level; currently the neutral rate may not be much higher than zero (Box 9.1).[3] Since 2014, the weakness in world oil prices, the recession in the

---

[3]Mendes (2014) estimates the neutral real interest rate in Canada at 1–2 percent, which translates to 3–4 percent in nominal terms. A neutral rate as high as 4 percent would imply that monetary conditions have been extremely expansionary since 2009, because the actual policy rate has not been above 1 percent. But this is difficult to square with subdued growth and inflation. If the latter are attributed to long-lasting economic headwinds, for operational purposes it would be simpler to regard these as part of the environment, rather than shocks, and to reduce the estimate of the neutral rate correspondingly.

Box 9.1. Downward Trends in the Global Equilibrium Real Interest Rate

The equilibrium real interest rate can be defined as the rate that would be consistent with equality between actual output and potential (full-employment) output in the absence of any short-term or cyclical shocks. In a standard macroeconomic model, an inflation-forecast-targeting central bank would vary the policy rate from this level only to gradually return inflation to the target rate after some disturbance. This involves a medium-term concept of equilibrium. For Canada, a very open economy with high capital mobility, the global (or as an approximation, the US) equilibrium rate drives the domestic rate.

Inflation-adjusted bond yields have seen a trend decline since the early 1980s (Rachel and Smith 2015). A renewed drop after the onset of the 2008 global financial crisis, accompanied by low inflation and weak output growth, has led to substantial downward revisions of the equilibrium real interest rate. But there is no consensus on how far the rate may have declined since the crisis. IMF (2014), the Council of Economic Advisers (2015), and Holston, Laubach, and Williams (2016) discuss the causes of the decline. Summers (2015) cites a –3 to 1.75 percent range from a survey of US studies. Mendes (2014) puts the range at 1–2 percent for Canada. The main difference arises from definitions of shocks. Higher estimates, above 1 percent, classify as shocks the repeated headwinds that have resulted in a systematically disappointing recovery. Lower estimates, near or below zero, classify these headwinds as a permanent part of the medium-term environment rather than as shocks that have transitory effects on real interest rates.

The second approach is preferred. At some point, if negative headwinds persist, they are no longer shocks that have transitory effects. Repeated downgrades of forecasts (Table 9.2) and below-target inflation, along with declines in actual real rates, suggest that monetary policy has been confronting a decline in the neutral rate that can be perceived only with a recognition lag. In the meantime, policymakers overestimating the equilibrium real interest rate would attribute persistent surprisingly weak output to unexpected headwinds.

Moreover, because of the evident steep drop in the global equilibrium rate, encounters with the effective lower bound are likely to become more frequent and longer lasting.

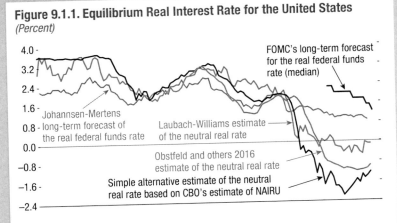

Figure 9.1.1. Equilibrium Real Interest Rate for the United States
(Percent)

Sources: Authors' calculations; Federal Reserve; Johannsen and Mertens 2016; Laubach and Williams 2015; Nomura; Obstfeld and others 2016.
Note: CBO = Congressional Budget Office; FOMC = Federal Open Market Committee; NAIRU = non-accelerating inflation rate of unemployment.

energy sector, and the weakness of other commodities markets has confronted Canadian monetary policy with the sharp end of the issue.

Fourth, a sound system of financial regulation and supervision, which includes a five-year updating of banking legislation, helped the Canadian financial system avoid the excesses that preceded the global financial crisis. As a result, Canada was one of the few advanced economies to escape severe financial sector stress during the global financial crisis. The banks were well-capitalized and did not need public sector support. The postcrisis tightening of credit, due to heightened risk aversion, was less severe in Canada than in other countries.

The core measure of CPI inflation has remained near 2 percent, but the widening of the negative output gap since 2014 portended further reductions in inflation. In response, the Bank of Canada reduced the overnight interest rate. With the overnight interest rate at that time at 0.5 percent, some room remained for cuts—the bank has revised its estimate of the effective lower bound on the overnight rate down to –0.5 percent from 0.25 percent (Witmer and Yang 2015).

However, in view of the drop in the global equilibrium rate, policy rate cuts, even of the maximum feasible extent, might not give much of a boost to the economy—unless, that is, they are supplemented by other measures. The central bank, drawing on the experiences of other central banks, has signaled that it is prepared to adopt unconventional monetary policy measures, such as large-scale asset purchases and funding for credit. While these less conventional options remain open for future contingencies, their efficacy is uncertain (Poloz 2015). And questions have been raised about the implications of negative rates maintained over an extended period for the efficiency and stability of the financial system (Bech and Malkhozov 2016).

Conventional forward guidance would strengthen an already-strong framework by making the interest rate instrument more effective—a strategic modification that would pay off in good as well as bad times. The change would move Canada back to the forefront of the inflation-forecast-targeting economies on transparency. It would improve the Bank of Canada's ability to manage the medium-term trade-offs as shocks drive the economy off course. In situations like a big downturn, it might obviate the need to consider a negative policy rate or the increased use of unconventional monetary instruments. And conventional forward guidance would be preferable to the suggestion to raise the inflation target from 2 percent, which raises issues of credibility (long-term inflation expectations have been very firm at 2 percent), effectiveness (a mere announcement would not do the job, the central bank would have to raise the actual inflation rate), and economic efficiency (such as inflation distortions caused by confusion between real and nominal changes, and by interactions with accounting and tax systems).

The essence of the argument is simple. In and of itself, the Bank of Canada's setting of the overnight rate for the next six weeks (the interval between policy meetings) has limited impact on inflation or output. The policy rate has an effect only insofar as it moves the longer-term interest rates at which households and firms borrow and invest. In effect, the bank must ensure that public expectations of the future overnight rate move in line with the current setting.[4]

Conversely, the central bank must have a view of how its policy decisions will affect the medium-term path of the short-term rate, because the transmission to inflation and output depends on this path. Thus, underlying every interest rate policy decision is a forecast—indeed, the best-informed forecast—of the rate path that will get inflation back to the 2 percent target over the medium term. The forecast rate path, moreover, is endogenous—in the literal sense that inflation-forecast-targeting central banks use forecasting models with an endogenous policy rate, as well as in the logical sense that with an inflation target the policy rate must vary to keep inflation on target within the medium-term forecast horizon. The policy rate path therefore responds to observed economic conditions to get the inflation rate back to the target over time in a manner that efficiently manages the short-term output-inflation trade-off. If markets have similar policy interest rate forecasts as the central bank, longer-term interest rates, the exchange rate, and asset prices generally are likely to move in support of the objectives of monetary policy.

This point has been long accepted with respect to publication of the forecast inflation rate path. There is a duality, in that expected inflation and the actual nominal interest rate are the two components of the real interest rate. The published inflation rate forecast generally influences the expected real interest rate in support of monetary policy. When nominal interest rates are constrained by the effective lower bound, this is more important.[5] The central bank might well envisage a strategy in which there is a temporary overshoot of inflation above the target. This would reduce the real interest rate and help move the economy away from a deflation or low-inflation dark corner. Under conventional forward guidance, the central bank would communicate the whole story underlying the strategy, allaying any risk to the credibility of the target that the planned overshoot might otherwise create.

The main objection to conventional forward guidance is the conditionality of the interest rate forecast. Monetary policy must allow the interest rate to vary to offset shocks. It cannot commit to a forecast path for the rate. Central bankers have worried that if it becomes necessary to deviate from a given path their credibility might be impaired. However, with effective communications, this issue need not arise: markets have readily adjusted in those countries where the central bank publishes its interest rate forecast (such as the Czech Republic, New Zealand, Norway, Sweden). Indeed, with a deeper understanding of the intentions of policymakers, markets are more likely to perform a strong buffering role against shocks. Model-derived confidence bands, and alternative forecasts based on shocks to the baseline forecast, are useful tools for communicating the conditionality of the projection and the impact of shocks should they materialize.

---

[4]Theory supporting this assertion can be found in Eggertsson and Woodford (2003) and Woodford (2005), for example.

[5]In Canada, the effective lower bound has not been tested in practice, but a recent Bank of Canada estimate puts it at about –0.5 percent (Witmer and Yang 2015).

The analysis and policy simulations presented here indicate that a strong policy framework for avoiding macroeconomic quagmires would be provided by a loss-minimizing monetary policy, with a quadratic loss function, which puts an increasingly heavy penalty on deviations of inflation from the inflation target and of GDP from potential output; and full publication of the central bank forecast. In addition, near the effective lower bound, there is a clear role for a fiscal stimulus (Freedman and others 2009). These features could be more effective than unconventional monetary policy measures, or negative interest rates, or raising the target inflation rate, for avoiding the dark corner of the effective lower bound–deflation trap.

EXPECTATIONS AND A THREATENING DARK CORNER

In normal times, following a contractionary shock, policy would react with an interest rate cut that has its effects on inflation and output through the usual transmission mechanism. At the effective lower bound a somewhat weakened version of the mechanism could still apply, transmitted through real interest rates and the real exchange rate. That is, expected inflation provides a channel through which forward guidance can stimulate the economy. If monetary policy is active and credible, it could persuade the public that it will eventually get inflation back up to the long-term target. With the promise of a sufficiently vigorous policy, which commits to holding the interest rate at the effective lower bound for an extended future period, the public—and financial market participants in particular—would expect increased inflation. This would reduce longer-term real rates of interest even if the nominal rate were stuck at the effective lower bound. These movements buffer the shock. Under such circumstances, to respond strongly to the initially very weak economy, the central bank might show a stimulative forecast in which, over the medium term, inflation overshoots before returning to the long-term target.

Moreover, the real exchange rate would depreciate, and asset prices would rise immediately in line with the drop in the real interest rate. And the longer the expected period for the policy rate at the floor, the larger are these effects (Annex 9.1). This equilibrating response of the real price of foreign exchange is a normal aspect of the transmission mechanism. Thus, the real interest rate channel would be amplified in the open-economy case by the real exchange rate channel.[6] A very similar argument to that for the real exchange rate applies to asset prices. An increase in the expected medium-term rate of inflation that reduces real interest rates would boost asset prices through the lower real discount rate and through the positive impact of exchange rate depreciation on profits. Increased asset prices would stimulate spending and help eliminate economic slack in the economy.

---

[6]Svensson (2001) emphasizes these expectations mechanisms as a way to jump-start the economy in Japan.

Figure 9.4. Inflation Paths for Different Policy Frameworks
(Percent)

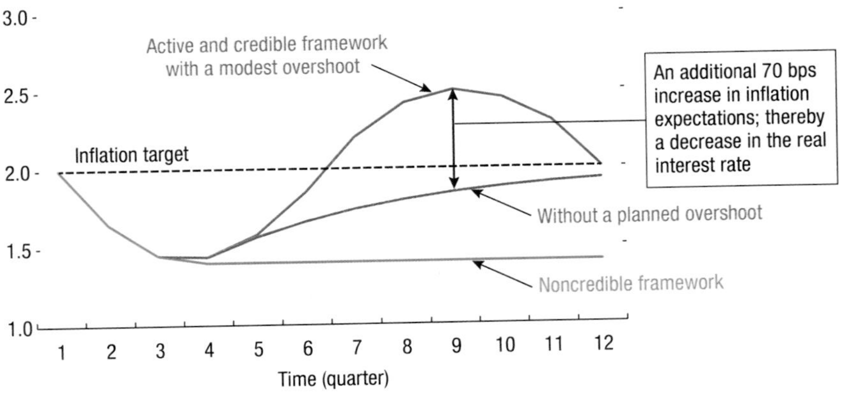

Source: Authors' calculations.
Note: bps = basis points.

To achieve this result, the central bank has to persuade people that the nominal interest rate will remain at the floor for an extended period and that the rate of inflation will rise over the medium term, possibly above the long-term target, but that the rate of inflation will eventually return to target. Is this a realistic prospect? The exchange rate policy used by the Czech National Bank from November 2013 until April 2017, which has relied heavily on influencing expectations, suggests that, under a transparent inflation-forecast-targeting framework, it can be (Chapter 10).

Figure 9.4 provides an illustration. The economy is hit by some contractionary shocks that cause economic slack and inflation to fall below the target. The orange line indicates a passive policy, with actual inflation well below a noncredible target of 2 percent and the interest rate stuck at the effective lower bound. The blue line is for a credible framework: starting in period 4, policy smoothly achieves the 2 percent target in period 12. But policy could be more aggressive. With conventional forward guidance, monetary policy deliberately causes inflation to overshoot the target for several quarters—at the peak, inflation reaches 2.5 percent. The medium-term increase in the inflation rate (over the blue line), which peaks at 0.7 percentage point, translates into temporarily higher inflation expectations, and hence a decrease in real interest rates of 70 basis points. This positive feedback is part of the boost provided by the more aggressive policy, which achieves the inflation target at a lower overall cost: it involves a smaller cumulative output gap, and provides better risk management, in that it moves the economy more quickly from the dark corner where the effective lower bound risks allowing potential deflationary forces if new contractionary shocks were to hit the economy in the future.

During a period in which the effective lower bound is binding, and where the main danger is on the deflation side, the forecast endogenous interest rate would be at the effective lower bound long enough to get inflation back on track (Eggertsson and Woodford [2003], with a different model, reach the same conclusion). To the extent that this forecast affects market expectations, it will result in medium- and long-term rates that are lower than their long-term equilibrium values. In this sense, publication of the forecast becomes an additional instrument, helping policy achieve its objectives, in the same way as the US Federal Reserve's forward guidance since 2008.

Conventional forward guidance emerges from a systematic framework, but it so happens that its advantages become most clear in the zone around the effective lower bound. A transparent lower-for-longer interest rate strategy would have the positive impact of reducing real interest rates by more than the actual cut in the overnight rate. A published forecast would encourage a desirable movement in medium-term expectations for both the nominal interest rate (down) and for inflation (up). Thus, longer-term market interest rates, the exchange rate, and asset prices would play a reinforced shock-absorber role in support of the economy.

DIFFERENT TYPES OF FORWARD GUIDANCE

Conventional Forward Guidance

Conventional forward guidance as practiced in the Czech Republic, New Zealand, Norway, and Sweden is a systematic part of the policy framework. It derives from the publication of a complete central bank macroeconomic forecast with an endogenous interest rate path and confidence bands around key variables. The endogenous policy rate moves to achieve the announced inflation target on a medium-term horizon in a way that reflects the policymakers' preferences for short-term trade-offs between output, inflation, and interest rate variability. The policy rate path is clearly conditional on a range of assumptions and subject to a range of uncertainty, as indicated by the confidence bands. In general, publication of the path should help steer public expectations in a way that is helpful to the attainment of policy objectives, in particular through the effect on medium- and longer-term interest rates.

Under inflation-forecast targeting, a type of forward guidance takes place on an ongoing basis, in that the central bank provides a regular flow of information on its current policy actions and on its view of the medium-term macroeconomic outlook. The rationale is that markets are more likely to operate in support of monetary policy objectives if they are well-informed about the central bank's view of the forces affecting inflation and output. At a minimum, under inflation-forecast targeting, forecast paths for inflation and the output gap or growth are published just after interest rate policy decisions are announced.

Systematic publication of the forecast interest rate path too would provide market participants with a seamless flow of information on how the changing state of the economy is likely to affect the monetary policy actions aimed at returning inflation to the target. This approach is robust in the sense that conventional forward guidance is a regular part of the policy framework—forward guidance is continuous in the routine format of the published forecast, not just in cases of major economic instability (Clinton and others 2015).

Publishing the path for the endogenous policy rate underlines that the policy action at any point in time involves more than just setting an interest rate until the next monetary policy meeting. In making any particular decision, policymakers must have in mind some view of the future interest rate path that will be necessary for the efficient achievement of the target over the medium term. A priori, releasing that path, along with a discussion of how it might change in response to new information that changes the outlook, would be the single most obvious way of clarifying for the public the central bank's view of the policy implications of the economic outlook, and, more generally, for revealing how it intends to manage the short-term output-inflation trade-off.[7] In contrast, a published forecast that shows a smooth return of inflation to target and output to potential, without the interest rate path, does not provide the public with a clear idea of the central bank's perception of the outlook, such as how strong the economic headwinds may be or how it intends to deal with them.

It is important, however, that communication on the policy rate path should avoid creating the false perception that the path is a promise rather than a conditional forecast. In practice, this has not proved to be an insuperable difficulty in the Czech Republic, New Zealand, Norway, and Sweden, where the central banks publish their forecasts for the short-term interest rate (Clinton and others 2015). These central banks communicate to the public not just a forecast path for the future policy rate (and for unconventional instruments where these are a factor), but also a sense of how and why this path might change in response to a variety of developments. At the same time, the central bank should make clear its evaluation of the risks and uncertainties that lie ahead. Effective communications are the key to avoiding false perceptions about the precision of the forecast. To underline the degree of uncertainty in the projections, conventional-forward-guidance central banks publish confidence bands, as well as the central tendency, for the path of the policy interest rate. In addition, the publication of alternative scenarios to the baseline, embodying large shocks for which the probability cannot be calculated from historical data, can indicate the nonnormal range of uncertainty perceived by the central bank.

A central bank using conventional forward guidance does not have to give special guidance as to when its guidance will switch on and off, or as to the threshold values of inflation and unemployment (or the output gap) that might trigger a policy move. In contrast, forward guidance as practiced in the United States has involved ad hoc central bank statements about when in the future—at

---

[7]This has been described by some policymakers as finding a path that "looks good" (Svensson 2002; Qvigstad 2005).

which calendar date—the policy interest rate might be changed, or about thresholds for the inflation rate and unemployment that might trigger a change in the rate (Alichi and others 2015).

Conventional forward guidance would generally influence expectations for the future policy rate, and for medium-term inflation, in a way that helps monetary policy—in good times as well as in times of heightened economic instability.[8] That is, it would encourage the longer-term real market interest rates that affect business and household demand to move in line with developments in the state of the economy and the Bank of Canada's output and inflation objectives. It would also improve the process of accountability, in that published forecast paths, confidence bands, and alternative scenarios provide a quantitative framework by which to account for central bank actions. Policymakers should be able to explain the events that caused deviations from the forecast path transparently, in terms of the specific deviations from forecast assumptions.

UNCONVENTIONAL FORWARD GUIDANCE

Forward guidance on the policy interest rate was employed by the Bank of Canada, the Federal Reserve, the Bank of England, and the Bank of Japan, among others, after the global financial crisis. These central banks used forward guidance to talk down the expected policy rate path and term premium, and thereby to reduce longer-term interest rates. In this respect, it did succeed (Engen, Laubach, and Reifschneider 2015; Charbonneau and Rennison 2015). This is called unconventional forward guidance because it was introduced along with other unconventional measures as an ad hoc tool when the effective lower bound put constraints on reductions in the policy rate.

Unconventional forward guidance has encountered difficulties in communicating its conditionality, in particular the time horizon over which the guidance is to apply. In the immediate aftermath of the global financial crisis, with raised risk premiums, central banks wanted to assure markets that policy rates would remain at the floor for at least as long as it took to restore a semblance of order. Indeed, the Bank of Canada emphasized that its policy rate would be kept at the floor (estimated at the time to be 0.25 percent) from April 2009 to April 2010, but that this commitment was conditional on the outlook for inflation. As the economy recovered and inflation returned to the 2 percent target, the bank exited this unconventional forward guidance (more or less as initially planned).

As such, the experience turned out quite well and Canada avoided difficulties that surfaced in other advanced economies, as discussed below. However, this was in large part fortuitous, in that, after 2009, Canada benefited from the favorable

---

[8]This corresponds to the observation by Eggertsson and Woodford (2003): "In fact, the management of expectations is the key to successful monetary policy at *all* times, not just in those relatively unusual circumstances when the zero bound is reached." See also Woodford (2005).

shock of booming demand for oil and other commodities from China and other emerging markets.

In the United States and the United Kingdom, things were more complicated. As these economies emerged, sluggishly and unevenly, from the postcrisis recession, their central banks tried to communicate when, and under what conditions, the policy rate would rise from the floor (and quantitative easing would taper off). For this purpose, they announced threshold values for the unemployment rate and the inflation rate.

A risk in this kind of announcement is oversimplification. Policymakers do not themselves use a simple threshold rule for decision-making. Their view of the future path of the policy rate depends on a much more complex assessment of what may be necessary to return the inflation rate to target: they have a clear perception of the objectives of policy, which are given, and the conditional nature of their projections for the policy instrument. Within central banks, such assessments are informed by forecasts derived with macroeconomic models that take account of numerous factors influencing the outlook and the judgment of the forecasters. Announcing thresholds for inflation and unemployment risks misguiding financial markets about the scope of other considerations that may influence policymakers' outlook for the interest rate.

This could lead financial market participants to underestimate the degree of uncertainty in the outlook, and hence make financial markets vulnerable to the arrival of unexpected news. For example, the strategy might misrepresent the amount of uncertainty in future long-term interest rates in the short term it might convince financial markets that short-term interest rates will stay low. A point will come, however, at which the interest rate has to be raised, upsetting market expectations and creating market volatility (as in the 2013 taper tantrum).

The Governor of the Bank of Canada has therefore expressed a concern that a conditional commitment to hold rates low might artificially reduce two-way rate volatility and prevent markets from properly assessing risks in the interest rate outlook, especially potential shocks of a size and nature in the distant tails of the statistical distributions (Poloz 2014). This risk is reduced with conventional forward guidance, which presents the central bank forecast as a conditional projection and is transparent about the underlying assumptions and their uncertain nature.

COUNTRY EXPERIENCES WITH UNCONVENTIONAL FORWARD GUIDANCE

United Kingdom

The Bank of England announced a threshold rule (August 2013), declaring that it would not raise its policy interest rate (or reduce its quantitative easing) until the following occurred:

- The unemployment rate fell below 7 percent or
- CPI inflation 18 to 24 months ahead rose above 2.5 percent or

- Inflation expectations became unhinged or
- The low interest rate threatened financial stability

Within a few months the unemployment rate had fallen below the threshold, yet there was no economic case for a rate increase: inflation was below 2 percent and falling and the financial system looked stable. In February 2014 the central bank reverted to qualitative guidance with no numerical thresholds.

United States

The Federal Reserve has changed the form of its unconventional forward guidance several times since its inception in 2008 (from qualitative to date-based, to threshold-based, and back to qualitative). Until 2013 the guidance succeeded in the operational objective of reducing the term premium and expected future short-term rates—and, hence, bond yields.

These changes nevertheless looked like improvisation rather than a consistent strategy. In 2013, a change in perceptions about policy triggered the taper tantrum, an outbreak of financial market volatility. Bond yields and term premiums rose sharply, to an extent way out of line with the modest eventual tightening envisaged in the cautious public statements of the central bank. Continuing communication difficulties with unconventional forward guidance are illustrated by this clarification from Federal Reserve Chair Janet Yellen (March 2015): "just because we removed the word 'patient' . . . doesn't mean we are going to be impatient . . . "

There is evidence that the communications difficulties have had material macroeconomic costs. The empirical study by Engen, Laubach, and Reifschneider (2015) concludes that if the public had understood beforehand the willingness of the Federal Open Market Committee (FOMC) to accommodate, the recession would have been less severe and the subsequent recovery more rapid (Figure 9.5).

Since January 2012, the Federal Reserve has released FOMC members' interest rate projections following each meeting. But it is difficult to "connect the dots" from the individual projections to form a single consistent forecast (Alichi and others 2015).

Filardo and Hoffmann (2014) look at experience in the United States, Japan, and the United Kingdom. They find that forward guidance has had moderately beneficial results. Charbonneau and Rennison (2015) provide a somewhat more favorable assessment of the international experience (including Canada), finding lower expectations of the future path of policy rates, improved predictability of short-term yields over the near term, and reduced sensitivity of financial variables to economic news. Engen, Laubach, and Reifschneider (2015) suggest the net stimulus to real activity and inflation was limited by the gradual nature of the changes in expectations for the interest rate and term premiums. In view of the limited sample size and of the shifts in the nature of forward guidance, the lack of a strong positive macroeconomic effect should not be surprising. More systematic, and more explicit, interest rate guidance might well yield material gains.

Figure 9.5. Predicted US Unemployment Rate, 2008–20
(Percent)

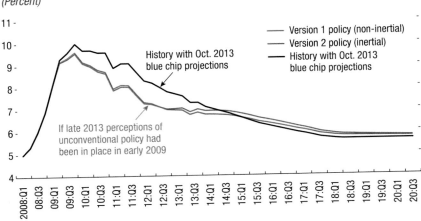

Source: Adapted from Engen, Laubach, and Reifschneider (2015).

Canada

The rate of inflation in September 2008, when the global financial crisis broke, was about 2 percent, and the Bank of Canada's policy rate was above 4 percent. Over the next two years, the central bank exploited the ample room for action during the global recession, cutting the policy rate to near zero. The Canadian dollar depreciated. Exports fell sharply with the drop in US demand, but the decline in GDP was limited to 2.7 percent, as domestic demand held up quite well. Inflation remained positive. In the Canadian case, policy actions helped keep expectations up, and the exchange rate acted as a shock absorber. Despite the proximity of Canada to the US epicenter of the crisis, and the drop in commodity prices, the Canadian recession was relatively mild.

By 2010, the Canadian economy was recovering. Rising global oil prices gave output as well as inflation a boost, as investment and output in the energy sector began to expand strongly. Even so, a considerable degree of slack, with weak employment, persisted. One might question the management of the output-inflation trade-off. The bank's forecasts for output were consistently overoptimistic. Over time, the forecasts in monetary policy reports repeatedly put back the date at which output was expected to reach potential, from the fourth quarter of 2011 in the July 2010 report, to the third quarter of 2017 in the April 2016 report (Table 9.2). In retrospect at least, such long-lasting headwinds, or negative output shocks, imply that the bank was overestimating the equilibrium real interest rate. An overestimate was to some extent inevitable, because this rate is not directly observable, and it would be impossible in real time to recognize a decline of the magnitude that now seems likely to have occurred.

TABLE 9.2.

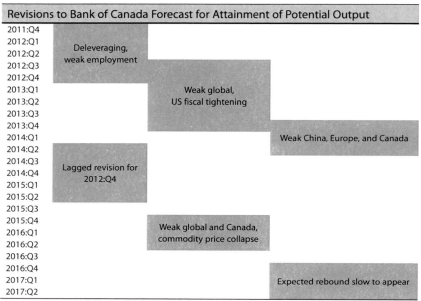

Revisions to Bank of Canada Forecast for Attainment of Potential Output

Source: Bank of Canada Monetary Policy Reports, 2009–16.

Notes: The first quarter in each shaded rectangle indicates when a revision was made. The last quarter in each shaded rectangle indicates when the output gap was expected to close, according to that revision. Rectangles do not always overlap exactly by one quarter, because small revisions are omitted.

MODEL SIMULATIONS OF ALTERNATIVE POLICY STRATEGIES

Simulation results based on a New-Keynesian model illustrate how conventional forward guidance might operate. The model used here for Canada bears similarities to those used at many central banks for forecasting and policy analysis. It has a standard core structure, with equations for the output gap, core inflation, the policy interest rate, and the exchange rate. Expectations are forward looking, consistent with the projections of the model itself, but the behavioral equations also embody lagged adjustments. In addition, the model has equations for headline inflation, food and energy inflation, the commodity terms of trade, trade and financial linkages with the rest of the world, and bond yields of various maturities.[9] Nonlinearities are in the Phillips curve—which becomes quite flat when there is a negative output gap—the effective lower bound constraint, and the monetary policy reaction function.

Monetary policy follows a loss-minimizing strategy in which the loss function has a weight, 1, on the squared inflation gap (the deviation from 2 percent) and

---

[9]Annex 9.2 outlines the model structure.

the squared output gap; there is a weight of 0.5 on the squared change in the policy interest rate, which implies a smoothed interest rate policy response; such smoothing is justified on theoretical grounds, and is a well-observed feature of actual central bank behavior. The quadratic loss function imposes an increasingly heavy loss as deviations from target increase; the loss-minimizing strategy would therefore be very averse to dark corners, in which the economy gets stuck in a bad equilibrium that is resistant to conventional policy instruments. In other words, the strategy takes a risk-avoidance approach to risk management.

It is interesting to see how a strategy of this nature, using conventional forward guidance, would have performed following the extreme event of the global financial crisis. A good place to start is in the second quarter of 2009. The dire situation then unambiguously called for maintaining the policy rate at the floor for some time and, in fact, the Bank of Canada provided forward guidance to this effect:

> With monetary policy now operating at the effective lower bound for the overnight policy rate, it is appropriate to provide more explicit guidance than is usual regarding its future path so as to influence rates at longer maturities. Conditional on the outlook for inflation, the target overnight rate can be expected to remain at its current level until the end of the second quarter of 2010 in order to achieve the inflation target. (Bank of Canada, 2009).

The central bank forecast, that this policy would return inflation to the target of 2 percent in 2011, was not far off (Figure 9.6, dashed line). However, this was largely due to the one-off effect of a rise in global energy and food prices in 2010–11. The forecast that the output gap would be closed in 2011 was overoptimistic. Core inflation languished below 2 percent, and within a couple of years headline inflation fell back below target. One might ask whether monetary policy should have maintained an easier stance, especially after 2010 as the postcrisis fiscal stimulus was being withdrawn. More productive questions, however, concern systematic strategy rather than the particular response to the circumstances of the time.

What would the macro forecast—the expected results—have looked like if a strategy combining conventional forward guidance with a loss-minimizing policy reaction function had been in place at the outset in the second quarter of 2009? How would the postcrisis economy, affected as it was by unexpected developments, have looked? What are the implications of other unconventional or supporting tools, such as a negative policy rate and a fiscal backstop?

In the simulations that follow, policymakers operate in quasi–real time: that is, the information available to them in any quarter is limited to what could have been available at the time. However, as vintage data sets are not used, the series employed contain revisions to the historical data. In other words, in these counterfactual reruns of history, the current historical data set unrolls one quarter at a time. The starting point, in the second quarter of 2009, had a large output gap, assumed to be –4.5 percent, an inflation rate of 1 percent, and a policy interest rate at the then-assumed effective lower bound of 0.25 percent. As for the real equilibrium interest rate, for the starting point, an estimate is assumed, based on

Figure 9.6. Optimal Control versus IFB Reaction Function, 2009–13

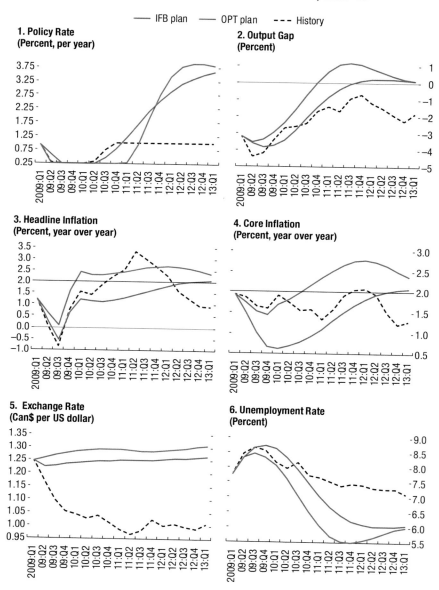

Source: Authors' simulations.
Notes: IFB = inflation-forecast-based; OPT = optimal control.

historical information available at the time, of 1.7 percent; it is revised downward thereafter on the basis of incoming new data.[10]

Forecast as of the Second Quarter of 2009 Plan

Figure 9.6 compares a plan made in the second quarter of 2009 under the loss-minimization strategy (OPT, red line) with one based on a linear inflation-forecast-based (IFB) reaction function (IFB, blue line). Under both illustrative plans, the central bank practices conventional forward guidance, so the forecast interest rate path has a direct impact on interest rate expectations. The red and blue lines—for the policy rate, output gap, headline inflation, core inflation, exchange rate, and unemployment—can be interpreted as the forecasts the policymakers would have before them in the second quarter of 2009. They would of course differ from subsequent actual outcomes because of unexpected changes: the counterfactual comparison of policies is purely a model-based exercise. The dashed lines in the figure show the realized historical paths of the variables. Monetary policy is constrained by an effective lower bound of 0.25 percent, which the Bank of Canada at that time viewed as the effective floor.

Key aspects of these policy simulations are as follows:

1. The derived loss-minimizing strategy (OPT) keeps the policy rate at the floor for two years, from the second quarter of 2009 to the same in 2011. The expectation under this plan, with the nominal interest rate held at the effective lower bound, is for the exchange rate to rise (the Canadian dollar to depreciate) about 4.5 percent for 2009 to the end of 2012. The wide output gap is closed quite quickly, to zero by the fourth quarter of 2010, and an excess demand gap opens. The unemployment rate comes down at the same pace. Inflation overshoots. Year-over-year core inflation peaks at 2.8 percent, from the fourth quarter of 2011 to the second quarter of 2012, before falling back to 2 percent. Headline inflation peaks slightly lower. One of the reasons for the strong stimulative impact of the policy is that the anticipated medium-term increase in inflation reduces real interest rates and causes the real exchange rate to rise (that is, a real depreciation).

2. The IFB strategy implies that the policy rate stays at the floor for only about a year, from the third quarter of 2009 to the second quarter of 2010. The medium-term rise in the exchange rate (depreciation of the Canadian dollar) is relatively modest. The output gap is closed more slowly than with the OPT strategy, reaching zero in the third quarter of 2011 and staying there. Unemployment at that time is 1 percentage point higher than under OPT. Inflation (core and headline) does not get back to target until a year later. By most standards, OPT would be regarded as the better strategy.

OPT wants inflation to overshoot and the output gap to close fast, because, given the initial conditions, the below-target inflation, and the wide negative

---

[10]A rolling filter determines the estimates of latent variables.

output gap in the second quarter of 2009, a quadratic loss function implies at the margin relatively high benefits from increases in both inflation and output. The constraint of the effective lower bound is an additional reason for the stimulative policy: given the loss function, forward-looking policymakers would be very averse to the bad equilibrium where deflation meets the effective lower bound. The idea is to put distance between the economy and that dark corner, fast.

Counterfactual History with Loss-Minimizing Strategy

The global financial crisis in fact had deeper and longer-lasting effects than anticipated in 2009. On top of this, additional negative shocks were to hit the Canadian economy. As a result, the history presents a much weaker picture than either of our two illustrative second-quarter 2009 policy strategies envisaged, and the negative output gap was never completely closed.

The simulations can be repeated, allowing the unanticipated shocks to affect the outcomes, including the loss-minimizing policy response (Figure 9.7).[11] The quasi-real-time results can be compared with the history, since the hypothetical central bankers are dealing with the same shocks as the real ones.

Key aspects of the results are as follows:

1. The loss-minimizing response to the historical shocks results in the policy rate at the effective lower bound until the first quarter of 2013 (the whole period shown in Figure 9.7). In contrast, the Bank of Canada raised the policy rate to 1 percent in 2010. The Canadian dollar appreciates less with the counterfactual strategy.

2. Under OPT, inflation overshoots the target by a substantial margin. Core inflation peaks above 3.5 percent in 2010, and headline inflation, driven by energy and food price shocks, peaks above 4 percent. The output gap closes to zero in the second half of 2011 before further negative shocks in 2012 reopen a gap.

3. OPT delivers a considerably narrower output gap than the historical output gap and an unemployment rate consistently below the historical rate—as much as 0.8 percentage point lower in 2010 and 2011.

4. In summary, OPT involves an aggressive response to the negative shocks in terms of the length of time the policy rate forecast is at the effective lower bound. It would quickly move the economy away from the deflation dark corner and closer to potential output and full employment.

5. The overshoot in the inflation rate with OPT may be regarded as a drawback. And the 2010–11 increase in the prices of oil and food exacerbates the cycle in headline inflation. In our view, the prospect of a medium-term overshoot is acceptable, as, over time, the strategy would involve deviations on both sides of the target. Such a pattern is evident in Figure 9.7, and is in line with the Canadian experience of inflation targeting and the maintenance of a firm nominal anchor (see Kamenik and others 2013).

---

[11]The shocks are estimated from historical filtration of the model.

Figure 9.7. Predicted Outcomes under Optimal Control with Historical Shocks, 2009–13

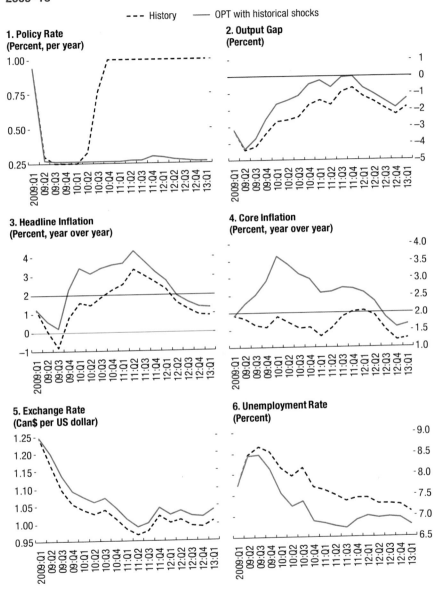

Source: Authors' simulations.
Note: OPT = optimal control.

Fiscal Stimulus

The simulations in Figure 9.8 investigate the extent to which more expansionary policies in the aftermath of the global financial crisis might have helped achieve policy objectives. The assumed shock involves a fiscal stimulus equivalent to 1 percent of GDP and a cut in the policy rate from 0.25 to –0.5 percent (reflecting the Bank of Canada's latest estimate of the effective lower bound). As before, each policy simulation refers to a forecast as of the second quarter of 2009. All cases considered are under the loss-minimizing strategy.

Key aspects are as follows:

1. Under the negative interest rate case (blue line), the policy rate is cut to the new floor and stays there a little less time than the base case with the 0.25 percent effective lower bound (red line). The lower rate causes a quick rise in the price of foreign exchange; these two changes close the output gap faster than the control. Because the nominal rate declines more, the decline in the real interest rates requires a smaller overshoot of inflation than in the base case. These changes are relatively modest compared with those achieved at the positive effective lower bound.

2. Fiscal policy has a more direct impact on the economy than monetary policy. The results are shown in the cross-hatched lines. Because fiscal policy works through the demand channel more directly, and is less reliant on the expectations channel, the implied inflation overshoot is smaller than in the baseline. The fiscal stimulus does appreciate the Canadian dollar relative to the base case—in line with the classic Mundell-Fleming result for fiscal policy in a small economy with perfect capital mobility. However, in this model, unlike in Mundell-Fleming, fiscal policy is effective in increasing output because monetary policy keeps its focus on the objectives for inflation and the output gap and holds the interest rate at the effective lower bound. The exchange rate decrease relative to control is not large enough to choke off the stimulus. As Lane (2016) has pointed out, amid sustained weak aggregate demand, relying primarily on monetary policy to provide stimulus may lead to financial vulnerabilities that macroprudential policy cannot, or should not, offset. In such circumstances, fiscal policy may be called upon to provide stimulus, particularly since it is likely to be more effective at low interest rates.

Alternative Scenario: Linear Policy Reaction Function, Backward-Looking Expectations

This illustrative case shows investigation into a situation where monetary policy places less emphasis on the avoidance of large risks and where the credibility of the inflation target is not strong. The specific assumptions are the following:

- Monetary policy follows an IFB reaction function

Figure 9.8. Optimal Control with Negative Interest Rate or Fiscal Backstop, 2009–13

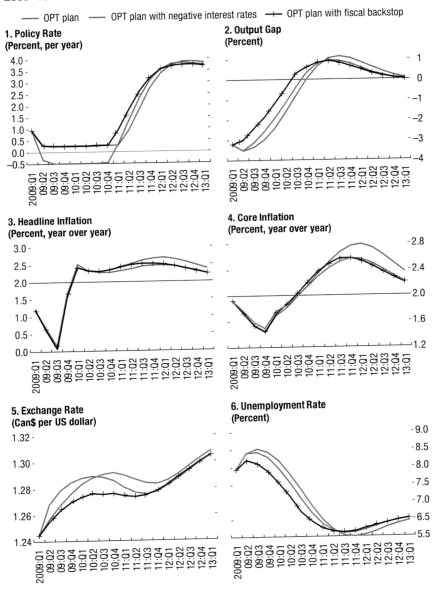

Source: Authors' simulations.
Note: OPT = optimal control.

- Expectations put a high weight on lagged inflation, such as because of imperfect credibility of the inflation target (Annex 9.2 gives detailed assumptions of this exercise).

The IFB reaction function does not have the same aversion to dark corners as the quadratic loss function, and will not lead to especially sharp corrective actions against negative shocks in the vicinity of deflation and the effective lower bound. Backward-looking expectations would reflect imperfect credibility of the announced inflation objective. If the target is not hit for a prolonged period, people are more likely to believe the rate they observe than the rate the central bank would like.

Negative shocks in this situation have bad results (Figure 9.9). Relative to history, starting in the second quarter of 2009 the output gap would have been wider, unemployment higher, and inflation lower. The counterfactual policy interest rate is lower for a couple of years. This does not reflect a more aggressive policy, but an endogenous response to the weaker economy.

CONCLUSIONS

Canada has a strong and well-proven inflation-forecast-targeting regime. Inflation expectations have been stable at the target rate of 2 percent for more than two decades. Core elements of this achievement have been the credibility of the target, which has been reinforced by sound monetary policy decisions, and the flexible exchange rate, which has helped stabilize the economy in the face of foreign disturbances, including large fluctuations in the commodity terms of trade.

However, the framework could be strengthened, especially in its capacity for avoiding dark corners. The case is strong for the Bank of Canada to use conventional forward guidance—that is, to publish its forecast of the short-term interest rate path as part of the information it releases following each of the eight annual policy decision meetings. Such an increase in transparency would strengthen the monetary policy framework for good times and times of greater economic instability. It would also improve accountability for monetary policy, in that the bank would be able to account openly for its interest rate decisions, against the guideline of the forecast path, justifying divergences from the path in terms of specific unexpected developments.

After the 2014–15 collapse of the boom in oil and other commodities, and the subsequent recession in the domestic energy industry, the Bank of Canada left open the options of unconventional policy instruments and a negative policy interest rate. However, these options have their own limitations and as yet uncertain effectiveness. Estimates of the equilibrium world real interest rate have been falling since the global financial crisis, in view of the lackluster performance of global output and low inflation. Various recent estimates are about zero (Summers 2015). This has implications for the framework of monetary policy and for fiscal policy.

If the 2 percent inflation target was right when the equilibrium real interest rate was 2 percent, is it still right when the equilibrium rate is near zero? The effective

Figure 9.9. Inflation-Forecast-Based Reaction Function and Backward-Looking Inflation Expectations, 2009–13

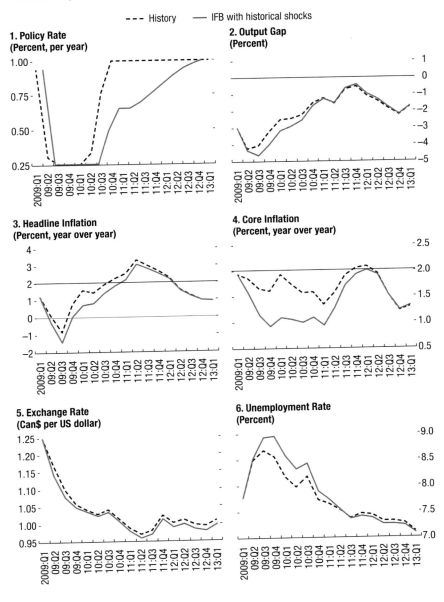

Source: Authors' simulations.
Note: IFB = inflation-forecast-based.

lower bound on the nominal interest rate would then impose a floor of about −2 percent on the gap between the actual and equilibrium real interest rate, which would not represent strong resistance to a downturn of typical cyclical amplitude. An increase of 1 percentage point in the inflation target, to 3 percent, would provide that much more space, still not a lot, for expansionary monetary policy.

However, merely announcing a higher target would not be enough—actions would be needed to get there—and the issue of how to achieve the more ambitious target would remain, especially given the firmness of expectations in Canada at 2 percent. Moreover, considering the price stability mandate for monetary policy, and the general performance of the economy over the past quarter-century, Canadian policymakers would reasonably be loath to recommend such a step.

From this viewpoint, an expansionary fiscal policy offers a better alternative for dealing with further negative shocks when monetary policy is constrained by the effective lower bound. And it would avoid any need to question the 2 percent inflation target, which has served well for a quarter-century as a firm nominal anchor to the economy.

ANNEX 9.1. POLICY CREDIBILITY: EXCHANGE RATE AND ASSET PRICES AS SHOCK ABSORBERS OR AMPLIFIERS

The risk-adjusted uncovered interest parity condition

This condition, under perfect foresight, may be written as

$$i_t - \left(i_t^f + u_t\right) = s_{t+1} - s_t,$$

where i_t is domestic interest rate, i_t^f is foreign interest rate, u_t is domestic risk premium, s_t is nominal price of foreign exchange. That is, the future change in the exchange rate compensates for any interest differential, such that the return adjusted for change in the exchange rate and the risk premium is the same in either currency.

One period ahead:

$$i_{t+1} - \left(i_{t+1}^f + u_{t+1}\right) = s_{t+2} - s_{t+1}.$$

Going forward:

$$i_{t+2} - \left(i_{t+2}^f + u_{t+2}\right) = s_{t+3} - s_{t+2},$$

. . .

such that this holds for any time $t + k$

$$i_{t+k} - \left(i_{t+k}^f + u_{t+k}\right) = s_{t+k+1} - s_{t+k}.$$

Summing up all the equations from time t to $t + k$, yields

$$i_t + i_{t+2} \ldots + i_{t+k} - \left(i_t^f + u_t\right) - \ldots - \left(i_{t+k}^f + u_{t+k}\right)$$
$$= (s_{t+1} - s_t) + (s_{t+2} - s_{t+1}) + \ldots + (s_{t+k+1} - s_{t+k}),$$

or equivalently,

$$\sum_{j=0}^{k} i_{t+j} - \sum_{j=0}^{k}\left(i_{t+j}^{f} + u_{t+j}\right) = s_{t+k+1} - s_{t}.$$

Rearranging the equation gets

$$\sum_{j=0}^{k} i_{t+j} = s_{t+k+1} - s_{t} + \sum_{j=0}^{k}\left(i_{t+j}^{f} + u_{t+j}\right).$$

The same condition holds in real terms,

$$\sum_{j=0}^{k} r_{t+j} = z_{t+k+1} - z_{t} + \sum_{j=0}^{k}\left(r_{t+j}^{f} + u_{t+j}\right),$$

where r_t is real interest rate, and z_t is real exchange rate defined as nominal exchange rate adjusted for the foreign (p_t^f) and domestic (p_t) price differential,

$$z_t = s_t + p_t^f - p_t.$$

Real Exchange Rate as Shock Absorber

In normal times with active policy, a negative demand shock reduces inflation in the short term, but does not affect the long-term real exchange rate (z_{t+k+1}). An inflation-forecast-targeting central bank is expected in normal times to reduce the policy rate sufficiently to steer inflation back to target. This expectation would, through the uncovered interest parity condition, lead to an immediate depreciation of the currency: the spot price of foreign exchange has to rise to the point that the expected decrease from then on compensates for the lower domestic interest rate.

Under a credible regime of aggressive policy responses, the expected medium-term inflation rate would also increase.[12] The decline in real interest rates would be greater than that in nominal rates. At the effective lower bound, the current nominal interest rate cannot go any lower, but under the aggressive regime people would expect the future nominal interest rate to be at the effective lower bound for longer, and because of the anticipated increase in inflation, real interest rates would decline. Thus, in both normal times and at the effective lower bound, there is $(\downarrow \sum_{j=0}^{k} r_{t+j})$. Given that the long-term real exchange rate (z_{t+k+1}) and expected paths for foreign real interest rates and domestic risk premium $\sum_{j=0}^{k} \left(r_{t+j}^{f} + u_{t+j}\right)$ do not change, this would result in a real depreciation $(\uparrow z_t)$,

$$\downarrow\sum_{j=0}^{k} r_{t+j} = z_{t+k+1} - \uparrow z_t + \sum_{j=0}^{k}\left(r_{t+j}^{f} + u_{t+j}\right).$$

This helps support demand, through both exports and domestic expenditure switching (from foreign goods to domestic goods).

---

[12] A regime that targets the path of the price level would systematically produce this kind of response (Svensson 1999).

Real Exchange Rate as Shock Amplifier

At the effective lower bound, the exchange rate can act as a shock amplifier. If policy is passive, and not credible, following a negative demand shock, people would expect the inflation rate in the future to be lower. Current and future short-term real interest rates could increase ($\uparrow \sum_{j=0}^{k} r_{t+j}$), resulting in a real appreciation ($\downarrow z_t$):

$$\uparrow \sum_{j=0}^{k} r_{t+j} = z_{t+k+1} - \downarrow z_t + \sum_{j=0}^{k} \left(r_{t+j}^{f} + \mu_{t+j} \right).$$

This would reduce net exports and further deepen the recession.

Asset Prices as Shock Absorber or Amplifier

A similar argument holds for other asset prices such as equity prices. A credible aggressive policy response would cause increases in equity prices (through the positive impact on profits of currency depreciation, and the effect of a lower real discount rate on asset valuations). A noncredible, passive response would do the reverse. Thus, depending on the policy regime, asset prices too may act as an absorber or an amplifier of the impact of shocks.

APPENDIX 9.2. THE NEW-KEYNESIAN MODEL FOR CANADA

1. IS Equation

The output gap ($\hat{y}_t$) is defined as the difference between the log-level of output (y_t) and potential output ($\bar{y}_t$). The investment-savings (IS) equation relates Canada's output gap ($\hat{y}_t$) to past and expected future output gaps, the deviations of the lagged one-year real interest rate ($r4_t$) and the real effective exchange rate ($reer_t$) from their equilibrium values, and the-rest-of-the-world output gap ($\hat{y}_t^{World}$). The terms-of-trade gap ($\widehat{tot}_t$) also affects the output gap in a significant way.

$$y_t = \bar{y}_t + \hat{y}_t$$

$$\hat{y}_t = \underset{(0.65)}{\beta_1 \hat{y}_{t-1}} + \underset{(0.15)}{\beta_2 \hat{y}_{t+1}} + \underset{(-0.15)}{\beta_3 \left(r4_{t-1} - \bar{r}4_{t-1} \right)}$$
$$+ \underset{(0.05)}{\beta_4 \left(reer_{t-1} - \overline{reer}_{t-1} \right)} + \underset{(0.3)}{\beta_5 \hat{y}_t^{World}} + \underset{(0.5)}{\beta_6 \widehat{tot}_t} + \varepsilon_t^{\hat{y}}$$

$$r4_t = \left(r_t + r_{t+1} + r_{t+2} + r_{t+3} \right)/4$$

2. Phillips Curve

In the Phillips curve, the core inflation rate (π_t^C) depends on inflation expectation ($E\pi_t^C$) and past year-on-year core inflation ($\pi 4_{t-1}^C$), with coefficients on both terms adding up to one. The lagged term reflects the intrinsic inflation inertia, resulting from contracts, costs of changing list prices and so on. Inflation expectation is pinned down by both the model-consistent solution of the year -over-year inflation one year ahead $(\pi 4^C_{t+4})$, as well as the inflation target (π^*), with the latter one having a small weight.[13] Core inflation depends on lagged output gap in a nonlinear way.

Core inflation also depends on the rate of real effective exchange rate depreciation, as well as on the deviation of the real effective exchange rate from its equilibrium value, as a real depreciation raises the domestic cost of imported intermediate inputs and final goods, creating upward pressure on prices.

Finally, we allow some small pass-through from oil and food price inflation to core inflation. This is captured by adding the two terms on the real price of oil and food adjusted for real exchange rate effects.

$$\pi^C_t = \lambda_1 E\pi^C_t + \left(1 - \lambda_1\right)\pi 4^C_{t-1} + \lambda_2 \frac{5\hat{y}_{t-1}}{5 - \hat{y}_{t-1}} + \lambda_3 \Delta \widehat{reer}_t$$
$$\quad (0.75) \qquad\qquad\qquad\qquad (0.25) \qquad (0.05)$$

$$+\lambda_4 \widehat{reer}_t + \lambda_5\left(\widehat{rp}^{Oil}_t + \hat{z}_t\right) + \lambda_6\left(\widehat{rp}^{Food}_t + \hat{z}_t\right) + \varepsilon^{\pi^C}_t$$
$$\quad (0.05) \quad (0.01) \qquad\qquad (0.01)$$

$$E\pi^C_t = \lambda_7 \pi 4^C_{t+4} + \left(1 - \lambda_7\right)\pi^*$$
$$\quad (0.8)$$

3. Policy Interest Rate: Reaction Function Options

Linear Inflation-Forecast-Based (IFB) Reaction Function

The equation is a fairly standard IFB reaction function:

$$i_t = \gamma_1 i_{t-1} + \left(1 - \gamma_1\right)\left[\bar{r}_t + \pi 4_{t+3} + \gamma_2(\pi 4^H_{t+3} - \pi^*) + \gamma_3 \hat{y}_t\right] + \varepsilon^i_t.$$
$$\quad (0.75) \qquad\qquad\qquad (1.5) \qquad\qquad (0.05)$$

In contrast to the conventional Taylor rule, the inclusion of the three-quarter-ahead inflation projection $(\pi 4^C_{t+3}$ and $\pi 4^H_{t+3})$ in the IFB reaction function implies that it discounts shocks to the system that are expected to reverse within the three-quarter policy horizon. More generally, the reaction function allows the central bank to take account of all relevant information available to it on future developments over the three-quarter forecast horizon.

Loss Minimizing Strategy—Risk Management

This strategy chooses the interest rate path to minimize the discounted current and future losses from inflation deviations from the target, output gaps, and changes in the policy rate. The loss function incorporates the principal objectives

---

[13]The sensitivity analysis (Figure 9.9) looks at the implications of more inertia in the inflation process, in other words, a case where λ_1 is reduced from 0.75 in the base case to 0.65, and at the same time the weight on the inflation target $(1 - \lambda_7)$ is reduced to 0.

of the central bank—expressing an aversion to deviations of output and inflation from desired values that grows ever larger as these deviations increase.

$$Loss_t = \sum_{i=0}^{\infty} \beta^i \left[\omega_1 \left(\pi 4_{t+i}^H - \pi^* \right)^2 + \omega_2 \hat{y}_{t+i}^2 + \omega_3 \left(i_{t+i} - i_{t+i-1} \right)^2 \right]$$

$$(0.98)\,(1.0) \qquad\qquad (1.0) \qquad (0.5)$$

The quadratic formulation implies that large errors or deviations are more important in the thinking of central banks than small errors or deviations. The term with the squared change of the policy interest rate prevents very sharp movements in the policy interest rate, which would otherwise occur in the model on a regular basis in response to shocks. Central banks in practice do not typically change interest rates in large steps, and there are sound theoretical reasons for this. By taking account of both current and expected future values of output and inflation, this formulation has the central bank incorporate into its decisions any information currently available that may affect its objectives over the next few quarters.

Effective Lower Bound

Under both cases, the interest rate is subject to an effective lower bound constraint (i^{floor}), which is assumed to be 0.25 percent in the historical simulation.[14]

$$i_t \geq i^{floor}$$

$$(0.25)$$

4. Real Interest Rates and Real Exchange Rates

The real interest rate (r) is defined as the nominal interest rate minus the expected core inflation (π_{t+1}^C).

$$r_t = i_t - \pi_{t+1}^C$$

The bilateral real exchange rate between Canada and the United States (z) is defined in terms of Canadian core CPI (p_t^C), and in such a way that an increase means a depreciation in the Canadian dollar. The real exchange rate is broken down into an equilibrium trend ($\bar{z}_t$) and deviation from that trend ($\hat{z}_t$). The equilibrium real exchange rate is assumed to be determined by the equilibrium terms of trade ($\bar{z}_t^{tot}$).

$$z_t = s_t + p_t^{US} - p_t^C$$

$$z_t = \bar{z}_t + \hat{z}_t$$

$$\bar{z}_t = \bar{z}_t^{tot}$$

---

[14]Historically the effective lower bound is assumed to be 0.25 percent. Recently, the central bank revised its estimate of the effective lower bound down to –0.5 percent. In simulations, the implications of the new effective lower bound are examined.

The real effective exchange rate that enters the output gap equation is the trade-weighted bilateral real exchange rates of Canada versus seven regions in the world (United States, euro area, Japan, China, emerging Asia, Latin America, and the rest of the world). The breakdown of the regions is consistent with the Global Projection Model.[15]

$$\widehat{reer}_t = w^{Trade,US}\hat{z}_t^{US} + w^{Trade,EU}\hat{z}_t^{EU} + w^{Trade,JA}\hat{z}_t^{JA}$$
$$(0.68) \qquad\quad (0.07) \qquad\quad (0.02)$$

$$+ w^{Trade,CH}\hat{z}_t^{CH} + w^{Trade,EA}\hat{z}_t^{EA} + w^{Trade,LA}\hat{z}_t^{LA} + w^{Trade,RC}\hat{z}_t^{RC}$$
$$(0.08) \qquad\quad (0.04) \qquad\quad (0.05) \qquad\quad (0.05)$$

Risk-Adjusted Uncovered Interest Parity Condition

The risk-adjusted uncovered interest parity condition links the bilateral exchange rate between Canada and the United States with the interest rates in the two economies (i_t and i_t^{US}).

$$i_t - i_t^{US} = 4(Es_{t+1} - s_t) + \sigma_t^{ctry} + \sigma_t^{tot} + \varepsilon_t^s$$
$$Es_{t+1} = \phi s_{t+1} + (1 - \phi)\{s_{t-1} + 2[\Delta \bar{z}_t - (\pi^{*,US} - \pi^*)/4]\}$$
$$(0.84)$$

The equation allows the expected exchange rate (Es_{t+1}) to be a linear combination of the model-consistent solution (s_{t+1}) and backward-looking expectations (s_{t-1}) adjusted for the trend exchange rate depreciation ($2[\Delta \bar{z}_t - (\pi^{*,US} - \pi^*)/4]$). The factor ¼, which multiplies the inflation differential ($\pi^{*,US} - \pi^*$), de-annualizes the inflation rates, which are expressed in annual terms, while the factor 2 is necessary as the nominal exchange rate in the past period (s_{t-1}) is extrapolated two periods into the future using the steady-state growth rate in the nominal exchange rate ($\Delta \bar{z}_t - (\pi^{*,US} - \pi^*)/4$). Conversely, in the condition that links Canadian and US interest rates, the factor 4 before the expected depreciation ($Es_{t+1} - s_t$) annualizes the expected quarterly depreciation rate, making it consistent with the interest rate quoted on the annual basis. A time-varying variable (σ_t^{ctry}) is included to account for shocks to country risk premium. Terms-of-trade shifts (σ_t^{tot}) is also an important factor that affects movements in the nominal exchange rate.

As the terms-of-trade premium should disappear when the economy is in the equilibrium, the following condition holds:

$$\bar{r}_t - \bar{r}_t^{US} = 4(\bar{z}_{t+1} - \bar{z}_t) + \sigma_t^{ctry}.$$

5. Relative Prices

Headline inflation is affected by the dynamics of relative price movements (core CPI (p_t^Q) relative to headline CPI (p_t^H)). In the long term the overall (headline)

---

[15]See Carabenciov and others (2008) and Blagrave and others (2013) for the Global Projection Model.

inflation is assumed to be equal to the underlying (core) inflation, though it can diverge over prolonged periods, when there is a trend in the relative prices of noncore items (mortgage interest rates, unprocessed food, energy). The dynamics of relative prices (rp_t) are modeled as the sum of the relative price trend ($\overline{rp}_t$) and the relative price gap ($\widehat{rp}_t$). The relative price gap depends on the real price of oil and food in the international markets adjusted for exchange rate effects, while the relative price trend growth is assumed to be an autoregressive process with mean zero. The parameters in the relative price gap equation are calibrated based on various information, such as the weights of energy and food in the CPI basket, and the degree and time profile of the pass-through from energy and food inflation to headline inflation.

$$rp_t = p_t^C - p_t^H$$

$$rp_t = \overline{rp}_t + \widehat{rp}_t$$

$$\widehat{rp}_t = \rho^{\widehat{rp}} \widehat{rp}_{t-1} - c_1^{\widehat{rp}}\left(\widehat{rp}_t^{Oil} + \hat{z}_t\right) - c_2^{\widehat{rp}}\left(\widehat{rp}_t^{Food} + \hat{z}_t\right) + \varepsilon_t^{\widehat{rp}}$$
$$\quad (0.43) \quad (0.012) \qquad\quad (0.02)$$

$$\Delta \overline{rp}_t = \rho^{\Delta\overline{rp}} \Delta \overline{rp}_{t-1} + \varepsilon_t^{\Delta\overline{rp}}$$
$$\quad (0.9)$$

6. Term Structure of Interest Rates

The model allows for long-term bond yields to shed light on the equilibrium real interest rates. Let $i_t^{Gov,k}$ be the nominal government bond yield with a maturity of k quarters, where k could be 4, 8, 20, or 40. The bond yield is equal to the average expected short-term interest rates k quarters into the future plus a term ($\sigma_t^{Term,k}$) that captures both government bond premium (same for bonds with all maturity) and term premium (a premium that increases with the maturity). A shock at the end of each equation ($\varepsilon_t^{Gov,k}$) reflects measurement errors.

$$i_t^{Gov,4} = i4_t + \sigma_t^{Term,4} + \varepsilon_t^{Gov,4}$$

$$i_t^{Gov,8} = \left(i4_t + i4_{t+4}\right)/2 + \sigma_t^{Term,8} + \varepsilon_t^{Gov,8}$$

$$i_t^{Gov,20} = \left(i4_t + i4_{t+4} + i4_{t+8} + i4_{t+12} + i4_{t+16}\right)/5 + \sigma_t^{Term,20} + \varepsilon_t^{Gov,20}$$

$$i_t^{Gov,40} = \sum_{i=0}^{9} i4_{t+4i}/10 + \sigma_t^{Term,40} + \varepsilon_t^{Gov,40}$$

$$i4_t = \left(i_t + i_{t+1} + i_{t+2} + i_{t+3}\right)/4$$

7. Unemployment Rate

The unemployment rate (u_t) is characterized by a "gap version" of Okun's law. The equation implies that a 1 percentage point increase in the unemployment gap ($\hat{u}_t$) is associated with approximately 2 percentage point decrease in the output gap. The non-accelerating inflation rate of unemployment (NAIRU) ($\bar{u}_t$) is assumed to follow a stochastic process that has both shocks to the level and to the growth rate.

$$u_t = \bar{u}_t + \hat{u}_t$$

$$\hat{u}_t = \underset{(0.4)}{\rho^{\hat{u}}} \hat{u}_{t-1} - \underset{(0.4)}{c_1^{\hat{u}}} \hat{y}_t + \varepsilon_t^{\hat{u}}$$

$$\bar{u}_t = \bar{u}_{t-1} + \Delta \bar{u}_t + \varepsilon_t^{\bar{u}}$$

$$\Delta \bar{u}_t = \underset{(0.9)}{\rho^{\Delta \bar{u}}} \Delta \bar{u}_{t-1} + \varepsilon_t^{\Delta \bar{u}}$$

8. Potential Output

The potential growth rate $(\Delta \bar{y}_t)$ is assumed to converge to its steady-state level $(\Delta \bar{y}^{ss})$ in the longer term. However, it can deviate from the steady-state level for prolonged periods.

$$\Delta \bar{y}_t = \underset{(0.97)}{\rho^{\bar{y}}} \Delta \bar{y}_{t-1} + \underset{(2)}{(1 - \rho^{\bar{y}})} \Delta \bar{y}^{ss} + \varepsilon_t^{\Delta \bar{y}}$$

9. The Rest of the World

The Canadian economy is linked to the rest of the world through both the trade linkage and the financial linkage. The rest-of-the-world output gap relevant for the Canadian economy is defined as a weighted average of output gaps in the seven regions (United States, euro area, Japan, China, emerging Asia, Latin America, and the rest of the world), using export shares as weights.

$$\hat{y}_t^{World} = \underset{(0.79)}{\varpi^{Exp,US}} \hat{y}_t^{US} + \underset{(0.04)}{\varpi^{Exp,EU}} \hat{y}_t^{EU} + \underset{(0.02)}{\varpi^{Exp,JA}} \hat{y}_t^{JA} + \underset{(0.04)}{\varpi^{Exp,CH}} \hat{y}_t^{CH}$$

$$+ \underset{(0.04)}{\varpi^{Exp,EA}} \hat{y}_t^{EA} + \underset{(0.02)}{\varpi^{Exp,LA}} \hat{y}_t^{LA} + \underset{(0.05)}{\varpi^{Exp,RC}} \hat{y}_t^{RC}$$

The equilibrium real interest rate in Canada is closely linked to that in the United States.

$$\bar{r}_t = \underset{(0.6)}{\rho^{\bar{r}}} \bar{r}_{t-1} + (1 - \rho^{\bar{r}}) \bar{r}_t^{US} + \varepsilon_t^{\bar{r}}$$

10. Commodity Terms of Trade

The real price of oil (rp_t^{Oil}) is defined as the global oil price (p_t^{Oil}) in US dollars relative to the US CPI (p_t^{US}). In the equilibrium, the real price of oil is assumed to grow at a rate of zero, although the actual growth rate can deviate from zero for long periods. The real price of oil gap $(\widehat{rp}_t^{Oil})$, defined as the difference between the real price of oil and its equilibrium value, is modeled as an autoregressive process with a shock.

$$rp_t^{Oil} = p_t^{Oil} - p_t^{US}$$

$$rp_t^{Oil} = \overline{rp}_t^{Oil} + \widehat{rp}_t^{Oil}$$

$$\Delta \overline{rp}_t^{Oil} = \rho^{\Delta \overline{rp}^{Oil}} \Delta \overline{rp}_{t-1}^{Oil} + \varepsilon_t^{\Delta \overline{rp}^{Oil}}$$
$$(0.95)$$

$$\widehat{rp}_t^{Oil} = \rho^{\widehat{rp}^{Oil}} \widehat{rp}_{t-1}^{Oil} + \varepsilon_t^{\widehat{rp}^{Oil}}$$
$$(0.7)$$

A similar modeling strategy is followed for the real price of food.

$$rp_t^{Food} = p_t^{Food} - p_t^{US}$$

$$rp_t^{Food} = \overline{rp}_t^{Food} + \widehat{rp}_t^{Food}$$

$$\Delta \overline{rp}_t^{Food} = \rho^{\Delta \overline{rp}^{Food}} \Delta \overline{rp}_{t-1}^{Food} + \varepsilon_t^{\Delta \overline{rp}^{Food}}$$
$$(0.95)$$

$$\widehat{rp}_t^{Food} = \rho^{\widehat{rp}^{Food}} \widehat{rp}_{t-1}^{Food} + \varepsilon_t^{\widehat{rp}^{Food}}$$
$$(0.7)$$

The terms-of-trade gap ($\widehat{tot}_t$) for Canada is determined by the real price of oil gap ($\widehat{rp}_t^{Oil}$) and the real price of food gap ($\widehat{rp}_t^{Food}$). The coefficients of the two terms represent the shares of these two commodities in Canada's GDP.

$$\widehat{tot}_t = c_1^{tot} \widehat{rp}_t^{Oil} + c_2^{tot} \widehat{rp}_t^{Food}$$
$$(0.03) \qquad (0.002)$$

The real exchange rate depreciation consistent with changes in the terms of trade (Δz_t^{tot}) is related to movements in the real price of oil (Δrp_t^{Oil}) and food (Δrp_t^{Food}), adjusted for their relative size in total exports. The same condition holds for those variables at their respective equilibrium values.

$$\Delta z_t^{tot} = -c_0^{\Delta z^{tot}} \left(c_1^{\Delta z^{tot}} \Delta rp_t^{Oil} + c_2^{\Delta z^{tot}} \Delta rp_t^{Food} \right) / \left(c_1^{\Delta z^{tot}} + c_2^{\Delta z^{tot}} \right)$$
$$(0.25) \ (0.03) \qquad (0.002)$$

$$\Delta \overline{z}_t^{tot} = -c_0^{\Delta z^{tot}} \left(c_1^{\Delta z^{tot}} \Delta \overline{rp}_t^{Oil} + c_2^{\Delta z^{tot}} \Delta \overline{rp}_t^{Food} \right) / \left(c_1^{\Delta z^{tot}} + c_2^{\Delta z^{tot}} \right)$$
$$(0.25) \ (0.03) \qquad (0.002)$$

The terms-of-trade premium that goes into the uncovered interest parity condition (σ_t^{tot}) is modeled as the "surprise" component in the real exchange rate movement consistent with the terms of trade.

$$\sigma_t^{tot} = 4 \left(z_t^{tot} - E_{t-1} z_t^{tot} \right)$$

REFERENCES

Alichi, A., K. Clinton, C. Freedman, M. Juillard, O. Kamenik, D. Laxton, J. Turunen, and H. Wang. 2015. "Avoiding Dark Corners: A Robust Monetary Policy Framework for the United States." IMF Working Paper 15/134, International Monetary Fund, Washington, DC.

Bank of Canada. 2009. Press Release. "Bank of Canada lowers overnight rate target by 1/4 percentage point to 1/4 per cent and, conditional on the inflation outlook, commits to hold current policy rate until the end of the second quarter of 2010." April 21. Bank of Canada, Ottawa.

Bank of Canada. 2012. "Monetary Policy." Backgrounders. Bank of Canada, Ottawa.

Bank of England. 2013. "Monetary Policy Trade-Offs and Forward Guidance." August. London: Bank of England.

Bech, M., and A. Malkhozov. 2016. "How Have Central Banks Implemented Negative Policy Rates?" *BIS Quarterly Review*, March. Bank for International Settlements, Basel.

Blagrave, P., P. Elliott, R. Garcia-Saltos, D. Hostland, D. Laxton, and F. Zhang. 2013. "Adding China to the Global Projection Model." IMF Working Paper 13/256, International Monetary Fund, Washington, DC.

Carabenciov, I., I. Ermolaev, C. Freedman, M. Juillard, O. Kamenik, D. Korsunmov, D. Laxton, and J. Laxton. 2008. "A Small Multi-Country Global Projection Model with Financial-Real Linkages and Oil Prices." IMF Working Paper 08/280, International Monetary Fund, Washington, DC.

Charbonneau, K., and L. Rennison. 2015. "Forward Guidance at the Effective Lower Bound: International Experience." Bank of Canada Staff Discussion Paper 2015–15, Bank of Canada, Ottawa.

Clinton, K., C. Freedman, M. Juillard, O. Kamenik, D. Laxton, and H. Wang. 2015. "Inflation-Forecast Targeting: Applying the Principle of Transparency." IMF Working Paper 15/132, International Monetary Fund, Washington, DC.

Council of Economic Advisers. 2015. "Long-Term Interest Rates: A Survey." July.

Dincer, N., and B. Eichengreen. 2014. "Central Bank Transparency and Independence: Updates and New Measures." *International Journal of Central Banking* 10 (1): 189–259.

Eggertsson, G. B., and M. Woodford. 2003. "The Zero Bound on Interest Rates and Optimal Monetary Policy." *Brookings Papers on Economic Activity 1:* 2003, Brookings Institution, Washington, DC.

Engen, E., T. Laubach, and D. Reifschneider. 2015. "The Macroeconomic Effects of the Federal Reserve's Unconventional Monetary Policies." Finance and Economic Discussion Series 2015–005, Board of Governors of the Federal Reserve System, Washington, DC.

Filardo, A., and B. Hoffmann. 2014. "Forward Guidance at the Zero Lower Bound." *BIS Quarterly Review*, March. Bank for International Settlements, Basel.

Federal Open Market Committee (FOMC). 2012. Press Release, Board of Governors of the Federal Reserve System, January 25.

Freedman, C., M. Kumhof, D. Laxton, D. Muir, and S. Mursula. 2009. "Fiscal Stimulus to the Rescue? Short-Run Benefits and Potential Long-Run Costs of Fiscal Deficits." IMF Working Paper 09/255, International Monetary Fund, Washington DC.

Holston, K., T. Laubach, and J. Williams. 2016. "Measuring the Natural Rate of Interest: International Trends and Determinants." Federal Reserve Bank of San Francisco Working Paper 2016–11.

International Monetary Fund (IMF). 2014. "Perspectives on Global Real Interest Rates." *World Economic Outlook,* April, Washington, DC.

Kamenik, O., H. Kiem, V. Klyuev, and D. Laxton. 2013. "Why Is Canada's Price Level So Predictable?" *Journal of Money, Credit and Banking* 45 (February): 71–85.

Johannsen, B. K., and E. Mertens. 2016. "The Expected Real Interest Rate in the Long Run: Time Series Evidence with the Effective Lower Bound." FEDS Notes, Board of Governors of the Federal Reserve System, Washington, DC.

Lane, T. 2015. "Inflation Targeting—A Matter of Time." Bank of Canada. Conference presentation, Halifax, Nova Scotia, October.

Lane, T. 2016. "Monetary Policy and Financial Stability—Looking for the Right Tools." Bank of Canada. Conference presentation, HEC Montréal, February.

Laubach, T., and J. C. Williams. 2015. "Measuring the Natural Rate of Interest Redux." Federal Reserve Bank of San Francisco Working Paper 2015–16.

Mendes, R.R. 2014. "The Neutral Rate of Interest in Canada." Bank of Canada Discussion Paper 2014–5, Bank of Canada, Ottawa.

Obstfeld, M., K. Clinton, O. Komenik, D. Laxton, Y. Ustyugova, and H. Wang. 2016. "How to Improve Inflation Targeting in Canada?" IMF Working Paper 16/192, International Monetary Fund, Washington, DC.

Poloz, S. S. 2014. "Integrating Uncertainty and Monetary Policy-Making: A Practitioner's Perspective." Bank of Canada Discussion Paper 2014–6, Bank of Canada, Ottawa.

———. 2015. "Prudent Preparation: The Evolution of Unconventional Monetary Policies." Speech at the Empire Club of Canada, Toronto, December 8.

Qvigstad, J. F. 2005. "When Does an Interest Rate Path 'Look Good'? Criteria for an Appropriate Future Interest Rate Path – A Practician's Approach." Norges Bank Staff Memo No. 2005/6, Norges Bank, Oslo.

Rachel, L., and T. D. Smith. 2015. "Secular Drivers of the Global Real Interest Rate." Bank of England Staff Working Paper No. 571, Bank of England, London.

Summers, L. H. 2015. "Low Real Rates, Secular Stagnation, and the Future of Stabilization Policy." Speech, Bank of Chile, November.

Svensson, L. E. O. 1997. "Inflation Forecast Targeting: Implementing and Monitoring Inflation Targets." *European Economic Review* 41: 1111–46.

———. 1999. "Price Level Targeting vs. Inflation Targeting: A Free Lunch?" *Journal of Money, Credit and Banking* 31: 277–295.

———. 2001. "The Zero Bound in an Open Economy: A Foolproof Way of Escaping from a Liquidity Trap." *Monetary and Economic Studies* (Special Edition), February.

———. 2002. "Monetary Policy and Real Stabilization." In *Rethinking Stabilization Policy, A Symposium Sponsored by the Federal Reserve Bank of Kansas City*, Jackson Hole, WY.

Witmer, J., and J. Yang. 2015. "Estimating Canada's Effective Lower Bound." Bank of Canada Staff Analytical Note 2015–2, Bank of Canada, Ottawa.

Woodford, M. 2005. "Central-Bank Communication and Policy Effectiveness." Presented at the Federal Reserve Bank of Kansas City Symposium, Jackson Hole, WY, August 25–27.

Yellen, J. 2015. Transcript of Chair Yellen's FOMC Press Conference, Board of Governors of the Federal Reserve System, March 18.

CHAPTER 10

Czech Republic: Transition to the Frontier

RANIA AL-MASHAT, KEVIN CLINTON, DOUGLAS
LAXTON, AND HOU WANG

The Czech experience with inflation targeting thus illustrates that the ultimate purpose of inflation targeting is not to announce inflation targets and then hit them mechanically. It is a mistake to confuse inflation targeting with inflation obsession. The aim is to design a rule-based monetary policy framework characterized by a high degree of transparency and accountability.—Z. Tůma, Governor of the Czech National Bank (2003)

Monetary policy in the Czech Republic moved in less than 10 years from a de facto fixed exchange rate to the frontiers of inflation-forecast targeting.[1] This chapter describes the evolution of monetary policy since the revolution of 1990 and how inflation-forecast targeting provided the economy with a firm nominal anchor.

Soon after the collapse of an exchange rate peg in 1997, the central bank adopted inflation targeting. It was a controversial decision, given the concerns at the time about objectives other than inflation control, about current inflation rising above 10 percent, and about the entrenched inflation psychology, and given the doubts about the effectiveness of monetary policy in an economy still in transition. Moreover, the central bank did not have an adequate internal setup to pursue an inflation target. A rapid fall in the inflation rate before 2000 nevertheless boosted the credibility of the new approach. As this was happening, the Czech National Bank (CNB) moved with due speed to establish a forecasting and policy analysis system, with an appropriate forecasting model. In 2002, policy switched from a basic, short-term approach to flexible, medium-term inflation targeting. The new regime used model-based forecasting and policy analysis. In recent years, the credibility of Czech monetary policy allowed the central bank to use an innovative exchange rate strategy to stabilize the economy in the face of disinflationary pressures emanating from other parts of the European Union, and to raise inflation to the 2 percent target. And the CNB has itself become an important provider of international technical assistance on monetary policy.

---

[1]The chapter draws from Coats 2000; Coats, Laxton, and Rose 2003; Alichi and others 2015; and Clinton and others 2017.

IMF technical assistance is also part of the story. After the Velvet Revolution opened the door to market-oriented reform, the State Bank of Czechoslovakia recognized the need for radical change to equip the institution for the job of monetary policy in a market economy. To help, the IMF assembled a team of staff members and specialists from various central banks, including the Bank of Canada, the Austrian National Bank, the Bank of Italy, and Norges Bank. They advised on the appropriate structure for all major areas of central banking, including monetary policy analysis and strategy, money markets and policy operations, and foreign exchange operations.

Following the division of the country in 2003, in support of the ongoing IMF program, the Bank of Canada contributed bilateral assistance to the CNB, providing training in Ottawa on money markets, monetary policy operations, model building, and policy strategy, and on the process of decision-making. Personnel from the CNB shared offices with Bank of Canada counterparts and attended key meetings over a period of weeks. Visiting CNB staff included money market traders who sat at the open-market operations desk, and senior managers who observed, from a policymaker level, the assembly of inputs of information for policy decisions and attended forecast and monetary policy committee meetings. The visit gave them insight into an effectively operating forecasting and policy analysis system for inflation targeting.

RECENT CZECH MONETARY POLICY

1991–97: De Facto Fixed Exchange Rate

Until 1997 the CNB ran monetary policy based on three pillars: a target for broad money growth, a one-year-ahead inflation-reduction objective, and a fixed exchange rate. In practice, the fixed exchange rate dominated, resulting in a de facto fixed exchange rate regime. This was a stabilizing factor for economic decision during the uncertainties of the economic transformation.[2] As long as capital mobility remained limited, monetary policy had a degree of independence to pursue the money growth target, despite the fixed exchange rate. But within a few years, increasing international financial integration exposed the "impossible trinity": the incompatibility of simultaneously open capital markets, a fixed exchange rate, and an independent monetary policy.

The three pillars never provided a firm nominal anchor. Inflation got stuck in the high single digits. In the mid-1990s, heavy capital inflows forced the CNB to accumulate a growing stock of foreign exchange reserves. The central bank tried to sterilize the monetary impact through the sale of bonds, which placed a burden on the budget since Czech interest rates were much above the rates on the reserve assets. Moreover, the sterilization operations were insufficient to prevent inflationary increases in money supply.

---

[2]See Capek and others 2003; Ötker-Robe and Vavra 2007.

To deter further volatile inflows, the CNB widened the tolerance band around the exchange rate peg to ±7.5 percent in 1996. However, ample supplies of liquidity, combined with inadequate banking regulation and supervision and lax lending standards, led to a credit bubble. Much of the lending covered losses in former state enterprises that bankers perceived to be too big to fail. The expansion of credit overheated the economy, one symptom of which was a large current account deficit.

The economic imbalances and financial weakness were unsustainable. Contagion from the Asian financial crisis and domestic political instability triggered capital flight in 1997. The CNB used 20 percent of Czech foreign currency reserves to defend the exchange rate peg, and hiked the policy interest rate from 12 percent to 26 percent—the one-week interbank rate peaked at 75 percent. Even so, the peg had to be abandoned, and the exchange rate depreciated 13 percent. As the impaired balance sheets of the banks became apparent, a full-blown banking crisis erupted. Real GDP decelerated, and inflation was well above the typical level in the European Union, and rising.

In the aftermath of the collapse in confidence, the CNB attempted a managed float, without a clear nominal anchor to keep inflation expectations under control. However, Czech policymakers were aware of the need for a domestic monetary standard to replace the fixed exchange rate, and they had noted the success of inflation targeting in several advanced economies.[3] As noted, several of them had witnessed its implementation in Canada. It did not take long for the central bank to decide in favor of inflation targeting for the nominal anchor.

But this decision was neither easy nor uncontroversial. Economists debated whether inflation targeting could work in a country that was still far from completing the transition to a market economy. Many feared that the Czech Republic did not satisfy so-called preconditions for the regime. Political support for inflation targeting was limited, and the banking system remained fragile. Furthermore, the central bank had focused on the analysis of monetary aggregates, the exchange rate, and the balance of payments, and did not have the resources appropriate for the macroeconomic forecasting and analysis required for inflation targeting.

Economic forecasting, meanwhile, was hindered by inadequate data series, structural shifts, and uncertainties about the transmission mechanism. Decision-making processes were not well-structured; for example, senior-level meetings would include time debating objectives versus how to adjust instruments to achieve objectives. The credibility of an objective for stable, low inflation was an issue because the population was accustomed to inflation in the high single digits, and was expecting sporadic jumps in the prices of various essential services as a wide range of controlled prices—including rents and utilities—were to be liberalized in the years just ahead. The market environment was still

---

[3]Money growth rules as a nominal anchor were completely discredited. Financial innovation, and resulting instability of the demand for money (on any definition), had led to the failure of numerous attempts at money growth rules in many countries. Their prospects were, if anything, worse in the Czech Republic, in view of the rapid, even hectic, changes taking place in the financial system.

incomplete after a half-century of repression, and the effectiveness of monetary policy in the control of inflation was untested.

Despite these uncertainties, in early 1998 the CNB introduced inflation targeting with an ultimate inflation target of 2 percent and a sequence of interim targets for inflation reduction. Since the CNB has goal and instrument independence, it could install the new regime without a lengthy political consultation. In adopting inflation targeting, the central bank took the lead in an atmosphere of doubt, confusion, and financial distress.

Perhaps not surprisingly, the announcement was met with widespread skepticism. Within the central bank itself, there was uncertainty about the reliability of the transmission of conventional monetary policy in view of the ongoing transformation of the economy, sparse macroeconomic data, and the lack of an appropriate forecasting and policy analysis system and models. Some policymakers worried that the central bank would be unable to make good on a commitment to durable inflation reduction, especially in view of the entrenched inflation mentality, the demands for high wage increases in current negotiations, and the eventual need for firms to restore normal profits.

Macroeconomic theory, however, supported by evidence from recent disinflation episodes in the advanced economies, suggested a more sanguine outlook. First, since the steep postcrisis recession and credit squeeze would alone open a disinflationary gap, without the need for further tightening by the CNB, the uncertainties—and probable weaknesses—of the transmission mechanism would not be a material factor in the early phases.

Indeed, in view of the widening output gap and the credit crunch brought on by the banking crisis, there was a high risk that inflation would fall more quickly than the interim targets envisaged—as had happened in Canada, New Zealand, and Sweden. Second, wage settlements tend to be a lagging indicator; they would moderate during the slowdown because of depressed profits and the inability of employers to pass on increased costs given the slack in the economy. And third, the procyclical rebound of productivity in the eventual recovery would hold unit labor costs down and promote a return to normal profitability without a resurgence of price inflation.

1998–2001: Inflation Targeting without a Forecasting and Policy Analysis System

For the most part, inflation targeting turned out reasonably well from the outset. The CNB handled the price decontrol problem by defining the initial inflation reduction targets in terms of *net inflation*—that is, consumer price index (CPI) inflation excluding the prices affected by the lifting of controls. It listed other special factors that might affect the inflation rate from year to year and that would justify a deviation from the announced targets. It recognized the risk of undershooting the target, announcing that such an outcome would represent unexpectedly rapid progress to the ultimate target and therefore justify a downshift in the target trajectory, rather than attempting to push inflation back up to the interim path originally announced. As it turned out, this risk did materialize—and the steep decline in inflation grabbed the public's attention and gave the credibility of the CNB's inflation targeting a needed boost. This experience resonates with the theme in Chapter 3 that when policy is confronted with a credibility problem, an assertive policy stance—which may result in a temporary under- or overshooting of target—can have a salutary, constructive impact on expectations.

Aspects of the fledgling regime, however, did call for improvement. In the absence of a forward-looking framework for policy analysis, policymakers focused excessively on current economic outcomes and were slow to take policy action in anticipation of projected future developments. Failing to take adequate account of the disinflationary impact of the output gap and credit crunch, the CNB kept interest rates too high for too long (Figures 10.1). While the faster-than-intended drop in inflation helpfully brought down long-term expectations, it came at the short-term cost of a deep slowdown and high unemployment, which put the CNB's independence into political jeopardy.[4] Learning from this, the CNB moved with all due speed to set up a forecasting and policy analysis system for forward-looking, flexible inflation targeting and to adopt a more transparent approach to monetary policy communications.

2002–07: Inflation-Forecast Targeting with a Forecasting and Policy Analysis System

In setting up the forecasting and policy analysis system, the CNB's collaboration with the IMF again proved useful. IMF staff members had already helped to design and put to work such frameworks at the Bank of Canada and the Reserve Bank of New Zealand.[5] They helped the CNB staff develop an appropriate core monetary policy model (QPM-gap), with forward-looking, model-consistent expectations, and with policy represented by an endogenous short-term interest rate. The specification put a high priority on credible simulation properties, with theoretically plausible responses to shocks. To this end, the model builders calibrated the parameters from a broad range of evidence in small open economies, rather than using traditional econometric estimation, which was not in any case feasible in the Czech Republic at the time, due to the very short time series for the relevant data. In 2002, the forecasting and policy analysis system was ready to go in support of an explicit inflation-forecast-targeting framework with flexible exchange rate.[6] This allowed a considerable increase in transparency, as the CNB was now able to make policy informed by an explicit model, the main properties

---

[4]The unemployment rate peaked at 9.3 percent in 2000. More detailed discussions of the history of monetary policy in the Czech Republic are in Laxton, Rose, and Scott (2009) and Ötker-Robe and Vavra (2007).

[5]Laxton, Rose, and Scott (2009) give a thorough description of how to set up a forecasting and policy analysis system for inflation-forecast targeting.

[6]For complete documentation of the forecasting and policy analysis system introduced in 2002 see Coats, Laxton, and Rose (2003).

Figure 10.1. Nominal and Real Interest Rates, 1993–2017
(Percent, per year)

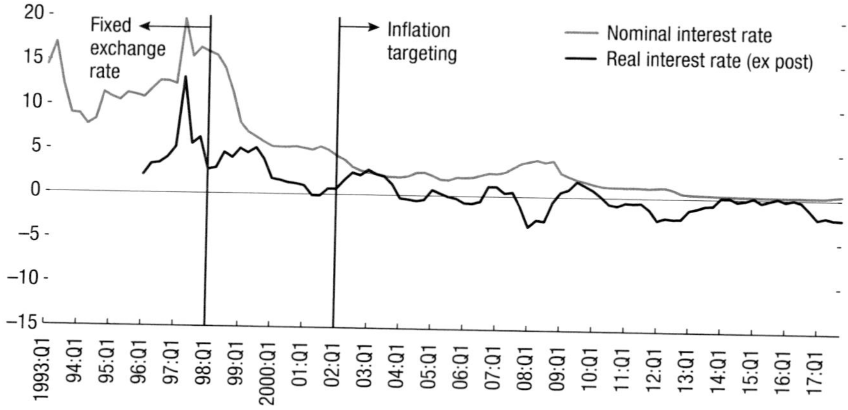

Sources: Czech National Bank; Czech Statistical Office; and Haver.
Note: Last observation: 2017:Q4.

of which reflected standard economic theory. Over time, this would become comprehensible and credible to financial markets and the public.

Work on the forecasting and policy analysis system benefited from the clarification provided by Svensson (1997), which showed that efficient flexible inflation targeting amounted to inflation-forecast targeting. The argument is that the central bank's inflation forecast represents an ideal intermediate target to manage and communicate the short-term output-inflation trade-off. That is, in the context of returning inflation to its long-term target rate following a shock, the central bank simulates the possible paths available to it and decides on one that accounts for the trade-off between the costs of forecast inflation being off target and the costs of a significant output gap.[7] This insight underlined the importance to policymaking of a systematic process to forecast the economy and to map the transmission channels between instruments and objectives in a credible macroeconomic model. The CNB would also have to adapt its organizational structure to support the provision of relevant macroeconomic analysis to policymakers. This included the internal and external communications necessary for transparency and accountability.

The Czech economy performed well over much of the 2000s, as did many other economies. Output grew strongly and unemployment fell gradually, from over 7 percent to under 5 percent (Figure 10.2). Longer-term inflation expectations became well anchored (Figure 10.3).

---

[7]In realistic models of economies with important lags in the monetary transmission mechanism it simply is neither feasible nor optimal to keep current inflation on target at all times.

Figure 10.2. Unemployment Rate and Real GDP Growth, 1993–2017
(Percent)

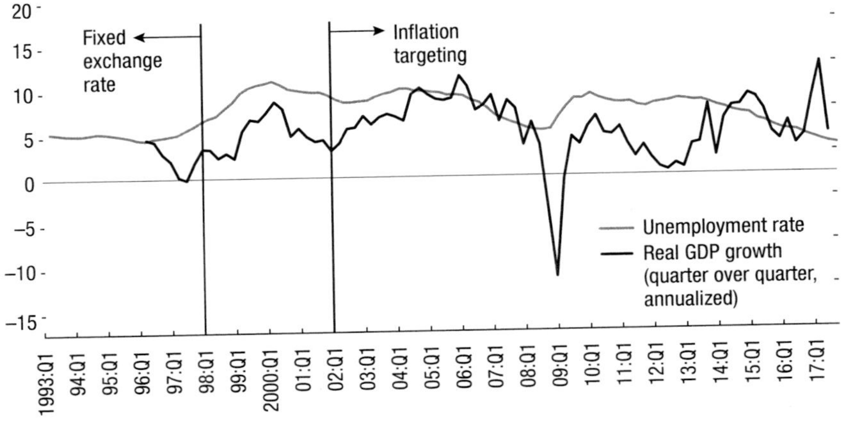

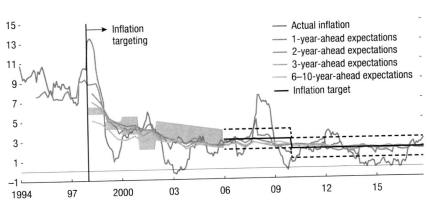

Sources: Czech Statistical Office and Haver.
Note: Last observation: 2017:Q4.

Figure 10.3. Inflation and Inflation Expectations, 1994–2017
(Percent)

Sources: Consensus Economics and Haver.
Note: Last observation: October 2017.

2008 and After: Management of Expectations and Mature Forecasting and Policy Analysis System

Monetary policy became more forward looking and preemptive, with the medium-term forecasts serving as the main basis for discussions of the CNB's strategy. The endogenous interest rate facilitated transparency and ease of communications. Whether an inflation-targeting central bank chooses to describe its policy path qualitatively or quantitatively, it can tell a coherent economic story in terms of policy reaction to pressures on inflation and output.

Over time, the CNB became comfortable with the decision-making process and more inclined to the view that publishing the complete forecast could be helpful in explaining what the central bank really meant. In the first quarter of 2008, the central bank started publishing the projected interest rate path, with confidence intervals to emphasize that the central bank is never committing to follow a baseline path for the policy rate, but is committed to adjust this path in response to new information.[8]

Overall Assessment

The Czech Republic has earned a reputation for successful inflation targeting even though actual inflation has often deviated from announced targets and the output gap has often been far from zero. The data show a bias to the downside, with inflation being more often below than above target (Šmídková 2008). According to a quadratic loss function, until 2006 the inflation-targeting error was the costlier facet (Figure 10.4).[9] Since then, and especially in the aftermath of the global financial crisis, output gaps have more often been dominant.

Undershooting the inflation target in the early years actually bolstered the CNB's long-term reputation (despite strong criticism at the time), because it helped dispel memories of double-digit inflation before 1998. From the viewpoint of an endogenous credibility model, the surprisingly low inflation rate at the turn of the century helped convince people that monetary policy had indeed reformed from the previous high-inflation regime to a low-inflation regime.[10] After the adoption of the inflation-forecast-targeting framework, strong exogenous macroeconomic shocks again led to significant deviations of inflation from the target and of economic activity from potential.

But the key to maintaining confidence in the system has been that the CNB has consistently and visibly adjusted monetary policy instruments to bring inflation back to target in the medium term (Franta and others 2014; Alichi and others 2015). In its communications, the CNB credibly demonstrated that its actions were indeed in line with its objectives. The forecasting and policy

---

[8]The CNB currently develops its confidence bands based on an analysis of past forecasting performance, but it is now technically possible to construct confidence intervals for nonlinear models. Relevant nonlinearities include the Phillips curve and the floor on nominal interest rates. See Clinton and others (2010).

[9]The loss function assigns a weight of 1, 1, and 0.5 on the squared deviation of inflation from its target, the output gap, and change in the policy rate, respectively. In practice, changes in the policy rate make empirically negligible contributions to the loss.

[10]Alichi and others (2009) present a model in which people are initially undecided as to whether monetary policy will adhere to a new announced low-inflation target or revert to a previous policy of high inflation. In their expectations of future inflation, some weight attaches both to the new target and to the old high rate. Over time, the central bank builds credibility by keeping inflation low: the weight on the announced target goes to one, while that on the old high rate goes to zero.

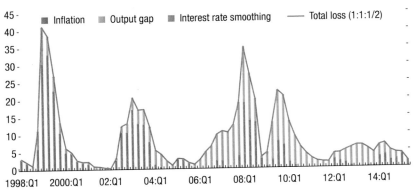

Figure 10.4. Loss-Function Values for the Czech Republic, 1998–2015

Source: Czech National Bank.

analysis system, with forecasts deriving from a coherent macroeconomic model, helped make explicit the economic rationale: crucial for building the credibility of the Czech inflation-forecast-targeting regime was the capacity to provide a coherent narrative of how interest rates, and the economy in general, might behave over the medium term as inflation was brought back to the announced target.

THE CNB'S FORECASTING AND POLICY ANALYSIS SYSTEM

The CNB's forecasting and policy analysis system has seen three distinct stages (Figure 10.5). The first was a preliminary phase from 1998 until mid-2002, with an incomplete framework that relied on data-driven, near-term forecasting (that is, the current quarter and the next) models. The second, 2002–08, used the small core model (QPM-gap) to give more emphasis to the medium term and, hence, to the explicit implications of the feedback between monetary policy settings and economic activity and inflation. In a key development, QPM-gap had forward-looking, model-consistent inflation expectations, and an endogenous policy interest rate determined by a policy rule to return inflation to target. The third stage started in mid-2008, when the dynamic stochastic general equilibrium (DSGE) model, QPM-g3, took over.

The accuracy of four-quarter-ahead inflation forecasts has improved with the more advanced models (Figure 10.6). Moreover, the decline in forecasting errors with QPM-g3 was achieved during the turbulence following the global financial crisis and despite the effective lower bound on interest rates. Negative external demand shocks resulted in overpredictions of inflation, in part because interest rate cuts were blocked by the effective lower bound constraint.

Figure 10.5. Stages of Czech National Bank Model Development, 1998–2008

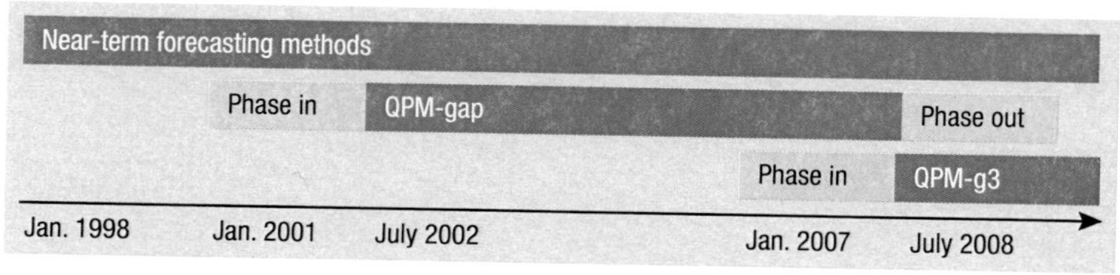

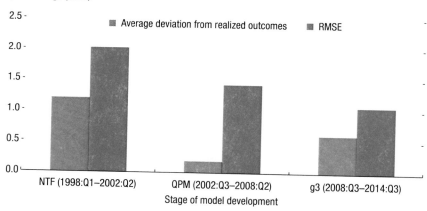

Source: Czech National Bank.

Figure 10.6. Accuracy of Czech National Bank's Four-Quarter-Ahead Inflation Forecasts
(Percentage point)

Source: Czech National Bank.
Notes: NTF = near-term forecasting; RMSE = root mean squared error.

Early Years: Near-Term Focus

Inadequate forecasting methods, together with the volatile macroeconomic environment and unstable inflation expectations, contributed to large forecast errors in the initial years of inflation targeting (Holub and Hurník 2008; Šmídková 2008). An important part of the sudden and unpredicted disinflation in 1998–99 could be attributed to a sudden fall in global and food prices in that period, that is, to exogenous shocks. However, in addition, near-term forecasting methods underestimated the disinflationary impact of the economic recession. Inflation fell very quickly almost to zero, that is, well below the target and the forecast. Monetary policy came under criticism for being overly tight and for contributing to an unnecessarily deep recession.

Near-term forecasting methods do have a comparative advantage for the short end of the inflation-forecasting horizon. This is true especially for quantifying the near-term impact of cost-push shocks, such as changes in indirect taxes, price deregulation, and global commodity price fluctuations. However, for horizons beyond a couple of quarters the monetary policy feedback cannot be ignored. Following a shock, a credible policy will reestablish the targeted inflation rate over the medium term, with the time profile of adjustment depending on the nature, size, and duration of the source of the shock. Depending on the preferences of policymakers in managing the short-term output-inflation trade-off, inflation may be brought back to target more or less quickly. A proper forecasting framework takes all this into account, with an explicit view of the monetary policy transmission mechanism and the time lags involved.

Next Phase: Model with Medium-Term Horizon

QPM-gap, a small-scale calibrated monetary policy model, was developed over several years, with technical assistance from the IMF (Coats, Laxton, and Rose 2003). The CNB began the process by committing the necessary staff resources: the model development and forecasting team, the team head, the model operators, and the relevant sectoral specialists. Modeling focused on the channels of policy transmission. Initial model calibration was based largely on theoretical considerations and evidence from other small, open economies, but accumulation of domestic data over time allowed modifications to better capture the dynamics of the Czech economy. CNB staff members did extensive tests of model properties to evaluate model-consistent estimates of unobserved variables such as the neutral interest rate and potential output and to identify historical demand- and supply-side shocks. Sectoral specialists were consulted on the magnitudes and timing of model responses to shocks. Forecasting properties were assessed through in-sample simulations and shadow forecasts. Policymakers and staff agreed upon a set of operational rules for an efficient flow of information from the forecasting and policy analysis system to the monetary policy committee (the Bank Board of the CNB). This involved the time frame of the forecast for timely presentation before board decision meetings, personal responsibilities, and clear deadlines at each stage.

The switch to QPM-gap in July 2002 kicked off inflation-forecast targeting in the Czech Republic: the model had the appropriate medium-term focus, it included forward-looking expectations and policy responses, the monetary policy transmission mechanism had an internal channel (through a forward-looking interest rate term structure) and an external channel (through the exchange rate), and, last but not least, it had an endogenous policy interest rate.

Figure 10.7 outlines the structure. The model disaggregates inflation, with separate Phillips curves for core, food, and fuel inflation, and exogenous administered prices. The latter aspect smoothed the transition from the previous near-term forecasting inflation-forecasting method. An aggregate output gap represents the real side of the economy. The team developed tools to decompose

Figure 10.7. Czech National Bank's QPM-Gap Model: Extended Version from January 2007

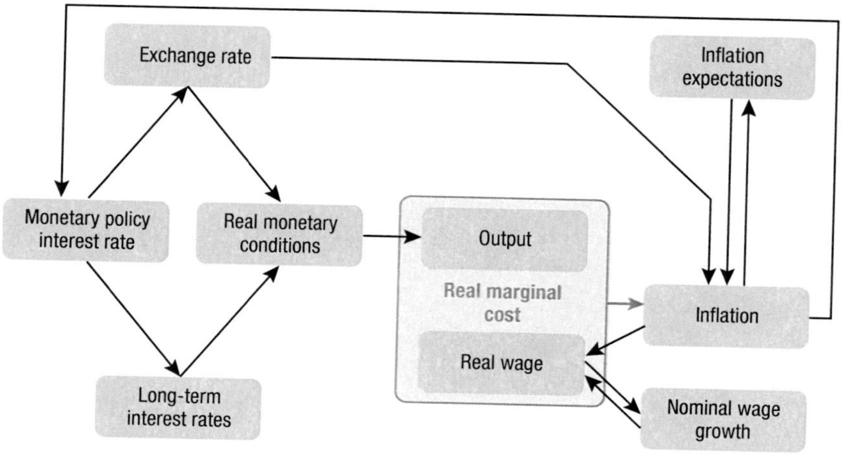

Source: Czech National Bank, Inflation Report, I/2007.

the aggregate GDP forecast from QPM-gap into expenditure components, as policymakers wanted to see forecasts for household consumption, government consumption, investment, exports, and imports.

The Czech experience bears out that QPM-gap–style models are a good, practical starting point in the early years of inflation targeting. They provide the necessary features to facilitate forward-looking monetary policy discussion. At the same time, they are adaptable to different—and evolving—country circumstances and are not too demanding on human and other resources. In the Czech case, there were three material modifications to QPM-gap during its six years as the core forecasting model.

First, staff members recalibrated the assumptions about long-term equilibrium paths, with an increase in the rate of appreciation of the equilibrium real exchange rate and a reduction in the domestic real equilibrium interest rate. These changes were motivated by forecast errors, in particular by an observed uptrend in the real exchange rate that was not having a visible negative effect on the real economy. The second modification explicitly recognized wage developments as a factor in CPI inflation. The real wage gap was added to the output gap as a component of the real marginal cost gap. This extension of QPM-gap drew on work for the new DSGE model, GPM-g3. Third, staff members reduced the second-round effects of administrative measures and other short-term cost-push shocks in the Phillips curve. This was in line with the observed weakening of pass-through effects and lower inflation persistence—developments that reflected the anchoring of long-term inflation expectations at the target rate.

TABLE 10.1.

Comparison of QPM-g3 and QPM-gap	
QPM-g3	**QPM-gap**
Explicit derivation using "behavioral principles"	Reduced form
Model-consistent expectations	Model-consistent expectations
Stock-flow consistency	Flows only
Basic national accounts disaggregation	No GDP structure
Works with level variables	Works with "gaps"
Balanced-growth path with technology trends	Equilibrium trends
Simple fiscal block	Implicit treatment
Inflation-forecast-based interest rate reaction function	Inflation-forecast-based interest rate reaction function
Carefully chosen "structural shocks"	Residuals for each equation

Sources: Andrle and others 2009; and Czech National Bank.

Advanced Inflation-Forecast Targeting: A DSGE Model

In 2008, the CNB switched to QPM-g3 as its core quarterly projection model.[11] Table 10.1 provides a comparison between QPM-gap and QPM-g3. The newer model is based on explicit behavioral principles. It preserves stock-flow consistency, whereas QPM-gap defined cyclical gaps from prefiltered trends. Since QPM-g3 disaggregates GDP on national accounts lines, it directly yields forecasts for the major components of spending.[12] However, for components of inflation, the modeling and projections team developed satellite models using Kalman-filter methods.

Although the use of DSGE models for forecasting has been questioned (Fukač and Pagan 2006), the forecasting performance for inflation on the monetary policy horizon has improved since 2008. Relatively large errors in the aftermath of the global financial crisis can be attributed to wrong assumptions rather than to a wrong model. The disaggregated nature and the structural form of QPM-g3 have provided ways to incorporate judgment in a consistent way (Brůha and others 2013). At the same time, the forecasting team has been able to develop procedures for using the QPM-g3 model to address the effective lower bound constraint on the policy interest rate (Franta and others 2014).

Near-Term Forecasts in the Forecasting and Policy Analysis System

The forecasting process should allow efficient use of expert judgment. This implies some near-term forecasting input in the baseline forecast. Sectoral experts

---

[11]The CNB was introduced to DSGE models by IMF technical assistance. However, CNB modelers developed QPM-g3 from scratch. It was the first DSGE model to be used as a core quarterly projection model in an inflation-forecast-targeting central bank.

[12]See http://www.cnb.cz/en/monetary_policy/inflation_reports/2008/2008_III/boxes_annexes/ir_2008_III_box_1.html for the sectoral and production structure of the QPM-g3 model.

pay close attention to short-term idiosyncratic factors and may use a variety of models to inform their forecasts, such as single-equation indicator models. Informed judgment easily outperforms model forecasts for current and next-quarter GDP.

Brůha and others (2013) provide several case studies from the CNB's experience to show how expert information can be usefully incorporated into a structural framework during turbulent times. Even when such adjustments have no effect on the policy outlook, their inclusion may reassure an informed audience that the forecast has not ignored material events. For example, after the global financial crisis, the "cash-for-clunkers" subsidies introduced in western Europe to boost slumping demand for new autos made headlines. They moderated the decline in Czech exports, but at the same time reduced selling pressure on the koruna: the forecast assessment of the overall impact on the Czech inflation rate and interest rate was neutral. It was nevertheless important to incorporate the subsidies explicitly into the forecast, because otherwise the CNB board and outsiders might have thought that the forecast story had forgotten something obvious.

A managerial issue is to make sure that the modeling team and sectoral experts cooperate effectively. At the CNB, before 2004, the near-term forecasting team and the modeling and projections team were in separate divisions (Real Economy Division and Economic Modeling Division) (Figure 10.8). This created tension during integration of near- and medium-term forecasts. In 2003, board members expressed dissatisfaction with the forecasting process.[13]

A restructuring in 2004 merged the two teams into a single Macroeconomic Forecasting Division (Figure 10.8). A division director became responsible for managing the whole forecast process and for making sure that both groups make cooperative input into the final forecast. A department-wide forecasting team of about 10 people now ensures that the other divisions of the department are actively involved in forecasting. All divisions send experts to the team, which reports to the management of the department and presents its work at several departmental meetings during each forecasting round. The team head, chosen from the core model operators, presents the forecast at meetings with the board.

Since 2004, CNB macroeconomic forecasts have used near-term forecasting estimates only for the most recent quarter (nowcasts) and for one quarter ahead. The team also prepares forecasts for regulated prices, indirect tax changes, and government consumption, which are exogenous inputs into the general-equilibrium core model over the whole forecast horizon. Similar treatment applies to the foreign economic outlook (from the External Economic Analyses Division), and to fiscal impulse estimates (from the Monetary Policy and Fiscal Analyses Division).

---

[13]For example, very critical remarks can be found in the transcript for the October 30, 2003, board meeting (Czech only): http://www.cnb.cz/miranda2/export/sites/www.cnb.cz/cs/menova _politika/br_zapisy_z_jednani/2003/2003_10_30/pt_10_SZ_30_10_03.pdf.

Figure 10.8. Evolution of the Organizational Structure at the Czech National Bank

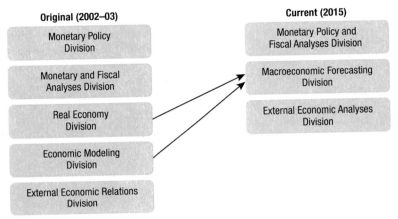

Source: Czech National Bank.

Reckoning for Uncertainty

Decision-making is trickiest amid high uncertainty—for example, during the global financial crisis, the European sovereign debt crisis, and following the first encounter with the effective lower bound. In such situations, the central bank's board may request alternative scenarios and sensitivity analyses to see how different assumptions would change the outlook. A model-based forecasting system greatly facilitates this process. In contrast, to produce even one such scenario under a pure near-term forecasting system would require time-consuming iterations and negotiations among sectoral specialists. Policymakers have found the capacity for systematic examination of alternative feasible outcomes reassuring (Tůma 2010).[14] Forecasting tools that help policymakers promptly, at the very time they are weighing risks of alternative actions, have special value (Hampl 2014).

The Human Resource Input

An effective forecasting and policy analysis system team does not have to be large, but it does need a balance of complementary skills. CNB experience suggests that the process can begin with a relatively small team and can be strengthened over time. Specialized modeling skills are not acquired quickly, either through training

---

[14]Tůma (2010): "The forecasting system must give the policymakers the comfort in making these ex ante decisions under uncertainty. This implies that forecasting accuracy is not as important as the ability to consistently differentiate between various alternative future developments. Our forecasting system has developed over the years to a truly disciplining tool for the policy debates and a platform for analyzing risks and their policy implications. These properties made it an acceptable tool for the policymakers."

of existing staff or through recruitment. In both cases, it is more important to have a good match between job requirements and individual skills than to fill open positions without delay. This said, narrow specialization is unhelpful, either from the cooperative viewpoint of team output or from the individual viewpoint of the careers of team members. Diversification of skills can be achieved over time through encouraging staff members to take an interest in the broader aspects of the work of the team and through timely job rotation—policies that are at the same time likely to improve the work environment and the quality of output.

In 1998, most economists in the CNB's Monetary Department worked as sectoral specialists, focusing on analyses of the real economy, monetary developments, and the balance of payments. The department's output was largely descriptive and statistically oriented material. Forecasting was based on judgment and simple near-term methods. There was a widespread belief within the CNB staff at the time, reflected in the models in use, that the short-term interest rate had a negligible effect on aggregate demand. Monetary policy modeling at the central bank involved few economists. When policy was mainly directed at maintaining the exchange rate peg, this lack of a core macroeconomic framework was of little importance.

In the 1990s the supply of well-qualified Czech macroeconomics graduates was very limited, but the Czech education system did provide high-quality training in mathematics and other technical subjects. The few economists at the CNB that did focus on modern macroeconomic analysis produced work of high technical quality. Moreover, by the turn of the century, graduates well-schooled in modern macroeconomics were emerging from the universities, and the CNB became a successful recruiter.

Purely technical knowledge, however, is insufficient—all forecasting and policy analysis system staff should have at least some acquaintance with modern, open-economy, macroeconomic theory, and the leadership should be experts in the field. Economists with a talent for synthesizing various strands of thought, and with drafting skills, can shape the central bank's economic story of a forecast into an intelligible narrative, without losing the technical insights. (The right amount of technical detail depends on the audience—for example, policymakers or academics would demand more than journalists or the general public.)

CNB senior management has continued to support the forecasting and policy analysis system. By acknowledging that its input made a difference to their decisions, policymakers have boosted morale and created a strong incentive for staff members to remain with the team and perform well. Moreover, the opportunity to acquire valuable know-how and to add to individual human capital is also a motivating factor.

Forecasting at a central bank involves an intensive schedule of meetings and rigid deadlines. Solutions must be found for unexpected economic or technical problems.[15] Compromises must be struck between differing staff views on various

---

[15]Time pressure on staff, as well as the risk of errors, can be reduced by investing in automated data management, production of charts, tables and presentations, and so on.

issues. Presentations for policymakers have to be prepared on short timelines. And at least once a quarter, forecast error evaluations should be made.[16] The nature of the work puts pressure on the forecasting team and can result in significant stress.[17]

The CNB allows forecast team members the opportunity to take breaks to work on other projects with less stressful deadlines and longer planning horizons (for example, model development, near-term forecast work, training, or even secondments to some other central bank or research institution). At the CNB, economists regularly switch between forecasting and research. Ideally, the selected research projects focus on some aspect of model development, for example, extensions with new blocks.[18]

Experience at the CNB (and also at other central banks) suggests that research by forecasting and policy analysis system members is more fruitful than external research for core model improvements—in part because the costs of knowledge transfer are so much less. On the other hand, research projects should not be vetted narrowly. It is never clear where the next good idea is going to come from.

Even an appreciative working environment and a system of job rotation that allows staff members time to pursue—and publish—other research interests cannot ensure that crucial staff members are retained. In principle, the economics staff should be sufficiently flexible that, between forecasts, the entire forecasting and policy analysis system team could be switched for another—with outgoing members taking over the functions of the incoming. Not that such a switch would ever be a good idea in practice, but the potential to do it defines an ideal standard for adequate backup.

To the same end, models and data sets should be fully documented and stored such that they are accessible to the whole team and not just to individuals who might leave at some point.

Ownership of the Forecast

Ownership of the forecast—who decides the guiding assumptions and judgments—reflects the management structure of the central bank, the nature of its monetary policy decision-making, the extent to which policymakers shape

---

[16]Each quarter, CNB staff do a forecast evaluation based on a detailed model-consistent analysis of the factors contributing to forecast errors. The results of these evaluations are presented to the policymakers. They help identify priority areas for model improvement.

[17]The modeling and projections team has grown to six economists. The enlargement of the team made it possible to create a rotational system composed of two three-member teams, which rotate every year between forecasting and model development. During each calendar year, one of the three-member teams is responsible for the forecast and the other does model development and economic research to support the forecasting and policy analysis system.

[18]During the initial period of the global financial crisis, policymakers were concerned with the role of financial frictions in the transmission mechanism. To test the forecasting model for the presence (and size) of shocks originated from the financial sector, the model was extended to include a financial block. This work was carried out by those members of the forecast team who were not responsible for forecasting at the time.

the assumptions, and existing requirements for accountability. Since these differ in important ways across countries, one cannot speak about universal best practices.

The main forecast considered for policy decisions can be labeled interchangeably as a board (or monetary policy committee) forecast, a staff forecast, or a central bank forecast.[19] There is no hard and fast delineation among these labels. They are all central bank forecasts, in that the institution is ultimately responsible for their production—it provides the resources, it publishes results, and it acknowledges their influence on policy decisions. Under any arrangement, one assumes that the central bank would always in the event of criticism defend the integrity of the forecasting process and the quality of the underlying research. At the same time, nobody would expect it to defend any particular aspect of any given projection.

The CNB Inflation Report describes forecast ownership in the following way:

> The forecast is the key, but not the only, input to our monetary policy decision-making. Unless the economic situation requires an extraordinary monetary policy meeting, the Bank Board meets eight times a year to discuss monetary policy issues. At four of the meetings (in February, May, August and November) we discuss a new forecast, while at the other four (in March, June, September and December) we discuss the risks and uncertainties of the most recent forecast in the light of newly available information on domestic and foreign economic developments. Due to the arrival of new information since the forecast was drawn up and to the possibility of the Bank Board members assessing its risks differently, the decision we adopt may not fully correspond to the message of the forecast prepared by our experts. (CNB Inflation Report, IV/2017)

The substantive difference between the CNB forecast and an official central bank forecast lies in the degree to which the forecast is the basis for actual policy. If the forecast by design reflects the view of policymakers, it is official, and the key aspects are theirs to defend. Operationally, an official forecast would apply when board or monetary policy committee members, or the central bank governor, are heavily involved in forecasting (for example, the Reserve Bank of New Zealand). Given their involvement, policymakers have little room to deviate from the official forecast: they are accountable for it.

Board responsibility for the shape of a forecast would not be feasible at the CNB. The board is not just a monetary policy decision-making body. It also oversees the management of the central bank as an institution, a function that involves a wide range of highly technical, sensitive, and time-consuming responsibilities, including the supervision of the whole Czech financial system. This limits the time that individual board members can devote to monetary policy. Time-tracking software used by the vice-governor overseeing the Monetary Department showed that he devoted only 10 percent of his time to monetary policy (Hampl 2014). Staff members meet with the board only twice during each

---

[19]Policymakers may have forecasts of their own. For example, the Federal Open Market Committee of the Federal Reserve publishes summaries of the economic projections of members.

forecasting exercise—once focused on assumptions and initial conditions and the other meeting on alternative and sensitivity scenarios. In effect, decision-making, and the communication strategy of board members, may be quite individualistic, as frequently surfaces in split votes.[20] On occasion, the board as a whole may differ from the staff forecast.

The question of ownership is related to issues of communications and transparency. When monetary policy decisions are made by votes in a committee—as opposed to consensus or by the governor—each member may be basing their vote on an independent, informal, forecast. The staff forecast, however, is likely to be the only fully coherent macroeconomic projection. It is also likely to be the point of departure for the various member outlooks and the basis of reference for policy discussions. So, it has intrinsic interest from the viewpoint of public accountability, even if it is not necessarily the overriding factor in a committee vote.

The fact that board members may express reservations may have eased the decision of the CNB to go for full disclosure. The central banks of Israel, Norway, Sweden, and the United States, which also maintain highly transparent communications, also make decisions by committee vote. This has not, however, been an overriding factor: in New Zealand, the Reserve Bank of New Zealand has full disclosure, yet the governor alone is accountable for policy actions and is engaged in the forecast process.

COMMUNICATIONS AND TRANSPARENCY

Early Awkwardness

At the outset of inflation targeting, when the CNB relied on near-term forecasting methods, interest rates (as well as the exchange rate) were assumed to be constant over the forecast horizon. There was no need to think about publication of the interest rate path. But such a forecast ignored the nominal anchor responsibility of monetary policy, and was thus not internally consistent (Skořepa and Kotlán 2006). Nor was it easily comparable to forecasts of financial market analysts and other institutions, which incorporated their best guess about future monetary policy. The forecast did not provide quantified guidance on the likely direction and speed of actions required to achieve policy objectives. And when the policy rate was changed, in a direction consistent with the inflation pressures in the most recent forecast, the CNB faced questions on whether this forecast was now still valid, and if not, what an updated forecast would look like. These were hard to answer with any clarity given the lack of well-defined monetary policy transmission in the existing CNB forecasting models.

---

[20]See http://www.cnb.cz/en/monetary_policy/bank_board_minutes/voting_of_the_bank_board .xlsx for voting of the CNB Bank Board.

Increasing Transparency with the Forecasting and Policy Analysis System

Following the introduction of QPM-gap and a properly structured forecasting and policy analysis system, in 2002, the forecast did include an endogenous interest rate path (for the three-month Prague interbank offered rate [PRIBOR]). Press conferences and inflation reports for some years gave only a qualitative description of the path.

This was, and still is, the most common approach. For example, Mishkin (2004) states the following:

> Although economists understand that any policy path projected by the central bank is inherently conditional because changes in the state of the economy will require a change in the policy path, the public is far less likely to understand this. When new information comes in and the central bank changes the policy-rate from its projected path, the public may see this as a reneging on its announced policy or an indication that the central bank's previous policy settings were a mistake.

However, the risk-of-confusion argument became less convincing in view of the combined experiences of inflation-forecast-targeting central banks, and their capacity to underline the conditionality of the projection through the presentation of confidence bands around the baseline path, and alternative scenarios.

Clear Language and Explanation

Modelers and forecasters do not necessarily write well. At the CNB, the managers of the Monetary Department, who typically are economists with good communications skills, play an important role in editing the final versions of the reports, using their experience with communications to the board to strike the right balance between technical rigor and digestibility.

Model changes require careful explanation to policymakers. When QPM-g3 replaced QPM-gap, some concepts familiar to the board members disappeared, replaced with new ones. For example, QPM-g3 replaced the output gap with endogenous real marginal costs of producing consumer goods and with firms' markups. The change was difficult for board members to digest.[21] Several rounds of nontechnical presentations of the new model to the board members were needed to facilitate the transition. Since then, staff give regular presentations to new board members on the forecast process and materials.

Toward Full Disclosure

While the qualitative description of the interest rate forecast generally helped move the term structure of rates in the desired direction, opinion in the board shifted toward explicit disclosure. In early 2008, the CNB decided to publish the forecast path for the three-month PRIBOR, in a fan chart with confidence bands

---

[21]Hampl 2014, slide 23.

based on past forecast errors.[22] This step was taken to enhance the transparency of the CNB forecast and the associated monetary policy decisions, and to increase the effectiveness of monetary policy transmission. At the same time, the confidence bands illustrated the degree of uncertainty, and the conditional nature, of the published path.

Over time the CNB has broadened, deepened, and quickened its communications on policy actions. The board issues a press release immediately after the decision is taken, and the Governor gives a press conference the same afternoon. The monetary policy decision is explained either in the context of a new macroeconomic forecast (four times a year), or, for interforecast policy meetings, of a risk assessment to the previous quarterly forecast (also four times a year since 2008).[23] The presentations give the votes cast by the board members on interest rate decisions. Since 2014, the governor has provided a written explanation of the decision, followed by a question and answer session. Eight days after the policy meeting, the CNB publishes the minutes (with the individual votes since 2008), and the Inflation Report, which has full details of the forecast. Over time, the structure of the Inflation Report has evolved to put more emphasis on the forward-looking content and to deliver a more concise message.

Another regular means of communication is a schedule of quarterly meetings with financial market analysts (both local and foreign), at which senior staff present the new macroeconomic forecast, followed by a discussion with one or two board members. These meetings take place one day after the policy decision announcement, along with the release of the Executive Summary of the Inflation Report, which includes a detailed forecast table.[24]

In all, outside observers see the CNB as in the *avant-garde* of transparency in the conduct of monetary policy. Dincer and Eichengreen (2014) calculate an index of central bank transparency based on five broad criteria (political, economic, procedural, policy, and operational), each of which has three subcategories. The index for 2014 places the CNB as the second-most transparent central bank in the sample of more than 100, with a score of 14.5 out of a maximum 15.

Has the CNB gone too far? Former Governor Tůma (2010), after his departure, expressed doubts about the net benefits of publishing board votes by name: "[O]n the margin, publishing of individual votes goes too far and may actually be detrimental to good policy . . . the greater transparency may lead to a more opportunistic behavior of the chairman and less frequent swing votes by the Board members." On the other hand, in 2013 some board members felt discomfort

---

[22]This decision was announced on March 8, 2007.

[23]Between 2009 and mid-2013, the CNB published a fan chart for the endogenous CZK/EUR exchange rate at the press conference—a practice that was suspended between November 2013 and January 2018, when the CNB used an exchange rate floor as an unconventional monetary policy instrument.

[24]The board publishes a full transcript of policy meetings with a delay of six years. The six-year lag was chosen to match the term in office of individual board members to avoid inhibiting frank and open debate. This publication has yet to attract much attention from academics or journalists.

when the board decided not to publish the individual votes and to restrict communication of individual opinions on the exchange rate. This was intended as a special measure to avoid any confusion among the public that differing individual voices within the board might create (Franta and others 2014).

MANAGING EXPECTATIONS—THE EXCHANGE RATE INSTRUMENT EXPERIENCE[25]

By 2010, the Czech economy seemed to be recovering from the postcrisis recession. But in late 2011, the marked slowdown in the euro area and continuing domestic fiscal consolidation began to put a damper on growth. By the second half of 2012, inflation was below the 2 percent target and output was below potential. As the CNB inflation forecast signaled further undershooting of the target, the central bank cut policy rates to the effective lower bound in November 2012. Yet the projections suggested that a further easing in monetary conditions was necessary. The central bank needed a new policy instrument to provide the monetary ease needed to reach the inflation target.

Svensson (2001) advocates that exchange rate management be a complementary monetary policy tool to escape the effective lower bound problem. CNB analysis concluded that weakening the nominal exchange rate would indeed be an effective strategy against a cyclical slowdown (Franta and others 2014). The modeling and projections team adapted QPM-g3 to derive model-consistent scenarios in which the exchange rate is effectively an additional instrument. Model simulations reported in Figure 10.9, which roughly replicate real-time results available in 2013, show the effects of a fully anticipated 5 percent weakening of the exchange rate for various projected durations at the effective lower bound. The combined effect of these interest rate and exchange rate channels—which depend entirely on expectations—produces a significant increase over the medium term in real GDP growth and inflation. Since 24 percent of the CPI basket is directly imported, and another 9 percentage points is imported as intermediate inputs, the strong impact is not surprising.

Implementation of such a strategy would require managing expectations because the exchange rate, unlike the policy interest rate, is not under the direct control of the central bank. To further complicate matters, the high degree of capital mobility imposes a link between expected short-term interest rates in the Czech Republic and the exchange value of the koruna. For example, the longer the expected interest rate stays at the floor, the greater the depreciation of the exchange rate. Macro models embody this link in an uncovered interest parity condition, modified to allow a time-varying risk premium.

In autumn 2013, the CNB announced that it would add the exchange rate as an additional tool for easing monetary conditions within the context of the inflation-forecast-targeting framework: "The CNB will intervene on the foreign

---

[25]For more on the CNB's experience of adding the exchange rate as a complementary monetary policy tool to stimulate the economy when the policy rate is at the effective lower bound, see Alichi and others (2015), Clinton and others (2017), and Franta and others (2014).

Figure 10.9. QPM-g3 Model Impulse Responses to a Fully Anticipated 5 Percent Weakening of the Exchange Rate for Different Lengths of Stay at the Effective Lower Bound

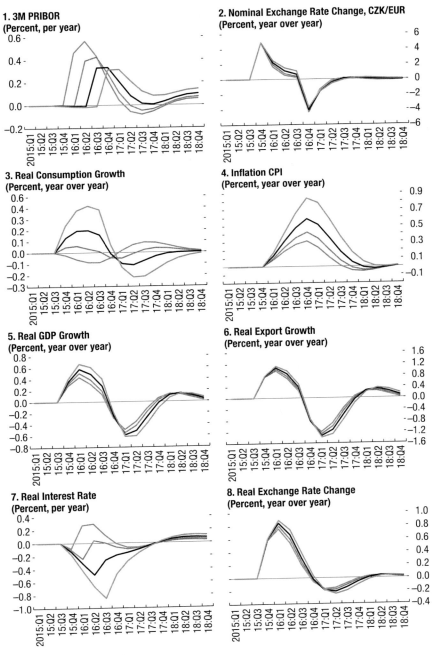

Source: Czech National Bank.
Note: CPI = consumer price index; PRIBOR = Prague interbank offered rate.

TABLE 10.2.

Czech Republic: Inflation Expectations (Annual percent)			
	2014	**2015**	**2016**	**Long-Term Target**
Sep. 2013 Survey	1.6	1.8	2.0	2.0
Apr. 2014 Survey	1.2	2.2	2.0	2.0
Change (percentage point)	−0.4	0.4	0.0	0.0

Source: Consensus Economics.

exchange market to weaken the koruna so that the exchange rate of the koruna against the euro is close to CZK27."[26]

Ideally, the strategy would increase short- to medium-term inflation expectations without deanchoring long-term expectations. For this purpose, the exchange rate must be perceived as a temporary tool, not an additional longer-term objective, so that the public believes that the central bank remains committed to its longer-term 2 percent inflation target. The CNB therefore underlined to the public that the exchange rate policy was subject to revision as conditions changed. The communications worked. Long-term expectations of inflation held firm at the target rate (Table 10.2).

In the exchange market, financial market participants understood that the CNB was using the exchange rate tool only temporarily to boost economic activity and to avoid the risk of deflation. They realized too that the CNB had unlimited intervention power to buy foreign currency since it could supply koruna indefinitely. The credibility of the policy was such that to achieve the desired depreciation the CNB bought foreign exchange over just two days. The koruna then traded at or above 27 per euro for three years, without any further CNB intervention.

During this period, growth picked up, and the output gap closed. Industrial production growth moved from a low of just over 3 percent in September 2013 to over 5 percent by August 2014, reflecting in part the effect of depreciation on exports. Inflation remained somewhat lower than expected, partly because of administered prices, some of which declined. The exchange rate depreciation nevertheless played an important role in the Czech Republic's averting the strong disinflationary tendencies evident elsewhere in the European Union.

---

[26]In a subsequent question and answer session, the CNB clarified that the intervention is one sided: "What does the CNB's exchange rate commitment mean for the future evolution of the koruna exchange rate? This means the CNB has undertaken to prevent excessive appreciation of the koruna below CZK27/EUR. On the stronger side of the CZK27/EUR level, the CNB is preventing the koruna from appreciating further by intervening on the foreign exchange market, that is, by selling koruna and buying euro. On the weaker side of the CZK27/EUR level, the CNB is allowing the koruna exchange rate to float. In other words, the exchange rate will be close to CZK27 to the euro or even weaker in the period ahead. Potential fluctuations to levels weaker than CZK27/EUR will be determined by supply and demand on the interbank foreign exchange market."

One should be careful about generalizing from the Czech experience with exchange rate policy. Its apparent success depended to a large extent on the strong credibility of the inflation-targeting program that has been built over a period of many years. And the CNB has cultivated streamlined links to the communications media, which allowed it to get out effectively to the public the nuances and conditions of the policy. Not all central banks possess these advantages. Furthermore, the Czech Republic is a small economy: its deliberate exchange rate depreciation did not create the same concerns about a beggar-thy-neighbor policy, and about retaliation, that would arise if a large economy employed the same strategy.

CONCLUSIONS

This chapter describes the development and practice of inflation-forecast targeting in the Czech Republic since the turn of the century. A remarkable feature of the history is that over the course of a decade, Czech monetary policy went from a primitive condition, in a country with very limited experience with the functioning of a modern market economy, to the state of the art.

The record of the CNB for controlling inflation under the inflation-forecast-targeting regime stands up well in any international comparison. Expectations for long-term inflation in the Czech Republic have been firmly anchored at the target rate of 2 percent. It is not too important that actual year-over-year inflation has often been significantly off target. The key to keeping public confidence has been that, in the event of any deviation from target, the central bank—consistently and visibly—has acted to return inflation to target over the medium term.

Underlying the transformation of policy conduct within the central bank was a commitment to establishing and maintaining a forecasting and policy analysis system adequate for the implementation of inflation-forecast targeting. This has required an ongoing investment in human capital, the development of up-to-date models for forecasting and policy analysis, institutional reorganizations to allow efficient provision of relevant economic intelligence to inform policy decisions, and improvements in the dialogue between economists and policymakers to ensure that they were working from mutually comprehensible assumptions. One of the benefits of model-based forecasting has been that the CNB can explain its policy actions with a transparent, coherent, economic narrative. This has enabled a bold opening of external communications, with complete disclosure of the central bank's economic forecast. Outside assessments of central bank transparency have placed the CNB near the top of the international ranking.

Within the Czech Republic, there is much more awareness today than at the start of the century about monetary policy issues. Media coverage has become better informed. More important for the long term has been the growth of interest in monetary policy at the universities and the emergence of a generation of highly qualified, policy-oriented monetary theorists and model builders. This has given the central bank and other institutions a deep pool of talent. The ability to recruit and maintain in-house human capital, of sufficient size and flexibility to cope with turnover, is crucial for the sustainability of an effective forecasting and policy analysis system.

Internationally, the CNB has become a recognized leader for the formulation and conduct of monetary policy. Despite its relatively small size, the Czech central bank has become an important contributor of technical assistance. Model builders from the CNB have had a major influence on the models used for inflation targeting at numerous central banks.

REFERENCES AND OTHER RESOURCES

Alichi, A., J. Benes, J. Felman, I. Feng, C. Freedman, D. Laxton, E. Tanner, D. Vavra, and H. Wang. 2015. "Frontiers of Monetary Policymaking: Adding the Exchange Rate as a Tool to Combat Deflationary Risks in the Czech Republic." IMF Working Paper 15/74, International Monetary Fund, Washington, DC.

Alichi, A., H. Chen, K. Clinton, C. Freedman, M. Johnson, O. Kamenik, T. Kışınbay, and D. Laxton. 2009. "Inflation Targeting under Imperfect Policy Credibility." IMF Working Paper 09/94, International Monetary Fund, Washington, DC.

Andrle, M., T. Hlédik, O. Kameník, and J. Vlček. 2009. "Implementing the New Structural Model of the Czech National Bank." CNB Working Paper 2/2009, Czech National Bank, Prague.

Antoničová, Z., K. Musil, L. Růžička, and J. Vlček. 2008. "Evaluation of the Quality and Success Rate of Forecasts—A Historic Overview." In *Evaluation of the Fulfilment of the CNB's Inflation Targets 1998–2007*, edited by K. Šmídková. Prague: Czech National Bank.

Arbatli, E., D. Botman, K. Clinton, P. Cova, V. Gaspar, Z. Jakab, D. Laxton, C. Lonkeng Ngouana, J. Mongardini, and H. Wang. 2016. "Reflating Japan: Time to Get Unconventional?" IMF Working Paper 16/157, International Monetary Fund, Washington, DC.

Archer, D. 2005. "Central Bank Communications and the Publication of Interest Rate Projections." A paper for a Sveriges Riksbank conference on inflation targeting, Stockholm, June.

Argov, E., A. Binyamini, D. Elkayam, and I. Rozenshtrom. 2007. "A Small Macroeconomic Model to Support Inflation Targeting in Israel." Bank of Israel, Monetary Department.

Argov, E., N. Epstein, P. Karam, D. Laxton, and D. Rose. 2007. "Endogenous Monetary Policy Credibility in a Small Structural Model of Israel." IMF Working Paper 07/207, International Monetary Fund, Washington, DC.

Batini, N., K. Kuttner, and D. Laxton. 2005. "Does Inflation Targeting Work in Emerging Markets?" Chapter IV in *World Economic Outlook*, September, International Monetary Fund, Washington, DC.

Benes, J., K. Clinton, R. Garcia-Saltos, M. Johnson, D. Laxton, P. Manchev, and T. Matheson. 2010. "Estimating Potential Output with a Multivariate Filter." IMF Working Paper 10/285, International Monetary Fund, Washington, DC.

Benes, J., K. Clinton, M. Johnson, D. Laxton, and T. Matheson. 2010. "Structural Models in Real Time." IMF Working Paper 10/56, International Monetary Fund, Washington, DC.

Benes, J., M. Kumhof, D. Laxton, D. Muir, and S. Mursula. 2013. "The Benefits of International Policy Coordination Revisited." IMF Working Paper 13/262, International Monetary Fund, Washington, DC.

Blanchard, O., and J. Galí. 2007. "The Macroeconomic Effects of Oil Shocks: Why Are the 2000s So Different from the 1970s?" NBER Working Paper 13368, National Bureau of Economic Research, Cambridge, MA.

Brázdik, F., Z. Humplová, and F. Kopřiva. 2014. "Evaluating a Structural Model Forecast: Decomposition Approach." CNB Research and Policy Note 2/2014, Czech National Bank, Prague.

Brůha, J., T. Hlédik, T. Holub, J. Polanský, and J. Tonner. 2013. "Incorporating Judgments and Dealing with Data Uncertainty in Forecasting at the Czech National Bank." CNB Research and Policy Note 3/2013, Czech National Bank, Prague.

Capek, A., T. Hledik, V. Kotlan, S. Polak, and D. Vavra. 2003. "Historical Perspective on the Development of the Forecasting and Policy Analysis System." In *The Czech National Bank's Forecasting and Policy Analysis System*, edited by W. Coats, D. Laxton, and D. Rose. Prague: Czech National Bank.

Clinton K., T. Hlédik, T. Holub, D. Laxton, and H. Wang. 2017. "Czech Magic: Implementing Inflation-Forecast Targeting at the CNB." IMF Working Paper 17/21, January, International Monetary Fund, Washington, DC.

Clinton, K., M. Johnson, O. Kamenik, and D. Laxton. 2010. "International Deflation Risks under Alternative Macroeconomic Policies." *Journal of Japanese and International Economies* 24 (2): 140–77.

Coats, W., ed. 2000. *Inflation Targeting in Transition Economies: The Case of the Czech Republic.* Prague: Czech National Bank.

Coats, W., D. Laxton, and D. Rose, eds. 2003. *The Czech National Bank's Forecasting and Policy Analysis System*. Prague: Czech National Bank.

Czech National Bank. 2008. Inflation Report I, February.

———. 2017. Inflation Report IV/2017.

Dincer, N., and B. Eichengreen. 2014. "Central Bank Transparency and Independence: Updates and New Measures." *International Journal of Central Banking* 10 (1): 189–253.

Filardo, A., and B. Hoffman. 2014. "Forward Guidance at the Zero Lower Bound." *BIS Quarterly Review*, March. Bank for International Settlements, Basel.

Franta, M., T. Holub, P. Král, I. Kubicová, K. Šmídková, and B. Vašíček. 2014. "The Exchange Rate as an Instrument at Zero Interest Rates: The Case of the Czech Republic." Research and Policy Notes 3, Czech National Bank, Prague.

Freedman, C., M. Kumhof, D. Laxton, D. Muir, and S. Mursula. 2010. "Global Effects of Fiscal Stimulus during the Crisis." *Journal of Monetary Economics* 57 (5):506–26.

Freedman, C., D. Laxton, and I. Ötker-Robe. "On Implementing Full-Fledged Inflation-Targeting Regimes: Saying What You Do and Doing What You Say." n.d. Unpublished.

Freedman, C., and I. Ötker-Robe. 2009. "Country Experiences with the Introduction and Implementation of Inflation Targeting." IMF Working Paper 09/161, July, International Monetary Fund, Washington, DC.

Filáček, J. 2007. "Why and How to Assess Inflation-Target Fulfillment." *Finance a úvěr— Czech Journal of Economics and Finance* 57 (12): 577–94.

———, and B. Saxa. 2010. "Central Bank Forecasts as a Coordination Device." CNB Working Paper 13/2010, Czech National Bank, Prague.

Fukač, M., and A. Pagan. 2006. "Issues in Adopting DSGE Models for Use in the Policy Process." CNB Working Paper 6/2006, Czech National Bank, Prague.

Gagnon, J., M. Raskin, J. Remache, and B. Sack. 2011. "The Financial Market Effects of the Federal Reserve's Large-Scale Asset Purchases." *International Journal of Central Banking*, 7 (1): 3–43.

Hájková, D., and J. Hurník. 2007. "Cobb-Douglas Production Function: The Case of a Converging Economy." *Czech Journal of Economics and Finance* 57 (9–10): 465–76.

Hampl, M. 2014. "Monetary Policy in a Small Open Economy: A Decision Maker's Perspective." Presentation at Africa Training Institute/IMF Institute for Capacity Development, Mauritius, June 25.

Holub, T., and J. Hurník. 2008. "Ten Years of Czech Inflation Targeting: Missed Targets and Anchored Expectations." *Emerging Markets Finance and Trade* 44 (6): 67–86.

Hunt, B., D. Rose, and A. Scott. 2000. "The Core Model of the Reserve Bank of New Zealand's Forecasting and Policy System." *Economic Modelling* 17 (2): 247–74.

Ingves, S. 2007. "Monetary Policy, Openness and Financial Markets." Speech at Skandinaviska Enskilda Banken, Stockholm, September 24.

Isard, P., and D. Laxton. 2000. "Inflation-Forecast Targeting and the Role of Macroeconomic Models." In *Inflation Targeting in Transition Economies: The Case of the Czech Republic*, edited by Warren Coates. Prague: Czech National Bank.

———. 2000. "Issues Relating to Inflation Targeting and the Bank of England's Framework." In *IMF Staff Country Report 00/106*. Washington, DC: International Monetary Fund.

———, and A. Eliasson. 2001. "Inflation Targeting with NAIRU Uncertainty and Endogenous Policy Credibility." *Journal of Economic Dynamics and Control* 25: 115–48.

Laxton, D. 2008. "Getting to Know the Global Economy Model and Its Philosophy." *IMF Staff Papers* 55 (2): 213–42.

———, and P. N'Diaye. 2002. "Monetary Policy Credibility and the Unemployment-Inflation Nexus: Some Evidence from Seventeen OECD Countries." IMF Working Paper 02/220, International Monetary Fund, Washington, DC.

Laxton, D., and P. Pesenti. 2003. "Monetary Rules for Small, Open, Emerging Economies." *Journal of Monetary Economics* 50 (5): 1109–46.

Laxton, D., D. Rose, and A. Scott. 2009. "Developing a Structured Forecasting and Policy Analysis System." IMF Working Paper 09/65, International Monetary Fund, Washington, DC.

Laxton, D., and A. Scott. 2000. "On Developing a Structured Forecasting and Policy Analysis System Designed to Support Inflation-Forecast Targeting." In *Inflation Targeting Experiences: England, Finland, Poland, Mexico, Brazil, Chile*. Ankara: Central Bank of Turkey, 6–63.

Mester, L. 2015. "The Outlook for the Economy and Monetary Policy Communications." Speech at the 31st Annual NABE Economic Policy Conference, sponsored by the National Association for Business Economics, Washington, DC.

Mishkin, F. S. 2004. "Can Central Bank Transparency Go Too Far?" NBER Working Paper 10829, National Bureau of Economic Research, Cambridge, MA.

Obstfeld, M., K. Clinton, O. Kamenik, D. Laxton, Y. Ustyugova, and H. Wang. 2016. "How to Improve Inflation Targeting in Canada." IMF Working Paper 16/192, International Monetary Fund, Washington, DC.

Ötker-Robe, İ., and D. Vavra. 2007. "Operational Aspects of Moving to Greater Exchange Rate Flexibility: Lessons from Detailed Country Experiences." Occasional Paper 256, International Monetary Fund, Washington, DC.

Plosser, C. 2014. "Systematic Monetary Policy and Communication." Speech at the Economic Club of New York, New York, NY.

Poloz, S. 2014. "Integrating Uncertainty and Monetary Policy-Making: A Practitioner's Perspective." Bank of Canada Discussion Paper 2014–6, Bank of Canada, Ottawa.

Qvigstad, J. 2005. "When Does an Interest Rate Path 'Look Good'? Criteria for an Appropriate Future Interest Rate Path—A Practician's Approach." Norges Bank Staff Memo 6/2005, Norges Bank, Oslo.

Skořepa, M., and V. Kotlán. 2006. "Inflation Targeting: To Forecast or to Simulate?" *Prague Economic Papers*, 2006 (4): 300–14.

Šmídková, K., ed. 2008. *Evaluation of the Fulfilment of the CNB's Inflation Targets 1998–2007*. Prague: Czech National Bank.

Svensson, L. E. O. 1997. "Inflation Forecast Targeting: Implementing and Monitoring Inflation Targets." *European Economic Review* 41 (6): 1111–46.

———. 2001. "The Zero Bound in an Open Economy: A Foolproof Way of Escaping from a Liquidity Trap." *Bank of Japan, Monetary and Economic Studies (Special Edition)* February: 277–319.

———. 2003. "Escaping from a Liquidity Trap and Deflation: The Foolproof Way and Others." NBER Working Paper 10195, National Bureau of Economic Research, Cambridge, MA.

————. 2007. "Monetary Policy and the Interest Rate Path." Speech presented at Danske Bank, Stockholm, August 22.

Tůma, Z. 2003. "Preface." In *The Czech National Bank's Forecasting and Policy Analysis System*, edited by W. Coats, D. Laxton, and D. Rose. Prague: Czech National Bank.

————. 2010. "Monetary Policy in the Golden Decade of the Czech Economy: What I Have Learnt." Keynote speech delivered at the Czech Economic Society's Biennial Conference, November 27.

Woodford, M. 2005. "Central-Bank Communication and Policy Effectiveness." Presented at the Federal Reserve Bank of Kansas City Symposium, Jackson Hole, WY, August 25–27.

————. 2012. "Inflation Targeting and Financial Stability." NBER Working Paper 17967, National Bureau of Economic Research, Cambridge, MA.

CHAPTER 11

India: Stabilizing Inflation

RANIA AL-MASHAT, KEVIN CLINTON, DOUGLAS
LAXTON, AND HOU WANG

The nominal anchor should be communicated without ambiguity, so as to ensure a
monetary policy regime shift away from the current approach to one that is centered
around the nominal anchor . . . The nominal anchor should be defined in terms of
headline CPI inflation, which closely reflects the cost of living and influences inflation
expectations . . . — Reserve Bank of India (2014)

India's history of inflation targeting is very short. An expert panel recommended its introduction in 2014, and formal adoption came through an amendment to the Reserve Bank of India Act in May 2016, which formally established an inflation target of 4 percent (and a tolerance band of ±2 percent). This chapter outlines the analytical framework for the implementation of the young policy, and describes some of the background to this development.[1]

Three specific challenges make monetary policy more difficult to manage in India than in more advanced economies. The policy transmission mechanism is weaker, food prices have a larger impact on the dynamics of inflation, and the economy has a long history of unstable prices and drifting inflation expectations. The chapter shows how a strategy of flexible inflation targeting by the Reserve Bank of India (RBI) may, over time, mitigate these problems.

In simple terms, the RBI's main job is to stabilize long-term expectations at the 4 percent target rate and thereby to install a firm nominal anchor to the economy. Svensson (1997) shows that in systematic, operational terms, efficient flexible inflation targeting amounts to inflation-forecast targeting. Policy simulations using an RBI macroeconomic model illustrate inflation-forecast-targeting policy options for dealing with different kinds of shocks, including food price shocks, in a situation where the RBI is still in the process of building credibility for its inflation target.

THREE PHASES OF INFLATION: A MACROECONOMIC VIEW

After 2000, there were three distinct phases in the RBI's policy responses to inflation (Figure 11.1).

---

[1]This is an abridged version of Benes, Clinton, George, John, and others (2016), which contains full references to the supporting technical work and official documents.

Figure 11.1. A Macroeconomic Narrative of Inflation in India, 2002–15
(Percent)

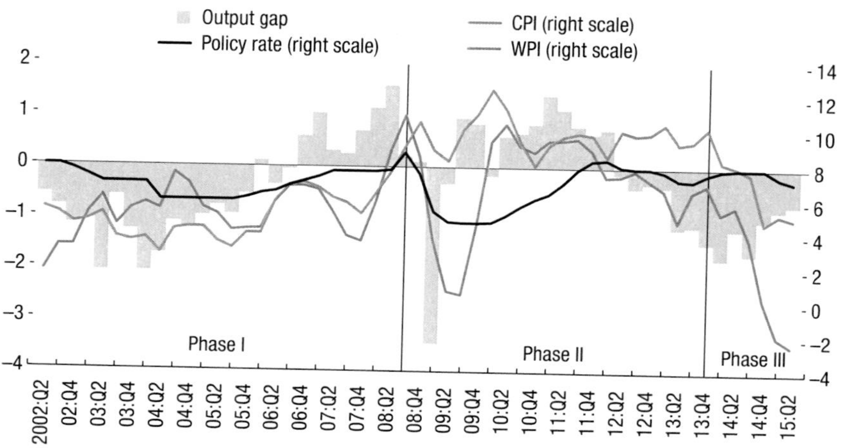

Source: Reserve Bank of India.
Notes: The consumer price index (CPI) inflation rates are on a year-over-year basis. The combined CPI since 2012; pre-2012, backcast using reweighted CPI-industrial workers data. WPI = wholesale price index.

Phase I: Moderate Inflation and Strong Growth, 2000–08

The RBI followed a multiple-indicator approach, with low and stable inflation as just one of the objectives.[2] To gauge inflation, the RBI used a slew of sectoral consumer price indexes (CPIs), but in its monetary policy communication it highlighted the all-India wholesale price index. The various price indexes can show quite different rates of inflation from one year to the next. With respect to instruments, the RBI regarded interest rates as the primary source of monetary policy transmission but did not focus on a single policy-controlled rate in the way that other major central banks have done for many years.

In the early 2000s output decelerated because of a combination of domestic and external factors, and this opened a negative output gap. Despite the fact that 2002 and 2004 brought deficient monsoons, food price inflation remained steady, in part because of the weakened demand and negative output gap. As headline inflation stayed inside its comfort zone, the RBI could support the recovery, reducing policy rates by 300 basis points in the period 2001–05.

---

[2]Under the multiple-indicator approach, policy perspectives were drawn by juxtaposing output data against interest rates or rates of return in different markets, along with movements in currency, credit, fiscal position, trade, capital flows, inflation rate, exchange rate, refinancing, and transactions in foreign exchange.

Output accelerated strongly, with GDP growth reaching almost 10 percent during 2006–08. As the output gap closed, the RBI began to tighten in 2005. Following passage of the Fiscal Responsibility and Budget Management Act, fiscal policy also tightened: the central government deficit was reduced from 4.3 percent in 2003–04 to 2.5 percent in 2007–08. In addition, steady capital inflows contributed to a real appreciation of the currency. These factors helped to moderate inflation pressures. Although commodity prices started to rise in 2005, the pass-through to consumer prices was temporarily muted by administered pricing of many products, especially fuel (Khundrakpam 2008). But as global commodity prices continued to rise strongly, especially crude oil prices, inflation accelerated, and in 2008 wholesale price inflation surged above 10 percent. Consumer prices also increased sharply. Second-round effects fed into the underlying inflation process, as workers sought to maintain real wages and firms to maintain profits. Large capital inflows led to an excess of liquidity in the banking system, fueling credit growth and an asset price boom. Although the RBI raised the policy rate, interest rates remained quite low in real terms, because of the increase in inflation. To contain domestic liquidity, the cash reserve ratio was increased. And to rein in the expansion of credit, macroprudential regulations were tightened, with higher risk-weighted capital requirements and stricter provisioning for bank lending.

Phase II: Persistently High Inflation, 2008–13

In the aftermath of the global financial crisis, GDP growth in India plummeted. In addition to a sharp contraction in external demand, the freeze in foreign financial markets quickly transmitted to a temporary disruption in short-term lending by banks, hurting domestic activity as well as foreign trade. However, as financial markets calmed and liquidity returned, growth rebounded by the second half of 2009. Countercyclical fiscal and monetary policies then kicked in, boosting growth to about 9 percent in 2010–11. The output gap turned from a large negative at the start of 2009 to a positive by the end of the year.

Inflation as measured by consumer and wholesale prices diverged during the crisis. This reflected the high share in the wholesale price index of primary commodities, which slumped in price after the global financial crisis. A series of commodity price shocks pushed the index up by about 10 percent in 2010, about the same increase as consumer prices that year. One of the proximate causes of the upturn was the deficient monsoon rains of 2009. Yet food prices continued to rise relatively quickly even after the monsoon shocks faded. This reflected three factors. The first was the impact of government interventions in the agricultural product and labor market—such as a sharp increase in minimum support prices, and enhanced coverage under the Mahatma Gandhi National Rural Employment Guarantee Act. The second was the pass-through of rapidly increasing world oil prices (agriculture and fertilizer production is highly energy intensive). The third were longer-term trends in food consumption in response to rising incomes, which led to demand-supply mismatches in specific food groups.

More generally, the increase in inflation reflected overall pressure on demand. Because of the postcrisis slowdown in potential output, strong acceleration of output opened a substantial positive output gap. Wages and materials costs rose quickly, and firms could pass on increased costs to consumers. Low monetary policy credibility led to drift in inflation expectations, contributing further to overall inflation persistence.[3]

Monetary policy during this period saw a normalization, from crisis-driven expansionary policies to a calibrated tightening in response to the resurgence of inflation. Policymakers were mindful that the durability of the postcrisis recovery was not assured. The uncertain extent of the loss of potential output implied by the global recession, and data issues, added to the difficulties of assessing the state of the economy. The continuation of the expansionary postcrisis fiscal stance added a further complication. As it became clearer that the inflation pressures were persistent, the RBI tightened more aggressively through 2011. However, following a slowdown in the economy and moderating commodity prices, policy rates were eased somewhat during 2012 and the first half of 2013.

Elevated inflation meant that real interest rates on bank deposits were negative and led to an erosion of savings. Higher demand for gold, which the population used as a hedge against inflation, worsened the trade deficit and diverted savings from productive investment. Concerns about macro-financial stability manifested in the market turmoil of the 2013 taper tantrum, when sovereign risk premiums rose abruptly and the rupee depreciated sharply on unfounded concerns that the US Federal Reserve was going to raise interest rates more rapidly than the market had anticipated.

These unsettled circumstances suggested a need to review the monetary policy framework. For this purpose, the RBI set up the Expert Committee to Revise and Strengthen the Monetary Policy Framework, which reported in 2014. Its report underlines that a fundamental factor underlying the unsatisfactory macroeconomic environment was the lack of a credible nominal anchor—that is, shifting long-term inflation expectations after what should have been one-off shocks to the inflation rate. The report notes that the large historical role of food price shocks in Indian inflation dynamics does not mean that monetary policy is not responsible for inflation over the longer term. It underscores the need for monetary policy to establish a firm nominal anchor so that changes in relative prices caused by real factors can take place without changing long-term inflation expectations.[4] The experience following the deficient monsoons of 2002–04 and 2009 suggested that a serious supply shock need not set off an outbreak of inflation if overall demand pressure was weak. After reviewing the economic history and the

---

[3]Studies on the inflation process in this period include Patra and Ray 2010; Basu 2011; Gokran 2011; Darbha and Patel 2012; Nadhanael 2012; Patra, Khundrakpam, and George 2014; Gulati, Jain, and Nidhi 2013; Sonna and others 2014; Mohanty and John 2015; Bhattacharya and Gupta 2015.

[4]See Rajan 2014; and Anand, Ding, and Tulin 2014.

feasibility of other options to establish a firm nominal anchor, the report recommends a flexible inflation-targeting framework.

Phase III: Disinflation and a New Framework, after 2014

The RBI began informally to put the Expert Committee recommendations into practice by endorsing a glide path for the reduction in CPI inflation—to 8 percent by January 2015 and 6 percent by January 2016. CPI inflation remained elevated through 2013, as the pass-through of exchange rate depreciation following the taper tantrum played out through the economy. But aggregate demand had started to wane, partly because of the tighter monetary policy, and a negative output gap had opened, creating sustained disinflation pressure. A fall in commodity prices, especially crude oil, and a more stable exchange rate, triggered a steep drop in inflation. Despite deficient monsoons, food price increases moderated toward the end of 2014 on a combination of better supply-management policies and a moderate increase in support prices. As a result, the 12-month CPI inflation rate dropped from 10 percent in December 2013 to 4 percent in December 2014, a significantly faster fall than had been expected in the glide path. Household inflation expectations moderated somewhat, and the expectations of professional forecasters became better anchored to the glide path. In 2015, inflation evolved roughly in line with the policy objective and was slightly below the target of 6 percent in January 2016. To moderate the disinflation pressure still evident in the domestic economy, and to resist the headwinds of a slowing global economy, the RBI cut the policy repo rate by 150 basis points between January 2015 and April 2016.

In the meantime, an agreement in February 2015 between the RBI and the government formalized the new approach. The Finance Act of 2016 amended the Reserve Bank of India Act to identify price stability as the primary objective of monetary policy, and to adopt flexible inflation targeting as the nominal anchor for monetary policy. The law also established a six-member monetary policy committee with responsibility for achieving the inflation objective. In August 2016, the government announced a CPI inflation target of 4 percent, with 6 percent and 2 percent as the upper and lower tolerance levels. The target applies until 2021.

SPECIAL CHALLENGES FOR INFLATION-FORECAST TARGETING IN INDIA
Transmission Mechanism Weaknesses

Empirical studies have focused on various channels of policy transmission for India.[5] These may work through interest rates, through the exchange rate,

[5]For the interest rate channel, see RBI 2005; Mohan 2008; Patra and Kapur 2010; Aleem 2010; Bhattacharya, Patnaik, and Shah 2011; Khundrakpam and Jain 2012; Kapur and Behera 2012;

Figure 11.2. Key Interest Rates in India, 2002–15
(Percent)

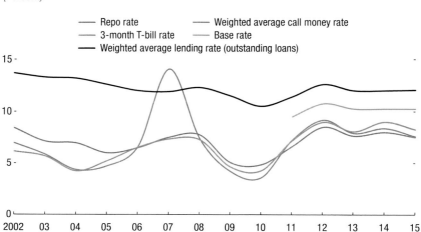

Source: Reserve Bank of India.
Notes: All rates other than the weighted average lending rate (WALR) represent the average rate for the month of March. WLAR is computed on March 31 of each financial year.

through easing or tightening of bank lending, and through asset prices. Because India's economy is relatively large, the exchange rate channel is not expected to be very strong. The interest rate transmission channel could in principle be quite strong, but in practice, although transmission of policy rates to money markets and financial market rates has been fairly complete, the transmission to medium-term bank lending rates has been sluggish (Figure 11.2). Changes in the policy rate in India evidently do not exert the immediate, almost one-for-one, effect on the costs of bank borrowing observed in most advanced economies. This implies a weak link in the Indian policy transmission mechanism for any market-based monetary policy regime.

The Expert Committee highlighted several impediments to the transmission of the policy rate to lending rates, the most prominent of which are administered interest rates, statutory preemptions, rigidities in deposit rate structure, and a lack of external benchmarks. Banks compute a lending base rate from the average cost of funds, which is not very sensitive to changes in the policy rate.[6] This may

Mohanty 2012; Kletzer 2012; RBI 2014; Das 2015. For the bank lending channel see Pandit and others 2006; Bhaumik, Dang, and Kutan 2011; Bhatt and Kishor 2013. For the asset price and exchange rate channel see Singh and Pattanaik 2012; Khundrakpam 2007; Bhattacharya, Patnaik, and Shah 2008; Khundrakpam and Jain 2012.

[6]The base rate for commercial bank loans refers to rates based on those elements of the lending rates that are common across all categories of borrowers, and as such it represents the "floor" for

have improved since April 2016, when the RBI made it mandatory for banks to calculate the base rate using the marginal cost of funds. The interest rate on small saving schemes is administered by government policy: it represents a sort of floor for deposit rates. During phases of monetary easing, if time deposit rates of banks fall below the administered small savings rates, a situation could arise wherein bank deposits migrate to small saving schemes in search of higher returns. This could be alleviated by government measures announced on February 16, 2016, to align the small saving interest rates with the market rates of some government securities. Furthermore, a large part of bank deposits are retail based and have a fixed tenure, which gives a rigidity to banks' cost of funds. Creation of floating deposit rate products faces the challenge of the lack of a transparent external money market benchmark for pricing. High statutory pre-emptions (requirements to hold reserves at the central bank or government debt) lead to crowding out of credit and impede transmission of policy rates to longer rates. State ownership of much of the system to some extent may be responsible for some of these rigidities.

Another factor with a significant bearing on the transmission process is the impact of international capital flows. These can be quite volatile, and if the flows are large the RBI may not be able to completely sterilize their impact on domestic liquidity, as occurred in the mid-2000s. At a much broader level, despite improved financial inclusion through institutional sources over the past decade, a considerable section of the population resorts to informal lenders, at interest rates that are not responsive to rates in the organized financial markets.

The Dominance of Food Prices in the CPI

Food constitutes about 46 percent of the CPI basket in India. This weight is a challenge to flexible inflation targeting for various reasons. First, food prices are highly susceptible to supply shocks because of the impact of variable monsoon rains on harvests. Second, government intervention—for example, changes to minimum support prices, employment guarantees, and minimum wages—sporadically affects food prices. These factors mean that, year over year, headline inflation can be quite different from measures of core inflation that exclude food and energy prices. And third, over the past decade, changes in the underlying structure of the economy and shifts in the composition of demand have caused food prices to rise faster than other prices (Figure 11.3).

Monetary policy affects the rate of inflation in the short and medium term largely through the effect of the output gap on sticky prices, such as those for services and manufactured goods. Thus, the typical Phillips curve of a macro model has core inflation as the dependent variable. The high weight on food dilutes the medium-term effect of policy rate changes on overall CPI inflation. In addition, the high variance of food prices introduces noise into the inflation rate

bank lending rates. Spread components are then added to arrive at the lending rate for a par-ticular borrower.

Figure 11.3. The Relative Price of Food in India, 2006–15
(Index, 2001 = 100)

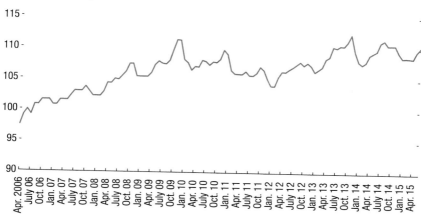

Sources: Haver Analytics; and Reserve Bank of India.
Note: The figure shows the ratio of the Food Group Index to overall consumer price index for industrial workers.

that makes it difficult for the public and policymakers alike to distinguish the influence of monetary policy.

This underscores the basic weakness of the former policy regime: it did not provide a firm nominal anchor to prevent the pass-through of food price shocks to a generalized spiral of inflation. With stable long-term inflation expectations, the relative price changes, which monetary policy is powerless to affect, could have taken place through one-off changes in the rate of inflation, without extended pass-through effects. In India, some lag in the adjustment of prices to shocks is inevitable, especially in those administered by the government. This, however, merely spreads out the shock: with stable expectations, the effect of supply shocks on inflation would still be transitory.

Inflation-forecast targeting can provide an effective strategy for minimizing the second-round effects of supply shocks. The central bank earns credibility over time by achieving the announced target for inflation on average. Years may be required for long-term inflation expectations to hold firm at the target rate. After each policy action, publication of a forecast showing a medium-term path back to target, along with an explanation of how policy actions should contribute to this outcome, helps to maintain such confidence. The medium-term path is conditional on events, but the ultimate target is not. Policymakers need flexibility to change interest rates in response to unforeseen developments. The important thing is not that they adhere to the medium-term path envisaged by a previous forecast, but that they consistently act to return inflation to target following shocks. Once long-term expectations are stabilized, this itself helps to reduce the effects of supply shocks on inflation, and to confine them to the short term.

The strong relative food price trend over time creates not only more substantive uncertainties but also a communications problem. If it continues, core inflation would turn out to be a systematically downward-biased indicator of headline inflation. The communication becomes challenging following a food price shock, because the authorities cannot point to core inflation to reassure the public that policy is on the right track. The challenge for monetary policy communication during a period of trending relative prices, therefore, lies in providing an assessment of the likely size and duration of the relative price trend, and a medium-term forecast in which headline inflation eventually returns to target.

No Track Record: The Challenge of Building Credibility

Before the official inflation target was introduced, the RBI did not have an explicit price stability mandate as its overarching objective. Therefore, the public had no historical record from which to judge either the central bank's commitment to the announced long-term inflation target or whether its actions to this end would prove effective. Despite the regime change, the history of high and unstable inflation has doubtless weighed heavily in the public mind. The RBI has therefore been mindful of the need to get inflation in line with the 4 percent long-term target and to be transparent in explaining how its policy actions are designed to return inflation to target following any deviation. While the RBI was building credibility, policy actions not consistent with stated objectives were liable to damage confidence in the target and thereby to unsettle the nominal anchor. As discussed in Chapter 3, expectations may then amplify the effects of shocks to the economy.

A QUARTERLY PROJECTION MODEL FOR INDIA

The RBI's forecasting and policy analysis system uses a quarterly projection model (QPM) which follows the broad outlines of the generic macroeconomic model sketched out in Chapter 4. Two variants of QPM exist. Production-QPM is the workhorse for deriving the forecasts. It contains significant structural detail to enable explicit forecasts of certain variables that are of particular interest to policymakers, including a linear policy rule for the short-term interest rate.[7] Core-QPM is a stripped-down version, which can be equipped with nonlinearities in the policy reaction function, the Phillips curve, and in a credibility-building process, along with other technical modifications. These enable the exploration of more complex problems and policy options than Production-QPM can examine. Here, the focus is on Core-QPM to show model properties and to illustrate policy options for returning inflation to target following various types of shocks.

As discussed in Chapter 2, flexible inflation targeting may be made operational through the concept of inflation-forecast targeting. Since the central bank forecast

---

[7]See Benes, Clinton, George, Gupta, and others (2016).

embodies all available information, including the policymakers' own preferences about short-term trade-offs, it provides an ideal target over any time horizon. That is, the forecast medium-term path to target includes the effects of current and expected disturbances and an appropriate policy reaction. The idea of inflation-forecast targeting underlies the policy reaction functions in the RBI's QPM. These reinforce the nominal anchor by ensuring that inflation returns to the 4 percent target over the medium term in the event of any deviation of actual inflation from the target. When policy consistently achieves this result, long-term expectations eventually solidify at the target rate.

Overview of Equations

Below is a list of the behavioral equations for Core-QPM.[8] It contains a quadratic policymaker loss function, which embodies a more realistic view of policymaking under flexible inflation targeting than a linear policy rule—whereas small deviations from desired outcomes may be tolerable, very large deviations can lead to dark corners (for example, inflation spirals or deflation traps) that should be avoided (Blanchard 2014).

Output gap:

$$\hat{y}_t = \alpha_1 E_t[\hat{y}_{t+1}] + \alpha_2 \hat{y}_{t-1} - \alpha_3 \hat{r}_t^m + \alpha_4 \hat{z}_t + \varepsilon_t^y \tag{11.1}$$

$\alpha_1 = 0.07; \alpha_2 = 0.60; \alpha_3 = 0.08; \alpha_4 = 0.05$

Definition of the real interest rate gap:

$$\hat{r}_t^m = i_t - E_t[\pi_{t+1}] \tag{11.2}$$

Definition of the real exchange rate gap:

$$\hat{z}_t = s_t + p_t^f - p_t \tag{11.3}$$

Inflation:

$$\pi_t = \beta_1 E_t[\pi 4_{t+1}] + (1 - \beta_1)\pi_{t-1} + \beta_2(e^{\beta_3 \hat{y}_t} - 1)/\beta_3 + \beta_4 \hat{z}_t + \varepsilon_t^\pi \tag{11.4}$$

$\beta_1 = 0.33; \beta_2 = 0.06; \beta_3 = 0.40; \beta_4 = 0.005$

Monetary policy loss function:

$$L_t = \sum_{i=0}^{\infty} \beta^i [\lambda_1 (\pi_{t+i} - \pi^*)^2 + \lambda_2 \hat{y}_{t+i}^2 + \lambda_3 (i_{t+i} - i_{t+i-1})^2] \tag{11.5}$$

$\beta = 0.98; \lambda_1 = 1; \lambda_2 = 1; \lambda_3 = 0.5$

Uncovered interest parity with risk premium:

$$i_t = i_t^f + \sigma_t + (E_t S_{t+1} - S_t)4 + \varepsilon_t^s \tag{11.6}$$

[8]The model follows the format depicted in Figure 2.1, Chapter 2.

Exchange rate expectation:

$$E_t S_{t+1} = \delta_1 S_{t+1} + (1 - \delta_1)\left\{ S_{t-1} + 2\left[\Delta \bar{Z}_t + \frac{\pi 4_{t-1} - \pi 4_{t-1}^f}{4}\right] + \delta_2 \hat{z}_t \right\} \qquad (11.7)$$

$$\delta_1 = 0.6; \delta_2 = 0.3$$

Weakened uncovered interest parity with risk premium:

$$\gamma_1 \left[i_t - (i_t^f + \sigma_t)\right] + (1 - \gamma_1)\left[\Delta \bar{Z}_t \times 4 + \left(\pi 4_{t-1} - \pi 4_{t-1}^f\right)\right] = \left(E_t S_{t+1} - S_t\right) \times 4 + \varepsilon_t^S \qquad (11.8)$$

$$\gamma_1 = 0.7$$

Inflation expectation:

$$E_t\left[\pi 4_{t+1}\right] = c_{t-1} \pi 4_{t+4} + (1 - c_{t-1})\pi 4_{t-1} + (1 - c_{t-1})b^\pi + \kappa \sum_{i=1}^{5} (1 - c_{t-1})^i \varepsilon_{t-i+1}^\pi \qquad (11.9)$$

$$b^\pi = 0.25; \kappa = 1$$

Change in real exchange rate trend:

$$\Delta \bar{Z}_t = 0 \qquad (11.10)$$

Notations: output gap $(\hat{y}_t)$, real interest rate gap $(\hat{r}_t^m)$, real exchange rate gap $(\hat{z}_t)$, shocks to aggregate demand (ε_t^y), domestic prices (p_t), foreign price (p_t^f), annualized quarterly changes in the seasonally adjusted logarithm of CPI (π_t), inflation expectation $(E_t[\pi 4_{t+1}])$, shocks to inflation (ε_t^π), interest rate (i_t), nominal exchange rate (S_t), expected exchange rate $(E_t S_{t+1})$, foreign nominal interest rate (i_t^f), time-varying country risk premium (σ_t), change in real exchange rate trend $(\Delta \bar{Z}_t)$, year-over-year inflation $(\pi 4_t)$, foreign inflation $(\pi 4_t^f)$, shocks to the exchange rate (ε_t^S), credibility stock (c_t).

Calibration of the model reflects India-specific features. The uncovered interest parity condition is modified to reduce the sensitivity of the rupee exchange rate to interest rate differentials. This captures frictions from capital controls and from incomplete financial markets. Expectations include a backward-looking component and a forward-looking, model-consistent component (also known as rational expectations).

Some Specific Features

The Phillips curve contains a nonlinear output gap. The term $(\beta_2(e^{\beta_3 \hat{y}_t} - 1)/\beta_3)$ implies an increasing marginal effect on the inflation rate as the gap increases. At wide negative output gaps, the curve becomes quite flat (Figure 11.4).

In the model, persistent food and fuel price shocks in a context of low monetary policy credibility can result in upward ratcheting in inflation expectations and can contribute to higher levels of inflation persistence. Specifically, inflation expectations are modeled as a linear combination of backward-looking (lags) and forward-looking, model-consistent (leads) components, with the weight on the former decreasing with the stock of credibility. In addition, when credibility is imperfect, inflation expectations are biased upward relative to the linear combination of backward-looking and forward-looking components. This strengthens the propagation mechanism from supply shocks, and therefore requires a more

Figure 11.4. Convex Phillips Curve
(Percentage point)

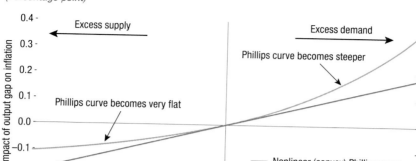

Source: Authors' calculations.

aggressive tightening in monetary conditions to contain inflationary pressures and anchor long-term inflation expectations. Over time, an established inflation-forecast-targeting regime provides an effective strategy for dealing with the second-round effects of supply shocks.

Credibility is earned, over time, by achieving announced objectives, and by effective, transparent communications. On the other side, it can be lost through policy actions inconsistent with stated objectives. There are two types of expectation-building processes. The first is optimistic yet watchful: it attaches a positive weight $(1 - \rho)$ to the central bank's intermediate target for inflation (that is, the inflation target π^*), but also some weight (ρ) to past inflation. The second type, conditioned by history, is skeptical, informed by the belief that inflation is likely to wander off back to some historical high level. This belief puts some weight on high inflation (π^H), as well as on past inflation, but ignores the central bank's inflation target. The credibility signal, as defined by the relative squared forecast errors under the two types, provides a measure of the extent to which an inflation outcome is consistent with the central bank's promise, where inflation falls to the target rate over time. High values of the credibility signals increase the credibility stock. However, it takes repeated good signals to improve credibility significantly.

Credibility stock building:

$$c_t = \rho^c \times c_{t-1} + (1 - \rho^c) \times \xi_t$$

$$\rho^c = 0.8$$

(11.11)

Signal for revision of credibility based on squared forecast errors:

$$\xi_t = \frac{(\varepsilon_t^H)^2}{(\varepsilon_t^H)^2 + (\varepsilon_t^L)^2} \tag{11.12}$$

Forecast errors:
Forecast error expected by optimists

$$\varepsilon_t^L = \pi 4_t - \left[\rho \times \pi 4_{t-1} + (1 - \rho) \times \pi^*\right] \tag{11.13}$$

Forecast error expected by skeptics

$$\varepsilon_t^H = \pi 4_t - \left[\rho \times \pi 4_{t-1} + (1 - \rho) \times \pi^H\right]$$

$$\rho = 0.5; \pi^* = 4; \pi^H = 8$$

Boundary conditions:

$$\text{If } \pi 4_t - \left[\rho \times \pi 4_{t-1} + (1 - \rho) \times \pi^*\right] < 0, \text{ then } \xi_t = 1. \tag{11.14}$$

$$\text{If } \pi 4_t - \left[\rho \times \pi 4_{t-1} + (1 - \rho) \times \pi^H\right] > 0, \text{ then } \xi_t = 0.$$

Monetary policy in the model minimizes a quadratic loss function, which penalizes squared deviations from output and inflation objectives and large short-term interest rate changes. It is common to use a linear (Taylor-type) rule to characterize monetary policy under inflation targeting. Such an approach may be adequate for situations in which there is no nearby risk to the credibility of the official inflation target. For India, however, long-term expectations of inflation are not yet firmly attached to the 4 percent target. Any substantial excess of actual inflation over target would likely cause expectations of inflation to ratchet up. To return inflation to target would then involve large losses to output and employment. Central bank policymakers would therefore react increasingly strongly to deviations above target as they grow—in effect, as if they had a quadratic loss function.

But policymakers avoid sharp interest rate changes. The penalty in the loss function for steep policy rate changes reflects the well-known preference of policymakers for gradual rate movements. This has the economic rationale that policymakers uncertain about the source or the duration of a shock will proceed cautiously. In addition, more variable changes in rates are liable to convey less information to the public about the stance of monetary policy. A given policy rate change has more effect on longer-term interest rates and the exchange rate if there is less noise in its movements.

ILLUSTRATIVE CORE-QPM MONETARY POLICY EXPERIMENTS

The most important function of a forecasting and policy analysis system model is as a tool for policymakers to assess the implications of alternate policy options under periods of uncertainty. A few plausible scenarios can be traced in the Indian context, which illustrate policy options and their likely implications using Core-QPM simulations.

Disinflation

This experiment derives paths for endogenous variables in a disinflation goal that would take inflation from 5 percent to 4 percent. Minimizing the loss function ensures that the latter is achieved at the lowest cost in loss in output, deviation of inflation from the target, and interest rate variability. An initial equilibrium with 5 percent inflation is assumed, and hence the nominal interest rate is 7 percent (or a real rate of 2 percent). With initial credibility not very high, the central bank should hike the policy rate in the baseline (Figure 11.5). The uncovered interest parity condition warrants a drop in the exchange rate (that is, appreciation of the rupee) when there are no further shocks to the system. The combination of interest rate increase and exchange rate appreciation reduces demand and opens a negative output gap. Inflation declines first by the impact of the stronger rupee, and then, increasingly over time, by the negative output gap. The cost in cumulative forgone output is 2 percent of annual GDP (that is, a sacrifice ratio of 2).

The credibility stock starts low initially, but as inflation declines toward the target, the central bank receives repeated high credibility signals, and as a result, it builds up the credibility stock over time. Eventually, as the credibility stock goes to one, the lagged term in inflation expectations and the bias term both disappear, which implies a much-improved short-term trade-off between output and inflation. Hawkish policymakers would achieve the long-term target slightly faster than the baseline. But they would raise the policy rate more, triggering a sharper appreciation, a wider medium-term negative output gap, and hence a larger sacrifice ratio. Dovish policymakers, in turn, with a higher weight on the output gap, would tighten monetary conditions less than the baseline and hence the sacrifice ratio would be lower.

Figure 11.6 shows a path generated under the assumption that the policy stance is fully credible. The 1 percentage point reduction in inflation is achieved within six quarters, at a reduced loss of cumulative output—1/2 percent of annual GDP. In the baseline, the tightening of policy is achieved without any increase in the policy interest rate—in effect, the required increase in the real rate is achieved entirely through the reduced expectations of inflation. If policymakers were to place more weight on deviations of output from the long-term equilibrium, the more gradual approach would further reduce the output cost. Were policymakers to exhibit willingness to tolerate short-term loss of output and employment, and so place less weight on the output gap, the policy rate would indeed increase slightly and the sacrifice ratio would be slightly higher. But clearly, policymakers' preference on the output gap makes little material difference to outcomes in the perfect credibility situation.

Mitigating Demand Shocks: Divine Coincidence

Under optimal policy, the central bank raises (or cuts) the policy rate to deal with positive (or negative) demand shocks (Figure 11.7). Dealing with such shocks does not create a conflict between output and inflation objectives because of the so-called divine coincidence (Blanchard and Galí 2007). With a prompt, active

Figure 11.5. Disinflation with Endogenous Policy Credibility

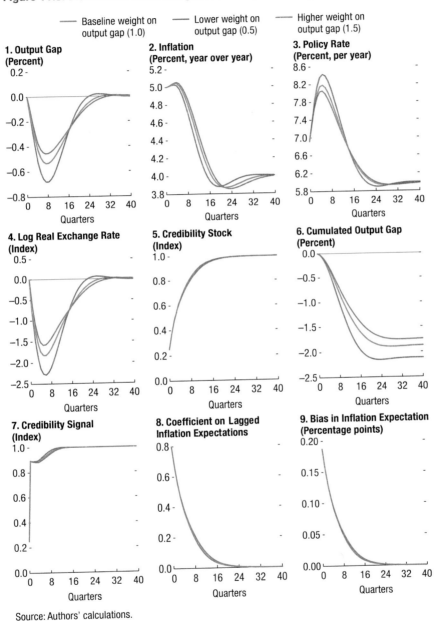

Source: Authors' calculations.

Figure 11.6. Disinflation with Perfect Policy Credibility

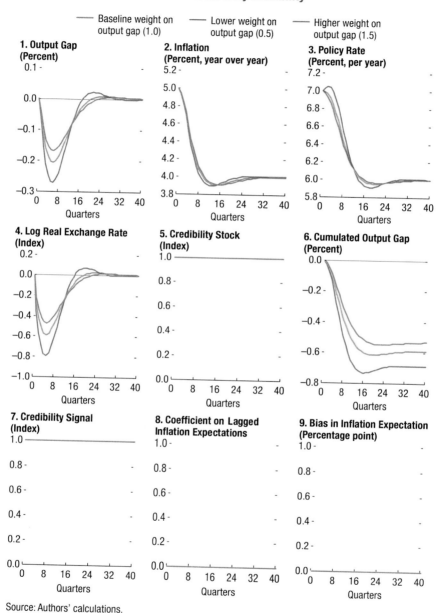

Source: Authors' calculations.

response to the shock, inflation is held close to baseline in each case. Given the flat Phillips curve under excess supply conditions, the widening of the output gap must be somewhat greater for the negative than for the positive shock. Because inflation is well controlled, demand shocks have no major impact on credibility.

Mitigating Supply Shocks: Trade-Offs

A nasty supply shock requires an increase in interest rates and a larger negative output gap (relative to baseline) to maintain the path to the 4 percent long-term target (Figure 11.8). The medium-term trade-off is between the speed of the approach to the target and the size of the output gap. A prompt and aggressive approach prevents long-term inflation expectations from ratcheting upward and preserves credibility, but it has higher costs to short-term output. By contrast, a favorable supply shock presents an attractive trade-off: inflation moderates relative to baseline and reaches 4 percent sooner; monetary policy eases; and the output gap closes faster.

Prompt versus Delayed Policy Responses

In the previous experiments, losses to both output and monetary policy credibility following supply shocks were reduced by prompt, effective action. The importance of timely policy action when credibility is imperfect can be shown with an experiment in which policymakers wait before responding to a nasty supply shock. If the policy action is delayed, the interest rate hike must be much greater than under a baseline response, and the cumulative output gap is larger, with higher inflation (Figure 11.9). Thus, a delayed policy response causes a substantial deterioration in the medium-term output-inflation trade-off.

CONCLUSIONS

India's experience with inflation targeting contrasts in several ways with that of most advanced economies. Structural factors result in changes in the RBI policy rate being transmitted weakly to output and inflation. Volatile food prices exert a large influence over the short- to medium-term dynamics of inflation. A history of high and variable inflation has left a legacy of skepticism about whether monetary policy will, or even can, achieve the announced inflation-control objective. Features such as these have implications for the conduct of policy, and they create challenges for macroeconomic modeling.

It is too early to judge whether the inflation targeting of the RBI will succeed in establishing a firm nominal anchor. So far, inflation has been brought down in line with the official target range. A strong test to the regime will come with the next major shock to food prices. Previous shocks set off second rounds of price and wage increases and hence a spiral of inflation. Public expectations of long-term inflation drifted with the actual rate. The intent under the new regime is that a bad harvest should have only a transitory effect on inflation, and

Figure 11.7. Demand Shocks

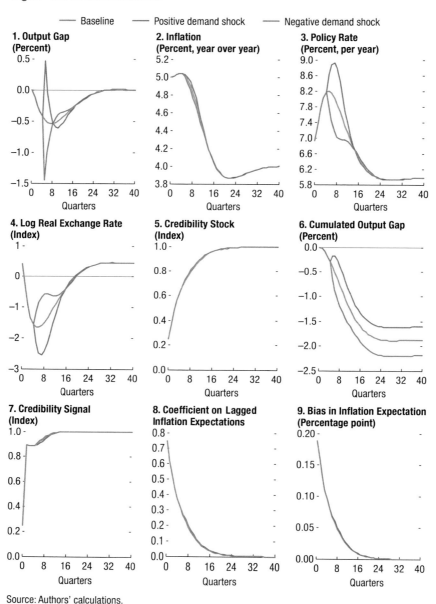

Source: Authors' calculations.

Figure 11.8. Supply Shocks

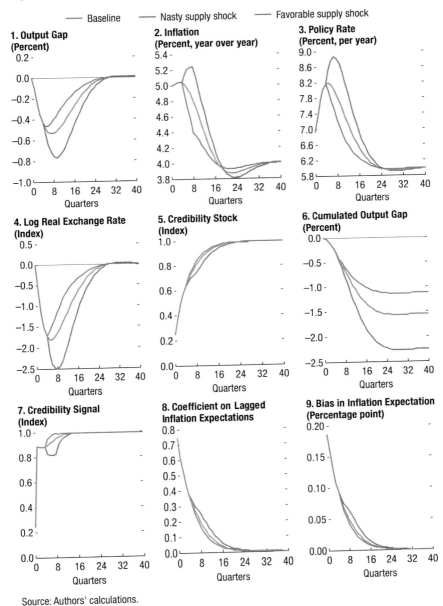

Source: Authors' calculations.

Figure 11.9. A Delayed Policy Response to Shocks

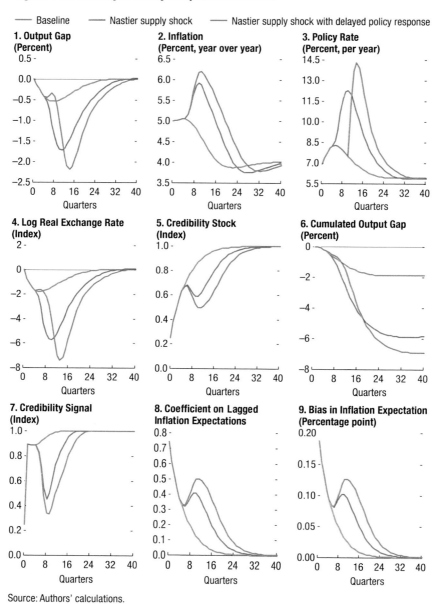

Source: Authors' calculations.

long-term expectations should hold steady at the official target rate. The change in relative prices, which monetary policy is powerless to affect, can be absorbed without a lasting change in the inflation rate. In other inflation-forecast-targeting countries, long-term inflation expectations have held firm following supply shocks, but the effect of such shocks on consumer prices in India is exceptionally large.

With respect to modeling, the RBI has been experimenting with ways to incorporate the special structural features of the Indian economy into a core macroeconomic forecasting model. A credibility-building process, according to which policy earns credibility over time by consistently returning inflation to target, will be a relevant part of the model during the early years of the new regime. Simulation results from the model indicate that delays in responding to shocks can be quite costly in terms of output losses and inflation, partly because of lost credibility.

There has also been a conjunctural difference with most advanced economies, in that the Indian economy has enjoyed robust growth since the global financial crisis. The relevant danger for India would be that long-term expectations of inflation get derailed on the upside. However, a theme in this book is that policy should respond assertively to disturbances that threaten to push the economy into a bad quasi-equilibrium, and this applies to India too. When there is a risk that inflation expectations may drift from inflation targets, prudent conduct of monetary policy may call for aggressive policy actions.

REFERENCES

Aleem, A. 2010. "Transmission Mechanism of Monetary Policy in India." *Journal of Asian Economics* 21 (2): 186–97.

Anand, R., D. Ding, and V. Tulin. 2014. "Food Inflation in India: The Role for Monetary Policy." IMF Working Paper 14/78, International Monetary Fund, Washington, DC.

Basu, K. 2011. "Understanding Inflation and Controlling It." *Economic and Political Weekly* 46 (41): 50–64.

Benes, J., K. Clinton, A. George, P. Gupta, J. John, O. Kamenik, D. Laxton, P. Mitra, G.V. Nadhanael, R. Portillo, H. Wang, and F. Zhang. 2016. "Quarterly Projection Model for India: Key Elements and Properties." Reserve Bank of India Working Paper Series 08/2016, Reserve Bank of India, Mumbai.

Benes, J., K. Clinton, A. George, J. John, O. Kamenik, D. Laxton, P. Mitra, G.V. Nadhanael, H. Wang, and F. Zhang. 2016. "Inflation-Forecast Targeting for India: An Outline of the Analytical Framework." Reserve Bank of India Working Paper Series 07/2016, Reserve Bank of India, Mumbai.

Bhatt, V., and K. N. Kishor. 2013. "Bank Lending Channel in India: Evidence from State-Level Analysis." *Empirical Economics* 45 (3): 1307–31.

Bhattacharya, R., and A. S. Gupta. 2015. "Food Inflation in India: Causes and Consequences." NIPFP Working Paper 2015–151 (June), National Institute of Public Finance and Policy, New Delhi.

Bhattacharya, R., I. Patnaik, and A. Shah. 2008. "Exchange Rate Pass-Through in India." NIPFP Macro/Finance Group, National Institute of Public Finance and Policy, New Delhi.

———. 2011. "Monetary Policy Transmission in an Emerging Market Setting." IMF Working Paper 11/5, International Monetary Fund, Washington, DC.

Bhaumik, S. K., V. Dang, and A. M. Kutan. 2011. "Implications of Bank Ownership for the Credit Channel of Monetary Policy Transmission: Evidence from India." *Journal of Banking and Finance* 35 (9): 2418–28.

Blanchard, O. 2014. "Where Danger Lurks." *Finance and Development* 51 (3): 28–31.

———, and J. Galí. 2007. "Real Wage Rigidities and the New Keynesian Model." *Journal of Money, Credit and Banking* 39 (s1): 35–65.

Darbha, G., and U. R. Patel. 2012. "Dynamics of Inflation 'Herding': Decoding India's Inflationary Process." Global Economy and Development Working Paper 48, Brookings Institution, Washington, DC.

Das, S. 2015. "Monetary Policy in India: Transmission to Bank Interest Rates." IMF Working Paper 15/129, International Monetary Fund, Washington, DC.

Gokran, S. 2011. "Food Inflation—This Time It's Different." Text of the Kale Memorial Lecture, Gokhale Institute of Politics and Economics, Pune.

Government of India. 2015. "Agreement on Monetary Policy Framework between the Government of India and the Reserve Bank of India." February.

———. 2016. "Amendments to The Reserve Bank of India Act, 1934, Chapter XII, Miscellaneous, Part I, The Finance Act 2016." May. 82–87.

Gulati, A., S. Jain, and S. Nidhi. 2013. "Rising Farm Wages in India: The 'Pull' and 'Push' Factors." Discussion Paper 5, Commission for Agricultural Costs and Prices, Delhi.

Kapur, M., and H. Behera. 2012. "Monetary Transmission Mechanism in India: A Quarterly Model." RBI Working Paper 09/2012, Reserve Bank of India, Mumbai.

Khundrakpam, J. K. 2007. "Economic Reforms and Exchange Rate Pass-Through to Domestic Prices in India." BIS Working Paper 225, Bank for International Settlements, Basel.

———. 2008. "How Persistent Is Indian Inflationary Process, Has It Changed?" Reserve Bank of India Occasional Papers 29 (2), Reserve Bank of India, Mumbai.

———, and R. Jain. 2012. "Monetary Policy Transmission in India: A Peep Inside the Black Box." RBI Working Paper 11/2012, Reserve Bank of India, Mumbai.

Kletzer, K. 2012. "Financial Friction and Monetary Policy Transmission in India." In *The Oxford Handbook of the Indian Economy*, edited by Chetan Ghate. Oxford/New Delhi: Oxford University Press.

Mohan, R. 2008. "Monetary Policy Transmission in India." Contributed paper in *Transmission Mechanisms for Monetary Policy in Emerging Market Economies* 35, 259–307. Basel: Bank for International Settlements.

Mohanty, D. 2012. "Evidence on Interest Rate Channel of Monetary Policy Transmission in India." RBI Working Paper 6/2012, Reserve Bank of India, Mumbai.

———, and J. John. 2015. "Determinants of Inflation in India." *Journal of Asian Economics* 36 (C): 86–96.

Nadhanael, G. V. 2012. "Recent Trends in Rural Wages: An Analysis of Inflationary Implications." RBI Occasional Papers 33 (1 & 2), Reserve Bank of India, Mumbai.

Pandit, B. L., A. Mittal, M. Roy, and S. Ghosh. 2006. "Transmission of Monetary Policy and the Bank Lending Channel: Analysis and Evidence for India." DRG Study No. 25, Reserve Bank of India, Mumbai.

Patra, M. D., and M. Kapur. 2010. "A Monetary Policy Model without Money for India." IMF Working Paper 10/183, International Monetary Fund, Washington, DC.

Patra, M. D., J. K. Khundrakpam, and A. T. George. 2014. "Post-Global Crisis Inflation Dynamics in India: What Has Changed?" In *India Policy Forum 2013–14*, Volume 10, edited by Shekhar Shah, Barry Bosworth, and Arvind Panagariya. New Delhi: Sage India.

Patra, M. D., and P. Ray. 2010. "Inflation Expectations and Monetary Policy in India: An Empirical Exploration." IMF Working Paper 10/84, International Monetary Fund, Washington, DC.

Rajan, R. 2014. "Fighting Inflation." Speech delivered at the Fixed Income Money Market and Derivatives Association of India—Primary Dealers' Association of India Annual Conference, Mumbai, February 26.

Reserve Bank of India (RBI). 2005. *Report on Currency and Finance, 2003–04*. Mumbai: Reserve Bank of India.

———. 2014. *Report of the Expert Committee to Revise and Strengthen the Monetary Policy Framework* (January). Mumbai: Reserve Bank of India.

Singh, B., and S. Pattanaik. 2012. "Monetary Policy and Asset Price Interactions in India: Should Financial Stability Concerns from Asset Prices Be Addressed through Monetary Policy?" *Journal of Economic Integration* 27 (1): 167–94.

Sonna, T., H. Joshi, A. Sebastian, and U. Sharma. 2014. "Analytics of Food Inflation in India." RBI Working Paper Series (DEPR) 10/2014, Reserve Bank of India, Mumbai.

Svensson, L. E. O. 1997. "Inflation Forecast Targeting: Implementing and Monitoring Inflation Targets." *European Economic Review* 41 (6): 1111–46.

CHAPTER 12

United States: Federal Reserve's Dual Mandate

Rania Al-Mashat, Kevin Clinton, Douglas Laxton, and Hou Wang

The FOMC is firmly committed to fulfilling its statutory mandate from the Congress of promoting maximum employment, stable prices, and moderate long-term interest rates. The Committee seeks to explain its monetary policy decisions to the public as clearly as possible. Such clarity facilitates well-informed decision making by households and businesses, reduces economic and financial uncertainty, increases the effectiveness of monetary policy, and enhances transparency and accountability, which are essential in a democratic society. — Federal Open Market Committee (2012)

The Federal Reserve's dual mandate—the pursuit of maximum employment and stable prices—provides an adaptable and flexible framework for monetary policy.[1] Over the years, the Fed has modified its objectives and operations in line with evolving views of the role of monetary policy and with changes in the economic environment.

A 2012 announcement clarified the longer-term goals and the strategy underlying the current policy regime (Box 12.1). It specified a 2 percent rate for consumer price increases (gauged by the personal consumption expenditure, or PCE, deflator) as the long-term goal for monetary policy. And it underlined a second goal of full employment, noting that while the inflation and employment objectives are generally complementary, the Federal Open Market Committee (FOMC) would take a balanced approach in promoting them. The announcement also reiterated the Fed's commitment to transparency, noting that it "seeks to explain its monetary policy decisions to the public as clearly as possible" (FOMC 2012).

For all intents and purposes, this revised dual-mandate framework amounts to flexible inflation targeting, or inflation-forecast targeting—although official Fed statements avoid such terminology.

Inflation-forecast targeting as practiced by the most transparent central banks does indeed provide a useful template, and that is true for US monetary policy. The main step in this direction would be for the Fed to publish the complete

---

[1] This chapter draws extensively from Alichi and others (2015).

Box 12.1. Federal Open Market Committee Statement of Longer-Run Goals and Policy Strategy

The FOMC is firmly committed to fulfilling its statutory mandate from the Congress of promoting maximum employment, stable prices, and moderate long-term interest rates. The Committee seeks to explain its monetary policy decisions to the public as clearly as possible. Such clarity facilitates well-informed decision making by households and businesses, reduces economic and financial uncertainty, increases the effectiveness of monetary policy, and enhances transparency and accountability, which are essential in a democratic society.

Inflation, employment, and long-term interest rates fluctuate over time in response to economic and financial disturbances. Moreover, monetary policy actions tend to influence economic activity and prices with a lag. Therefore, the Committee's policy decisions reflect its longer-run goals, its medium-term outlook, and its assessments of the balance of risks, including risks to the financial system that could impede the attainment of the Committee's goals.

The inflation rate over the longer run is primarily determined by monetary policy, and hence the Committee has the ability to specify a longer-run goal for inflation. The Committee judges that inflation at the rate of 2 percent, as measured by the annual change in the price index for personal consumption expenditures, is most consistent over the longer run with the Federal Reserve's statutory mandate. Communicating this inflation goal clearly to the public helps keep longer-term inflation expectations firmly anchored, thereby fostering price stability and moderate long-term interest rates and enhancing the Committee's ability to promote maximum employment in the face of significant economic disturbances.

The maximum level of employment is largely determined by nonmonetary factors that affect the structure and dynamics of the labor market. These factors may change over time and may not be directly measurable. Consequently, it would not be appropriate to specify a fixed goal for employment; rather, the Committee's policy decisions must be informed by assessments of the maximum level of employment, recognizing that such assessments are necessarily uncertain and subject to revision . . .

In setting monetary policy, the Committee seeks to mitigate deviations of inflation from its longer-run goal and deviations of employment from the Committee's assessments of its maximum level. These objectives are generally complementary. However, under circumstances in which the Committee judges that the objectives are not complementary, it follows a balanced approach in promoting them, taking into account the magnitude of the deviations and the potentially different time horizons over which employment and inflation are projected to return to levels judged consistent with its mandate.

Source: Extracted from Federal Open Market Committee 2012.

baseline staff forecast presented to FOMC policy decision meetings at the time policy decisions are announced. This would include showing a future interest rate path consistent with achievement of the FOMC's announced longer-term goals. The data on the individual forecasts of FOMC members currently released allow for various interpretations and do not provide a coherent macroeconomic vision of the path ahead.

A complete published forecast, including the path of the short-term interest rate, would help guide public expectations and thereby reinforce the effectiveness of monetary policy actions. The central bank's capacity to influence inflation and employment relies, in large part, on its influence over expectations for the future path for short-term interest rates and inflation.

The United States should also adopt an active risk-avoidance strategy strongly averse to large deviations from the desired macroeconomic equilibrium. The strategy could be almost indifferent to small targeting errors. But it would preemptively and aggressively keep the economy well away from bad quasi-equilibriums in which conventional monetary policy tools lose their effectiveness and expectations of inflation go adrift.[2]

During the global financial crisis, the Fed cut the federal funds rate to the floor; since then, it has employed unconventional measures to further ease monetary conditions. It used *extended forward guidance* to announce its intention to keep short-term interest rates lower for longer than might have otherwise been expected (Yellen 2016). *Large-scale asset purchases*—otherwise known as *quantitative easing*—were used to remove bond supply from the market, pushing down term premiums and adding liquidity to the financial system more durably than regular open-market repurchases. The effect is a reduction in bond yields beyond the decline in average future expected short rates that had been induced by its forward guidance.

The use of these measures during the postcrisis recession is the type of prompt corrective action advocated in this chapter (although the model simulations here focus on the interest rate instrument). Managing expectations becomes even more important in unusual circumstances, such as when the effective lower bound on interest rates is binding, or in the presence of unconventional measures, since markets then need clear guidance through the unfamiliar territory.

Empirical studies find a positive and economically significant impact from forward guidance and quantitative easing, confirming that the Fed's messaging has, by and large, been effective. However, the 2013 bond market "taper tantrum" caused a sharp and unhelpful jump in yields on mistaken assumptions that the Fed would soon be returning to more normal policy conditions. This episode suggests that more complete, quantitative statements on likely future unconventional measures may be useful for the winding down phase. In addition, by highlighting the uncertainties in the outlook through the publication of confidence bands and relevant alternative scenarios, the Fed could further moderate the risk of a bond market snap-back.

This chapter illustrates the argument for an active risk-avoidance strategy by presenting simulation results comparing a linear policy rule for the federal funds rate with an alternative strategy in which the rate adjusts to minimize a quadratic loss function. In each case, the central bank acts over time to close deviations of inflation from the long-term target rate and gaps between actual and potential

---

[2]They are quasi-equilibriums in that a favorable transitory shock could move the economy toward an equilibrium that monetary policy would support. Blanchard (2014) argues that macroeconomic policy should make a high priority of avoiding "dark corners." Dudley (2012) and Evans and others (2015) use the term "risk management."

output. The quadratic loss function penalizes large deviations from objectives heavily and small deviations negligibly, as per the recommended strategy.

The analysis examines negative shocks in an economy where the starting point already has a negative output gap and below-target inflation, and where the short-term interest rate is already at the effective lower bound. The main risk here is a trap in which inflation expectations slide below zero, real interest rates rise, and the economy goes into a downward spiral. To minimize the loss function would imply an aggressive monetary easing, which under these circumstances would mean holding the federal funds rate at the floor until the inflation and output gaps are almost closed and which may imply, over the medium term, a temporary overshoot of the inflation target.[3]

The behavior of public expectations is critical. In the model, the public as well as the central bank have forward-looking (model-consistent) expectations. The extended duration at the floor of the nominal interest rate affects aggregate spending through a drop in real longer-term interest rates. This is because the prospect of a longer period with short rates at the effective lower bound reduces the average expected nominal short-term interest rate over the life of a bond and increases the expected rate of inflation—possibly above the target for the medium term. Given the importance of expectations and the complexity of describing a quadratic loss function to the public, effective communication of central bank forecasts becomes a key policy instrument. The publication of a baseline staff forecast and alternative scenarios based on different policy reaction functions, as well as on different assumptions about the outlook, can be helpful in communicating to the public the rationale for interest rate settings and the majority view of the FOMC, with room to also explain dissenting views of FOMC members.

RECENT DEVELOPMENTS AT THE FEDERAL RESERVE

Increased Transparency

Since 2011, the FOMC has taken several steps to shed light on its policy actions and strategy (Table 12.1).[4] The 2012 announcement of an explicit 2 percent inflation objective was the most striking, which, as noted, amounted to adoption of inflation-forecast targeting—although official statements avoid such terminology. This established a firm nominal anchor without ignoring the objective of high employment and output (such as Gurkaynak and others 2006; Gurkaynak, Levin, and Swanson 2010). One principle underlying an inflation-forecast-targeting regime is a high degree of transparency, and inflation-forecast-targeting central banks that have taken this principle furthest have had particularly good policy outcomes.

---

[3]English, López-Salido, and Tetlow (2013) report a similar finding.

[4]English, López-Salido, and Tetlow (2013) describe and analyze these steps in more detail. Yellen (2012) discusses the Fed's nonconventional policy instruments introduced since the global financial crisis of 2008. Yellen (2014) outlines developments in the FOMC communications framework.

TABLE 12.1.

Postcrisis Steps to Increase US Monetary Policy Transparency

Date	Action	Description
Dec. 2008 to Mar. 2015	Forward guidance	Qualitative (Dec. 2008–Aug. 2011), date-based (Aug. 2011–Dec. 2012), threshold-based (Dec. 2012–Mar. 2014), qualitative (Mar. 2014–Mar. 2015)
Nov. 2008 to Mar. 2015	Balance sheet guidance	Volume of purchases, pace of purchases, assets purchased, criteria for revising asset purchases, reinvestment and shrinking of the balance sheet
Apr. 2011	Postmeeting press conference	More comprehensive and timely information on the Federal Open Market Committee (FOMC) policy decision and views, including Summary of Economic Projections
Jan. 2012	Statement on Longer-Run Goals and Monetary Policy Strategy	Clarify the Federal Reserve's objectives and policy strategy, including the introduction of a long-run 2 percent inflation goal
Jan. 2012	Policy rate projections	Individual FOMC members' policy rate projections were added to the quarterly Summary of Economic Projections published after the FOMC meetings

Source: Adapted from Alichi and others 2015.

The Fed, which has long enjoyed a reputation for transparency, has also enhanced its policy communications. Notably, it expanded the Summary of Economic Projections—released four times a year shortly after FOMC meetings—to provide members' projections of the federal funds rate path, GDP growth, the unemployment rate, and inflation. For each variable, the summary provides a range of the individual forecasts. A chart presents the range for the federal funds rate as a dot for each member's forecast; this "dot plot" attracts considerable financial market attention. The summary has become an important element in FOMC communications.[5]

Expanded Toolkit of Instruments

In normal times, an established pattern of policy behavior, consistent with the central bank's stated policy objectives, itself provides a strong basis for credibility and predictability. During temporary shocks, long-term inflation expectations stay in line with the official target without need for any special communications effort. However, in unusual circumstances, the central bank may need to resort to unusual measures, which require more explicit explanations (Woodford 2012). This need raised the profile of communications as a policy tool in the recession that followed the global financial crisis, when policy interest rates approached their effective lower bound and central banks introduced unconventional instruments, that is, forward guidance on interest rates and quantitative easing (large-scale asset purchases and maturity extensions). "Beyond the task of

---

[5]For example, Yellen (2015) cites the document several times in a discussion of monetary policy "normalization."

describing the new policies, extensive communication was needed to justify these unconventional policy actions and convincingly connect them to the Federal Reserve's employment and inflation objectives." (Yellen 2013).

Forward guidance—assuring markets that the short-term interest rate would remain low for an extended period—was intended to reduce expected short-term rates.[6] Large-scale central bank asset purchases combined with extensions of term reduce the supply of bonds available to private investors, squeezing long-term premiums lower through a portfolio rebalancing effect (the purchases might also reduce interest rate expectations). Outright purchases of assets—especially those of extended terms—also add reserves to the banking system in a way that might be expected to have more permanence than the normal short-dated repurchase operation. The proximate objective of both measures was to reduce longer-term rates. The bigger goals were to underline the Fed's commitment to bringing inflation back to 2 percent and to stimulate the economy.

Although the rationale for these instruments followed standard monetary theory, success was not guaranteed at the outset. Indeed, their use was controversial. A famous open letter to the Fed chair signed by several eminent economists argued the following:

> We believe the Federal Reserve's large-scale asset purchase plan (so-called "quantitative easing") should be reconsidered and discontinued. We do not believe such a plan is necessary or advisable under current circumstances. The planned asset purchases risk currency debasement and inflation, and we do not think they will achieve the Fed's objective of promoting employment. (Hoover Institution 2010)

Evidence has debunked this argument. Empirical studies find unambiguously that the unconventional measures eased financial conditions and gave a material boost to US economic growth and inflation, as the Fed expected (Gagnon and others 2010; Gagnon 2016; Engen, Laubach, and Reifschneider 2015.) Evidence in Europe is similar (Churm and others 2015 for the United Kingdom; Andrade and others 2016 for the euro area).

Gagnon and others (2010) conduct an event study, considering the response of interest rates over one-day windows around the FOMC's quantitative easing announcements, measured from the closing level the day prior to the announcement to the closing level the day of the announcement. Table 12.2 displays the changes in interest rates on each day in the baseline event set. The cumulative change indicates that the effects were in the expected direction and of lasting duration. Yields on all categories of bonds declined—10-year Treasuries by 91 basis points, 10-year agency debt by 156 basis points, and mortgage-backed securities by 113 basis points. The large change in the 10-year yield relative to the 2-year yield suggests that the announcements reduced yields principally through the term premium, as opposed to expectations. The relatively large changes in agency and mortgage-backed security yields demonstrate that quantitative easing helped to

---

[6]Bernanke (2013) provides an authoritative description of the evolution of forward guidance at the Fed.

TABLE 12.2.

Interest Rate Changes around Baseline and Extended Event Set Announcements

Date	Event	2y UST	10y UST	10y Agy	Agy MBS[2]	10y TP	10y Swap	Baa Index
11/25/2008[1]	Initial LSAP Announcement	−2	−22	−58	−44	−17	−29	−18
12/1/2008[1]	Chairman Speech	−8	−19	−39	−15	−17	−17	−12
12/16/2008[1]	FOMC Statement	−9	−26	−29	−37	−12	−32	−11
1/28/2009[1]	FOMC Statement	10	14	14	11	9	14	2
3/18/2009[1]	FOMC Statement	−22	−47	−52	−31	−40	−39	−29
04/29/2009	FOMC Statement	1	10	−1	6	6	8	−3
06/24/2009	FOMC Statement	10	6	3	2	4	4	5
8/12/2009[1]	FOMC Statement	−2	5	4	2	3	1	2
9/23/2009[1]	FOMC Statement	1	−3	−3	−1	−1	−5	−4
11/4/2009[1]	FOMC Statement	−2	6	8	1	5	5	3
12/16/2009	FOMC Statement	−2	1	0	−1	1	1	−1
01/28/2010	FOMC Statement	−6	−1	0	−1	1	−1	0
01/06/2009	Minutes Release	0	−4	3	−17	−1	−9	−14
02/18/2009	Minutes Release	9	11	4	6	8	9	16
04/08/2009	Minutes Release	2	−4	−7	−9	−4	−6	−6
05/20/2009	Minutes Release	−5	−5	−5	−7	−4	−4	−10
07/15/2009	Minutes Release	7	13	16	16	10	16	7
09/02/2009	Minutes Release	−1	−6	−6	−4	−7	−8	−5
10/14/2009	Minutes Release	1	7	10	3	7	7	8
11/24/2009	Minutes Release	0	−5	−5	−9	−5	−6	−3
01/06/2010	Minutes Release	−2	6	5	4	6	7	−1
Baseline Event Set		**−34**	**−91**	**−156**	**−113**	**−71**	**−101**	**−67**
Baseine Set + All FOMC		**−19**	**−62**	**−140**	**−123**	**−50**	**−83**	**−74**
Cumulative Change: 11/24/08 to 1/28/2010		**−39**	**30**	**−96**	**−109**	**21**	**20**	**−482**

Source: Gagnon and others 2010.
Notes: Agy = agency; FOMC = Federal Open Market Committee; MBS = mortgage-backed security; TP = term premium; UST = US Treasury.
[1]Included in the baseline event set.
[2]Two-day change for agency MBS on March 18, 2009, due to a Bloomberg data error.

lower risk premiums on these assets. Declines in the swap rate and the Baa corporate bond index yield show that quantitative easing had effects beyond those on the securities targeted for purchase. Gagnon and others (2010) also contains a model estimated on monthly data, January 1985 to June 2008. The results are in line with the event study, implying an overall reduction in the 10-year term premium in the range of 30 to 100 basis points as a result of the program.

Engen, Laubach, and Reifschneider (2015) use estimates of the interest rate effects of the Fed's forward guidance and quantitative easing programs in the FRB/US macroeconomic model to assess the economic stimulus provided by unconventional policy. The effect of forward guidance is derived from estimated changes in the expected FOMC federal funds rate rule, while the estimates of the effect of the quantitative easing program on term premiums are taken from Ihrig and others (2012). The latter show a maximum cumulative impact on the 10-year term premium of about 120 basis points in 2013 (Figure 12.1).

In the FRB/US model, these estimated interest rates have a peak effect of −1¼ percentage points on the unemployment rate and of ½ percentage point on the

Figure 12.1. Estimated 10-Year Term-Premium Effect of Federal Open Market Committee Quantitative Easing: Large-Scale Asset Purchases, Phases LSAP1–LSAP3; and Maturity Extension Program, Phases MEP1–MEP2, 2009–20
(Basis points)

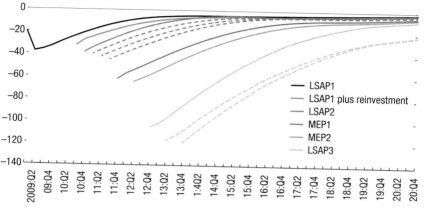

Sources: Engen, Laubach, and Reifschneider 2015; Ihrig and others 2012.
Notes: LSAP = large-scale asset purchases; MEP = maturity extension program.

inflation rate relative to what would have occurred absent the unconventional policy actions (Figure 12.2). Note, however, that the peak unemployment effect does not occur until early 2015 and the peak inflation effect until 2016. The net stimulus to real activity and inflation was apparently limited in part by the gradual nature of the changes in policy expectations and term premium effects. Had the FOMC revealed earlier the full extent of the eventual quantitative easing program, the boost to output and inflation would have been quicker. This suggests that although the Fed's communications were effective, there may have been room for improvement.

The importance of communications was underlined by the taper tantrum of May 2013, when concerns in the market about a tapering of purchases—following Chairman Benjamin Bernanke's testimony to the US Congress's Joint Economic Committee—raised the expected future federal funds rate (Figure 12.3) and longer-term rates and risk premiums (Figure 12.4). These increases were much larger than those implied by the modest increases envisaged by FOMC policy rate forecasts. This suggests that more explicit, quantitative statements on likely future unconventional measures may be useful, especially for the winding down phase of the quantitative easing program.

The tantrum took place as the Fed began to consider renormalization of its policy stance, with the economic recovery at last gathering steam. The main communications challenge for the FOMC later became how to communicate a gradual upward path in the federal funds rate and a scaling down of the Fed's large balance sheet without triggering another market overreaction.

Figure 12.2. Predicted Evolution of the Economy If Late-2013 Perceptions of Unconventional Measures Had Been in Place in 2009
(Percent)

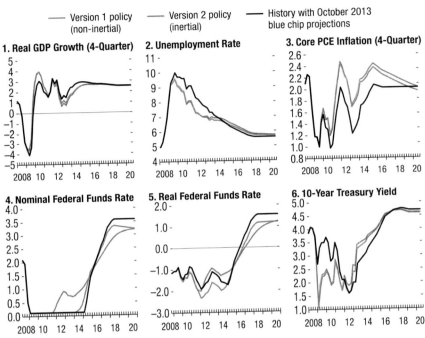

Source: Engen, Laubach, and Reifschneider 2015.
Notes: The version 1 simulation assumes that agents in the historical baseline always view the funds rate rule as non-inertial. In the version 2 simulations, agents in the historical baseline perceive the funds rate rule becoming inertial (lambda = 0.8) beginning in 2012. PCE = personal consumption expenditures.

LOSS-MINIMIZING MONETARY POLICY BASED ON A SIMPLE MODEL

The Federal Reserve Board staff has considerable experience with optimal control approaches to monetary policy (English, López-Salido, and Tetlow 2013; Brayton, Laubach, and Reifschneider 2014).[7] This chapter provides an example of this approach applied to a simple model of the US economy that captures the

---

[7]Considerable technical literature focuses on robust control of monetary policy, in particular, the analysis and determination of optimal policy under model uncertainty. See Cogley and Sargent 2005; Svensson and Williams 2005; Brock, Durlauf, and West 2003; Durlauf and West 2007; Brock and Durlauf 2005. This chapter is intended to be a very practical illustration of how models can be used to improve the policy dialogue and how different models can provide different policy insights when combined with simple policy rules or optimal-control techniques.

Figure 12.3. Federal Funds Futures (24 months ahead) and Treasury Rates, 2008–14
(Percent)

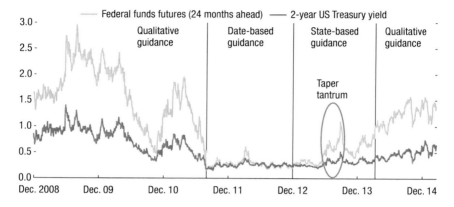

Source: Alichi and others 2015.

Figure 12.4. Ten-Year Treasury Yield and ACM Term Premium, 2008–14
(Percent)

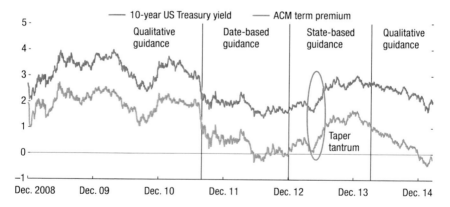

Source: Alichi and others 2015.
Note: ACM = Adrian, Crump, and Moench 2013.

trade-off between inflation and output. It sets up the model in a stylized version of the below-par postcrisis economy. It examines three policy reaction functions, in the same model and context, and compares outcomes. In each case the model derives a projected path for the federal funds rate that will achieve the official target over the medium term, while taking account of the welfare costs of output gaps.

The policy decision frameworks considered are a simple Taylor rule, an inflation-forecast-based (IFB) reaction function, and minimization of a loss function that reflects the preferences of the policymakers.

It is interesting that the loss-minimization approach could, in a situation near the effective lower bound for the interest rate with a negative output gap and undesired disinflationary pressure, result in an ex ante planned overshoot of the inflation target. Under the circumstances, this represents prudent risk avoidance—policymakers would place a high priority on getting away from the dark corner of the deflation spiral. Increased medium-term expectations of inflation lower the real interest rate, and hence stimulate consumption and investment demand.

Outline of the Model

The simple closed-economy model used is based on the standard closed-economy, inflation-targeting model.[8] It has equations for output (investment/saving curve) and inflation (based on an expectations-augmented Phillips curve), and embodies a policy reaction function that ensures that inflation returns to target within a medium-term horizon. The model is forward looking, in that expectations and policy reactions are driven in part by the model's own future solved values (in the long term, both expectations and outcomes converge to steady-state paths). The output gap equation contains a bank-lending-tightening variable, which captures exogenous changes in credit conditions. Demand shocks are represented by the stochastic term in the output gap equation, and supply shocks by that in the inflation equation.

For present purposes, the only aspect that needs discussion in any depth is the form of the policy decision for the federal funds rate. The analysis here experiments with three alternatives. They all have in common that the real interest rate rises and falls with the inflation rate and the output gap (excess demand).

Taylor rule. The variant used in this chapter, as shown below, is like that proposed in Taylor (1993):

$$i_t = \bar{r}_t + \pi 4_t + 0.5 \times (\pi 4_t - \pi^*) + 0.5 \times y_t + \varepsilon_t^i, \tag{12.1}$$

where i_t is the federal funds rate; $\bar{r}_t$ is the equilibrium real interest rate; $\pi 4_t$ is average annualized inflation over the past four quarters; π^* is the inflation objective, assumed to be 2 percent; and ε_t^i is a policy deviation shock. The nominal federal funds rate is a function of the equilibrium real interest rate; the inflation rate; the deviation of inflation from target with a coefficient of 0.5; and the output gap, also with a coefficient of 0.5. The exogenous increase over time in the equilibrium real interest rate assumes that the extremely low level of real interest rates in the aftermath of the crisis reflected contractionary forces and heightened uncertainties in the economy, which gradually dissipate over time.

---

[8]The main equations of the model are presented in appendices of Alichi and others (2015). The model is based on a stripped-down version of the IMF's Global Projection Model.

Inflation-forecast-based reaction function. The IFB reaction function used in this chapter focuses on the forecast for year-over-year PCE inflation three quarters in the future.

$$i_t = 0.71 \times i_{t-1} + (1 - 0.71) \times \left[\bar{r}_t + \pi 4_{t+3} \right.$$
$$\left. + 0.91 \times \left(\pi 4_{t+3} - \pi^* \right) + 0.21 y_t \right] + \varepsilon_t^i. \tag{12.2}$$

Here the nominal federal funds rate is a function of its lagged value (a way of smoothing the reactions to changes in inflation and output), the equilibrium nominal interest rate (as measured by the sum of the equilibrium real interest rate and the projected year-over-year core PCE rate of inflation), the forecast deviation of projected inflation from its target value, and the output gap. Interest rate smoothing is a well-known feature of monetary policy, and can be justified on various grounds.[9] In contrast to the Taylor rule, the IFB formulation ignores inflation shocks that are expected to reverse within the three-quarter policy horizon. It also allows the central bank to take account of known developments that might affect inflation over this horizon, including lagged effects of the policy itself that are still in the pipeline.

Minimizing a loss function. The loss function incorporates the principal objectives of the central bank in policy making.

$$L_t = \sum_{t=1}^{\infty} \left[\alpha \times \left(\pi 4_{t+i} - \pi^* \right)^2 + \beta \times y_{t+i}^2 + \gamma \times \left(i_{t+i} - i_{t+i-1} \right)^2 \right] \tag{12.3}$$

The quadratic formulation implies that large deviations from desired levels weigh disproportionately more in the objective function than small deviations—that is, that there is a rising marginal cost of inflation deviations from the target, output gaps, and interest rate volatility. Given that policy actions are subject to imprecision and uncertainty, this is reasonable, since policymakers should focus principally on avoiding larger errors instead of trying to fine-tune the economy. Policymakers would want to keep their economies well away from dark corners where recovery from shocks becomes much more difficult because of nonlinearities like the effective lower bound (Blanchard 2014). In other words, the central bank might tolerate small deviations from targets, but would be strongly against large recessions or destabilized inflation expectations.[10]

The squared change of the federal funds rate in the equation represents aversion to interest rate volatility. This term smooths the policy response of the federal funds rate, reflecting the behavior of central banks. By taking account of both current and expected future values of output and inflation, this formulation incorporates currently available information about likely future developments into the policy response.

---

[9]For example, Woodford (2003) presents a theoretical argument that some policy rate smoothing is optimal for clear signals to the market about the intent of policy.

[10]A lesson from endogenous credibility models is that an episode of excessive inflation can result in a costly loss of the nominal anchor (such as Argov and others 2007). A deflation trap destabilizes inflation expectations on the downside.

In the baseline calibration, equal weight (1.0) is put on inflation and output gaps, reflecting a dual mandate or, equivalently, inflation-forecast targeting. The smoothing coefficient for the change in the nominal interest rate is set to 0.5. In sensitivity analyses, variants of the baseline calibration are considered where the weights on inflation and output differ from the baseline case.

The feedback loops are also worth underlining. Any shock of material size and duration, in any equation, reverberates through the whole system, and brings into play the policy response, which eventually, through the transmission mechanism, will stabilize inflation at the long-term target rate, and output at its long-term equilibrium, or potential level.

Illustrative Simulation Results

The illustrative simulations of possible policy responses are based on assumed initial conditions in the US economy as of the fourth quarter of 2014, with an output gap of –2 percent (that is, excess capacity), a rate of PCE inflation of about 1.5 percent, and a federal funds rate of about zero. In Figure 12.5, the policy implications of the IFB reaction function (the blue line) and the loss function DM1 (green circles) are compared.

The simulations incorporate an estimate of the time-varying real equilibrium federal funds rate (the so-called neutral rate, reported as the dashed line in Figure 12.5, panel 2). While there is considerable uncertainty about estimates of the neutral rate, which is unobservable, estimates in Pescatori and Turunen (2015) suggest that it is currently likely to be close to zero and to increase only gradually over time (see also Dudley 2012; Yellen 2015).

Consistent with these results, in the simulations it is assumed that the neutral rate rises from 0 in the fourth quarter of 2014 to about 1.3 percent in the fourth quarter of 2020 (close to, but below the median of the FOMC members' forecast of the long-term real federal funds rate [about 1.75 percent]). The rising trend is put forward here to depict the return of the equilibrium rate to a more normal value after the damaging effects on investment and confidence of the global financial crisis.[11] Equivalently, with a 2 percent inflation target, the equilibrium nominal rate rises from 2 percent in the fourth quarter of 2014 to 3.3 percent in the fourth quarter of 2020.

The federal funds rate gradually rises starting almost immediately under the IFB reaction function, whereas under the DM1 loss function it remains at the floor until mid-2016, before beginning to rise. The much earlier increase under the IFB reaction function is related to the anticipated increase in the equilibrium real interest rate in the IFB function specification. The IFB policy tightening means a slower closing of the output gap, and inflation below target for longer, with the output gap and the rate of inflation moving gradually to the long-term equilibrium. In contrast, the output gap and the inflation rate overshoot somewhat under the DM1 policy, with the output gap moving to a positive

---

[11]Taylor (1993) assumes a constant 2 percent equilibrium real rate.

Figure 12.5. Illustrative Example: IFB Reaction Function versus a Dual Mandate CB Loss Function, 2014–20

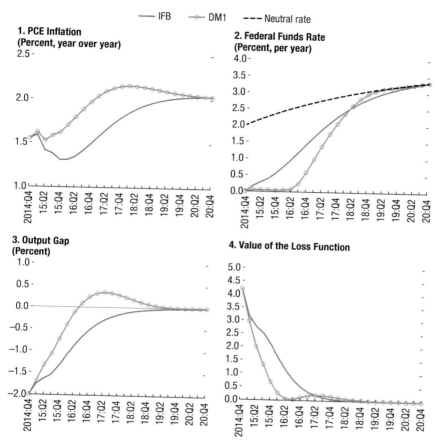

Source: IMF staff calculations.
Notes: CB = central bank; DM = dual mandate; IFB = inflation-forecast based; PCE = personal consumption expenditures.

0.3 percent (that is, modest excess demand) at the maximum, and the rate of inflation to 2.2 percent at the maximum. That is, equilibrium is reached via a modest cycle, which is optimal given the symmetric weight attached to inflation or the output gap being above or below the long-term goals.

Sensitivity Analysis: Variants of the Model

The loss function in the baseline analysis puts equal weight (1.0) on inflation and output gaps. To examine the robustness of these results, a second loss function calibration (DM2) is considered, which has half the weight on the output gap as

Figure 12.6. Comparison of Four Reaction Functions, 2014–20 (Part 1)

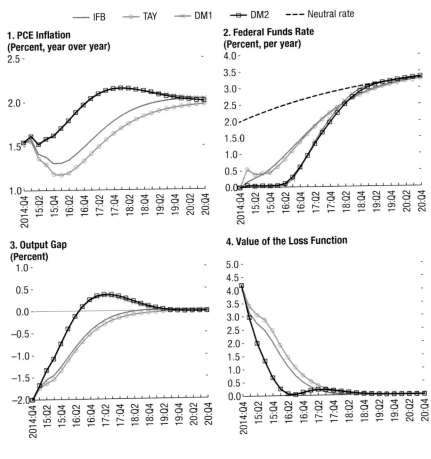

Source: IMF staff calculations.
Notes: DM = dual mandate; IFB = inflation-forecast based; PCE = personal consumption expenditures; TAY = Taylor rule.

that on the inflation gap. Figures 12.6 and 12.7 present all four policy approaches (Taylor, IFB, DM1, and DM2). In these figures, DM1 is represented by a red line with crosses and DM2 by a black line with squares.

The two DM lines sit almost on top of each other—the halving of the weight on the output gap in DM2 makes hardly any difference to the outcome. The two reaction functions (blue line for the IFB reaction function, green line with circles for the Taylor rule) show very similar results to each other. Thus, the major difference is seen in the pair of loss-function minimizations versus the pair of policy rules. To repeat, the much lower real interest rate under the loss-minimization approach has a significant effect on the movements of output and inflation. Higher medium-term inflation, with forward-looking expectations, means that

Figure 12.7. Comparison of Four Reaction Functions, 2014–20 (Part 2)

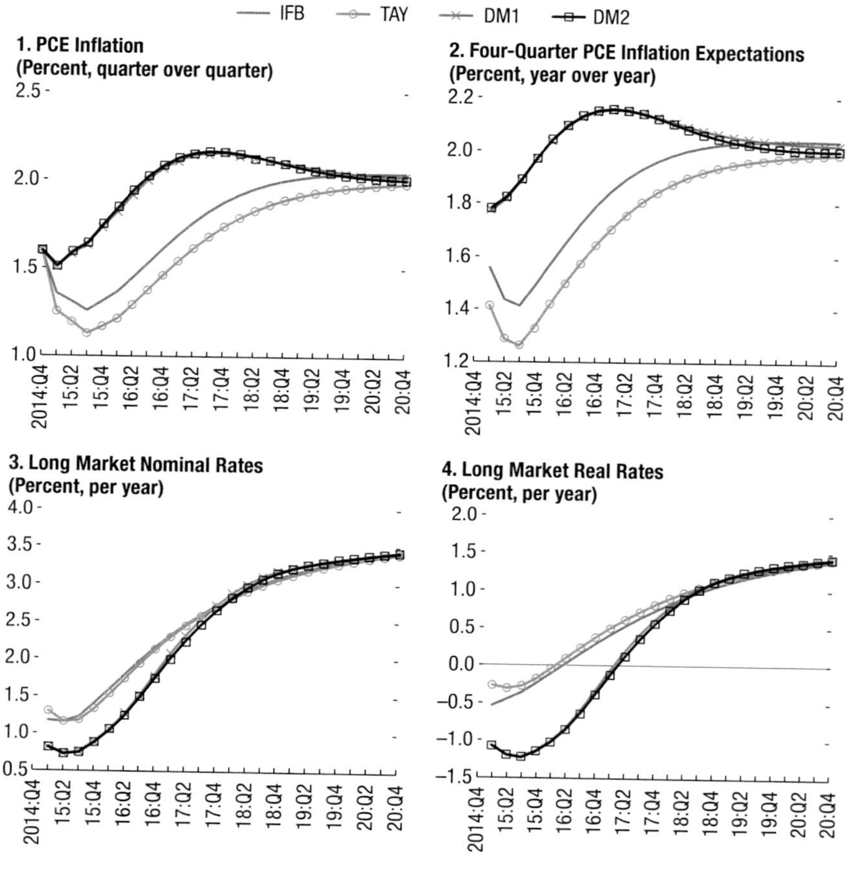

—— IFB   —○— TAY   —✕— DM1   —□— DM2

**1. PCE Inflation
(Percent, quarter over quarter)**

**2. Four-Quarter PCE Inflation Expectations
(Percent, year over year)**

**3. Long Market Nominal Rates
(Percent, per year)**

**4. Long Market Real Rates
(Percent, per year)**

Source: IMF staff calculations.
Notes: DM = dual mandate; IFB = inflation-forecast based; PCE = personal consumption expenditures; TAY = Taylor rule.

the difference is even larger for real long-term rates than for nominal short-term rates—compare the bottom pair of panels of Figure 12.7. This drives stronger growth (as shown in the output gap) and a higher inflation rate, as compared with the linear reaction functions. The overshooting of inflation and output under DM1 and DM2 is the deliberate result of the very stimulative policy stance. From the viewpoint of the loss functions, the starting point for the economy (with output well below potential and inflation below the target rate) is very inefficient. Given the rising marginal cost of the negative output and inflation gaps, and given the effective lower bound, which deprives policy of a stimulative tool in the event of a negative demand shock, the central bank takes a minor upside risk to insure against a much costlier downside risk.

Figure 12.8. Two Different Reaction Functions for Expansionary Demand Shock with Nonlinear Phillips Curve, 2014–20

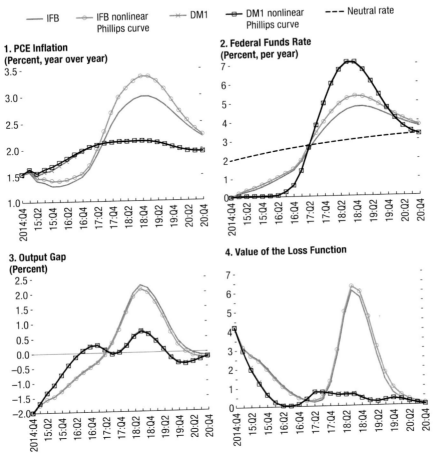

Source: IMF staff calculations.
Notes: DM = dual mandate; IFB = inflation-forecast based; PCE = personal consumption expenditures.

To illustrate upside risks to inflation, overheating scenarios with a nonlinear Phillips curve are considered, which has inflation increase sharply as slack diminishes. Figure 12.8 presents two policy approaches (IFB and DM1) toward an expansionary demand shock that has appreciable inflationary potential.

The baseline linear Phillips curve is

$$\pi_t = \lambda_1 \times \pi 4_{t+4} + (1 - \lambda_1) \times \pi 4_{t-1} + \lambda_2 \times y_{t-1} + \varepsilon_t^\pi \qquad (12.4)$$
$$\lambda_1 = 0.70; \ \lambda_2 = 0.10.$$

The alternative nonlinear model is[12]

$$\pi_t = \lambda_1 \times \pi 4_{t+4} + \left(1 - \lambda_1\right) \times \pi 4_{t-1} + \lambda_2 \times \frac{5y_{t-1}}{5 - y_{t-1}} + \varepsilon_t^\pi$$
$$\lambda_1 = 0.70; \; \lambda_2 = 0.10. \tag{12.5}$$

In the first equation, inflation responds symmetrically to negative and positive output gaps. In the second, the marginal impact of an increase in the gap is small when the gap is negative, but large when the gap is positive. The analysis calibrates the curve for inflation to have a floor of –5 percent and to rise without limit as the output gap approaches +5 percent.

Under the loss-function approach, the central bank raises the interest rate much more aggressively in response to the expansionary shock than under the IFB approach. Inflation is lower and the output gap is smaller. The loss-function approach quickly eliminates the inefficiency associated with output and inflation gaps being simultaneously positive. The alternative specifications in the Phillips curve make hardly any difference for the outcomes. The reason is that the loss-function approach foresees the stark potential implications of the nonlinearity, and adjusts the interest rate aggressively. As a result, the economy stays in the region where nonlinearity is a minor factor. In contrast, under the IFB rule, both output and inflation increase significantly more than in the linear case.

Forecast Confidence Bands and Alternative Simulations

Model-based confidence intervals, derived from the historical record of ex post prediction errors, are useful both in the assessment of risks during the formulation of policy, and in communicating the magnitude of the risks to the public.

Figures 12.9, 12.10, and 12.11 show forecast confidence intervals for the federal funds rate, year-over-year inflation rate, and the output gap for the monetary policy responses under IFB, and for the two calibrations of the loss function.

The right-hand panels show the results if the initial output gap were believed to be –4 percent rather than –2 percent. The shaded bands show the confidence intervals, from 10 to 90 percent, in 10-percentage-point increments.

These bands show a wide range of uncertainty. For example, the 30 to 70 percent confidence bands are wide relative to the planned medium-term overshoot of the inflation target discussed in the preceding subsection. This gives a better perspective on the challenges facing policymakers.

Since the loss-function approach implies aggressive interest rate responses to shocks, it results in wider confidence bands for the interest rate but much narrower bands for output and inflation than the IFB reaction function.

Confidence bands for the policy rate under the loss-function approach are skewed because of the floor to the interest rate. And the volatility of the economy

---

[12]See Laxton, Meredith, and Rose (1995) and Laxton, Rose, and Tambakis (1999) for discussions of the nonlinear Phillips curve.

Figure 12.9. Illustrative Examples of Confidence Bands for Federal Funds Rate, 2014–19

(Percent, per year)

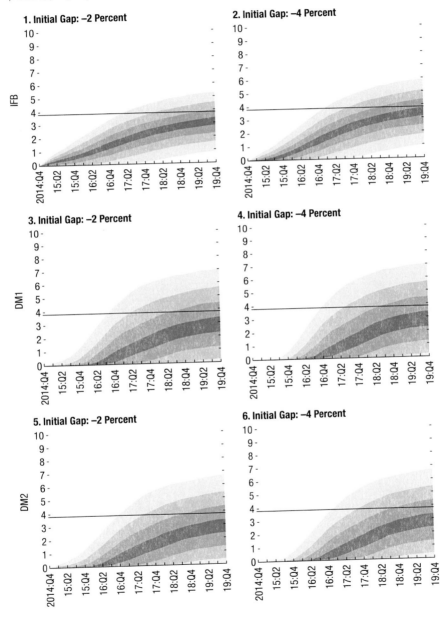

Source: IMF staff calculations.
Notes: DM = dual mandate; IFB = inflation-forecast based.

Figure 12.10. Illustrative Examples of Confidence Bands for PCE Year-over-Year Inflation, 2014–19
(Percent)

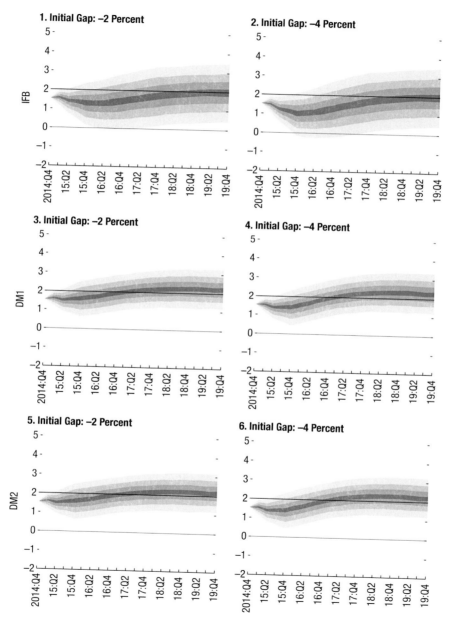

Source: IMF staff calculations.
Notes: DM = dual mandate; IFB = inflation-forecast based; PCE = personal consumption expenditures.

Figure 12.11. Illustrative Examples of Confidence Bands for Output Gap, 2014–19
(Percent)

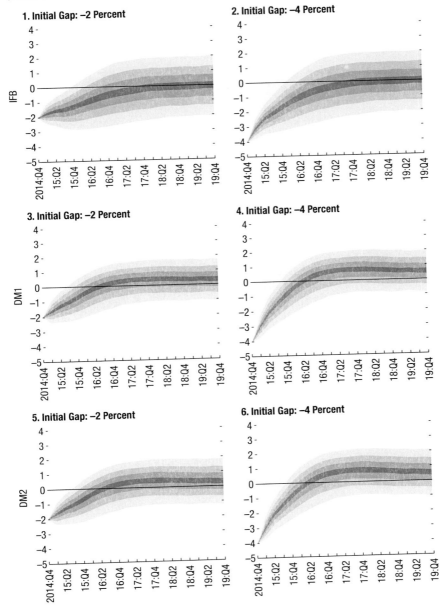

Source: IMF staff calculations.
Notes: DM = dual mandate; IFB = inflation-forecast based.

is somewhat greater under the –4 percent output gap case versus the –2 percent case, because of the higher likelihood that the floor will impede an effective stabilizing policy response.

A Summing Up of the Policy Simulations

While the linear reaction functions tested here may give reasonable results in normal times, they have difficulty in abnormal times. When policy interest rates are near the effective lower bound, the quadratic loss-function approach appears to give better results because its response to disinflationary conditions involves an extended commitment to keep the rate at the floor. As the effective lower bound approaches, a policy that avoids extreme outcomes (the quadratic loss function) provides ever stronger policy reactions to contractionary shocks, to keep the economy away from the deflation dark corner.

At the effective lower bound, this becomes a commitment to hold the short-term interest rate there for long enough that inflation will rise, perhaps for a while above the long-term target rate. The boost to inflation expectations reduces the real medium-term interest rate, even though the nominal short rate can go no lower. Under the circumstances, where there is very little risk of sustained inflationary pressure, but a high risk of getting stuck in the deflation trap, such a strategy represents prudent risk avoidance.[13] This is consistent with Evans and others (2015), who show that monetary policy, under uncertainty and close to the effective lower bound, is better placed to deal with risks from inflation temporarily above the central bank's objective than with a scenario where inflation falls short of it.

PROPOSALS FOR FURTHER ADVANCES IN TRANSPARENCY

Publishing the Forecast

Moves toward a more transparent framework—publishing the inflation objective, providing tentative estimates of the equilibrium (or natural) rate of unemployment, and forecasts of the policy rate path—have supported the Fed's efforts to stimulate the economy in the decade after the global crisis. FOMC members have discussed further enhancements to communications. Plosser (2014) suggests that the Fed publish a quarterly Monetary Policy Report, endorsed by the FOMC.[14] This would convey more detail about the FOMC's central forecast, the nature of uncertainties,

---

[13]Isard, Laxton, and Eliasson (1999) make a more general argument for stronger policy reactions to avoid bad outcomes in the presence of model uncertainty, especially where nonlinearities may be involved.

[14]IMF (2014) too recommends publishing a quarterly monetary policy report, to convey more detail about the majority view of the FOMC on the outlook, policies, and the nature of uncertainties around the baseline.

and the rationale for actual policy decisions given the relevant options. The latter could be illustrated with alternative projections for the short-term interest rate paths from "a few Taylor-like rules." These might at the same time shed light on the differing risks associated with the various alternatives, and help communicate the risk-management aspect of policy making. Mester (2015) raises the option of releasing a complete forecast for each FOMC member. While the existing Summary of Economic Projections reveals the central tendency in the range of FOMC projections, and the associated array of interest rate forecasts, it does not present a coherent forecast of the kind that would emerge from an explicit model. Nor does it convey the degree of uncertainty that members may feel around their forecasts.

Extensive international experience with monetary policy reports at inflation-targeting central banks suggests that these proposals have merit. Such reports help prepare the public for the likely response of monetary policy to evolving economic conditions, and hence reduce the surprise component of policy.[15] A report that releases all key macroeconomic variables from a complete, consistent forecast, can be an important tool for communicating how the central bank is balancing its short-term output and inflation objectives (IMF 2014; Levin 2014). Monetary policy reports also play a role in the process of democratic accountability of the central bank: policymakers provide a justification—which may be challenged—for their past and current actions, in terms of how policy decisions help meet the announced objectives of monetary policy.

Advantages and Disadvantages of Explicit Publication of the Rate Path

Publishing the Fed's forecast in full, including the explicit endogenous interest rate path, would have advantages and disadvantages. Publication of the interest rate scenario should be helpful for managing expectations of future interest rate movements.

This argument is particularly applicable to a situation in which markets are faced with unfamiliar developments. Currently, the case in point is the eventual "normalization" of policy, following almost a decade of exceptional monetary ease. Longer-term interest rates might snap back if markets perceive that the very low rates have achieved their purpose as output and inflation pick up. For example, early in this decade, the announcement of numerical thresholds, for the unemployment rate and so on, to indicate when rates might rise from the floor oversimplified the outlook for policy. The glitch of the taper tantrum illustrates the danger. This risk could be reduced by releasing a complete central bank forecast, with the gradually rising medium-term policy rate path that this would

---

[15]The Czech National Bank, which ranks near the top in rankings of central bank transparency, provides an example of how open communications, in the context of a well-articulated program of action, may increase the effectiveness of unconventional policy measures. Chapter 9 discusses the exceptional use of the exchange rate as an additional tool for easing monetary conditions in the Czech Republic, 2013–17.

involve. Accompanied by confidence bands and relevant alternative scenarios, the published forecast would highlight the uncertainties surrounding the projected rate path. This also would reduce the probability of a bond market snap-back.

The Fed's Summary of Economic Projections currently provides information about the likely path of policy. However, the Summary of Economic Projections does not reveal the specific interest rate path consistent with the baseline economic outlook. This leaves an awkward information gap. While the interest rate dots provide information about individual policymakers' expectations, they do not necessarily represent the FOMC's majority view of the expected policy rate path. Also, it is hard to judge internal consistency since for each dot there is presumably a distinct individual view of the associated growth, interest rate, and inflation paths. And the median path through the interest rate dots may not be internally consistent with the median forecast for other variables.

The principal perceived risk in publishing an explicit path for projected interest rates appears to be that some market participants might believe that the Fed is making a commitment to bring about the projected interest rate path, regardless of changing developments. In any case, one of the most important messages that the Fed communicates is that the forecast is conditional upon information available at the time of writing and is liable to change as new information becomes available. With respect to release of the interest rate forecast, the central bank should underline the conditionality.

For example, when Sveriges Riksbank decided to publish the interest rate scenario underlying its forecast, the governor noted that "it is important to emphasize . . . that we are talking about a forecast for the repo rate. This is the repo rate development that currently appears most likely given the information available. We are not making any promises. The fact that the Riksbank is presenting its own interest rate path does not mean that we are laying down a policy that we will commit ourselves to following" (Ingves 2007). Swedish central bankers anticipated that there might be an awkward learning period: "it is natural that it will take some time for the new system to become established" (Svensson 2007). In view of this caution, it is somewhat surprising that the experience—in New Zealand since June 1997, Norway since November 2005, Israel since July 2007, and the Czech Republic since February 2008, as well as in Sweden—suggests that financial market participants learn quickly about the conditional nature of the forecast interest rate path.

A more substantive difficulty for the FOMC would be the practical difficulties of forging agreement on a published path for policy rates within a large and diverse group. Mishkin (2004) and Goodhart (2001), for example, have argued that attempting to agree on a path in a committee setting could complicate the decision-making process.

Whose Forecast Should Be Published?

Two options are considered to illustrate the issues. In the first, policymakers take direct ownership of the published forecast. This would be feasible for central banks that reach policy decisions by consensus, or by the governor alone. However, it would be much more difficult at the Fed, or other central banks where decisions are made by vote. FOMC members may have divergent views about the forecast. When there is no consensus, the Fed might have to publish up to 12 complete projections for the voting FOMC members (Mester 2015). How would all this be accommodated in the write-up explaining policy? Such an approach could be inefficient internally and confusing externally.

The second option is for the staff to produce and publish the baseline forecast that the FOMC could then endorse. The published report would include alternative scenarios to represent substantive differences of opinion among members, and hence to give a sense of the dispersion of views around the baseline.[16] This has worked quite well in several central banks that make policy decisions by committee, such as the Czech National Bank. The Czech National Bank emphasizes that the baseline provides an important input into monetary policy decision-making, but only one input, as some policymakers may disagree with the staff forecast. In practice, with appropriate internal communications between policymakers and forecasters in the production process, the staff baseline forecast should not wander far from the consensus view of the committee.[17] The range of views among policymakers would be reflected in alternative scenarios prepared by the staff, if not in confidence bands around the baseline, and in the highlighting of specific uncertainties in official publications and statements. Policymakers would not be obliged to defend any given forecast beyond expressing their confidence in the process that produced it. However, they should have solid economic arguments for any substantive disagreement with the staff. For example, at times they may be uncertain whether a recent change is persistent or transitory. In the former case, central bank action may well be required, while in the latter the problem unwinds itself without any central bank action. Another example would be where the baseline projection sees a development that is not yet reflected in the data. Whether the central bank should act now or wait and see can be the subject of legitimate disagreement. Clear and transparent airing of such differences would help outsiders understand the action (or absence of action) by the central bank. It might even increase the credibility of the central bank, since open debate would shed light on how policy would react when future data reveal which of the opposing views was more valid.

---

[16] A significant investment has been made by Fed policymakers and staff to develop the scenarios that are presented in the "dots." The scenarios could serve as the basis for constructing a baseline scenario, highlighting key risks and communicating the width of the confidence bands around the baseline forecast.

[17] Chapter 4 discusses the structure of a forecasting and policy analysis system for inflation-forecast targeting, including the communications between policymakers and forecasters that are needed for the production of useful forecasts.

CONCLUSIONS

This decade, the Federal Reserve has effected major reforms to clarify its policy framework while maintaining the dual mandate for price stability and maximum employment. It has adopted an explicit inflation objective (2 percent). It has increased the transparency of policy in other ways too, notably through the timely publication of FOMC member forecasts, including projections for policy interest rates, and more open communications. It has employed unconventional instruments, motivated by the need to stimulate the economy under the constraint of the effective lower bound on the federal funds rate. The maturing expansion of the economy provides evidence that these initiatives have been successful.

The changes, however, amount to more than a set of measures to boost policy effectiveness during an abnormal period. They have brought about a more transparent framework for monetary policy that is appropriate for normal times, as well as for the unusual situation, post–global crisis, of chronic excess capacity, undesirably low inflation, and a rock-bottom federal funds rate. The revised arrangements can be regarded as equivalent, for all intents and purposes, to an inflation-forecast-targeting approach. And from this perspective, the Fed might consider further enhancements to the policy framework.

A simulation under conditions of a negative output gap, below-target inflation, and a binding interest rate floor results in a modest, planned overshooting of inflation. The monetary stimulus comes from expectations that under this policy the short-term policy interest rate will be held at the effective lower bound for an extended period, and from the boost that this gives to the expected rate of inflation, which reduces the current and expected real interest rate. Since this policy gets the economy away quite quickly from the dark corner of the deflation spiral, it can be viewed as a risk-management strategy.

Much of monetary policy relies on management of public expectations. Central bank communications always have an important role here, as changes in the policy rate—a very short-term money market rate—must influence the longer-term rates at which households and firms borrow and lend to have the desired macroeconomic impact. Effective communications are especially valuable when policy embarks on new initiatives. Thus, early adopters of inflation targets quickly recognized, in view of widespread skepticism about the proposed regime, the need for an intensive effort to explain what the new policy was about, for regular reports on the policy actions intended to achieve the targets, and so on. In the same way, since the global financial crisis, the Fed and other central banks have taken care to provide information on the introduction and use of less conventional monetary instruments—extended forward guidance and large-scale asset purchases (quantitative easing). That these operations have been broadly successful in their outcomes demonstrates that execution and communication of the program has been effective. At the same time, the short-lived but unhelpful taper tantrum suggests room for further improvement in the mode of communication.

In this regard, there is a strong argument for full transparency about the Federal Reserve's estimates of the quantities and interest rates that it projects. Publication of the complete staff forecast, with the explicit path for the short-term interest rate, would make transparent the main economic input into the conduct of policy. Uncertainties would be communicated by the presentation of confidence bands and relevant alternative scenarios to the baseline. This would make redundant the current incomplete set of information provided by the "dot plot." Dissenting outlooks among members would be revealed in the published alternative scenarios. Open communications of this kind would clarify the rationale for federal funds rate decisions and, just as important, raise the profile of the relevant uncertainties. In turn, better-informed expectations for inflation and policy rates would strengthen the effectiveness of policy actions, and allow the Federal Reserve to reach its goals at lower cost.

REFERENCES

Alichi, A., K. Clinton, C. Freedman, O. Kamenik, M. Juillard, D. Laxton, J. Turunen, and H. Wang. 2015. "Avoiding Dark Corners: A Robust Monetary Policy Framework for the United States." IMF Working Paper 15/134, International Monetary Fund, Washington, DC.

Andrade, P., J. Breckenfelder, F. De Fiore, P. Karadi, and O. Tristani. 2016. "The ECB's Asset Purchase Programme: An Early Assessment." European Central Bank Working Paper 1956, European Central Bank, Frankfurt.

Argov, E., N. Epstein, P. Karam, D. Laxton, and D. Rose. 2007. "Endogenous Monetary Policy Credibility in a Small Macro Model of Israel." IMF Working Paper 07/207, International Monetary Fund, Washington, DC.

Bernanke, B.S. 2013. "Communication and Monetary Policy." Herbert Stein Memorial Lecture, Washington, DC, November.

Blanchard, O. 2014. "Where Danger Lurks." *Finance and Development* 51 (3): 28–31.

Brayton, F., T. Laubach, and D. Reifschneider. 2014. "Optimal-Control Monetary Policy in the FRB/US Model." FEDS Notes, Board of Governors of the Federal Reserve System, Washington, DC.

Brock, W., and S. Durlauf. 2005. "Local Robustness Analysis: Theory and Application." *Journal of Economic Dynamics and Control* 29 (11): 2067–92.

———, and K. West. 2003. "Policy Evaluation in Uncertain Economic Environments." *Brookings Papers on Economic Activity* 34 (1): 235–322.

Churm, R., M. Joyce, G. Kapetanios, and K. Theodoridis. 2015. "Unconventional Monetary Policies and the Macroeconomy: The Impact of the United Kingdom's QE2 and Funding for Lending Scheme." Bank of England Staff Working Paper 542, Bank of England, London.

Cogley, T., and T. J. Sargent. 2005. "The Conquest of US Inflation: Learning and Robustness to Model Uncertainty." *Review of Economic Dynamics* 8 (2): 528–63.

Dudley, W. 2012. "Conducting Monetary Policy: Rules, Learning and Risk Management." Remarks at the C. Peter McColough Series on International Economics, Council on Foreign Relations, New York City, May 24.

Durlauf, S., and K. West. 2007. "Model Uncertainty and Policy Evaluation: Some Theory and Empirics." *Journal of Econometrics* 136 (2): 629–64.

Engen, E. M., T. Laubach, and D. Reifschneider. 2015. "The Macroeconomic Effects of the Federal Reserve's Unconventional Monetary Policies." Finance and Economics Discussion Series 2015–005, Board of Governors of the Federal Reserve System, Washington, DC.

English, W. B., J. D. López-Salido, and R. J. Tetlow. 2013. "The Federal Reserve's Framework for Monetary Policy—Recent Changes and New Questions." Federal Reserve Board, Paper presented at the 14th Jacques Polak Annual Research Conference, Washington, DC, November.

Evans, C., J. Fisher, F. Gourio, and S. Krane. 2015. "Risk Management for Monetary Policy Near the Zero Lower Bound." Brookings Papers on Economic Activity (Spring).

Federal Open Market Committee (FOMC). 2012. "Statement on Longer-Run Goals and Monetary Policy Strategy." Federal Reserve.

Gagnon, J. E. 2016. "Quantitative Easing: An Underappreciated Success." Peterson Institute for International Economics Policy Brief PB16–4, Peterson Institute for International Economics, Washington, DC.

Gagnon, J.E., M. Raskin, J. Remache, and B. Sack. 2010. "Large-Scale Asset Purchases by the Federal Reserve: Did They Work?" Federal Reserve Bank of New York Staff Report 441, Federal Reserve Bank of New York, NY.

Goodhart, C. 2001. "Monetary Transmission Lags and the Formulation of the Policy Decisions on Interest Rates." Federal Reserve Bank of St. Louis Review (July/August).

Gurkaynak, R., A. Levin, A. Marder, and E. Swanson. 2006. "Inflation Targeting and the Anchoring of Inflation Expectations in the Western Hemisphere." *Journal Economía Chilena (The Chilean Economy)* 9 (3): 19–52.

Gurkaynak, R., A. Levin, and E. Swanson. 2010. "Does Inflation Targeting Anchor Long-Run Inflation Expectations: Evidence from the US, UK, and Sweden." *Journal of the European Economic Association* 8 (6): 1208–42.

Hoover Institution. 2010. "Open Letter to Ben Bernanke." Hoover Institution, November 15.

International Monetary Fund (IMF). 2014. "United States: 2014 Article IV Consultation—Staff Report." Washington, DC: International Monetary Fund.

Ingves, S. 2007. "Monetary Policy, Openness and Financial Markets." Speech at SEB, Stockholm, September 24.

Ihrig, J., E. Klee, C. Li, B. Schulte, and M. Wei. 2012. "Expectations about the Federal Reserve's Balance Sheet and the Term Structure of Interest Rates." Federal Reserve Board Finance and Economics Discussion Series 2012–57, Board of Governors of the Federal Reserve System, Washington, DC.

Isard, P., D. Laxton, and A.-C. Eliasson. 1999. "Simple Monetary Policy Rules under Model Uncertainty." IMF Working Paper 99/75, International Monetary Fund, Washington, DC.

Laxton, D., G. Meredith, and D. Rose. 1995. "Asymmetric Effects of Economic Activity on Inflation." *IMF Staff Papers* 42 (2): 344–74.

Laxton, D., D. Rose, and D. Tambakis. 1999. "The U.S. Phillips Curve: The Case for Asymmetry." *Journal of Economic Dynamics and Control* 23: 1459–85.

Levin, A. 2014. "The Design and Communication of Systematic Monetary Policy Strategies." *Journal of Economic Dynamics and Control* 49: 52–69.

Mester, L. 2015. "The Outlook for the Economy and Monetary Policy Communications." Speech at the 31st Annual NABE Economic Policy Conference, sponsored by the National Association for Business Economics, Washington, DC.

Mishkin, F. 2004. "Can Central Bank Transparency Go Too Far." NBER Working Paper 10829, National Bureau for Economic Research, Cambridge, MA.

Pescatori, A., and J. Turunen. 2015. "Lower for Longer: Neutral Rates in the United States." IMF Working Paper 15/135, International Monetary Fund, Washington, DC.

Plosser, C. 2014. "Systematic Monetary Policy and Communication." Speech delivered at the Economic Club of New York, New York.

Svensson, L. E. O. 2007 "Monetary Policy and the Interest Rate Path." Speech presented at Danske Bank, Stockholm, August 22.

———, and N. Williams. 2005. "Monetary Policy with Model Uncertainty: Distribution Forecast Targeting." NBER Working Paper 11733, National Bureau of Economic Research, Cambridge, MA.

Taylor, J. 1993. "Discretion versus Policy Rules in Practice." *Carnegie-Rochester Conference Series on Public Policy* 39 (1):195–214.

Woodford, M. 2003. "Optimal Interest-Rate Smoothing." *Review of Economic Studies* 70 (4): 861–86.

————. 2012. "Methods of Policy Accommodation at the Interest-Rate Lower Bound." Presented at the Federal Reserve Bank of Kansas City Symposium, Jackson Hole, WY, August.

Yellen, J.L. 2012. "Perspectives on Monetary Policy." Speech at the Boston Economic Club Dinner, Boston, MA.

————. 2013. "Communication in Monetary Policy." Speech at the Society of American Business Editors and Writers 50th Anniversary Conference, Washington, DC, April.

————. 2014. "Monetary Policy and the Economic Recovery." Speech at the Economic Club of New York, April.

————. 2015. "Normalizing Monetary Policy: Prospects and Perspectives." Presented at "The New Normal Monetary Policy," a research conference sponsored by the Federal Reserve Bank of San Francisco, San Francisco, CA, March.

————. 2016. "The Federal Reserve's Monetary Policy Toolkit: Past, Present, and Future." Speech at "Designing Resilient Monetary Policy Frameworks for the Future," a symposium sponsored by the Federal Reserve Bank of Kansas City, Jackson Hole, WY, August.

Tobias, A., R. K. Crump, and E. Moench. 2013. "Pricing the Term Structure with Linear Regressions." *Journal of Financial Economics* 110 (1): 110–38.

PART **IV**

A Widened Perspective for Inflation-Forecast Targeting

CHAPTER 13

Low-Income Countries

Rahul Anand, Andrew Berg, and Rafael Portillo

The farmers care a lot more about the rain than they do about interest rates. But the central bank has a lot more influence over the interest rate than it does over the rains.
—Anonymous African central banker

In recent decades, many central banks in low-income countries have succeeded in reducing inflation to single digits while also deepening their financial markets and achieving high growth, the result in no small part of better macroeconomic management. Monetary policy has gained traction due to increased central bank independence, reduced fiscal dominance, and greater reliance on market-based procedures. More recently, though, policymakers in low-income countries have begun to ask that monetary policy do more than achieve a basic degree of stabilization.

This ambition is stymied by the general lack of clear and effective monetary policy frameworks, which impairs central banks' ability to steer financial conditions, respond appropriately to shocks, and avoid policy misalignments. Many central banks are therefore in the process of modernizing their policy frameworks to address these limitations. To further enhance their ability to anchor inflation and inflation expectations and to promote macroeconomic and financial stability, many of these central banks are moving toward more flexible and forward-looking frameworks for formulating, implementing, and communicating monetary policy.

The factors that contribute to the success of inflation-forecast-targeting regimes, as documented in previous chapters of this book, provide useful lessons for central banks in low-income countries that seek to improve their monetary frameworks. At the same time, these central bankers face unusual monetary policy challenges, such as relatively small financial systems and a heavy dependence on agriculture and commodities.

This chapter charts a way forward for monetary policy in low-income countries, drawing on the IMF's experience in helping build capacity in these central banks, notably in establishing forecasting and policy analysis systems. The discussion draws heavily on the experience of countries in sub-Saharan Africa, but the issues are broadly similar across low-income countries. Furthermore, monetary

---

This chapter is based on the work done at the IMF on monetary policy regimes in low-income countries. In particular, it draws heavily from Berg and Portillo (2018). It also draws on our work on IMF policy papers on the topic, notably IMF (2015) and on our engagement with central banks in Africa and Asia (Uganda, Kenya, Tanzania, Sri Lanka, and so on) on building their capacities for forward-looking monetary policy analysis and implementation.

policy issues in low-income countries differ in degree—but not fundamentally in kind—from those of more developed countries.

THE EVOLUTION OF MONETARY POLICY IN SUB-SAHARAN AFRICA

Starting in the mid-1980s and through the late 1990s many countries in sub-Saharan Africa began economic reform programs that often included the unification of multiple exchange rates; a movement toward more market-determined, flexible exchange rates; and the dismantling of exchange and trade controls. The conditions prevailing at the start of these programs (that is, heavily managed or even de facto pegged exchange rates, pervasive capital controls, and fiscally driven monetary policy) explain the appeal of such a monetary policy framework, anchored on control over money financing of the fiscal deficit.

Other key elements of this two-decade transition were sharp reductions in central bank financing of government and financial liberalizations that eliminated interest rate controls and introduced competition into the banking sector. The reestablishment of fiscal control provided support for the introduction by the late 1990s of money-based programs to bring down inflation to (or near) single digits in the context of higher economic growth and higher international reserves, in line with the experience of other developing countries. The liberalization of direct controls over the commercial banking system helped alleviate the prolonged financial repression (Adam and O'Connell 2005).[1] These developments also coincided with greater use of open market operations by central banks in the region. All of these developments had the effect of increasing the role of market signals and the importance of managing expectations in the implementation of monetary policy.

By the early 2000s, then, countries such as Ghana, Kenya, Nigeria, Tanzania, Uganda, and Zambia were beginning to enjoy sustained growth with low and stable inflation (see, for example, Kessy, O'Connell, and Nyella 2016). Macroeconomic stability was increasingly accompanied by the deepening and development of domestic asset markets and, in some cases, by moves to liberalize the capital account to encourage greater private capital inflows, including into sovereign debt.

The reduced role for the exchange rate as a nominal anchor and increasingly developed financial markets revealed weaknesses with existing policy frameworks. In particular, the money-targeting regimes did not provide effective frameworks for formulating and implementing policy. At the same time, the ambition grew for monetary policy to promote smoother functioning of interbank markets, to provide clearer interest rate signals, and more generally to play a greater stabilizing role.

---

[1]For countries in sub-Saharan Africa with available data (and without exchange rate pegs), the financial reform index reported by Giuliano, Mishra, and Spilimbergo (2010) more than doubled on average in the decade between 1985–1990 and 1995–2000. (The countries are Ghana, Kenya, Madagascar, Mozambique, Nigeria, South Africa, Tanzania, and Uganda.)

CHALLENGES FOR MONETARY POLICY IN LOW-INCOME COUNTRIES

Undertaking to modernize the monetary policy frameworks in low-income countries requires a reasonably accurate view of how these economies work. Standard macroeconomics does not fully capture the situation in low-income countries given that it was developed based on the experience of fairly stable institutions and consistent data series and thousands of research papers in advanced economies and more recently in emerging markets. Low-income countries face specific characteristics and challenges that influence the way in which their central banks conduct monetary policy.

The Monetary Transmission Mechanism

There are many reasons to think that the transmission mechanism in low-income countries may be different. Low-income countries have shallow financial markets, so that changes in financial conditions brought about by monetary policy may directly affect a smaller share of the population (Table 13.1). Furthermore, the nature of the policy itself decisively shapes the nature of transmission, and the opacity of existing frameworks may undermine the effectiveness of policy. Where exchange rates are heavily managed, or the capital account is closed, transmission through exchange rates is also likely to be attenuated. Moreover, reviews of the empirical literature (mostly based on vector autoregressions, VARs) have had difficulty finding a clear transmission mechanism (Mishra and Montiel 2012).

Some policymakers and researchers conclude from this assessment that the transmission mechanism is weak or even nonexistent (see Mishra, Montiel, and Spilimbergo 2013, for example). However, much of the empirical evidence may result in part from difficulties in applying standard empirical approaches to low-income countries rather than a lack of underlying transmission. Typical features of low-income country data, including short sample lengths, measurement error, and frequent policy regime changes, can greatly reduce the power of VARs to uncover the monetary transmission mechanism (Chapter 6 of Berg and Portillo 2018).

In addition, the policy regime itself strongly shapes transmission, in addition to and sometimes in lieu of deeper structural factors. Monetary policy relies on a clear understanding from financial market participants of current and likely future actions by the central bank, and existing arrangements in low-income countries make such a clear understanding difficult; the combination of money target misses, noisy short-term interest rates, and incipient communications makes it difficult to assess policymakers' intentions. Under these conditions, monetary policy decisions have a smaller impact on longer-term rates, inflation, and output than they do under interest-rate-based frameworks, even when policy intentions are the same and even when the underlying economic structure is supportive of monetary policy effectiveness.

TABLE 13.1.

Financial Sector Indicators: Low-Income Countries versus Other Economies

Group	Credit to the Private Sector (Percent of GDP)	Bank Credit to the Private Sector (Percent of GDP)	Five-Bank Asset Concentration (Percent)[1]	Stocks Traded, Total Value (Percent of GDP)	Dollarization[2]	Chinn-Ito Financial Openness Index[3]
Low-Income Countries	19.6	18.8	80.0	4.9	12.8	−0.4
Emerging Market Economies	60.9	49.1	69.6	26.6	4.0	0.3
Advanced Economies	145.3	133.7	84.8	70.2	0.5	2.2

Sources: Data is 2011 World Bank data except as noted; and IMF staff estimates.

[1] Assets of five largest banks are shown as a share of total commercial banking assets.

[2] Foreign currency deposits are shown as a share of total deposits in the banking system.

[3] Index values are for 2010. The index takes a maximum value of 2.5 for the most financially open economies, and a minimum of −1.9 for the least financially open (see Chinn and Ito 2008).

TABLE 13.2.

Economic Structure: Low-Income Countries versus Other Economies

Group	Exports (Percent of GDP)	Imports (Percent of GDP)	Aid (Percent of GDP)	Rural Population (Percent of total)	Commodity Exports (Percent of exports)[1]
Low-Income Countries	28.3	48.4	13.1	69.2	64
Emerging Market Economies	42.2	41.4	1.8	34.5	27.9
Advanced Economies	65.5	61.0	0	20.5	19.5

Source: Organisation for Economic Co-operation and Development; World Bank; and IMF staff estimates.
[1]Includes exports of food, agricultural raw materials, and ore and minerals (2011 data).

A study of the effects of a dramatic tightening in monetary policy in the East African Community in 2011 finds a well-functioning transmission mechanism, especially in those countries where the stance of monetary policy was communicated clearly. It also finds that the depth of financial markets is a less clear indicator of the strength of transmission than of the clarity of the regime (Chapter 5 of Berg and Portillo 2018).

It still may be that transmission in low-income countries is generally weaker and more uncertain than in other countries, which would caution against trying to fine-tune monetary policy. However, this point can easily be overemphasized. First, deep uncertainty about the transmission mechanism is not unique to low-income countries but rather is a general characteristic, perhaps especially of countries implementing new policy frameworks, often in the face of rapid structural change or financial crises. Second, this does not justify inaction. Indeed, weak transmission may explain the much larger policy movements that are often observed in sub-Saharan Africa.

Supply Shocks and Macroeconomic Volatility

The economies of low-income countries are typically commodity dependent in terms of both domestic production and trade and are thus dominated by supply shocks (Table 13.2). Indeed, it is difficult to identify a Phillips-curve-type relationship in the data because of the dominance of supply shocks, which tend to generate a negative correlation between the output gap and inflation in low-income countries (Figure 13.1). Many of these supply shocks call for adjustments to the real exchange rate. In general, developing economies with more flexible exchange rate regimes do a better job of shielding their economies from the effects of these shocks, thanks to the shock-absorbing role of the exchange rate.[2]

---

[2]See Broda (2004) and Edwards and Levy-Yeyati (2005) for evidence on the effect of terms-of-trade shocks in developing countries across exchange rate regimes, and Hoffmaister, Roldos, and Wickham (1998) and Ahmad and Pentecost (2010) for similar analyses for countries in sub-Saharan Africa.

Figure 13.1. Correlation between Inflation and the Output Gap, by Level of Income per Capita

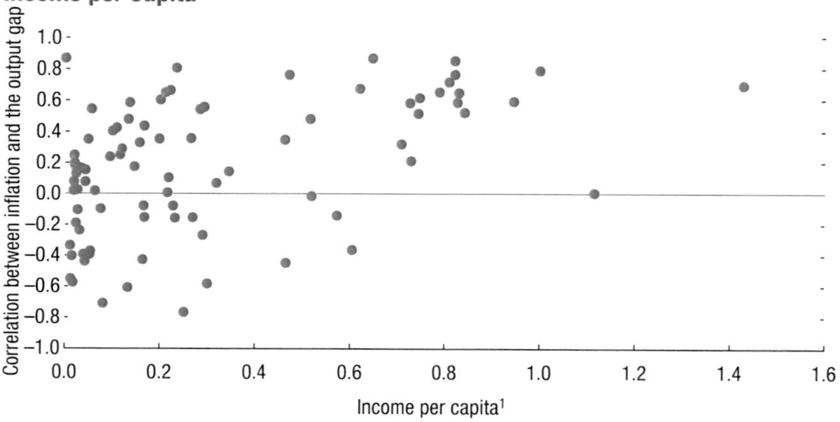

Sources: Haver Analytics; Organisation for Economic Co-operation and Development; World Bank Development Indicators; and IMF staff estimates.
[1]Income per capita (2012) is normalized by income per capita for the United States.

Shocks to international food and fuel prices pose an additional set of challenges. In the African context, food makes up a large share of the consumer basket, so that the direct impact of food price shocks is larger. In addition, sub-Saharan African countries are net food importers on average, and many are net oil importers, so that the inflationary impact from higher international prices could be compounded by the real and nominal depreciation required for external adjustment (see Adam 2011; Chapter 11 of Berg and Portillo 2018). These shocks have therefore been a source of inflation pressures; at the same time, the direct effect of these shocks may mask underlying monetary policy misalignments that can amplify the overall inflationary effect (see Chapter 15 of Berg and Portillo 2018, for example).

Domestic supply shocks are an even larger source of inflation volatility. This is because the agricultural sector is heavily exposed to weather-related shocks. One implication is that inflation is inevitably more volatile in low-income countries, with the larger volatility reflecting supply-side changes to relative food prices. Much of this volatility is unlikely to disappear even as countries modernize their policy frameworks.[3]

Traditionally less open to foreign capital, many low-income countries have substantially opened their capital accounts in recent decades, significantly exposing them to a full range of external shocks. Given that international aid inflows can be large and unpredictable, this creates difficult challenges both for fiscal policy and for monetary policy (Table 13.2).[4]

---

[3]See Anand, Prasad, and Zhang (2015) for a discussion of some of the analytics of food prices and monetary policy.

[4]See Chapter 10 of Berg and Portillo (2018); Buffie and others (2008); and Buffie, O'Connell, and Adam (2010) on the advantages and disadvantages of various policy responses.

Fiscal Policy as a Source of Volatility and Pressures on Monetary Policy

Fiscal dominance—where the need to finance the government deficit through money printing determines the rate of inflation—remains a fundamental challenge to monetary policy in only a few countries in sub-Saharan Africa. In a much larger group of countries, however, fiscal policy can greatly complicate the conduct of monetary policy. Central banks in Africa must contend with highly volatile and procyclical fiscal policy. Sometimes the source of fiscal volatility is a high dependence on revenues from the commodity sector and the lack of binding fiscal rules to ensure intertemporal smoothing. In other cases, fiscal procyclicality stems from the political cycle. Certain features of African economies, for example, the large share of the population that lives on their current income, amplify the effect of these shocks on aggregate demand.

Even if fiscal dominance is a (not-so-) distant memory, the volatility and procyclicality of fiscal policy creates other forms of fiscal pressures on monetary policy. One stems from the cost of monetary operations.[5] This is a source of contention with the government, particularly where the financial system is in a situation of structural liquidity surplus, for example, due to sizable interventions in foreign exchange markets, and a legacy of quasi-fiscal operations have left the central bank with low or negative net worth. In this case sterilization operations, which are necessary to maintain an appropriate policy stance, can have sizable effects on central bank profits.

Another type of pressure occurs when the central bank tightens policy less aggressively out of concern for the effect on fiscal solvency. This may be one possible reason why many central banks in sub-Saharan Africa have yet to formally adopt interest-rate-based frameworks and why those that do often implement changes to the policy stance without changing the more visible policy rate.

THE CURRENT MONETARY POLICY LANDSCAPE

Many policy changes have been institutionalized in sub-Saharan Africa through reforms that have cemented central bank independence and through the adoption of new central bank charters. Most of the region's central banks have a de jure (legislated) independence, and their de facto independence score (0.26) has been on average very close to the developing countries' average (0.25), using the measure in Lucotte (2009).[6] The de facto policy regime in most countries is best characterized as a hybrid regime. An overview of the objectives and targets of monetary policy in the region reveals a set of managed floaters with a variety of

---

[5]Berg and Portillo (2018) Chapter 2 provides a discussion of these issues in the case of Uganda.

[6]Indices of central bank independence combine assessments of tenure protection of central bank's senior management, operational independence, clearly legally defined objectives for monetary policy, and limits to central bank lending to the government. The construction of the indices is based on the methodology outlined in Cukierman (1992) for de facto independence and Cukierman, Webb, and Neyapti (1992) for de jure independence.

conventional-looking objectives (price and exchange rate stability), but with money aggregates still present as both operational and intermediate targets.

Price Stability, the Medium-Term Inflation Target, and the Pursuit of Other Objectives

Most central banks in sub-Saharan Africa have bought into the idea that price stability is the primary goal of monetary policy, at least de jure. In many countries, however, the primacy of price stability remains to be established. Most central banks without inflation-targeting regimes do not have an explicit inflation objective, and those that do tend to adjust the objective in line with changes in the near-term inflation forecast, which reduces its anchoring role. Many central banks continue to pursue other objectives, for example, supporting growth, deepening the financial sector, or improving external competitiveness. This multiplicity of objectives and the lack of a clear hierarchy among them typically results in erratic policies, although to a smaller degree than in the past: the monetary stance is loosened, for example, to support financial deepening, only to be tightened later once inflation pressures appear.

This state of affairs is most visible in the central role that the exchange rate plays in policy frameworks of many countries in sub-Saharan Africa, including those with de jure exchange rate flexibility. Though some attention to the exchange rate is inevitable given its importance for inflation dynamics, in some countries exchange rate stability often takes precedence over price stability. The exchange rate is the de facto anchor, at least temporarily, and operations aimed at influencing the exchange rate end up determining the stance of policy, for example, through the use of unsterilized interventions in the foreign exchange markets. Of course, this is a feature of many emerging market economies as well, although it features more prominently in low-income countries (Figure 13.2).

Operational Frameworks

Low-income countries of sub-Saharan Africa use reserve money targeting as the de jure operational framework of choice, in contrast with the now standard practice of setting operational targets on (and controlling) very short-term interest rates adopted by most advanced and emerging market central banks.[7]

Money targeting is implemented very flexibly, with frequent economically significant misses of money targets. These misses mainly seem to represent accommodation of money demand shocks, although some may involve policy shifts. Flexible implementation of money targeting is also evident in the process of adjustment after misses. In "textbook" money targeting, where a constant growth rate of money serves as the nominal anchor, deviations from targets would be undone in

---

[7]Targets on reserve money are part of a broader monetary programming exercise in which targets are also set for broad money, which is considered an intermediate target of policy. With a few exceptions, however, targets on broad money play a smaller role in policy discussions in practice.

Figure 13.2. Intervention to Foreign Exchange Market Index in Low-Income Countries and Emerging Market Economies[1]

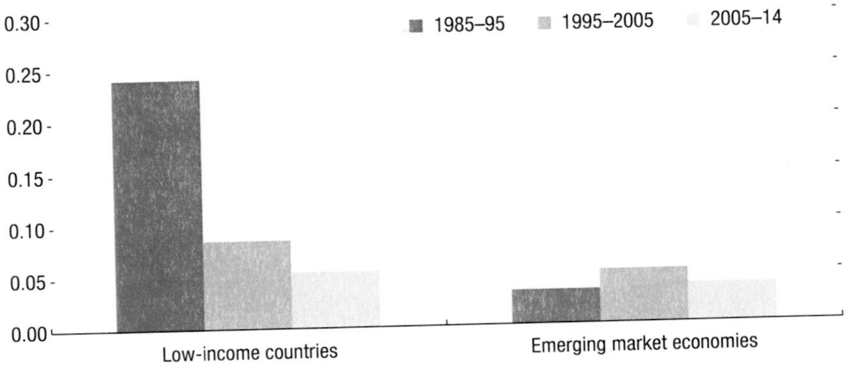

Sources: IMF International Financial Statistics; and IMF staff calculations.
[1]Following Levy-Yeyati, Sturzenegger, and Gluzmann (2013), the index is calculated as the annual average absolute change in net international reserves relative to the monetary base in the previous quarter, both in US dollars.

subsequent quarters as the actual stock would be brought back to the predetermined target path. This does not seem to be what happens, however. Rather, the new targets themselves tend to accommodate, at least partly, deviations from previous targets. There is no sign that actual money growth itself moves to reduce earlier deviations from target. There is also little sign that inflation responds to these misses, at least in countries with inflation below the mid double digits.

More recently, many central banks have introduced policy rates to signal the stance of policy, but deviations between policy and actual rates are common, and tensions between money targets and interest rate policy are inevitable. Reserve money targeting can lead to highly volatile short-term interest rates, as the authorities respond partially and unpredictably to money demand shocks.[8] In addition, tensions between money targets and desired interest rate outcomes frequently lead to complex regulations and interventions in short-term financial markets and a multiplicity of short-term interest rates. All this discourages financial market development (IMF 2015).

In addition, reserve money targeting makes the stance of policy noisier and more difficult to interpret on the part of both financial market participants and the central bank itself. Not all money demand shocks are accommodated, so that interest rates are a volatile and noisy indicator of the current and expected stance of policy. Greater de facto flexibility relative to money targets reduces this volatility but at costs of greater discretion and opacity about the true operational

_____
[8]Berg and others (2013) describe the implications of strict money targeting for interest rate volatility in Uganda.

framework. Of course, not all deviations from target represent accommodation of money demand, but it is very hard to tell in any particular situation. The effectiveness of the operational framework is hampered as a result (see Chapters 8, 9, and 16 of Berg and Portillo 2018).

An additional layer of complexity is brought about by recurrent interventions in foreign exchange markets, which are the main tool for managing the exchange rate in most sub-Saharan African countries. There is often insufficient coordination between interventions in foreign exchange markets and other operations. As a result, interventions influence the stance of policy in unintended and undesired ways.

Given all this flexibility, and given the difficulty of inferring the stance of policy from the money targets or target misses and the failure of money targeting itself to provide a nominal anchor, how can these policy regimes be understood? The answer seems to be that these countries tend to practice an opaque version of "inflation targeting lite," in which decisions about the setting and achievement of the money targets depend on progress relative to inflation, output, exchange rates, and in many cases other objectives (see Stone and Bhundia 2004).

MODERNIZING MONETARY POLICY

Central banks in sub-Saharan Africa are well aware of the limitations of their existing frameworks and are looking to improve along the various dimensions we have discussed. Ghana was an earlier adopter of inflation targeting. Uganda was next in line. Outside of sub-Saharan Africa, the Sri Lankan central bank has publicly announced its commitment to adopt inflation targeting. Several other central banks, including Kenya, have explicitly discussed the possibility, even if they have yet to formally commit. Many other countries, while not explicitly considering the move, are working to improve their operational framework by giving more prominence to policy interest rates, and by improving on the design and use of open market operations and standing facilities.

Although there is no one-size-fits-all approach to monetary policy modernization, central banks can learn from the experience of many countries outside sub-Saharan Africa, as well as from early movers within the region. One key lesson is that progress is not possible without sufficient operational independence nor with a sufficiently clear central bank mandate for price stability, even if adherence to these two principles is always a work in progress. Building and maintaining political commitment are therefore critical. The central bank has a leading role to play in building the necessary consensus for reform.

Another lesson is that central banks can make progress in many areas simultaneously. Progress can be self-reinforcing: the development of analytical capacity is more likely to impact policy making if it is consistent with the way policy is designed and implemented, which requires clarity about the strategy and the operational framework. The adoption of an explicit numerical objective can provide impetus to investing in analytical capacity and the communication strategy, while an effective operational framework can make central banks more comfortable about explicitly committing to an inflation objective. These synergies call for a comprehensive approach to reform.

A related issue is whether to explicitly adopt a new regime, namely inflation targeting, and if so whether to do so at a specific stage of the modernization process. What the international evidence corroborates, and the above discussion implies, is that countries do not need to satisfy a strict number of preconditions before they can adopt inflation targeting (Batini and Laxton 2007). If anything, the opposite is true. A clear framework is more conducive to reform. This should not be surprising in view of the observation above that current reserve money targeting frameworks already amount to an obscure form of "inflation targeting lite."

Another critical part of modernization is the development of analytical tools for policymaking and techniques for effective communication. Despite limited availability and reliability of the macroeconomic data in low-income countries, and regardless of the monetary policy framework in place, there is significant room for improvement in macroeconomic analysis of the already available data. Central banks of low-income countries have a great need for models to undertake policy analysis. In our view, these models must meet two criteria. First, they must reflect modern thinking on monetary policy, drawing on both state-of-the-art macro theory and current practice in central banks in advanced and emerging markets. Second, they must be tailored to address key low-income-country-specific issues. Despite the importance of the topic, there has been very little work in the academic and policy literature tailored to low-income countries. Several chapters in Berg and Portillo (2018) review analytic frameworks useful for policymaking in low-income countries.

Forecasting and Policy Analysis System

The efforts involved in deriving and applying these models have led to a more systematic collaboration between the IMF and central banks in low-income countries on the topic of analytical frameworks for policy analysis and forecasting. Partly as a result, several central banks have been developing and using their own variant of these models to organize their internal discussion and forecasting systems.[9] This is an important part of the policy modernization efforts and points to the synergies between research, IMF surveillance or program work, and capacity development on the ground.

Besides these challenges, there is a need to gain more experience with using the analytical tools (including core medium-term forecasting models) in low-income countries. Although these tools have proven to be useful in advanced economies and emerging markets, the practical experience with using them in low-income

---

[9]This includes the central banks in Ghana, Kenya, Malawi, Mozambique, Rwanda, Sri Lanka, Tanzania, and Uganda.

countries is limited so far. Berg and Portillo (2018) present several efforts to adapt these tools to characteristics of low-income countries. However, practical experience from real-time use of these tools to support policy decision-making remains to be built over time.

The Role of the IMF

In response to demand from country authorities (mostly governors of central banks in sub-Saharan Africa), the IMF's review-based conditionality toolkit was adapted to support countries' efforts in strengthening their monetary policy frameworks. In 2014, the IMF's Executive Board approved a new review-based conditionality for programs with countries with evolving monetary policy frameworks that have a good record of policy implementation or are committed to a substantial strengthening of their policy framework through the introduction of a monetary policy consultation clause (IMF 2014). This will help align conditionality in IMF programs to the policy reality in some low-income countries, and strengthen the IMF role as a trusted advisor. The new toolkit is being integrated into IMF-supported programs and Article IV consultations in low-income countries, building on countries' progress in modernizing frameworks.

CONCLUSIONS

Central banks in low-income countries have come a long way. They played a critical role, though perhaps subordinate to fiscal policy, in improving macroeconomic stability. In sub-Saharan Africa, for example, this has helped set the stage for the growth resurgence since the mid-1990s. The challenges, however, seem to be getting tougher. Perhaps foremost is the difficult global economic environment: will low-income countries be able to keep growth going in the face of shocks related to China's growth slowdown and swings in commodity prices? Are monetary policy institutions strong enough? Have central banks achieved effective enough monetary policy frameworks to adjust to these shocks, keep expectations anchored, and resist political pressures? Much progress has been made and much more is under way. Will pressures expose weaknesses that spur further reforms or rather derail them?

Many of the most serious challenges lie in the domain of fiscal policy and more broadly still in the resilience of a broad range of institutions both public and private. Most of the shocks are real rather than monetary: commodity prices, resource output, foreign direct investment flows, foreign demand, and fiscal policy. However, in our view the agenda for monetary policy outlined here can play a critical supporting role.

Central banks can work to implement clear forward-looking policy regimes that respond coherently to the full range of shocks. This will help avoid macroeconomic and financial crises, allow exchange rate flexibility to avoid persistent misalignments due to commodity price shocks, and keep inflation expectations anchored while avoiding unnecessary swings in interest rates, inflation, exchange rates, and output. All this can keep bad times from exploding into vicious circles of macroeconomic disarray and allow policymakers time to address the full range of challenges.

REFERENCES

Adam, C. 2011. "On the Macroeconomic Management of Food Price Shocks in Low-Income Countries." *Journal of African Economies* 20: i63–i99.

———, and S. O'Connell. 2005. Monetary Policy and Aid Management in Sub-Saharan Africa. Unpublished. Oxford: University of Oxford; Swarthmore, PA: Swarthmore College.

Ahmad, A., and E. Pentecost. 2010. "Terms of Trade Shocks and Economic Performance under Different Exchange Rate Regimes." Loughborough University Working Paper 2010–08, Loughborough UK.

Anand, R., E. Prasad, and B. Zhang. 2015. "What Measure of Inflation Should a Developing Country Central Bank Target?" *Journal of Monetary Economics* 74: 102–16.

Batini, N., and D. Laxton. 2007. "Under What Conditions Can Inflation Targeting be Adopted? The Experience of Emerging Markets." Central Banking, Analysis, and Economic Policies Book Series 11: 467–506.

Berg A. and R. Portillo. 2018. Monetary Policy in Sub-Saharan Africa. Oxford: Oxford University Press.

Berg, A., J. Vlcek, L. Charry, and R. Portillo. 2013. "The Monetary Transmission Mechanism in the Tropics: A Narrative Approach." IMF Working Paper 13/197, International Monetary Fund, Washington, DC.

Broda, C. 2004. "Terms of Trade and Exchange Rate Regimes in Developing Countries." *Journal of International Economics* 63: 31–58.

Buffie, E., C. Adam, S. O'Connell, and C. Pattillo. 2008. "Riding the Wave: Monetary Responses to Aid Surges in Low-Income Countries." *European Economic Review* 52 (8): 1378–95.

Buffie, E., S. O'Connell, and C. Adam. 2010. "Fiscal Inertia, Donor Credibility, and the Monetary Management of Aid Surges." *Journal of Development Economics* 93 (2): 287–98.

Chinn, M., and H. Ito. 2008. "A New Measure of Financial Openness." *Journal of Comparative Policy Analysis* 10(3), 309–22.

Cukierman, A. 1992. *Central Bank Strategy, Credibility, and Independence—Theory and Evidence.* Cambridge, MA: MIT Press.

———, S. Webb, and B. Neyapti. 1992. "Measuring the Independence of Central Banks and Its Effect on Policy Outcomes." *World Bank Economic Review* 6: 353–98.

Edwards, S., and E. Levy-Yeyati. 2005. "Flexible Exchange Rates as Shock Absorbers." *European Economic Review* 48 (9): 2079–105.

Giuliano, P., P. Mishra, and A. Spilimbergo. 2010. "Democracy and Reforms: Evidence from a New Dataset." *American Economic Journal* 5 (4): 179–204.

Hoffmaister, A., J. Roldos, and P. Wickham. 1998. "Macroeconomic Fluctuations in Sub-Saharan Africa." *IMF Staff Papers* 45 (1): 132–60.

International Monetary Fund (IMF). 2014. "Conditionality in Evolving Monetary Policy Regimes." IMF Policy Paper, Washington, DC.

———. 2015. "Evolving Monetary Policy Frameworks in Low-Income and Other Developing Countries." IMF Policy Paper, Washington, DC.

Kessy, P., S. O'Connell, and J. Nyella. 2016. "Monetary Policy in Tanzania: Accomplishments and the Road Ahead." In *Tanzania: The Path to Prosperity*, edited by C. Adam, P. Collier, and B. Ndulu. Oxford: Oxford University Press.

Levy-Yeyati, E., F. Sturzenegger, and P. A. Gluzmann. 2013. "Fear of Appreciation." *Journal of Development Economics* 101(C), 233–47.

Lucotte, Y. 2009. "The Influence of Central Bank Independence on Budget Deficits in Developing Countries: New Evidence from Panel Data Analysis." Laboratory of Economics in Orleans, University of Orleans.

Mishra, P., and P. Montiel. 2012. "Monetary Transmission in Low-Income Countries: Effectiveness and Policy Implications." *IMF Economic Review* 60: 270–302.

Mishra, P., P, Montiel, and A. Spilimbergo. 2013. "How Effective is Monetary Transmission in Developing Countries: A Survey of the Empirical Evidence." *Economic Systems* 37 (2): 187–216.

Stone, R., and A. Bhundia. 2004. "A New Taxonomy of Monetary Regimes." IMF Working Paper 04/191, International Monetary Fund, Washington, DC.

CHAPTER 14

A Robust and Adaptable Nominal Anchor

Tobias Adrian, Douglas Laxton, and Maurice Obstfeld

> *Even if it is now all too evident that the stabilization of inflation and inflation expectations does not by itself guarantee that macroeconomic instability will never be an issue, there remain excellent reasons to believe that success on this dimension is conducive to macroeconomic stability more broadly.* —M. Woodford (2013)

Over the past quarter-century, flexible inflation targeting has provided a resilient nominal anchor for monetary policy. Inflation-forecast targeting is an efficient, operational form of this regime, and countries that have adopted it have had relatively good macroeconomic outcomes. In fact, no central bank that has implemented inflation-forecast targeting has later abandoned it. Its adoption does not, however, confer automatic credibility. Monetary policy under any regime earns credibility by delivering, over an extended period, a stable monetary standard.

With respect to inflation targeting, earning credibility does not mean that the inflation rate must always remain close to the official target rate. The nature of economic disturbances is such that actual inflation may sometimes be well wide of the target. Lags in the effect of monetary policy and the short-term trade-off between inflation and output make it unfeasible to quickly eliminate inflation shocks. The important thing for credibility is that the central bank consistently acts in a way that returns inflation to target within the usual time lag for the effect of monetary policy (in practice, a couple of years or so). Survey evidence and financial market data from countries that have adhered to inflation-forecast targeting show that, over time, long-term expectations do converge to, and hold steady at, the official target rate, notwithstanding variations in the actual rate of price increases.

ANCHORING POLICY EXPECTATIONS

The nominal anchor under inflation targeting is the firm expectation that long-term inflation will adhere to the announced target rate. It follows immediately that monetary policy is fundamentally about expectations. As Woodford (2005) puts it, "For not only do expectations about policy matter, but, at least under current conditions, very little else matters."

One might ask why inflation-forecast targeting has apparently provided a wider range of economies with a superior means of managing expectations than other regimes, including a fixed exchange rate (or an announced path for the rate), rules for money or central bank credit growth, or eclectic systems with multiple objectives. The answer would lie in the transparency and flexibility of inflation-forecast targeting. It does so by anchoring long-term inflation expectations, while allowing policy to guide short- to medium-term interest rate expectations. Announcing a fixed numerical target for the rate of increase in consumer prices over the long term clarifies without ambiguity the policy objective and sets an objective standard for monetary stability. It concerns the behavior of a variable that affects everybody directly and materially. The regime does not ignore real variables such as output and employment but recognizes them consistently with macroeconomic theory and evidence: the short-term trade-off between output and employment and inflation affects the speed with which policymakers will return inflation to target; and in the long term steady inflation at the target rate is consistent with output at the highest sustainable level.[1] Furthermore, the flexibility of the exchange rate under inflation targeting helps the economy adjust to shocks with minimal harm to output and employment. The consistency of the objectives with basic economic principles makes it easier for an inflation-forecast-targeting central bank to communicate policy and to build confidence that its targets will be met.

Under alternative regimes it is more difficult to manage expectations.

- For many small open economies, a fixed exchange rate regime can provide a clear target that is publicly understood. However, history shows that a fixed exchange rate standard is liable to collapse, especially following an asymmetric shock: the fragility of the official commitment undoes the usefulness of its clarity.

- Monetary standards based on rules for money or credit growth have had major communications problems, as well as substantive issues. The aggregates that are targeted are neither objectives of interest to the general population nor instruments under the control of policymakers.

- Financial innovation has undermined attempts to target money growth. Policymakers have been drawn into arcane discussions about the definition of money and about the instability of the links from money and credit aggregates to inflation and output caused by financial innovation. This can detract from their more important policy commitment: holding inflation to a low rate.

---

[1] For various inflation-forecast-targeting central banks (for example, Bank of Canada, US Federal Reserve) maximizing employment or output is part of the statutory central bank mandate. However, output or employment objectives are not defined numerically, either in the mandate or in the specification of inflation targets. The dual mandate as defined by the Fed in 2012 is equivalent to flexible inflation targeting or inflation-forecast targeting.

- Central banks espousing systems with eclectic objectives—inflation control, high employment, money growth, credit conditions, the balance of payments, exchange rate management, and so on—may have worried less about financial innovation, but they have often been unable to present a clear vision to the public of what they ultimately sought to achieve.

Effective management of expectations is important to ensure both the potency of the policy instrument and confidence in the objective. Again, inflation-forecast targeting benefits from clarity. In normal times, the instrument is typically a key short-term money market interest rate. At times when the policy rate is constrained by the effective lower bound, managing expectations becomes even more important as a means to reduce longer-term rates. A preannounced schedule of dates for setting the policy rate draws the attention of the public and provides a basis for pricing in financial markets—spot, forward, and futures. Media commentary highlights both the issues that a monetary policy committee may consider at its decision meeting and the pros and cons of any change in the policy rate. Academics test policy reaction functions for the rate in macroeconomic models. All this attention serves a useful purpose, since the focus on central bank decisions about the policy rate strengthens their impact on financial market expectations.

USING TRANSPARENCY TO PROMOTE ACCOUNTABILITY

All this attention matters, because, in and of itself, the policy interest rate is of negligible importance to the economy as a whole. If nobody notices the policy rate, nothing much will happen when it changes.[2] The effectiveness of monetary policy stems from its impact on interest rates in the longer term, which are the rates at which households and firms borrow and lend. To shift the entire yield curve, changes in the policy rate must change expectations about future short-term interest rates. Under inflation-forecast targeting, the central bank prompts expectations to move in line with policy objectives by explicitly indicating the likely course of the policy rate at future monetary policy committee meetings. Given how clearly central banks now communicate their policy objectives, it is somewhat astonishing to recall that in the early 1990s central banks did not even disclose the level at which they intended to set the key interest rate under their control.

Policymakers have managed to clearly define for the public the nature and limits of the commitments imposed by inflation-forecast targeting. To achieve an inflation target, the policy instrument must be free to move in response to new developments—which is why the effective lower bound poses special

---

[2]In some non-inflation-targeting regimes, the central bank has not highlighted a policy rate. Not surprisingly, changes in an official rate then have had little impact on other interest rates. The lack of emphasis breaks a key link in the policy transmission mechanism.

difficulties. There can be no commitment to a given interest rate or to a given future path for the interest rate. Instead, the policy interest rate responds to the need to return inflation to target under inflation targeting. Thus, inflation-forecast-targeting central banks use models for forecasting and policy analysis in which the path of the short-term interest rate is endogenous, determined by a policy reaction function. Policymakers underline the conditionality of their forecasts of future interest rates by emphasizing the uncertainties in the outlook. In practice, it has proved relatively straightforward to communicate to financial markets and to the public in general the difference between the commitment to the fixed long-term inflation target and the conditional projections for the interest rate.

Inflation-forecast-targeting central banks have stepped up communications programs to maximize the impact on public expectations of the increased availability of information. Immediately after monetary policy committee meetings, there are press releases and press conferences with the central bank governor and other senior officials to explain the rationale for the committee's decision. Monetary Policy Reports (usually quarterly) analyze recent outcomes relative to prior expectations and explain in detail how the central bank expects current policy actions to assist in the return of inflation to target. In most cases, this involves a verbal, qualitative description of the interest rate forecast. A few central banks publish their entire forecast, including the explicit numerical path of the short-term interest rate. By doing this, they provide forward guidance for the policy rate routinely after each policy decision. Based on the existing evidence, this increased openness has reduced the element of surprise in policy rate changes and strengthened the transmission of policy.

Feedback from increased political accountability, both formal and informal, reinforces the influence on expectations and credibility. The formal aspect involves relations between the central bank and the government or parliament. The informal aspect is more general, relating to the obligation of the central bank to explain itself to the public: what objectives it is trying to achieve; how its past, present, and future actions are in line with those objectives; and the reasons behind any failure to achieve its objectives. Transparency is therefore a key component of accountability. In turn, clear political accountability buttresses public trust in the system.

There is no free lunch. Communications activity absorbs time and energy of senior management and staff. Furthermore, inside the central bank, inflation-forecast targeting implies an increased cost of policy implementation and an increased reliance on economic analysis, compared with a system that targets an intermediate variable like the exchange rate or a monetary aggregate. The direct focus on the objectives of inflation and output requires policymakers to make decisions based on an understanding of the complex linkages from the policy instrument. Between each monetary policy committee meeting a vast amount of new, relevant, data becomes available. The transmission mechanism famously involves long and variable lags and short-term trade-offs between goals. Inflation-forecast-targeting decisions are therefore based on forecasts and on judgments about the best path back to target, for example, fast or gradual. Each inflation-forecast-targeting central bank therefore invests in a structured forecasting and policy analysis system, which is designed to process the economic implications of the new data and to efficiently provide relevant macroeconomic information for each policy meeting. The forecasting and policy analysis system involves a team of economists who produce a model-based baseline forecast and alternative scenarios based on different assumptions about exogenous factors or policy responses.

The model at the core of the forecasting process has standard economic properties. These include an endogenous short-term interest rate set by a policy reaction function and forward-looking, model-consistent expectations on the part of policymakers and the public. The model provides an organizing framework for the mass of relevant data and solutions for the paths of endogenous variables that would otherwise be intractable, as well as for model-based bands of uncertainty around these paths. The internal economic consistency of model-derived forecasts helps central bank economists deliver a coherent economic narrative for their forecasts and related policy analyses, which is an asset in explaining the conduct of monetary policy.

INFLATION-FORECAST TARGETING IN PRACTICE

Effective implementation of monetary policy requires frequent operations by the central bank, in wholesale money markets, to translate policy decisions into changes in economic incentives. The operational framework facilitates such actions and comprises the *operating target*—the variable the central bank targets to implement its policy stance—and *monetary instruments*—used to align market conditions with the operating target.

In most cases the operating target is a very short-term interest rate, although there are exceptions. Some countries, where financial markets are undeveloped or shares of imports in the consumption basket are exceptionally large, target the growth rate of base money or an exchange rate. In addition, central banks that generally target interest rates may also use the size of their balance sheet as an operational target as interest rates approach the effective lower bound, as happened in the wake of the global financial crisis.

While the traditional monetary instruments—reserve requirements, open market operations, and standing facilities—are well known, there are numerous variations on the choice of operating target and the configuration of the operating framework. Central banks generally choose between targeting a market rate (for example, the overnight unsecured interbank rate) or attaching their policy rate to a central bank instrument (either in the middle or at the floor of an interest rate corridor). The aim is to ensure strong transmission by establishing a stable and predictable relationship between the policy rate and the interest rates that have a direct bearing on economic activity.

In settling on an operational framework, central banks need to consider their own circumstances and constraints, and decide how to balance the trade-offs across different criteria. For instance, operational frameworks differ in the degree of liquidity risk they impose on participants with consequent impact on market activity and development. Operational and financial costs and risks, and the capacity of staff to calibrate and conduct operations, also matter.

The question naturally arises as to whether monetary policy should pursue the additional objective of minimizing risks of major financial crises, and occasionally raise interest rates more than required by regular flexible inflation targeting. Systemic financial crises may be infrequent, but their occurrence can impose heavy costs on the economy. Micro- and macroprudential policies would seem the most appropriate policy tools as they are designed to tackle specific financial vulnerabilities, and thereby mitigate the probability of financial crises. However, their effectiveness remains somewhat uncertain, though initial evidence is encouraging. Nevertheless, adding financial stability as a separate objective for monetary policy seems ill-advised. Historical evidence suggests that raising interest rates more than warranted by the price stability mandate in an attempt to preempt risks of a crisis generally implies costs that outweigh potential benefits.

This does not imply that monetary policymakers should remain oblivious to financial sector frictions and vulnerabilities, captured in financial conditions indices. These carry important information that can help the central bank manage the short- to medium-term inflation-output trade-off more efficiently, with an unchanged mandate—that is, with lower variance of inflation and output around the desired path. Financial conditions are shown to contain important information on continuously evolving downside risks to economic activity over the policy horizon—to be distinguished from risks of devastating, though infrequent, systemic crises.

A few country experiences are worth highlighting:

- Canada is an advanced economy with a mature policy framework. The Bank of Canada's record for inflation control is excellent. Expectations of long-term inflation have been steady at the 2 percent target rate through all the fluctuations of the actual rate. One change is recommended: publication of the forecast path for the short-term interest rate. This, combined with an aggressive risk-avoidance strategy, might be especially useful in the event of another large negative shock, to reinforce the effectiveness of a stimulative policy when the policy rate is near the effective lower bound.

- The Czech economy went through a deep structural reform and a transition from an emerging market to an advanced economy. In the middle of this process the Czech National Bank adopted inflation-forecast targeting. It has implemented the regime with remarkable success. Like the Bank of Canada, it has managed to establish firm long-term expectations of 2 percent inflation. The Czech National Bank has become an international leader in central bank transparency.

- India is an emerging market that more recently embarked on flexible inflation targeting. The Reserve Bank of India has had to deal with various special issues, among which are a weak transmission mechanism and the strong influence of volatile food prices on the short- to medium-term dynamics of inflation. Time will tell if the new regime will help to anchor the previously drifting inflation rate, but the early days indicate that the approach holds promise, with a decline in inflation in line with the announced long-term target.

- The United States had a lower rate of inflation than the preceding countries in the late twentieth century and therefore did not face the same imperative to reform its monetary policy framework. Internally, the Federal Reserve had all the elements of an efficient forecasting and policy analysis system for inflation-forecast targeting: a well-honed process of internal communication between forecasters and policymakers and a long-standing schedule for policy meetings and announcements. It also had sophisticated communications arrangements. By 2012, when it announced the 2 percent inflation objective, the US monetary policy committee, the Federal Open Market Committee (FOMC), was already following an inflation-forecast-targeting policy in all but name. That the regime has been adopted gradually, over many years, indicates that at each step the Fed liked how it worked. The FOMC kicked the tires and took a long test drive before buying the vehicle.

- Finally, an examination of issues in low-income countries confirms that a wide range of countries might benefit from espousing the principles at the heart of inflation-forecast targeting.

A broader summary of the international history is in order.

The 15 years before 2008 comprised a period of remarkable economic stability for advanced economies, with steady growth and low, stable inflation. During that time, emerging market economies achieved an enormous expansion of output and vastly improved standards of living. This period was not without shocks, however. In 1997–98, severe financial crises in Asia and Russia, and the related failure of the giant hedge fund Long-Term Capital Management, exposed large systemic weaknesses and imbalances. In 2000–02, trillions of dollars were wiped from stock markets with the bursting of the dot-com bubble. The September 11, 2001, terrorist attacks on the United States shook confidence further, causing severe damage to the financial infrastructure of New York City and triggering another plunge in stock markets. Yet with adept monetary policy actions, the global economy weathered these crises.

One could have been forgiven for concluding that central bankers had found the key to providing a firm nominal anchor while avoiding cyclical instability. Stock and Watson (2002) wrote of "the great moderation." Nobel Laureate Robert Lucas declared that the "central problem of depression-prevention has been solved, for all practical purposes, and has in fact been solved for many decades" (Lucas 2003). Blanchard and Galí (2005) noted a "divine coincidence" in that under certain conditions the appropriate policy interest rate response to hold inflation at the target rate following a demand shock would also stabilize output—for example, following a negative demand shock the central bank would cut the rate to keep inflation on target and to keep the output gap at zero.

Blanchard (2009)—the initial draft of which was written before the failure of Lehman Brothers in September 2008—surveyed the field and concluded that "The state of macro is good." It seemed to be smooth sailing.

The global financial crisis that began with the failure of Lehman Brothers made it clear that the lessons about financial stability offered by previous crises had not been absorbed. The Great Recession in the United States spread and exposed underlying weaknesses that contributed to a decade of lackluster growth in advanced economies. Adverse longer-term trends—the decline in the global real equilibrium interest rate, lower productivity growth, aging populations—became more visible. Key macroeconomic variables fell significantly out of line with historical business downturns. It became untenable to continue applying convenient assumptions about the linearity of trends in existing forecasting and policy analysis. For example, these models were ill-equipped to handle the effective lower bound on interest rates or the strains in the financial sector.

Conjunctural problems have been aggravated by a decline in manufacturing and international trade. A strong rebound in China from 2009 to 2011 contributed to a commodities boom—often referred to as a commodities "supercycle"—that lifted exporters of industrial materials, including many emerging market economies. But commodity prices too have retreated. Negative output gaps and below-target inflation rates have persisted around the globe. Forecasts of growth were repeatedly downgraded, and the risk assessments of the IMF and the World Bank have been conspicuously tilted to the downside.

The decline in the global equilibrium interest rate is evident in the large drop in long-term bond yields since the 1990s and in the fact that historically low interest rates have not stimulated a strong increase in private investment or consumption. With inflation expectations at—or in the euro area and Japan, below—target rates (typically 2 percent), the global level of nominal rates consistent with maintaining output at its potential level today is well below the pre-2008 level; estimates group around zero (for example, Summers 2015).

This poses a serious obstacle to the main instrument of monetary policy, since the effective lower bound on the policy rate is about zero.[3] With rates already extremely low, central banks have had little room to cut further. It is therefore questionable whether monetary policy can effectively respond in the event of a new negative shock to the international economy. A relevant danger is a shock that is big enough to push a large part of the global economy into a trap of low inflation or deflation. In this dark corner, with the nominal policy interest rate at the effective lower bound, the real rate rises as expectations adapt to the central bank's failure to raise the inflation rate to the target rate. The feedback loop, through a further weakening of demand, puts the economy deeper into the hole. A breakdown in the management of expectations is obviously a big part of the problem.

---

[3]Depending on institutional arrangements, and on the opportunity costs of holding large stocks of cash, the effective lower bound may be a fraction above or below zero.

The situation is one in which the best policy response would involve concerted action on all macroeconomic policy fronts: fiscal, monetary, financial stability, and structural (Gaspar and others 2016). The focus though in this book is on monetary policy. Central banks have resorted to less conventional tools to stimulate output when the policy rate is near the floor. For example, forward guidance on the future path of the rate brings down the expected rate, and hence longer-term bond yields. Quantitative easing and outright purchases of longer-term bonds lower longer-term interest rates by reducing term risk premiums. The evidence suggests that these tools have had positive, albeit small-scale, results.

CREDIBLE FORECASTS ILLUMINATE DARK CORNERS

Without doubt, assertive, credible policy actions under a transparent inflation-forecast-targeting regime reinforce the potency of monetary policy. The essence of avoiding a bad equilibrium, when expectations of interest rates and inflation get stuck in an undesirable place, is to continue to effectively manage expectations. The most expeditious way to do this is for the policy framework to incorporate this principle rather than to rely on ad hoc forms of forward guidance. This principle has long been accepted with respect to the objective of monetary policy. Central banks that target inflation have always insisted that they will achieve their explicit targets, and they have used the communications tools at their disposal to convince the public to expect long-term inflation at the target rate. From the outset, they have published a forecast path for the inflation rate that achieves the target over the medium term.

Expectations are, as argued throughout the book, just as important with respect to the instrument of monetary policy. The simplest, most transparent way for central banks to encourage appropriate movements in longer-term interest rates is to publish their own forecast paths for the endogenous short-term rate, along with the inflation rate and the other main variables in its macroeconomic forecast. For the few central banks that have been this transparent, including the Reserve Bank of New Zealand and the Czech National Bank, the results have been good. We call such an open communications strategy *conventional forward guidance* to distinguish it from the unscheduled forward guidance used on occasion by the Federal Reserve and other central banks. Financial markets have readily understood that the rate forecast (unlike the long-term inflation forecast) is subject to change and conditional on unpredictable economic developments.

Assertive policy measures can illuminate dark corners. From a weak starting point, any further large negative shock to the global economy should be met with an aggressive, stimulative monetary policy response. When the policy interest rate is already at the effective lower bound, this would mean making a conditional public commitment to holding the rate at that low level for an extended time to bring long-term rates further down. Inflation might then temporarily overshoot the official target.[4]

---

[4]Simulations in which policymakers minimize a quadratic loss function often show this result. The quadratic loss function implies a risk-avoiding policy strategy.

There is nothing alarming in such a prospect. Indeed, the implied increase in medium-term inflation expectations would reduce real interest rates, even if nominal rates are at the floor, and thereby boost the desired monetary stimulus. In view of the costly losses of output and employment that would ensue from a slide into a trap of low inflation or deflation at the effective lower bound, tolerance for a brief period of high inflation would constitute prudent risk avoidance.

Credibility widens the tactical room for discretionary policy actions. When policy has established a reputation for consistent actions in line with announced goals, the occasional tactical detour does not raise concerns that these goals have been abandoned. Short-term room for maneuver might be useful for dealing with short-lived financial stability issues. There is a debate about the extent to which financial stability considerations should affect the conduct of monetary policy. Svensson (2015) argues that monetary policy should focus on inflation control and that other instruments should be used to maintain financial stability. The Bank for International Settlements (2017) criticizes inflation targeting as the basis for monetary policy on grounds that it does not adequately recognize the financial stability objective. The position emphasized in this book is closer to that of Svensson (2015): the comparative advantage of the monetary policy instrument is for inflation control; inflation-forecast-targeting central banks should not generally pursue the additional mandate of mitigating the risks of major financial crises (IMF 2015).

Confidence in the underlying policy framework likewise underlies the effectiveness of some unconventional measures. It also allows policymakers to experiment with new tactical approaches, without a material risk of sending long-term inflation expectations off target—the recent Czech experiment with exchange market intervention being a case in point. Conversely, a tactical deviation is necessarily short-lived, because the stability of the nominal anchor depends on a consistent strategy of returning inflation to the official target rate.

CONCLUSIONS

The global financial crisis and its aftermath exposed challenges for the effective conduct of monetary policy that have yet to be adequately resolved. Monetary policy at the frontier faces substantial unknowns and challenges. These include heightened uncertainty about underlying variables previously thought to be relatively stable, for example, potential growth and the equilibrium interest rate. The effective lower bound on nominal interest rates limits the extent to which central banks can stimulate output growth and raise inflation back to target. In recent years, with the policy interest rate already near its lowest feasible level, the main danger has been the risk of a bad quasi-equilibrium in which inflation becomes stuck at a very low, even negative, rate. Some analysts fear that extremely low interest rates, and the associated expansion of central bank liquidity, might eventually have negative effects on financial stability.

Central bankers will doubtless be confronted with major surprises as monetary policy is normalized. Our main argument is that inflation-forecast targeting provides superior management of expectations compared with alternative regimes. It bolsters confidence in the long-term inflation target and strengthens the transmission of policy actions. It is consistent with proactive, assertive measures that avoid bad quasi-equilibriums, when expectations of long-term inflation drift with the actual inflation rate. The regime has proved to be resilient and adaptable to advanced and emerging market economies with very different structures. Inflation-forecast targeting offers a state-of-the-art standard of monetary stability for the unpredictable challenges that lie ahead.

REFERENCES

Bank for International Settlements. 2017. *Annual Report 2016/17*. Basel.

Blanchard, O. 2009. "The State of Macro." *Annual Review of Economics* (1): 209–28.

———, and J. Gali. 2005. "Real Wage Rigidities and the New Keynesian Model." NBER Working Paper 11806, National Bureau of Economic Research, Cambridge, MA.

Gaspar, V., M. Obstfeld, R. Sahay, D. Laxton, D. Botman, K. Clinton, R. Duval, K. Ishi, Z. Jakab, L. Jaramillo Mayor, C. Lonkeng Ngouana, T. Mancini-Griffoli, J. Mongardini, S. Mursula, E. Nier, Y. Ustyugova, H. Wang, and O. Wuensch. 2016. "Macroeconomic Management When Policy Space Is Constrained: A Comprehensive, Consistent and Coordinated Approach to Economic Policy." IMF Staff Discussion Note 16/09, International Monetary Fund, Washington, DC.

International Monetary Fund (IMF). 2015. "Monetary Policy and Financial Stability." IMF Policy Paper (August), Washington, DC.

Lucas, R.E. Jr. 2003. "Macroeconomic Priorities." *American Economic Review* 93 (1): 1–14.

Stock, J., and M. Watson. 2002. "Has the Business Cycle Changed and Why?" *NBER Macroeconomics Annual*, National Bureau of Economic Research, Cambridge, MA.

Summers, L.H. 2015. "Low Real Rates, Secular Stagnation, and the Future of Stabilization Policy." Keynote speech to the Annual Conference of the Bank of Chile, Santiago, November 20.

Svensson, L.E.O. 2015. "Monetary Policy and Financial Stability." Presentation to Financial Liberalization, Innovation, and Stability: International Experience and Relevance for China, the Third Joint Conference, People's Bank of China and International Monetary Fund, Beijing, March.

Woodford, M. 2005. "Central-Bank Communication and Policy Effectiveness." Presented at the Federal Reserve Bank of Kansas City Symposium, Jackson Hole, WY, August 25–27.

———. 2013. "Inflation Targeting: Fix It, Don't Scrap It." In *Is Inflation Targeting Dead? Central Banking after the Crisis*, edited by L. Reichlin and R. Baldwin. London: Centre for Economic Policy Research.

Index